LABOR COMMITMENT
AND SOCIAL CHANGE
IN DEVELOPING AREAS

Edited by
WILBERT E. MOORE
and
ARNOLD S. FELDMAN

SOCIAL SCIENCE RESEARCH COUNCIL
NEW YORK 1960

The Social Science Research Council was organized in 1923 and formally incorporated in 1924 for the purpose of advancing research in the social sciences. Its members are chosen from seven associated professional organizations in the social sciences and from related fields.

ASSOCIATED ORGANIZATIONS

American Anthropological Association

American Economic Association

American Historical Association

American Political Science Association

American Psychological Association

American Sociological Association

American Statistical Association

PREFACE

There is a kind of unification going on in the world. This unification represents a trend so strong that it is sweeping out of the way many differences in attitudes and beliefs. It proceeds apace despite political difficulties and international tensions, some of which are indeed a direct product of the very force that gives political entities similar goals but without necessarily creating mutual friendship. The unification reflects a commitment to improved material well-being and conditions of life as a goal of public policy and private endeavor. It turns up in the oddest places, and in fact in most places. A worldly doctrine, it is the single most successful conversion movement in the history of ideological diffusion. Its missionaries have been poorly organized, often unwitting, and certainly dissentious. They have succeeded to an often embarrassing extent.

The areas outside the historic homelands of industrialism are poor, and in many instances growing poorer, at least relatively. But they are changing, and in most instances the change represents both intended and unanticipated consequences of "economic development." This volume is concerned with those areas, which we have called "newly developing." Its particular focus is quite specialized—the problem of labor motivation in unfamiliar tasks or, in the technical language used in this volume, the problem of *commitment* of industrial labor, by which we mean *both* the short-run objective performance of modern kinds of economic activity *and* the long-run and deep-seated acceptance of the attitudes and beliefs appropriate to a modernized economy. It turns out on even superficial inspection or contemplation, however, that it is the developmental process itself that engages and excites attention, for the worker (factory hand, manager, merchant, purveyor of services) is simply the protagonist for the major drama of socio-economic change.

This book is by many hands and gains thereby much more in depth and breadth of expert knowledge than it loses in details of language and style. It is the outgrowth of a conference, sponsored by the Committee on Economic Growth of the Social Science Research Council, and held in Chicago on March 28–30, 1958. From the inception of the conference plans and selection of authors and discussants to completion of the major revisions of papers for the present volume, the central problem and its ramifications have been kept in sharp focus. The perspectives of authors differ, as they should, but the field of vision has been the same.

The sequence of steps leading to publication of this volume may be briefly noted. After exploration by the sponsoring committee sufficient to establish the importance of the subject and the availability of persons actively interested and working on aspects of it, a planning subcommittee was appointed, consisting of Bert F. Hoselitz, Melville J. Herskovits, and Wilbert E. Moore (chairman). The final conference program and the selection of authors and other participants were that subcommittee's responsibility. That responsibility was discharged with the aid of a number of minor miracles.

Papers were solicited and circulated in three stages: (1) A background paper, designed to be speculative and wide-ranging, and therefore provocative of controversy, was first circulated to all other authors. (2) Some eleven papers, grouped into four major topics, were solicited from various social scientists well-informed on particular subjects and areas. (3) These basic papers were in turn sent, by groups, to four other scholars for comment and criticism.

The organization of this volume is consistent with that procedure. Part I is by the undersigned, who are both authors and editors. The basic analyses are presented as the earlier chapters in each subsequent Part (Chapters 5–7, 9–11, 13–14, and 16–18). The final chapters of each Part (Chapters 8, 12, 15, and 19) are of a more general character than their predecessors and represent a critical but also creative approach to the four major topics. All papers have been revised in the light of the conference discussion as well as the authors' own afterthoughts and the editors' suggestions. Our initial paper has been extensively revised on the basis of the superior wisdom of our colleagues, and now appears as the four chapters of Part I. We have added a concluding, retrospective chapter on moot issues.

The conference that resulted in this volume was one of a series sponsored by the Committee on Economic Growth, aided by a grant from the Ford Foundation to the Council for support of the committee. The suggestion of the particular subject was made several years ago by Frederick H. Harbison, then of the University of Chicago and now of Princeton University, and Charles A. Myers of Massachusetts Institute of Technology. Their work and that of others associated with the Inter-University Study of the Labor Problems in Economic Development were vital ingredients in the assembly of the reports and analyses presented here. In addition, Messrs. Harbison and Myers served as "general discussants" at the conference. Their comments and criticisms have aided many of the authors, including the editors.

Mr. Feldman's work as both author and editor was aided by the sponsoring committee, which provided funds for critical exploration of the theoretical literature on economic development. Mr. Moore's work was aided by a Grant-in-Aid from the former Behavioral Science Division of the Ford Foundation. Besides incidental clerical expenses, part of these funds was used to secure the research assistance of Mrs. Jane Kronick and of Kermit Gatten and David Chaplin for tracking down some of the growing body of significant literature. In addition, Mr. Moore's work as Faculty Associate of the Center of International Studies at Princeton, on our continuing study of the dynamics of industrial societies, made possible an allocation of both writing and editorial time since the summer of 1958. Mr. Feldman also spent the academic year 1959–60 and the summers of 1959 and 1960 as a Visiting Research Associate at the Center, thus making possible our firsthand cooperation on this volume as well.

Various authors have recorded acknowledgments as notes to their papers, and we in turn wish to note our appreciation for their willingness to participate in this enterprise.

Betty B. Bredemeier has given valiant editorial aid, ranging from checking references and maintaining uniformity of format to the rendering of scholarly prose into communicative English.

We record here, therefore, our thanks to the many individuals and organizations that helped make this volume possible.

Finally, we note for ourselves as authors and editors that we have worked jointly. Since we are quite unable, and indeed unwilling, to single out our individual contributions, we should not think it worth while for others to attempt it. We have found the whole experience immediately rewarding, and now hope others may share part of the excitement.

WILBERT E. MOORE
ARNOLD S. FELDMAN

November 1960

CONTENTS

ix

PART II   THE ORGANIZATION OF WORK

PART III   THE MARKET MATRIX

1 COMMITMENT OF THE
INDUSTRIAL LABOR FORCE

Arnold S. Feldman
Wilbert E. Moore

THE continuing expansion of market-oriented and often even industrially organized economic activities into "newly developing" areas of the world is a crude empirical fact. However, the speed of transition, its relative success in economic terms, the amount of social disorganization, and the prospective future viability of the emerging social systems are all highly variable. This volume explores the social correlates of economic change, using labor commitment as a convenient focus for the whole complex process of social transformation.

THE CONCEPT OF COMMITMENT

Commitment involves both performance and acceptance of the behaviors appropriate to an industrial way of life. The concept is thus concerned with overt actions and with norms. The fully committed worker, in other words, has internalized the norms of the new productive organization and social system. By implication, therefore, there are degrees of commitment and partial substitutions, as on the part of the external conformist whose performance remains satisfactory only so long as immediately available bribes and discipline suffice to win his compliance.

Any social system can, and does, survive some outright deviance and some external conformity. Of the two, the latter is perhaps more troublesome because it is less easily detected and controlled. It is a fundamental postulate of this volume that full commitment of an industrial labor force is both important for continuous economic development and problematical—for reasons that are explored in some detail.

The scope of the discussion of labor force commitment is rather broader than the phrase may imply. On the one hand, the industrial labor force includes not only manual workers in factory operations, but the whole range of occupations appropriate to an industrialized economy—clerical, managerial, and professional. In the broad sense, indus-

1

trial production involves financial and distributive activities, as well as the production and processing of materials. On the other hand, the phrase "appropriate to an industrial way of life" refers to more than the production of goods and services that move through the market and thus acquire economic valuation. For example, adjustment to new residential patterns, ways of assigning status, political orientations, and social goals are critically involved. These processes of social transformation that accompany economic change demand attention and justify theoretical and practical concern for the performance and acceptance of behaviors consistent with that transformation.

Why Is Commitment Important?

A competent answer to this question requires analysis of the problematics of social change, to which the remainder of this chapter, and indeed of this volume, is largely devoted. Because the question is often asked from a practical point of view, in the context of advancing economic growth, a preliminary answer may be put in that context. Labor commitment in any occupation is of practical importance for several reasons: (1) The committed worker requires less supervision, and certainly less disciplinary supervision, and his performance is more likely to be at the upper end of the tolerable range than at the lower. (2) The worker who has accepted the norms appropriate to his particular role behaves more predictably in optional or choice situations than the one who appears to be governed entirely by external circumstances. (3) This reliability of behavior is especially noteworthy in crisis situations, which indeed comprise effective tests for distinguishing the partially committed (or external conformists) and the fully committed. There are, then, tests of commitment that do not require "depth psychology"; the behavioral consequences of commitment presumably are reflected in social systems as well as in the structure of individual personalities.

It is probably true that different levels of commitment are required for different functional positions. However, the cynical position that makes the performer's attitudes unproblematical or unimportant has limits at both extremes—ranging from his negative capacity for sabotage to his positive capacity for outstanding performance.

This preliminary reply to the question concerning importance of commitment has been put in terms of work roles. A little further analysis reveals the fundamental importance of norms in the conduct of a viable social system. Concepts like equity, honesty, trust, confidence in money and credit arrangements, mutuality of contractual obligations, and many others cannot be taken for granted when they have not previously existed, or have not been specifically applied in the social contexts fostered by economic modernization. Considerable attention will be paid here to these broader contexts of commitment, since they underlie the specific performance requirements of workers and also serve to place work within a system of social relationships.

Criteria of Judgment

Discussion of commitment in terms of performance of work and other roles may seem spuriously easy. Under the fictitious assumption of a "perfectly integrated" society, without conflicts of interests between persons or groups and without role conflicts, expectations of performance might be perfectly symmetrical and reciprocal. In all actual situations the criteria of adequacy of performance are multiple and often inconsistent. This difficulty has continued to plague sociological analysis of industrial organizations.

Since the managerial bias of American industrial sociology has been only partly eradicated, industrial sociologists who study industry in newly developing areas may perhaps not be free of this and other biases of their specialty.

There are additional reasons for the introduction of the managerial bias in the study of labor force commitment in newly developing areas. First, it is the manager who is most clearly and consistently perceived as upholding the goal of industrialization. The research investigator typically enters the situation with an implicit bias in favor of industrialization. Thus there is a kind of value-affinity between them. Second, many newly developing areas are characterized by exceedingly great social distances between their various social strata. The investigator is almost always in a stratum equivalent to that of the managers and, because of the tremendous gulf between the strata, he has little accessibility to the workers and easy accessibility to the managers. Problems of language also enter the situation. The investigator's reliance on selected bilingual informants frequently results in an overrepresentation of management. This source of error is being corrected by recent research based on adequate cross-sectional samples, for example, by Gregory (Chapter 9 infra). Third, the problem of commitment is frequently seen as one faced by managers. Thus the investigator finds himself sliding into the position that his task is to provide the kind of information that will allow management or other social engineers to design programs that will reduce unproductive behavior by the work force. Questions concerning commitment are consequently perceived as within the field of applied research.

The result of the promanagement bias deriving from these various sources is that the investigator is likely to confuse, or fail to distinguish between, commitment to industrial labor and commitment to managerial practices. For example, various kinds of labor unrest are frequently interpreted as evidence of low levels of commitment. It is quite possible that exactly the reverse is the case. A strike, a slowdown, or other demonstration may be evidence of high levels of commitment, in that only a committed labor force would undertake and be able to carry out effective antimanagement organization and activity. One view is that an antimanagement ideology is part of the tradition and culture of industrial labor, and that commitment includes the acceptance of such an ideology. At the very least, the committed worker (manager, distributor) is alert to special as well as common interests.

The Unit of Observation

The focus of this volume is on the effects of industrial labor force commitment on programs of social and economic change in newly developing areas or, more specifically, on the extent to which low levels of labor force commitment impede efforts to industrialize newly developing areas. It should be clear, then, that the relevant unit of observation is the labor force viewed as a collectivity. The individual worker becomes a valid unit of observation only if two conditions obtain: if his commitment level is additive with that of other workers so that they can be averaged; and if such an average of the commitment levels of individual workers is a valid expression of the commitment level of the labor force as a collectivity.

Determining whether individual levels of commitment are, in fact, additive is a technical problem. Presumably one way of solving this problem is through the construction of scales. Although a number of factors—for example, problems of language, radically different cultural milieux, and sampling difficulties—make the construction and use of attitude scales in newly developing areas technically challenging, the difficulties can be resolved, given a favorable balance of economic resources and ingenuity.

Ascertaining whether an average of individual commitment levels is a valid measure of the level of commitment of the labor force viewed as a collectivity is methodologically much more intricate. First, there is the question of the predictability of the behavior of the collectivity from a summary measure of its component individuals. This is the familiar problem of the relations between the distribution of a set of scale scores and a measure of their central tendency. Again, given an adequate sample and sufficient caution on the part of the investigator, the difficulties are surmountable. For example, even if it is not feasible to predict for the labor force as a whole, predictions may be made for relatively homogeneous substrata of the labor force, if the sample has been adequately stratified. This technical problem is related to the theoretical one involved in the use of differing criteria of performance in various sectors of the labor force. This subject is touched on at a number of points in this volume, but without final resolution. The fact is that it is easier to analyze the general problems of commitment—and that is difficult enough—than the differential ones.

In our discussion the individual to whom commitment processes and results are attributed is thus a typological representative of a social system in process of change: change brought about largely by the transformation of representative individual actions and beliefs.

COMMITMENT AND ECONOMIC DEVELOPMENT

The growth and diffusion of the desire for a common minimum level of living is an outstanding feature of the postwar world. In a sense, for perhaps the first time in the history of the modern world a universal goal is gradually evolving. Even in cultures traditionally based on a normative system that emphasizes otherworldliness, the desire for change for the better in this world is constantly increasing. Further, the desire for such change has itself become a spiritual force of great importance in these areas of the world.[1]

Development as End and Means

The type and degree of change needed can be understood in part through examination of the desired goal. Although it may be impossible to state in detail the specific content of this goal, it undoubtedly includes a certain minimum economic standard, particularly in regard to the material conditions of life. The type of change required, then, is to a considerable extent change in the socioeconomic institutions. This is especially true of those areas where the discrepancy between actual levels of living and the desired levels is greatest. Where this discrepancy between actual and desired levels of living remains high,

[1] Wilbert E. Moore, "Creation of a Common Culture," *Confluence*, 4:231–233 (July 1955).

and the prospects for continuation of the discrepancy are also high and visible, the world is faced with a source of social strife.[2] Here is the crucial problem in social engineering, outweighing all the particular questions of developmental strategy and tactics.

Since both the common goal involved and the means of achieving this goal include economic change, the concept of economic development can be interpreted as both an end and as a means to that end. It is precisely this duality of the concept of economic development that defines the central problem of this volume. The desire for or commitment to economic development as an end does not necessarily include desire for or commitment to economic development as a means. The fact that these two aspects of development can vary somewhat independently means that even though the desire for development as a goal may exist and be physically achievable, commitment to development as a process of change may not exist. When physical capabilities are partially blocked, commitment to the means of development is even less probable, particularly since greater sacrifices are likely to be involved.[3]

We are here mainly concerned with the acceptance and performance of the actions necessary for economic change, i.e., with means. Where the process of change includes a gradual achievement of the end, i.e., where the end itself is viewed as a continuum rather than a distinct state, the two types of commitment will probably be mutually reinforcing and perhaps indistinguishable.[4] In such a situation the problem of gaining commitment to development as a means should be minimal.

[2] On differences in current economic levels and in rates of growth, see: Norman S. Buchanan and Howard S. Ellis, *Approaches to Economic Development* (New York: Twentieth Century Fund, 1955), pp. 3–22; Karl W. Deutsch, *Nationalism and Social Communication* (New York: John Wiley & Sons, 1953); Paul K. Hatt, ed., *World Population and Future Resources* (New York: American Book Co., 1952); Eugene Staley, *The Future of Underdeveloped Countries* (New York: Harper & Brothers, 1954), pp. 1–26. The demographic and social correlates of underdevelopment are emphasized by A. J. Jaffe and Charles D. Stewart, *Manpower Resources and Utilization* (New York: John Wiley & Sons, 1951), pp. 401–414.

[3] See Deutsch, *op. cit.;* Gunnar Myrdal, *International Economy: Problems and Prospects* (New York: Harper & Brothers, 1956), pp. 160–221, 319–321; Talcott Parsons and Neil J. Smelser, *Economy and Society* (Glencoe: Free Press, 1956), pp. 255–271, especially pp. 260–261. See also references listed in *International Social Science Bulletin* (special issue on "Factors of Economic Progress"), 6(2):288–289 (1954); Keith Simpson and Hazel C. Benjamin, *Manpower Problems in Economic Development: A Selected Bibliography* (Princeton: Industrial Relations Section, Princeton University, 1958).

[4] For an exposition of the reciprocity of stimulation between wants (ends) and activities (means), see Alfred Marshall, *Principles of Economics* (8th ed.; London: Macmillan and Co., 1938), pp. 86–91.

The end can appear as a continuum only in certain situations, primarily where development is more a process of intensification than of transformation. In areas where incomes are very low, the sheer amount of change required to achieve the desired goal rules out the intensification of current economic institutions. The type of economic change required in these areas calls for the transformation of the basic character of the economy and concomitant social structure. Furthermore, other characteristics of currently underdeveloped areas impose limits on the possibility of immediate gains even from transformation. Of particular importance here is the economic position of these areas vis-à-vis the remainder of the world; in many such areas rapid growth is still less rapid than in advanced countries.[5]

Commitment to Economic Development as a Means

When the two types of commitment are not mutually reinforcing, the differences between them are likely to become sharper through time. In other words, where the given goal of economic development involves major transformations of the socioeconomic structure, their acceptance is problematical and uncertain. The "means" prove to be new patterns of daily existence and thus are in conflict with an intricately interrelated social, including normative, structure.

These patterns of behavior and their normative sanctions in turn relate to goals and values other than economic development or material well-being.[6] Since such well-being is not the sole goal of any society, and cannot be if it is to survive as a viable system, the value conflict is not trivial or simply based on temporary ignorance or misunderstanding.

Even if it is argued that in some underdeveloped areas the aspiration for economic development is so high and firm that it has a temporal or strategic primacy, it does not follow that the goal would or could be pursued "at *all* costs." The question is: What are the minimum and probable "costs" if the goal is pursued at all, as it certainly will be? These costs prominently include value conflicts arising from necessary transformations in hitherto accepted ways of life. Acceptance and per-

[5] Simon Kuznets, "Underdeveloped Countries and the Pre-Industrial Phase in the Advanced Countries," *Proceedings of the World Population Conference, 1954* (New York: United Nations, 1955), Vol. 5, pp. 947–968.

[6] Wilbert E. Moore, *Economy and Society* (Garden City: Doubleday and Co., 1955), p. 6, and *Industrialization and Labor* (Ithaca: Cornell University Press, 1951), especially pp. 166–199; Talcott Parsons, "The Motivation of Economic Activities," in his *Essays in Sociological Theory, Pure and Applied* (Glencoe: Free Press, 1949), Chapter 9.

formance of these new ways of life are important as necessary means and are problematical because of the lack of appreciation of their necessity (cognitive element) and the resistance to sacrifices of values (normative element).[7]

VARIABILITY OF SYSTEMS AND SEQUENCES

Societies that are currently considered highly developed show considerable differences in their economic and social organization. There is no reason to believe that the alternative patterns are exhausted. On the contrary, there is every reason to expect that extremely novel forms of high development will result when and if currently underdeveloped societies achieve their goals. The cultural similarities among the developed countries arise in part from the "historical accident" that these countries (with the exception of Japan) share a cultural heritage far more ancient than their common use of industrial forms of economic organization. A central theoretical question, therefore, is the extent to which subscription to the goal of economic growth prejudges the possible range of other cultural characteristics. The question is sharpened when alternative means for achievement of the common goal are taken into account.

The evidence already at hand indicates that sequences, rates, and results of socioeconomic change differ in both time and space. The ultimate refuge of the social scientist is, of course, "cultural relativism," which essentially denies the possibility of any repeated relations or predictive propositions. He is then limited to "culture bound" static generalizations or retrospective descriptions. This issue arises in various contexts throughout this volume. Herskovits, for example, takes the position (Chapter 8) that the *processes* of culture change are more general than the sequence of social and cultural *forms*. Kerr, on the other hand, implies the probability of variety in transitional forms but emphasizes the probable similarity of end results (Chapter 19). In Part I of this volume we attempt to provide the basis for recognizing and identifying variety without abandoning claims that a generalized theoretical system for social dynamics is possible.

---

[7] John M. Clark, *Preface to Social Economics* (New York: Farrar and Rinehart, 1936), pp. 44–65; Everett E. Hagen, "The Process of Economic Development," *Economic Development and Cultural Change*, 5:193–215 (April 1957); Talcott Parsons, *The Social System* (Glencoe: Free Press, 1951), pp. 55–57; Wilbert E. Moore and Melvin M. Tumin, "Some Social Functions of Ignorance," *American Sociological Review*, 14:791–792 (December 1949).

The methodological question is partly one of desired detail. Generalization loses information, which must be reintroduced if the generalization is to be "applied" to a concrete social system at a particular junction in its somewhat unique evolution. In this volume the interplay between analysis of developments in particular areas, on the one hand, and the search for structural and sequential types or universals, on the other hand, is a recurrent theme.

Despite differences in particular social systems and in the historic paths to the present, problems of variability are partly resolved by recognition that the analysis deals with *systems*. Thus the elements of social behavior associated with productive systems are not randomly variable. The possible sequences of change are substantially short of infinite in their variety.

If the analysis of social change starts from a consideration of economic development, no crude theory of economic determinism is implied. Rather, the concern is with a value change that is major in both degree and scope and with the implications of this change for the whole socio-economic fabric of existence. Economic development thus represents as serious a challenge to social science as it does to social engineering.

Elements and Organization of Analysis

Defining commitment as the acceptance and performance of behaviors appropriate to new social forms gives three main components for analysis: (1) actions and norms, appropriate to (2) varieties of social forms and contexts (the *loci* of commitment), acquired through (3) varieties of sequential socialization via the agencies of exposure.

The tests of commitment thus lie in both acceptance and performance—norms and actions. Both may vary in level and degree. Performance provides inferential but not conclusive evidence of acceptance, which may also be tested by persistence in the face of adversity or competing opportunities, performance in the absence of external sanctions, and emotional condemnation of normative violations by others. In other words, *acceptance refers to the phenomenon of internalization or moral conformity.*

The appropriateness of actions and norms is of course always relative to a specific *locus* of action. This locus cannot be limited properly to a particular form of work organization, such as the factory system, for two reasons: (1) Social systems display some degree of functional interdependence and integration, so that a change in modes of productive organization has consequences for other social structures in which any individual participates. (2) Thus, the initial agency of exposure and sequential socialization is not necessarily the work organization.

The broad organization of hypothetical relations then consists of (a) a taxonomy of social contexts (loci), for each of which there are (b) actions and norms that are appropriate, under the assumptions of a functionally integrated industrial society, and (c) the agencies of exposure at various points in the socialization sequence. The assumption of functional integration does not preclude multiple bases of status in a social system; it leaves open the question of their coherence and integration, as Singer suggests (Chapter 14).

Social Contexts of Commitment

Three major contexts can be distinguished with respect to the loci of commitment; and each can be further subdivided into a variable number of subcontexts:

I. The Work Place: Action patterns specific to a job and to the organization of that job. The subcontexts are:
   A. Workers and Machines: The pattern of interaction between human and nonhuman disposable resources as they are typically utilized in a process of factory production.
   B. Division of Labor: The specialized, sometimes hierarchical system of interdependence, resulting from either the dilution of previous skills or the creation of new skill *Gestalten,* in the flow of production.
   C. Authority: The alternative systems of communication and coordination, including the alternative bases of legitimation.

II. Market System: The extensity and purity of a generalized medium of exchange. The subcontexts are:
   A. Labor Market: Including managerial and professional labor, as well as the different levels of skill.
   B. Commodity Market: Including capital and producers' goods, as well as consumers' goods.

III. Social Structure: The institutional order of society, and particularly major functional complexes, their associated norms and concrete groups, and also various common orientations and integrative norms. The subcontexts are:
   A. Kinship: The patterns of reciprocities and strains between family and economy.
   B. Stratification: Competing patterns of invidious social differentiation and the individual's equitable position therein. Unions, occupational groups, and education as aspects of stratification.

C. Political System: Patterns of political loyalty and participation resulting from the structural position of the state as the focus of national
   integration and identity and the ultimate enforcement agency for
   social codes.
D. Common Orientations: Minimum levels of cognitive consensus, acquiescence in a normative order, and minimal consensus on ultimate
   values.

Agencies of Exposure

With respect to the agencies of exposure to new kinds of social action,
the analysis distinguishes (a) precommitment or predisposing agencies
and processes, (b) transitional phenomena, and (c) the ways in which
internalization is effected and maintained.

Predisposing agencies include those elements in the premodern sectors
of an underdeveloped area that facilitate the acts and norms appropriate to the social behavior systems characteristic of integrated industrial societies. For example, a stratification system that is at least normatively open-class, with institutionalized modes of status achievement—
such as traditional Chinese society—presumably would encourage
ready acceptance of the comparable norms applicable to an industrial
labor force.[8]

Transitional phenomena refer primarily to the agencies and processes
of adult socialization, which is a neglected area of investigation with
regard to the many changes in the position of adults in industrial societies.[9] Adult socialization is of critical significance in the transformation
of socioeconomic systems, for without it, new social patterns could be
neither self-generated nor self-maintained. The process of socialization
clearly involves both cognitive and affective elements.[10] These are, of
course, analytical distinctions, since there is no human action without
affect or, at some level, cognition. Nevertheless the distinction is important, as the agencies of major relevance may differ with respect to
the two elements. Cognitive learning often takes place in predominantly formal and impersonal social relations, but the internali-

[8] Marion J. Levy, Jr., "Contrasting Factors in the Modernization of China and
Japan," *Economic Development and Cultural Change*, 2:167 (October 1953).

[9] The significance of adult socialization is related to recent interest in "reference
group" phenomena. See Peter M. Blau, "Social Mobility and Interpersonal Relations,"
American Sociological Review, 21:290–295 (June 1956); Everett E. Hagen, *op. cit.*

[10] See Talcott Parsons and James Olds, "The Mechanism of Personality Functioning with Special Reference to Socialization," in Talcott Parsons and Robert F. Bales,
Family, Socialization and Interaction Process (Glencoe: Free Press, 1955), Chapter 4.

zation of norms always involves strongly affective relations and thus something approximating the specifications for "primary" groups. The family may turn out to be as crucial for socialization of the adult as for that of the child, both by way of adult interaction and, especially, by way of children in a transitional situation.

For maintenance of commitment it is assumed, *at least in the locus under discussion,* that the transition has been completed. But just as there is an important range of phenomena involving adult socialization (contrary to prominent Freudian and neo-Freudian conceptions), the socialized or committed individual will not necessarily remain so unless the learned actions and ideas and the believed values are more or less consistently buttressed by a system of rewards and expectations. The maintenance processes relevant here are presumably most effective when the transition is no longer segmental and partial (e.g., in a new kind of employment), and when all other individual involvements (as consumer, city dweller, father, citizen, etc.) actually or potentially help maintain the specific commitment. This is one implication of the conception of a functionally integrated industrial system.

Interdependence and Expanding Commitment

Functional interdependence implies that the various loci of commitment (work place, market, family, community) constitute potential agencies of socialization for intrinsically relevant actions and norms, and also, theoretically, for any or all others. The order of our classification of social contexts implies a sort of order of expanding commitment.[11] However, other sequences are both theoretically possible and empirically observable, at both societal and individual levels. For example, rapid urban growth may occur without substantial industrialization,[12] and individuals may join labor unions while remaining peasant proprietors and living in small villages. The kind of conceptual apparatus used here would permit an empirical typology of action and commitment sequences, their frequency, and determinants, but we do not offer such a typology. The taxonomy of contexts, actions, and agencies is here restricted to partial or segmental sequences, which are noted fairly systematically.

[11] This is related to MacIver's analysis of the "dynamic assessment." See Robert M. MacIver, *Social Causation* (Boston: Ginn and Co., 1942), pp. 291–350.

[12] Kingsley Davis and Ana Casis, "Urbanization in Latin America," *Milbank Memorial Fund Quarterly,* 24:2–22, 43–45 (April 1946); Moore, *Industrialization and Labor,* p. 263.

2 THE WORK PLACE

Arnold S. Feldman
Wilbert E. Moore

In Part I of this volume we try to specify the patterns of working and living to which commitment is required if economic development is to be pursued. It is assumed that certain actions and norms are required for sustained economic development; and that, although the margin of error may be uncomfortably large, knowledge is sufficient for specifying the character of these actions and norms. It must be admitted that these assumptions are quite optimistic.

Any attempt of this kind is largely dependent on historical and current knowledge of highly industrialized societies. This dependence introduces the possibility of an ethnocentric bias,[1] a charge made in several later chapters, but here effort is made to minimize the potential bias and distortion from these sources. First, limited parts of the social system (the individual loci) are analyzed seriatim, a procedure that hopefully discourages excessively broad generalizations. Second, the processes of change considered to be most immediately relevant to each of the loci of commitment are much more limited than the total number of processes commonly designated by the term "economic development." This chapter deals with the place of work and its corresponding process, industrialization, somewhat narrowly conceived.

INDUSTRIALIZATION AND THE FACTORY

Industrialization is defined as one aspect of economic development: the development of a factory system of production. So defined, indus-

[1] On the applicability of "Western" developmental patterns and sequences to newly developing areas see Kingsley Davis, "The Controversial Future of the Underdeveloped Areas" in Paul K. Hatt, ed., *World Population and Future Resources* (New York: American Book Co., 1952), pp. 14–24; *International Social Science Bulletin*, 4:243–339 (1952); Wilbert E. Moore, *Industrialization and Labor* (Ithaca: Cornell University Press, 1951); Irene B. Taeuber, "The Future of Transitional Areas" in Hatt, *op. cit.*, pp. 25–38, and "Population Increase and Manpower Utilization in Imperial Japan" in *Modernization Programs in Relation to Human Resources and Population Problems* (New York: Milbank Memorial Fund, 1950), pp. 121–141; Irene B. Taeuber and Edwin G. Beal, "The Dynamics of Population in Japan" in *Demographic Studies of Selected Areas of Rapid Growth* (New York: Milbank Memorial Fund, 1944), pp. 2, 11–15, 19–21, 26, 32–34.

trialization is more limited in scope than the growth of the secondary or manufacturing industry per se. Our concern is with the acts and norms required for effective factory labor.

The Factory as System and as Situation

Industrial sociologists typically conceive of the factory as a self-contained and complete social system,[2] a point of view aptly labeled "plant sociology" by Kerr and Fisher.[3] In this conception of the factory there is an intriguing, if paradoxical, combination of breadth and narrowness, which creates a dilemma for the analysis of commitment to factory labor. The breadth of the conception is a consequence of the important empirical discovery that many previously unsuspected relationships exist within the factory.[4] The narrowness of the conception is a consequence of the plant sociologists' insistence on including all these relations and "interactions" under the rubric of work relations in order to support their view of the factory as a self-contained social system.[5]

The dilemma comes about in the following manner. First, any analysis of the factory as a place of work and thus as a place where commitment occurs must take cognizance of the empirical evidence. Many relations not intrinsic to the work roles of the participants do exist within the factory, and this fact is at least equally relevant for the analysis of factory work in newly developing areas. Thus, the thinking of plant sociologists suggests that commitment to factory labor is only partly commitment to certain forms of work. It follows that a great deal of what the new factory worker must commit himself to in the factory cannot be derived directly from job specifications.

Second, the plant sociologists' conception of the factory as a complete and single social system means that place of work and the factory are perceived as different labels for a single phenomenon, since all the

---

[2] Conrad M. Arensberg and Geoffrey Tootell, "Plant Sociology: Real Discoveries and New Problems" in Mirra Komarovsky, ed., *Common Frontiers of the Social Sciences* (Glencoe: Free Press, 1957), pp. 312–315; Clark Kerr and Lloyd H. Fisher, "Plant Sociology: The Elite and the Aborigines" in Komarovsky, *op. cit.*, pp. 302–305; William F. Whyte, *Money and Motivation* (New York: Harper & Brothers, 1955), p. 218.

[3] Kerr and Fisher, *op. cit.*, p. 285.

[4] Arensberg and Tootell, *op. cit.*, pp. 317, 320–321, 328–333; Elton Mayo, *The Human Problems of an Industrial Civilization* (Boston: Harvard Graduate School of Business, 1933), pp. 55–121; F. J. Roethlisberger and W. J. Dickson, *Management and the Worker* (Cambridge: Harvard University Press, 1940), pp. 493–510.

[5] Arensberg and Tootell, *op. cit.*, pp. 333–337; Kerr and Fisher, *op. cit.*, pp. 302–305.

social relations present are functionally interdependent.[6] Thus, if this position is adopted, all these relations should be included in any analysis of the place of work as a locus of commitment. Since so much occurs within the factory, it would appear that the work place becomes the most salient locus of commitment.

Attributing primary salience to the place of work as a locus of commitment is quite unpalatable to us. In the preceding chapter it was argued that the commitment process involves many areas of a person's life and that no single locus is intrinsically more important than any other.

The analytical problem then is as follows: if the place of work is to be treated as a locus of commitment equivalent in rank to the other loci, certain acts and norms present in the factory must be excluded. Moreover, the exclusion should not be capricious, but based on principle. The principle basic to the present analysis is that the factory is a concrete structure whose boundaries are *never coterminous with any single* analytical system; aspects of different analytical systems manifest themselves within the factory.[7] In the terminology used here the factory is a physical place where elements from the various loci of commitment are found, but the factory itself is not a locus of commitment. The factory is more than a place of work; it is also a market place for labor, a place where some of the actions of different occupational and union groups occur, and where the norms of the communal or societal status systems influence people's behavior.

As the physical place where parts of the different loci of commitment intersect, the factory has great situational relevance for any study of labor force commitment. Parts of the processes of commitment for almost all the loci may be observed in the factory. As a theoretical entity, however, the factory is less significant and less relevant for the study of commitment. Indeed, treating the factory as if it were a single theoretical system is an error.

In specific factories, elements from the different loci of commitment may be so closely connected as to appear indistinguishable. Since the foreman may also be the employer, the norms of the work place and of the market place may be combined in a single status. But it would be an error to deduce from this the theoretical proposition that the respective

6 Arensberg and Tootell, *op. cit.*, pp. 315–321, 334–337.

7 Marion J. Levy, Jr., *The Structure of Society* (Princeton: Princeton University Press, 1952), pp. 88–89; Talcott Parsons and Neil J. Smelser, *Economy and Society* (Glencoe: Free Press, 1956), pp. 14, 42, 79–81.

norms and acts must be so integrated. The considerable and increasing separation of these two statuses suggests that they should be regarded as parts of separate analytic systems.[8]

"Naturalness" of Conflict

The failure to distinguish between a concrete organization and its component analytic systems leads to a number of conceptual errors. Prominent among these is the manner in which conflict within the factory is treated. This error is quite apparent in the analysis of differentiation between line and staff, that is, between coordinating functions and informational functions.

The empirical observation that separation of line and staff is associated with conflict frequently evokes the interpretation that such conflict is unnatural, the result of artificial barriers to communication and thus of a lack of mutual understanding. In turn, the barriers to communication are attributed to the artificial division of hierarchical positions necessitated by an increase in the size of an organization.[9] Thus if communication channels were maximally efficient, the common interests would become apparent to those involved. It is argued that separation makes efficient communication difficult. The social distance separating the newly created positions is said to introduce a sense of conflict where none should exist.

An alternative interpretation is that conflict between line and staff is a "natural" consequence of the interaction between two distinct and sometimes opposing systems of action that simultaneously exist within the same concrete organization. Indeed, there is evidence that the conflict is present whether or not the positions are separated.[10] The separation allows the conflict between the market place and the work place

---

[8] Melville Dalton, "Conflicts Between Staff and Line Managers," *American Sociological Review*, 15:342–351 (June 1950), and "Unofficial Union Management Relations," *ibid.*, 15:611–619 (October 1950); Wilbert E. Moore, *Industrial Relations and the Social Order* (New York: Macmillan Company, 1955), pp. 74–84; Eugene V. Schneider, *Industrial Sociology* (New York: McGraw-Hill Book Company, 1957), pp. 81–83.

[9] Keith Powlison, "Explaining the Facts to Employees," *Harvard Business Review*, 25:145–157 (Winter 1947); Roethlisberger and Dickson, *op. cit.*, pp. 448–458.

[10] Robert K. Merton, "The Role-Set: Problems in Sociological Theory," *British Journal of Sociology*, 8:106–120 (June 1957); F. J. Roethlisberger, "The Foreman: Master and Victim of Double Talk," *Harvard Business Review*, 23:283–298 (Spring 1945); Donald E. Wray, "Marginal Men of Industry: The Foremen," *American Journal of Sociology*, 54:298–301 (January 1949).

to be external to any one person and thus manifest itself as organizational (or status) conflict rather than personal (or role) conflict.

Conflict and Commitment

This view of conflict within the factory has some implications for the process of commitment. First, if it is correct that much of the conflict internal to the factory is "natural," it is possible that the process of commitment may generate as much conflict as it dissipates. The extent to which different statuses in the factory conflict with one another may become increasingly apparent to workers and managers as their levels of commitment increase. The conflicting issues will, of course, change quite radically. In any case the sheer presence or absence of conflict by itself should not be made the test of commitment. A committed labor force (managerial and operative) is not necessarily a docile one: the opposite is more likely to be the case.

There is a high probability that the newly industrialized worker and manager will have a distorted perception of the factory quite similar to that held by the plant sociologist. They may expect a much more unitary and integrated system than can ever exist. If the worker comes from a preindustrial economic organization, his initial socialization to work occurred within a system in which many different statuses (and thus different systems) were combined in the same concrete position. The classic example of this is the integration of family and economic status in the peasant economy. The preindustrial work norms are then bolstered by the outward appearance that statuses in the factory duplicate the unitary character of nonfactory work statuses.

The sociological consequence is that the newly created industrial labor force perceives a single set of norms, when actually the situation is structured by sets of diffierential norms. The inability to perceive the full extent to which norms are differentiated within the factory may severely inhibit the ease of commitment.

THE THREE INTRINSIC WORK FACTORS

From the totality of elements present in a factory, the elements intrinsic to work may be isolated by considering the three primary aspects of any industrial job: any factory worker must typically interact with machines, other workers, and bosses.

The effects of mechanization on the nature of industrial work and workers remains a controversial issue for the social sciences. Analyses of relationships of workers and machines have tended to be argumentative, value-laden, and extreme—thus obscuring the considerable heterogeneity that now characterizes machine work.[11] Both machines and workers have experienced extensive specialization, and mechanized labor is quite variable with regard to number of workers and levels of skill and knowledge required for a given operation. The relation between men and machines is a truly interactive one, always involving the physical instrument, the unit of labor, and the required levels of skill and knowledge. All are, in a basic sense, the tools of production.[12] The proportions in which they are combined impart a typical pattern of behavior to any process of production.

"Fetishism" of Machines

The relations between worker and machine in a factory system of production are frequently misrepresented, particularly in the popular finding that workers' acts are machine-determined.[13] Technological determinism frequently results from an artifact in the collection of data. Specifically, whether the behavior patterns are determined by men or machines is a function of the particular point in the process of production at which the investigator makes his observations. If observations are made at the point where machines are designed, one type of determinism can be found. Men design machines in accordance with their own criteria, as well as estimates or assumptions regarding the physiological, psychological, and social capabilities of potential workers.

Even after the machines are designed and installed, such decisions as the speed of the assembly line and the rate of production are made by men. A curious and perverse romanticism of the machine frequently colors analysis of this part of the relation between man and machine. Writers allude to the evils of machines, the speeds they force on workers, etc.; they do not seem to recognize the anthropomorphic character of such judgments.

[11] Perhaps the most complete treatment of these factors is in Georges Friedmann, *Industrial Society* (Glencoe: Free Press, 1955).

[12] Herbert S. Frankel, *The Economic Impact on Underdeveloped Societies* (Oxford, England: Basil Blackwell, 1953), pp. 1–17.

[13] The term "fetishism of machines" is, of course, copied from Marx's analysis of the fetishism of commodities. See Karl Marx, *Capital* (New York: Modern Library), pp. 81–96. For analyses of machine determinisms see Daniel Bell, "Work in the Life of an American" in William Haber and others, eds., *Manpower in the United States* (New York: Harper & Brothers, 1954), pp. 9–14; Friedmann, *op. cit.*, pp. 42–43.

Once machines are designed, installed, and in operation, the reverse determinism can be observed. At this point in the cycle of relations between man and machine, the immediate "lead" comes from the machine. Since we are here concerned with the latter stage of these relations, the following presentation deals with an essentially machine-determined pattern of behavior. It may be noted that the men whose acts determine the machine are never the men whose acts are determined by it.

The Rhythm and Pace of Factory Work

The principal behavior patterns common to factory workers can be described as acts whose pace and rhythm are set by the machine. Within the restrictions just described, the worker typically reacts to leads initiated by the machine. Thus he is paced by the machine, in the sense that he is led through the day's work activities. It is important to avoid the hyperbole common to descriptions and analyses of machine pacing. The worker's role is not completely passive; he does not become a literal automaton. However, for the newly industrialized labor force, factory work will mean an increase in the proportion of acts wherein the machine paces the worker, rather more frequently than it means the reverse.

One consequence of machine pacing is a particular rhythm in the worker's activities. The extent to which a machine, once designed, can vary the periodicity of its acts is limited. The worker pays a penalty for his greater flexibility at this stage of the man-machine cycle. He adjusts and thus conforms to the rhythm of the machine. Although many different and varied motions may be combined into a pattern, which could be called a "stanza," succeeding stanzas will be almost exact duplications of each other.[14]

It is important to locate with some precision the commitment problems associated with the initial exposure to a work pace and rhythm determined by the machine. Too often the problems associated with factory labor in industrialized societies are assumed to exist also in the newly developing areas, without sufficient regard for differences in the standards of comparison and in the criteria of evaluation. This is particularly true of the physiological and psychological effects of highly

[14] For a more detailed description of pacing and rhythm see W. Baldamus, "Incentives and Work Analysis," *University of Birmingham Studies in Economics and Society,* Monograph A-1 (University of Birmingham, England: Research Board, Faculty of Commerce and Social Science, 1951), pp. 42–49.

mechanized labor. Problems of commitment in newly industrializing societies are surely not due to any increase in the dullness or hardness of work. If anything, in many areas these are likely to diminish as a consequence of factory work. The village peasants' labor is not a source of mental stimulation, nor is it "easy" work.[15]

Machine pacing and rhythm impart an increased rigidity to the structure of work activities.[16] The difficulty of either learning or performing such highly structured activities is at worst a temporary barrier to commitment; for as operative skills develop, the structure of activities per se should pose fewer problems. Routinization of work activities may be morally objectionable, but it makes their learning and efficient performance much easier.[17]

The worker may regard subordination to machine-structured work as personal and social degradation. If so, this phenomenon represents a major barrier to commitment. The extent and permanence of subordination to the machine in industrial societies are therefore of crucial importance for this analysis. Specifically, it is most important to see whether factors that reduce some of the adverse effects of machine subordination in industrial societies can operate early enough to prevent serious blockage of labor commitment in developing areas.

Two kinds of correctives serve to reduce the degradation associated with subordination to the machine in industrial societies. The first is the re-establishment of technical mastery as a result of ever higher levels of skills in the blue-collar segments of the labor force. The second may be the redistribution of property rights in machines to produce a partial sense of social mastery.

Industrialization and Levels of Skill

In industrial societies workers at the two extremes of the range of skill are usually less affected by machine pacing and rhythm than at the middle. The least-skilled segments of the work force (loaders, cleaners, etc.) are to some extent removed from the machine and are correspondingly less affected. As the level of skill required increases, the worker moves closer to the machine, and his actions are thereby increasingly affected. After a certain point, however, highly skilled personnel (mockup men, designers, tool and die makers) begin to move away from the

---

[15] Arnold S. Feldman, "Men and Machines," *Challenge: The Magazine of Economic Affairs,* 7(3):62–66 (December 1958).

[16] Wilbert E. Moore, *Industrialization and Labor,* pp. 90–94.

[17] *Ibid.*

machine or are less subject to its pacing. Of course, even the most casual observer of industrial production can cite exceptions at both extremes.

The skill distribution of an industrial labor force can be conceived as resembling a diamond standing on one of its points. The two extremes are somewhat constricted, relative to the bulk of workers who are moderately skilled. Nevertheless, highly skilled workers (those who are least likely to be subordinated to the machine) are present in sizable numbers, and current trends in technology indicate that future expansion of the labor force in factories is likely to take place at these high skill levels.[18] The new recruit to blue-collar labor in industrial societies can realistically aspire to work of that kind.

Most newly developing areas present a completely different picture of the industrial labor force. The skill distribution in such areas can be drawn as a large and relatively flat base, from which a spindle protrudes. The spindle represents the extremely small proportion of moderately and highly skilled workers, typical of labor force composition in preindustrial societies.

The process of industrialization first leads to the gradual emergence of a pyramidal structure as the moderately skilled occupations expand. This transitional stage is likely to take a long period of time. The final emergence of a diamond-shaped labor force completes the process. At each of the successive stages a somewhat higher level of skill is reached. The transitional phase is characterized by the expansion of moderately skilled and thus more machine-paced occupations; the highly skilled occupations are not likely to experience any significant growth during that phase.

If this description is at all accurate, blue-collar occupational mobility within the industrial sector of newly developing areas is toward jobs that are increasingly machine-paced. The probability of post-recruitment blocks to commitment as a result of this situation is high.

Machines and Property Norms

Property norms frequently become the most sacred elements in the ideologies of industrial societies. This seems to be the case whether the norms favor "private property" or "public ownership." The belief in (if not the fact of) private or public property may be a prerequisite for

18 Friedmann, op. cit., pp. 186–188, 197–200; A. J. Jaffe and Charles D. Stewart, *Manpower Resources and Utilization* (New York: John Wiley & Sons, 1951), pp. 255–260.

industrialization in different societies. One consequence of industrialization, however, is to alter property norms and particularly the application of these norms to machines. These alterations frequently have a
homogenizing effect on property norms despite different ideologies.

Property is best defined as the totality of rights to a socially relevant
good or service. The norms of property in the main prescribe the extent
to which these rights should be concentrated or dispersed. Actually, no
industrial society assigns to a single individual all the rights to a good
or service, although the extent to which the rights are dispersed varies
with the type of good or service. The very concept of property is social,
for only when a good or service becomes relevant to the interaction between people does the concept become meaningful. Social relevance is
what is usually meant by "scarce." [19]

The rights that are involved in machines are principally the rights of
use. These are differentiated in several respects: (a) types of use, e.g.,
rational, for a particular purpose, etc.; (b) situations of use, e.g., emer-
gencies, circumstances of overwhelming need; and (c) rights to rewards
resulting from the use of the machine. These property rights in machines are dispersed according to the number of rights assigned to a
single party and the number of parties who share a single right.[20]

Our major interest in property rights in machines is in the extent
to which these rights are shared between workers and "others." Therefore, the treatment of the latter is greatly simplified. The term "other"
is used as a matter of convenience, without distinguishing among entrepreneurs, investors, publicly or privately appointed managers, and
governmental officials.

The norm in industrial societies sanctions extensive dispersion of
machine property rights between workers and others. In a completely
socialistic society the workers (who are nominally the owners) are quite
limited in the uses to which they can put machines. In the absence of
"the people's manager," the workers are limited to "rational" use of
machines for a particular product. In all societies some of these limitations are built into the machine by the designer, who in this sense functions as a part of the others. In socialist societies the manager frequently
has more rights assigned to him than does his counterpart in a capitalistic society.

[19] Kingsley Davis, *Human Society* (New York: Macmillan Company, 1949), pp.
452–470; see also the references on pp. 476–477.

[20] Wilbert E. Moore, "The Emergence of New Property Conceptions in America,"
Journal of Legal and Political Sociology, 1:34–39, 42–44 (April 1943).

In a capitalistic society workers' rights to machines are incorporated in formal laws, as well as informal norms and procedures. Legislative acts concerning lockouts, collective bargaining and arbitration, seniority, unemployment and retirement benefits, etc. all work to foster the workers' rights to machines. Informal norms such as disapproval of idle machinery, and feelings of responsibility and obligations for employees' welfare, have much the same consequence.

In both capitalistic and socialistic industrial societies the dominant form of economic organization is the large-scale corporation—whether public or private. In regard to corporations, the claim that all rights are exclusively assigned to one party (the stockholders or the state) actually serves to bolster the dispersion of these rights; for the single party to which these rights are assigned is frequently an amorphous group that enters the situation only upon provocation. Since such an "owner" can be located only in the rare case, his "say" in the operating situation is limited unless he delegates these rights to the corporate managers. In this circumstance managers operate under this proxy instead of through legal ownership of the particular rights involved. Indeed, the fact that the manager becomes accountable in case of provocation may dispose him to favor amicable settlement with workers in order to maintain the quiescence of those who have delegated their authority and power to him.

In contemporary capitalistic societies, where a considerable amount of propaganda is given to stockholding workers, the fiction of management acting as a legal owner is obvious. In a socialistic society the manager in theory holds the proxy of the people with whom he deals.

Most discussions of the extensive sharing of a single machine property right have dwelt on the consequences of dispersing corporate "ownership" rights among an ever-expanding body of stockholders. A roughly comparable situation is also the case for those machine property rights assigned to workers. A functionally important characteristic of industrial production is the transferability of both machines and workers.[21] In theory, the norms prescribe that those rights to machines

---

[21] Donald J. Bogue, "Residential Mobility and Migration of Workers," in Haber and others, *op. cit.*, pp. 143–153; Clark Kerr, "The Balkanization of Labor Markets" in E. Wight Bakke and others, *Labor Mobility and Economic Opportunity* (Cambridge: Technology Press; and New York: John Wiley & Sons, 1954), pp. 92–110; Moore, *Industrial Relations and the Social Order*, pp. 244–245, 455–478; Charles A. Myers, "Patterns of Labor Mobility" in Haber and others, *op. cit.*, pp. 154–165; Gladys L. Palmer and Ann R. Miller, "The Occupational and Industrial Distribution of Employment, 1910–50," *ibid.*, pp. 83–92. On the general institutional require-

that are assigned to workers are given to the work force and only temporarily to any specific member of it.

The operation of this aspect of machine property norms is most obvious in situations involving changes of employers. In transferring from one employer to another, the worker loses his rights to the machines he has been using but assumes the comparable rights of the work force he joins. The rights he loses are, of course, still assigned to the work force of his previous place of employment.

The sharing of the rights assigned to workers applies within the factory. Ideally, there should be reasonably complete transferability of workers and machines. Actually, the reassignment of machines to different workers often is associated with considerable conflict. Anyone who has observed stenographers' possessiveness of "company" typewriters is well aware of the difficulties involved in enforcing the norms in this respect. Factory workers show the same kind of possessiveness in respect to certain types of manufacturing equipment. Unfortunately, this aspect of property norms has received little attention, and it is impossible to state with any certainty what rules seem to operate. Some machines are frequently viewed as individual property, while others in the same factory are treated as collective property. The basis of such differentiation is often obscure.

A rationale commonly employed in claiming exclusive ownership of certain machines is the necessity of sensitive mutual adjustments between workers and machines. Available evidence does not indicate the extent to which such sensitive mutual adjustments operate nor the amount by which productivity is increased through these adjustments. It is improbable that most possessiveness of machines is technologically determined, but this variable needs further study.[22]

---

ments of an industrial system, see Max Weber, *The Theory of Social and Economic Organization* (New York: Oxford University Press, 1947), pp. 232–250.

[22] Given the high frequency of possessive attitudes toward company property, it is somewhat surprising to note the avoidance of this relationship in the literature. One possible explanatory factor is the common assumption that workers will not become directly or positively involved with machines. This assumption is most basically the consequence of the technological determinism so pervasive in this area. See Robert Dubin, *The World of Work* (Englewood Cliffs: Prentice-Hall, 1958), in which the coverage of workers' relationships is quite comprehensive, yet there is no material on this particular subject.

Friedmann, *op. cit.*, refers to man's possessiveness toward machines but alleges that it occurs rarely and only in unique situations, i.e., in the highly skilled worker in the small plant (pp. 194–195) or the uniquely satisfactory human relations program

Machine Property Rights and Commitment

The norms prescribe that the worker enters the labor force with the expectation of always using machines that legally belong to others. When these norms have to be learned by an adult worker, blockages are quite likely to occur. In industrial societies, future workers are socialized to such norms quite early in life. Schools, playgrounds, and libraries all conform to roughly analogous norms. It is quite unlikely that the socialization of workers in newly industrializing areas proceeds apace in respect to dispersion of machine property rights. The difficulty of commitment to these norms varies jointly with the type of dispersion and the norms prevalent in the preindustrial economy.

The obvious hypothesis quite commonly employed for predicting ease of commitment to industrial property norms is: the ease of commitment varies directly with the similarity of property norms. According to this hypothesis, the worker in the preindustrial society whose norms are most like those of industrial societies will be most easily and quickly committed to the new norms. Several serious objections to this hypothesis can be seen in a comparison of the property norms of feudal societies with those of contemporary industrialized societies. Superficially, the property norms of these two kinds of societies show great similarity.[23] The relation between the serf and the lord of the manor, with different property rights assigned to each, and the property relations between peasants of equal status, as manifested in the use of the commons and in the annual reapportionment of crop lands, may appear similar to the dispersion of machine property rights. However, appearances are deceiving in regard to both comparisons.

Feudal societies are small communities lacking occupational specialization and exhibiting *"gemeinschaftlich"* social relationships. Quite the opposite social organization is present in industrial communities. It is one thing to share property with a feudal chieftain; it is something else

---

(p. 360). Nevertheless, his discussion of mass-mechanized industry explicitly rules out this phenomenon (pp. 195–197), which may be a consequence of observational difficulty rather than nonoccurrence.

[23] For a general discussion of property relations in contemporary peasant societies see John Gulick, *Social Structure and Culture Change in a Lebanese Village* (New York: Viking Fund Publications in Anthropology, 1955); and Robert Redfield, *The Primitive World and Its Transformations* (Ithaca: Cornell University Press, 1953), pp. 1–153. For a discussion of peasant property relations in currently highly developed societies, especially England, see Maurice Dobb, *Studies in the Development of Capitalism* (London: Routledge and Kegan Paul, 1946), pp. 221–254.

to share rights with thousands of stockholders and a highly proliferated management. Sharing usage rights in an almost completely undifferentiated good (land) with a minimum number of covillagers, frequently kinsmen, who are almost exactly the same occupationally, is very different from sharing usage rights in highly differentiated machines with a large number of occupationally specialized people with whom relations are much more segmental.

Perhaps a more basic difficulty with the hypothesis that ease of commitment is directly associated with normative similarity is that the newly recruited industrial worker in a developing area is often motivated by great dissatisfaction with preindustrial property norms. The similar elements, if visible to the worker, may prove to be obstacles to commitment. This situation may occur frequently since the apparently similar element in social structure may have higher visibility than the basic dissimilarities.

Property Rights, Job Rights, and Mobility

The preceding discussion of machine property norms leads to an illustration of the natural conflict that can exist between the various loci of commitment. To the extent that the worker becomes committed to the property norms described above, he begins to assume the rights to machine use that the norms prescribe. But to a considerable extent machine rights are the basis of job rights. Thus as these norms become structured they tend to commit the worker to a particular job, in the process of committing him to rights in machines.

Seniority rules are a case in point. If hiring a worker is tantamount to assigning him property rights or common stock in certain machines, then seniority rules can be considered analogous to preferred stock. Unlike common stock, preferred stock is not freely transferable. Thus seniority rules aid in commiting a worker to job stability, but they may also weaken his commitment to the norm of job mobility. A high level of commitment to intrinsic work factors may have negative consequences for commitment to the norms of the labor market and vice versa.[24]

The high level of commitment to machines in a particular factory may have additional positive consequences. Once the availability of particular machines is fully accepted by the worker, he may be encouraged to requisition superior maintenance. Since the expense of

[24] Kerr, "The Balkanization of Labor Markets," *op. cit.*, pp. 92–110, especially 93–96; Palmer and Miller, *op. cit.*, pp. 83–92.

such maintenance is not borne by the worker, his decision may be on "noneconomic" grounds, i.e., appearance, personal comfort, etc.[25] To the extent that superior maintenance keeps the machines operating at peak efficiency for longer periods of time, management may sanction the additional costs on economically rational grounds. However, the type of maintenance the worker requisitions may appear to be "irrational" from the manager's point of view, in that the contribution to the machine's upkeep may be obscure. From the worker's point of view superior maintenance may be justifiable because it makes important contributions to the "amenities" of the work place, but management may demur on precisely these grounds.

DIVISION OF LABOR

The division of labor is defined here as the system of specialized work activities within a factory. By limiting this analysis to the factory, many important levels of the division of labor are excluded; but even within the factory, three different levels of this phenomenon can be observed:

1. The division of labor within the work team;
2. The division of labor between different work positions (some of which are occupied by work teams), which constitutes what we call the flow of production;
3. The division of labor that accompanies the system of authority.

Division of Labor within the Work Team [26]

Since the primary manifest function of the work team is efficient utilization of both men and machines, the team exists as a substitute for the individual operator within the flow of production. Some of the norms and acts that characterize the work team are much like those of the worker and his machine. However, the work team is a social unit in its own right; some of its norms and acts are equally characteristic of a broader level of the division of labor. As a consequence of the work team's dual nature, the interaction between these two sets of norms and

[25] When these norms are violated, the same desire for mastery leads to exactly the opposite consequences. See Moore, *Industrial Relations and the Social Order*, p. 243.

[26] For discussions of the work team as an operating unit see Dubin, *op. cit.*, pp. 104–105, 292–293; Fred H. Blum, *Toward A Democratic Work Process* (New York: Harper & Brothers, 1953), pp. 69–72; William J. Goode and Irving Fowler, "Incentive Factors in a Low Morale Plant," *American Sociological Review*, 14:618–624 (October 1949); Nicholas Babchuk and William J. Goode, "Work Incentives in a Self-Determined Group," *American Sociological Review*, 16:679–687 (October 1951).

acts—those of the operator and those of the division of labor—brings about a special set of conditions that are unique to the work team.

These unique work-team factors may be called "ecological." Since the work team is less than a full division of labor, less than a complete social unit, its characteristic properties may best be conceived as being subsocial or ecological. The properties that stand out in any description of the work team are its size, its spatial distribution, and particularly its specialized activity in space.[27]

Once these ecological characteristics of the work team are set, they impose certain additional restrictions on the members of the team. These team characteristics act as an increment to, and a substitute for, the pace and rhythm imposed by the machine. The machine almost exclusively sets the pace for the individual operator, but the team member receives many leads from other members. These leads are both relays of and additions to the leads from machines. Since most team members work quite close to machines, the reduction of machine pacing for nonoperating members seems likely to be minimal. If this is correct, the increments in pacing from team characteristics alone may more than compensate for any reduction of machine pacing. The net result is that the team member receives increased pacing, most of which comes from another person rather than a machine.

These two characteristics of work teams—(1) that the total amount of pacing may be greater for the team member than for the individual operator, and (2) that a greater proportion of pacing leads may come from other team members rather than directly from the machine—are the most salient for commitment. In examining the relevance of the work team for commitment the two characteristics must be considered jointly, since their relation to ease of commitment may be quite different. If the sheer amount of pacing, independent of its source, represents a major barrier to commitment, then recruiting labor directly into a work team inhibits commitment. However, if machine pacing is more objectionable than pacing from another person, the work team may facilitate commitment.

A positive relation between team labor and commitment in many newly developing areas is the more reasonable hypothesis. Although the machine may still be an effective pace setter, the fact that leads may

---

[27] For discussions of the ecology of work in a factory see Leo F. Schnore, "Social Morphology and Human Ecology," *American Journal of Sociology*, 63:620–634 (May 1958); Émile Durkheim, trans. by George Simpson, *The Division of Labor in Society* (Glencoe: Free Press, 1947), pp. 266–270.

be relayed by or come directly from other members of the work team conceals or diminishes the amount of machine subordination visible to the worker. This is not to say that all varieties of pacing by other workers are preferable to machine pacing. The social characteristics of other team members are likely to be such as to maximize the willingness of newly recruited workers to accept their pacing leads. Thus, the substitution of work teams for operators may be as efficient for commitment as it is for the employment of surplus labor.

Specialization

As defined here, the division of labor proceeds through various processes of specialization, two of which are particularly relevant to the factory. They are skill dilution and the creation of new combinations of skill. Skill dilution, which has enjoyed much attention from social scientists concerned with industrialization, is associated with or alleged to be the cause of innumerable social evils, among which are demoralization, dehumanization, loss of skill, loss of self-respect, and loss of a feeling of worth. Some analysts go so far as to claim that it was and is responsible for the devaluation of work as an acceptable and desirable human activity.[28]

Nevertheless, skill dilution is a minor part of the specialization that currently accompanies industrial development. The limited applicability of skill dilution to contemporary industrial development is the result of several factors. Such dilution occurs primarily in the reorganization of existing industries. For example, the bootmaker's craft was diluted into a number of different and less skilled activities or "specialties," as shoe manufacturing became mechanized. It was, however, another method of producing an article previously produced in the commercial sector of the economy. In other words, manufacturing skills that could be diluted were present in the occupational system. It is, of course, quite misleading to talk of skill dilution when the skills have not existed previously. Many newly recruited factory workers cannot have their industrial skills diluted for the obvious reason that the society has not had a tradition of industrial skills.

The economic systems of most of the industrializing areas have been limited either to sources of raw materials or to noninvolvement in the world economy. Many areas have no tradition of industrial skills of any consequence, but abound in the nonindustrial skills of a peasant

28 Bell, *op. cit.*, pp. 9–22; David Riesman and others, *The Lonely Crowd* (Garden City: Doubleday & Company, 1953), pp. 32–48.

agriculture or hunting and gathering. Although factory labor there does not dilute industrial skills, it results in a "lamentable" loss of nonindustrial skills. However, the extent to which the Indian or Egyptian village peasant is "debased" by factory labor is certainly debatable. If the current accounts of lower-class life in these areas are at all accurate, further debasement and increased squalor is hardly possible. Laments for the "poor but noble savage" about to lose a life of hunting and root-gathering freedom are unnecessary.[29]

The second process of specialization leading to the division of labor, the creation of new combinations of skill, can occur either when new elements of skill are introduced by themselves or in conjunction with a new product economy. This process is likely to be more typical of newly developing societies, where industrialization simultaneously involves both the reorganization of the social structure of work—which by itself might be a process of skill dilution—and the introduction of new products. The agricultural peasant moving into the factory does not experience a dilution of his skills. His social status may or may not suffer from the switch to factory labor; when status degradation does occur, it is not importantly attributable to the loss of skill. On the contrary, the agricultural peasant or the tribal native moving into the factory must learn new skills, even though they may not be valued as a source of status in his culture. When these new skills are so valued in the culture, however, the move to factory labor may represent upward status mobility.

In many newly developing areas the status norms of industrial societies are adopted before the industrial labor force is of any importance. At the same time, a low value is placed on the status of factory hand. This low prestige is not necessarily the result of any rejection of industrial prestige norms; it frequently is the result of a premature but extreme identification with them. Factory labor is devalued relative to white-collar, administrative, or managerial jobs within the industrial or commercial sector of the economy. In newly developing areas the father does not desire his son to return to peasantry but to achieve high white-collar status within the new prestige system. Thus, lack of

[29] For extensive discussion of these points see Feldman, "Men and Machines"; also Wilbert E. Moore, "Technological Change and Industrial Organization," and Arnold Feldman, "The Interpenetration of Firm and Society," papers prepared for the Conference on the Social Implications of Technological Progress, held in conjunction with the Fourth General Assembly of the International Social Science Council, Paris, March 18–25, 1959. These papers are to be published in a symposium edited by Georges Balandier for the Council.

commitment to factory labor may be the result of overcommitment to industrial prestige norms rather than of their rejection.

The Process of Flow

Interdependence is the obvious counterpart to specialization. Increasing specialization and interdependence eventually create a complex system of organizational interaction. In the productive process the primary function of such a system is the maintenance of flow—the performance of the necessary acts upon the product at the appropriate times.

Most analyses of flow have stressed the participants' functional contribution to the over-all organization. The analysts have incorrectly extrapolated from the functional concern the proposition that maintenance of flow depends on the participants' assumption of the goals of the over-all organization. Actually, this does not follow at all. Flow may also be analyzed as a structure of activities. The structure imposed on any single participant by flow is a highly specialized or limited interdependence. Although the entire organization is dependent on every part, any one part within the process of flow directly interacts with but few other parts.

Because the primary emphasis is on the system of production within the factory, the following analysis is limited to a segment of the occupational types and their patterns of action. Among those occupations and patterns of action omitted because of this limitation are those that relate the organization to its external environment. The limitation is, of course, consistent with the importance of distinguishing between the concrete organization and the analytical systems applicable to it.

Specialized interdependence means that the ability of any single work position adequately to perform its task within the flow of production depends immediately on adequate performance in the preceding adjacent work positions, and in turn makes possible adequate performance in the subsequent adjacent work positions. Thus the performance of each worker's task can be conceived as a service provided the immediately adjacent workers. A complex network of services evolves from the specialized, interdependent character of industrial production. For each worker, the network is not so visible or pertinent as the particular service he receives from the man who precedes him on the line, and the service he performs for the man who follows him in the flow process. Indeed, it is most important that these services never transcend certain rigidly defined limits.

The limited character of these service acts frequently appears arbitrary and dysfunctional. Limitation requirements may demand at times more energy and effort from the worker than the actual service performed, for it may be easier to perform a succeeding act than to refrain from performing it. The full importance of limited service acts can be seen if one imagines the situation that would result from violating the limits. The worker who for some reason decides to impinge on the service performed by his neighbor, or voluntarily increases the scope of his own service, would soon cause a chaotic situation. Even if the worker decided to enlarge the scope of his services because of an identification with the over-all goals of the organization, the results of such expansions would be catastrophic for orderly flow of the production process.

If it is not necessary for the production worker to identify with the over-all goals of the organization and if such an identification sometimes has negative consequences for the organization itself, the appropriate normative orientation must be a combination of specificity and affective neutrality.[30] The norm is that of recognizing the requirements of a limited number of fellow workers and accepting fairly rigid boundaries for the acts assigned. The specificity and "minimal" character of the acts and norms to which commitment is required, however, may represent a major barrier to the commitment process.

It was argued above that the socialization for work in developing societies predisposes the workers to seek out or impose unitary statuses and norms in the factory situation. The new recruit to factory labor may be more than willing (perhaps, anxious) to identify with the goals of the entire organization. He may be quite willing to accept paternalistic treatment from management and establish "primary" relationships with his co-workers. However, the resulting social organization would not be very efficient for industrial production. This kind of over-commitment may represent a much more serious obstacle to the development of an industrial labor force than the undercommitment found in many newly developing areas.

Patterns of Deference and the Evaluation of Performance

The division of labor has here been conceived as leading to a system of limited service acts. However, the division of labor also results in an

[30] For Talcott Parsons' treatment of affective neutrality and the evaluation of performance see his *The Social System* (Glencoe: Free Press, 1951), pp. 59–66.

ordering of positions, invidiously differentiated. Ordered ranks accompany the division of labor because of differences in training periods and in the ascribed functional importance of the specialized positions, if for no other reason. The training period and the functional importance of a position may be culturally determined in part, although it is difficult to imagine a situation in which these factors are not highly correlated with the required amounts and kinds of skill.

The differentiation that results from the division of labor within the flow of production is not an authority rank system, but rather a rank system that may be labeled a "pattern of deference." The workers in the positions at the lower ranks of the system defer to the acts emanating from the higher. In this sense, organizational interaction involves asymmetrical service relationships, in that the lower positions provide services but do not receive a commensurate number of services in return. For example, the skilled worker interacts asymmetrically in the service sense with the sweeper, accepting the services offered by the latter without the expectation of any return. Clearly, this is not an authority relationship since both the skilled operator and the sweeper are under the same authority figure, the unit foreman. The relation is one of deference by the unskilled to the skilled; it is not a worker-boss relationship.

The normative orientation underlying the deference pattern concerns the evaluation of performance. To understand this normative orientation, the concepts of deference and authority must be clearly distinguished. The deference pattern is based on the evaluation of performance, not on the evaluation of status in the organization. Using these two concepts synonymously obscures a distinction that is crucial in analysis of industrial work. It is quite possible to value and differentially reward types of performance on a functional basis without setting up an authority system. Indeed, this distinction lies at the heart of line and staff problems.

Although the deference system and the authority system frequently come into conflict in the organization, there is little evidence that such conflict can be avoided by giving authority status to positions in the deference system. Any attempt to merge the two systems would probably increase the amount of conflict. Specific amounts and types of skill or knowledge bring about a deference pattern, where the positions involved are not arranged in a formal hierarchy.[31]

[31] For a distinction similar to that made here between deference and authority see Dubin, *op. cit.*, pp. 47–54.

AUTHORITY

The development of mechanized and rationalized systems of production involves some relatively sharp breaks with the norms and acts of preindustrial labor. The magnitude of the discontinuities between factory and prefactory labor ensures their high visibility to the worker as well as to the analyst. Moreover, avoidance of such sharp breaks is contingent on avoidance of the factory system of production. One might argue that a development pattern stressing cottage industries minimizes such discontinuities and their correlative commitment problems, but if the emphasis is on the creation of a factory system, sharp breaks inevitably will accompany the transition process.

The following analysis of changing patterns of authority examines the commitment problems associated with the transition from a "traditional" normative system to a normative system that sanctions authority on the basis of task performance, or function. Unfortunately, a number of factors complicate the analysis of authority systems.

The basis of authority is itself normative in that its allocation is always normatively sanctioned.[32] Thus, allowance must be made for possible divergence between the ideologies of authority and its functional role. The functions performed by managers do not determine the systems of belief that legitimize their authority. Rather, managerial rights and prerogatives are often assigned on the basis of certain "moral" qualities.

Even in industrial societies managers of factories have inherited and thus enjoy some of the moral sanctions applied to their occupational ancestors—the owner entrepreneur of early industrialism. It is no longer *de rigueur* for managers to affirm their "God given" rights, but they and many others may still think in these terms, though perhaps in a more irreligious vein.

The incomplete character of the transition from a traditional type of authority to a functional administrative model is especially clear in the case of managers at the apex of the organization. Weber makes this point: "There is no question but that the 'position' of the capitalistic

---

[32] For a general discussion of authority and economic development see Reinhard Bendix, *Work and Authority in Industry* (New York: John Wiley & Sons, 1956); Moore, *Industrialization and Labor*, pp. 119–147; Feldman, "The Interpenetration of Firm and Society," and Moore, "Technological Change and Industrial Organization"; Herbert A. Simon, "Authority," and Solomon Barkin, "Commentary on Mr. Simon's Chapter" in Conrad M. Arensberg and others, eds., *Research in Industrial Human Relations* (New York: Harper & Brothers, 1957), pp. 103–118.

entrepreneur is as definitely appropriated as is that of a monarch. Thus at the top of a bureaucratic organization there is necessarily an element which is at least not purely bureaucratic." [33] Because the man at the top is generally loathe to justify his position as merely another job, he develops an ideology that makes the amount of his authority independent of his functional role in the organization and correlatively keeps his accountabilities at a minimum.

The relation between the authority figure and organizational property also tends to widen the distance between the functions of authority and its normative sanctions. Even in the modern corporation with its proliferated body of stockholders, the property rights of managers are relevant to the legitimation of their authority. The manager, especially the one at the apex of the organization, is the concrete representative of a "diaphanous" group of owners. Although his ability independently to dispose of property and to determine the contractual terms for labor is impinged on by both the stockholders (via proxy fights, the power residual to boards of directors, etc.) and the labor force (via unions, occupational and professional organizations, etc.), he maintains some independent property control. There is therefore a tendency for executives to have normatively sanctioned authority beyond that attributable to their assigned organizational tasks.

Functional Legitimation of Authority

There is apparently a large discrepancy between strict functional considerations and the ways in which authority is normatively sanctioned in the factory. It is consequently quite impossible to conceive of the work organization without some charismatic or traditional authority norms, without some special nonfunctional control over organizational property by managers, without amorphous and ambiguous accountabilities.

Although such aspects of authority are always present, they do not distinguish the modern economic organization. On the contrary, it is their *limited* presence that distinguishes the general aspects of a factory system of authority; for the normative sanctions of authority in the factory are, in the main, based on functional considerations.

The functional authority of factory managers is sanctioned in terms of their performance of the tasks that satisfy the organization's need for direction, coordination, and communication. So structured, author-

[33] Weber, *op. cit.,* p. 335.

ity means the hierachical system of flow—the content of which is information. The acts appropriate to this pattern of authority are those that fit the worker into the hierarchical flow of information. The worker should be able to recognize the appropriate source of messages (orders), to understand their nature, and to provide the appropriate response. The norms that correspond to these patterns of action include affective neutrality, or submission to the goals of the organization as stated by the authority figure. Performance rather than quality becomes the basis for allocating authority status. Finally, functional specificity sanctions the scope of authority allocated to any given manager.

These patterns of norms and acts become incredibly complex and difficult to follow. Functions are "notorious" for the extent to which they overlap, partly because of the concrete impossibility of perfect planning. Allocating authority on the basis of function means a corresponding degree of overlap. Overlapping authority in turn creates difficulties in the recognition of the appropriate source of authority; the source of orders becomes ambiguous, even when visible.

The sanctioning of authority on the basis of performance rather than ascribed quality raises barriers to commitment. The norms of authority common to many types of preindustrial labor are frequently more extreme than those typical of the factory. The plantation *mayordomo* and the feudal landlord are more distant from the worker than the unit foreman, and the scope and degree of their authority is greater partly as a consequence of this distance. The legitimacy of authority is not as clear to the newly recruited worker in the factory as to the worker in the preindustrial sector of the economy.

The transition is from a system of authority that is both general and personal to one that is both specific and impersonal. This shift affects the workers' ability to understand the information contained in the orders received. A premium is placed on understanding language, in a "severely" specific manner, and simultaneously conceding the legitimacy of its source. When the manager is a member of an alien culture, i.e., when he is imported from an industrial society, the language problems undoubtedly are more acute and inhibit commitment.

Dual Nature of Functional Authority

These obstacles to commitment are partly a consequence of the inability of newly industrialized workers to perform adequately under an authority system whose norms derive primarily from the functional requirements of the process of production. Thus, two somewhat distinct sets of functional requirements serve as sanctions for authority: the needs for coordination, communication, and direction imposed by the production process; the needs for authority imposed by the "state" of the labor force, i.e., the ability of workers to perform assigned tasks at any given level of authority. Moreover, the type and amount of authority can be very different, depending on which of the two managerial functions is involved.

Under the unrealistic assumptions of clear and constant goals, a perfect match of talents and tasks, and unproblematical motivation for performance, authoritative coordination could be eliminated. Since these unrealistic assumptions constitute the conditions for "efficiency," the correlative goal of the organization is to minimize the necessity of authoritative direction.

The task of bridging the gap between a trained and committed labor force and one that is neither—of socializing newly recruited factory workers to the "proper" type of authority—is usually assigned to the authority system itself. The assumption is that the lack of labor force commitment can be compensated by an increase in the amount of authority allocated to managers. In this situation, authority is simultaneously (1) the agency of socialization and (2) the pattern of norms and acts to which commitment is required.

Commitment and Continuity

The double task imposed on the authority systems of factories in newly developing areas has led many analysts to recommend that traditional patterns of authority and types of sanctions be maintained in the factory, at least during the initial period of industrialization. Many argue that the duplication of preindustrial authority structures (and authority figures if possible) in the newly established factory will significantly reduce barriers to commitment.[34]

The argument for continuing traditional authority systems in the

[34] For arguments favorable to continuing preindustrial authority structures see James C. Abegglen, *The Japanese Factory* (Glencoe: Free Press, 1958); G. C. Allen, *A Short Economic History of Modern Japan, 1867–1937* (London: George Allen and Unwin, 1946); Horace Belshaw, "Industry and Agrarian Reform," *Far Eastern Survey*, 16:153–156 (July 2, 1947); Harry Elkin, "The Northern Arapaho of Wyoming," in Ralph Linton, ed., *Acculturation in Seven American Indian Tribes* (New York: D. Appleton-Century Company, 1940), pp. 207–258; G. E. Hubbard, *Eastern Industrialization and Its Effect on the West: With Special Reference to Great Britain and Japan* (London: Oxford University Press, 1935), pp. 112–117, 165–166; Moore, *Industrialization and Labor*, pp. 142–147.

factory is bolstered by evidence adduced from the experience in Japan. The apparent success of Japanese industries in "easily" gaining high levels of labor force commitment (what Abegglen has called "permanent commitment") is attributed to the maintenance of the *status quo ante* with regard to authority.[35]

The high positive value placed on the continuity of authority structures has some roots in cultural relativism. Although values are not of primary relevance to this discussion, the argument for maintenance of traditional authority structures seduces some observers into apologizing for the establishment of "sweatshops" in newly developing areas. Their position is that the newly recruited factory worker expects and desires the exploitation that traditional authority would bring into the factory. Many of these observers believe that the maintenance of traditional authority structures avoids the dehumanization of work and workers that accompanies industrialization. They do not seem to see any dehumanizing elements in traditional authority systems. More to the point, the argument for continuing traditional sanctions of authority is consistent with the existing predisposition to assign the determining role in economic development, including labor force commitment, to managers or entrepreneurs: a position we discuss in the next chapter as the "theory of entrepreneurial determinism."

Viewing managers as experts in human relations is closely related to this approach. When the management of factories in industrialized areas is viewed as a logical "elite" in charge of illogical and backward "natives," it is not surprising that such a conception should be doubly attractive when the labor force is actually made up of inexperienced natives.

Fallacies of Continuity

The various arguments in favor of maintaining the normative *status quo ante* with respect to the authority allocated to factory managers ignore a number of inherent difficulties. Whether continuity of authority systems aids commitment in other respects or not, it obviously makes commitment to a new system of authority impossible.

[35] For a discussion of Japanese experience see Abegglen, *op. cit.;* Marion J. Levy, Jr., "Some Social Obstacles to 'Capital Formation' in 'Underdeveloped Areas,'" in Moses Abramovitz, ed., *Capital Formation and Economic Growth* (Princeton: Princeton University Press, 1955), pp. 441–501. Harry Oshima in his "Comment," pp. 513–518, argues that the transition in Japan was accompanied by considerable conflict and "commitment problems."

First, it is hardly self-evident that newly developing areas can choose only those elements of industrialism they desire and reject those that offend them. Indeed, it is precisely the lack of complete variability and flexibility in industrial organizations that gives rise to problems of commitment. The traditional pattern of authority appears to be at variance with certain other organizational requirements. It may be possible to imagine the sanctioning of "line" managers in traditional terms, but it is quite difficult to imagine how the system could incorporate "staff" managerial positions.

Second, it is uncertain that managers, no matter how much authority they are given, can bridge the gap between a committed and trained labor force and one that is neither. Even "good" managers are not likely to have powers of persuasion and training adequate to accomplish a general transformation of the social structure and norms. If one excludes the unlikely possibility that tribal chieftains or feudal landowners could perform managerial roles, it is probable that those who are trained to do so are socialized to the functional legitimation of authority. Even if the barriers to labor force commitment could be reduced through continuing preindustrial authority structures, managers themselves are likely to be incapable of wielding this type of authority. The recruitment and training of future managers would certainly be adversely affected.

Finally, the rejection of the *status quo ante,* although incomplete and frequently naive, is one of the strongest forces motivating economic development in many preindustrial societies. Correlatively, rejection of the previous conditions of work is one of the motivations involved in the willingness to accept factory employment. Thus maintenance of the traditional order of authority may raise its own barriers to commitment.

The Permanent Process of Commitment to Authority

The difficulties involved in any attempt to insure the acts and norms of a factory system of authority are the consequences of (a) the potential discrepancy between the ideology of authority and its functional role and (b) the increments to the authority system that result from the ill-trained and uncommitted "state" of the labor force. When a third relation is added—that the ideology of authority is also related to the "state" of the labor force—the circle is completed. As one of these factors undergoes change, the other also changes. Commitment to acts and norms of authority is permanent as a process, *not* as a stable structure.

Where industrialism developed in some "natural" sequence, the circle of relations shows considerable correspondence; all three factors changed simultaneously and with at least minimal integration. As stated elsewhere: "it appears possible that each 'stage' of [physical] technological development (together with secular changes in the education of workers and in accumulated industrial traditions) may have got the administrative theory it deserved." [36]

However, the correspondence among these three factors—the technology of production, the "state" of the labor force, and managerial ideology—is much less in the newly developing areas of the world. Both physical and social technology is primarily imported, often in the heads of managers, but the labor force comes directly from the existing cultural milieu. Since technology is not likely to stand still, the process of commitment by the labor force cannot be one of "catching up."

A number of intriguing possibilities suggest themselves. If new social and physical technologies develop as a consequence of the "state" of the labor force, these three factors may draw closer to each other as they change. This does not mean that an eventually stable equilibrium will necessarily be achieved, but that an entirely different sequence of change may evolve. (This may represent a more adequate picture of the Japanese experience.) Alternatively, the factors may "pass" each other along the way, maintaining the same low degree of correspondence, but one of a different type. A third alternative is that physical and social technology may continue to reflect, and thus change along with, "Western" technology. In this situation the lack of correspondence between these factors and the labor force would continue to be very great and of the same relative type.

Thus the process of commitment is a permanent one. It is likely to be associated with even severer conflict than that which characterizes the continuing process of commitment to managerial authority in established industrial societies.

[36] Moore, "Technological Change and Industrial Organization."

3 THE MARKET

Arnold S. Feldman
Wilbert E. Moore

In this chapter the area of potential labor force commitment is broadened by viewing the work situation in a market context. This context is at least dual: a labor market and a commodity market. Indeed, one could argue in formal terms that a typological sequence would be: labor market involvement, employment, consumption.[1] However, market orientations are in some degree integrated and thus appropriately viewed with reference to both employment and exchange of goods.[2] Moreover, meaningful involvement of employees in a labor market is frequently and paradoxically a consequence of their initial employment rather than antecedent to it.[3]

A market system in the sense used here is more than a system of exchange (which exists in all societies): it rests on a generalized medium of exchange as the link between the specialized producer and the generalized consumer.[4] Only in such a system can the concept of "labor" be operationally defined with any reliability, and only in such a system is the conception of consumer choice and "consumer sovereignty" likely to have any substantial significance.[5] Markets so conceived may differ in respect to two significant variables, *extensity* and *purity,* each of which may be subdivided.

MARKET VARIABLES

The extensity of a market may be considered in terms of both proportions and absolutes: Of the total goods and services produced and consumed in a society, what proportions and which kinds "move

---

[1] For a more detailed breakdown of the most general levels in this sequence, see Talcott Parsons and Neil J. Smelser, *Economy and Society* (Glencoe: Free Press, 1956), pp. 120–123.

[2] Wilbert E. Moore, *Industrialization and Labor* (Ithaca: Cornell University Press, 1951), pp. 306–308.

[3] Parsons and Smelser, *op. cit.,* pp. 116–117.

[4] See Max Weber, *The Theory of Social and Economic Organization* (New York: Oxford University Press, 1947), p. 182.

[5] Wilbert E. Moore, *Economy and Society* (Garden City: Doubleday & Company, 1955), p. 10.

through the market"? How large are the total amounts of goods and services, both as additive units and as distinguishable entities?

It is a commonplace assumption that economic development involves increases in both the magnitude and variety of products and services, on the one hand, and the proportion of these moving through market channels, on the other. Although tangential to our central concerns here, it is worth noting that the size and proportion of market transactions are theoretically distinguishable. Failure to make the distinction prejudices interpretations of the increasing scale of *market-measured* production and consumption as a valid index of "welfare" improvement on a total or per capita basis. Acts long performed and even goods long produced may simply have been transferred to new modes of exchange. This changing relative position of the market in a social system has a further significance that is of central importance here. At whatever "stage" of economic development we look, there is a kind of competition between market and nonmarket ways of implementing interdependence. The change from the latter to the former poses the problem of commitment to the market system.[6]

With regard to industrial forms of production, then, one may properly ask about the lower and upper limits of market operations. The empirical lower limit may well be the "company town" where not even local scrip is used, but all transactions are purely bookkeeping entries. (Note, however, that such towns are likely to be part of a broader national market organized on conventional bases.) The upper limit of market operation, if not its violation, may be exhibited by modern industrial societies where almost any "service," including love and loyalty, is partially performed through market transactions. It is a fundamental principle in Marxian economics that an "impersonal" market system—in services and in goods—conceals but does not eliminate considerations of power and other social relationships among participants.[7] This is suggestive of issues posed in the overt extension of the market for services to include personal loyalty. In particular, the bureaucratization of employment and the stabilization of employment relations may represent a partial vindication of the Marxian position. The question, however, remains: what are the upper limits to market extension? If

6 Karl Polanyi, Conrad Arensberg, and Harry W. Pearson, eds., *Trade and Market in the Early Empires: Economics in History and Theory* (Glencoe: Free Press, 1957); Moore, *Industrialization and Labor,* pp. 20–35.

7 Karl Marx, *Capital: A Critique of Political Economy* (Chicago: Charles H. Kerr and Co., 1909), Vol. 1, pp. 185–196.

the key to the market principle is transferability, the limits of the market would appear to be set by types of interpersonal social relations necessarily characterized by durable and particularistic affectivity. The extension of the market in economic development poses this question persistently, and in every industrialized society. The problems of commitment to a market system may never be completely resolved, if only because this *locus* of performance and acceptance is not unchanging.

The market for persons as such, as in commercialized slavery, represents another upper limit. This kind of transaction is a form of labor recruitment and utilization that could not produce the range of occupations and skills required for a modernized economy. Slavery, moreover, involves extensive inconsistencies with reference to the norms appropriate to a developing economy, including notably status mobility.[8]

The major goal of economic development is presumably to increase the number, and possibly the variety, of consumable units. But since the allocation of these units via the market is a principal reward to participants, this also constitutes a major mechanism for effecting commitment. Much has been written concerning the tolerable limits of long-term sacrifices by workers (or, alternatively, the use of nonfinancial and thus nonmarket incentives) in economies attempting to maximize capital or military production. The theories and evidence cannot be reviewed here, but it should be noted that the communist countries, for example, use extensive market organization and even elaborate financial incentives, despite various restrictions on the total production of consumer commodities and even on access to the various markets that operate.

Market extensity also often involves the question of purity. The illustration just used exemplifies one form of impurity, namely, the simultaneous existence of various closed or partially closed markets. Other impurities include rationing, the bureaucratic or political allocation of perquisites not otherwise obtainable regardless of funds; multiprice systems (by class of buyer); and all sorts of restrictions on transfer and use, based on public or private policy. They shade into other impurities that constitute violations of the norms necessary for the ideal conception of a free market—that is, impersonality, ethical universalism, functional specificity, contractual equality, etc. Preindustrial exchange systems are impure in precisely these ways; they are often one aspect of complex patterns of interaction, an aspect that is

[8] Weber, *op. cit.*, pp. 276–277.

perhaps analytically distinguishable but not concretely distinct.[9] The relevant commitment problem, therefore, is again the acceptance and performance of new modes of interdependence at the cost of violating long-standing expectations.

Market purity may be asymmetrical, as in the cases of the "loyal" employee of an "irresponsible" or "hard boiled" employer, and the loyal patron of an indifferent producer or distributor. Reversed relations are at least theoretically possible, as in tenure arrangements binding on the employer but not the employee. Such asymmetrical relations may be actively encouraged by those who benefit, e.g., through the organization of training courses to teach the manipulation of pseudo-friendship. The point of more general significance, however, is that the institutional structure of the pure market is always somewhat fragile and subject to the "intrusion" of other norms. If the process of economic development may be viewed as involving the purification as well as the extension of markets, it does not follow that "conservative reactions" may not take place. They may be inevitable precisely because every proportional or relative extension of the market provides new challenges to previously accepted norms of conduct.

Although the model of the market implicit in much of the foregoing discussion has been the impersonal buying and selling of consumer goods, the market system is also applicable to capital transfers and the contractual provision of services—the labor market. That market is the one most intimately related to labor force commitment.

Labor Market

A key feature of modern economic development is the establishment of a market system for allocating and rewarding activities, which thereby become "labor" in a technical sense.[10] This process thus involves not only the transfer of activities and their performers into a market context, but also the potential transfer of activities within that context. An industrial system involves a wide range of appropriate activities, many of which are novel in an underdeveloped area, and most of which are novel in their particular combinations into specific occupations.[11] A labor market functions to provide both the mechanism

9 Parsons and Smelser, op. cit., p. 140.

10 Wilbert E. Moore, "The Exportability of the 'Labor Force' Concept," American Sociological Review, 18:72 (February 1953).

11 Bert F. Hoselitz, "The Recruitment of White-Collar Workers in Underdeveloped Countries," International Social Science Bulletin, 6:3–11 (December 1954).

for matching people and jobs (there are administrative alternatives) and the financial rewards for motivating the training and sorting processes (there are alternatives and supplements).

Need for New Occupations

Even if attention is limited to industrial production, narrowly conceived, the range of needed occupations is wide in both rank and diversity. It has been persuasively argued that the critical occupational groups for economic development are the entrepreneurial and managerial [12] not only because such talents and skills are generally in short supply, thus limiting the pace of growth, but also because these groups have the opportunity and responsibility for determining the specific characteristics of the intrinsic work situation, and thus the ease or difficulty of labor commitment among other groups.

The importance of managerial skills, however, should not be exaggerated into a doctrine of "entrepreneurial determinism," which would imply that the notable barriers to effective labor supply of all types could be erased by the comparatively simple expedient of training managers with appropriate leadership and even manipulative talents. The supply of executives and coordinators depends on educational and motivational qualifications. *The same is true for other occupations.* Concentration only on skilled management would repeat in newly developing areas the persistent errors in industrialized societies, namely, the failure to appraise correctly the motivational resistance to manipulation on the part of the "managed," and the cynical view that only minimal, bribed cooperation can be expected in any event.

The very diversity of occupations provides the basis for one class of market impurities—the existence of noncompeting markets over long periods. This phenomenon is buttressed by the training time required

---

[12] See Yale Brozen, "Entrepreneurship and Technological Change," in Harold F. Williamson and John A. Buttrick, eds., *Economic Development: Principles and Patterns* (New York: Prentice-Hall, 1954), Chapter 6; Frederick H. Harbison, "Entrepreneurial Organization as a Factor in Economic Development," *Quarterly Journal of Economics*, 70:364–374 (August 1956); Frederick H. Harbison and Charles A. Myers, *Management in the Industrial World* (New York: McGraw-Hill Book Company, 1959); Harvard University Research Center in Entrepreneurial History, *Change and the Entrepreneur* (Cambridge: Harvard University Press, 1949); Bert F. Hoselitz, "Entrepreneurship and Economic Growth," *American Journal of Economics and Sociology*, 12:97–110 (October 1952); Joseph A. Schumpeter, *Business Cycles* (New York: McGraw-Hill Book Company, 1939), and *Capitalism, Socialism, and Democracy* (3rd ed.; New York: Harper & Brothers, 1950), especially pp. 131–139.

for occupational access, as well as by such "extrinsic" factors as the lack of a correlation between occupational prestige and income, ignorance of alternative opportunities, and artificial barriers to occupational access.

The implication of noncompeting labor markets in the present context is that, almost independent of the degree of economic development, the phenomena and problems of commitment may follow particular occupational lines rather than the general labor market system.

Criteria of Performance

The factors in performance appropriate to labor market commitment are well known and can be quickly summarized. They include such criteria for entrance and exit as age and thresholds of employability; a wage or income orientation to jobs, which does not exclude other orientations but constitutes a minimum essential for participation; and job mobility. Of these the most significant is mobility, partly because some initial movement is essential for the establishment of an industrial labor system at all, and partly because continued growth and modification of industrial systems require reallocations of labor—short of theoretically conceivable perfect correspondence among demographic trends, completion of training before entrance into the labor force, and occupational demands exactly geared to supply factors.

Job mobility. Job mobility covers at least four distinguishable types of movement, involving (1) segment of the economy or specialized labor market, (2) geographical location, (3) employer, and (4) relative rank or position.[13] These may be designated, respectively, *situs, locus, patronus,* and *status*—to keep the terminology consistently classical. Any particular job transfer may involve only one or any combination of these positional categories, and different occupations vary substantially in the normal incidence of movement of each type.

The *economic* function of mobility in a labor market is the facilitation of "correct" or "optimum" occupational placement relative to given states of capital, technology, and organization. This function

---

[13] Although the terminology is different, the distinctions used here are not novel. See Emile Benoit-Smullyan, "Status, Status Types, and Status Interrelations," *American Sociological Review,* 9:151–161 (April 1944); Ely Chinoy, "Social Mobility Trends in the United States," *ibid.,* 20:180–186 (April 1955); David Glass, *Social Mobility in Britain* (Glencoe: Free Press, 1954); Natalie Rogoff, *Recent Trends in Occupational Mobility* (Glencoe: Free Press, 1953), especially Chapters 1 and 2; Melvin M. Tumin and Arnold S. Feldman, "Theory and Measurement of Occupational Mobility," *American Sociological Review,* 22:281–288 (June 1957).

theoretically may be performed by a minute but highly mobile minority of workers in any relevant positional category.

The *sociological* functions of mobility include exposures and rewards, which are instruments of commitment. It may also be argued that mobility contributes to the preservation of the purity of the market in terms of both actions and norms. That is, the norms associated with an impersonal labor market and the corresponding actions are subject to the constant threat of particularistic and diffuse relations, and of designation of status by ascription rather than by achievement. These pressures tend to increase with the persistence of particular patterns of personal relations. Mobility presumably serves to prevent or retard the institutionalization of such patterns, and even to restore the efficacy of the general norms. The sociological functions accordingly are performed only by widespread mobility.[14]

These functions or consequences of mobility have correlative costs, in the loss of elements of loyalty, friendship, and security. The costs help to account for observed restrictions and failures to move.[15]

Such costs are also attributable to the economics of labor mobility, especially in *locus* and *status*. If these costs are normally borne by the worker or, say, his family, as in the transportation of persons and household goods or the more significant costs of training, commitment to the system must be correspondingly greater. Similarly, an additional cost is attributable to the sociology of *status* mobility, namely, that positions of higher rank and reward commonly carry higher responsibility. The significance for commitment is again clear.

Intersector mobility. Industrialization typically means a shift of workers from the primary or agricultural sectors of the economy to secondary or manufacturing sectors. The bulk of the potential labor supply is likely to be concentrated in agriculture in the preindustrial economy, and a considerable amount of this supply is likely to be wastefully employed because of disguised unemployment and underemployment in agriculture. Although this shift from the primary sectors is economically attractive to the social planner and perhaps in the long run should be so to the laborer, the latter is often not the case.

It cannot be assumed that the hostility to shifts of this nature is

---

[14] Talcott Parsons, *The Social System* (Glencoe: Free Press, 1951), pp. 182–187.

[15] Peter M. Blau, "Occupational Bias and Mobility," *American Sociological Review*, 22:392–399 (August 1957), and "Social Mobility and Interpersonal Relations," *ibid.*, 21:290–295 (June 1956); Melvin M. Tumin, "Some Unapplauded Consequences of Social Mobility in a Mass Society," *Social Forces*, 36:32–37 (October 1957).

groundless. Quite the contrary, this kind of population movement has been associated historically with some of the most severe brutalities of the industrialization process. The cities to which people are urged to migrate are hardly "green belts," and the sections of these cities that receive migrants from the rural districts today represent the world's worst slums. Although in the long run a shift to manufacturing may mean an increased level of living, in the short run the advantages are not so immediately obvious. Levels of insecurity are high and visible. Even if the laborer were to act on the basis of economic rationality, his decision would not be necessarily favorable to the shift.

Forced migration into extractive industry sometimes represents the first stage of a sectoral shift. Because of the definition of underdeveloped areas of the world as suppliers of resources, the first taste of modern industry is often in mining. Recent developments in Africa come particularly to mind. Such developments are highly unlikely to perform an intermediate adaptive role vis-à-vis the cultural factors. Where recruitment is voluntary, the time orientations of the labor force are typically extremely temporary. Thus, signing up for a period in the mines is likely to be seen as a forced choice enabling the laborer to accumulate enough resources to give him an entree into the traditional status structure back in his village. Where recruitment is forced, of course many more negative associations are fostered in the minds of the laborers. Further, the isolated character of the mining industry is in many ways conducive to minimum exposure to new ways of thinking as well as to new knowledge.

In sum, the short-run factors as perceived by the working class stress the disadvantages of sectoral shifts. First, there is a strong pull to remain within the traditional social organization. Second, the "new" elements are likely to be perceived as highly repellent and, indeed, are likely to be so both socially and economically as far as the labor force is concerned. Finally, participation in labor camps, particularly in mining, whether forced or voluntary, is extremely inefficient as an intermediate exposure to new ways of work.

One possible way of overcoming these blockages is to reverse the movement and locate the factories in the rural districts. However, this "solution" is liable to create other problems. Because few rural areas in preindustrial societies have the type of capital developments necessary for industrialization—forms of transportation, sources of power, etc.—the initial costs would be prohibitive. Also, moving industry to rural areas would not necessarily change the normative order; on the contrary, leaving the worker in the rural state might well encourage the maintenance of a normative system hostile to industrial labor. However, the movement of factories to the location of potential labor supplies, where feasible, represents an economic advantage to the worker in that it saves him the costs of mobility. These costs are transferred to the entrepreneur, but are frequently prohibitive.

Assuming that the sheer physical transfer of large portions of the labor force has taken place, their acceptance of factory work and their adaptation to the new environment are not foregone conclusions. Indeed, many of the most severe problems of industrial labor force development are presented only after the initial period of exposure. It is at that point that the full scope of the changes in patterns of living is experienced by the new industrial worker.

Adaptation to urban life. The initial shock of urban life frequently results in a problem of labor supply, which can be called rejection. The worker is thrust into a different and quite alien cultural milieu. His integration into this subculture is likely to be anything but orderly, since he typically lacks the social skills necessary for urban life. As a result of his disorganization he develops attitudes hostile to the industrialization process. These attitudes may lead him to support political movements with ideologies that are anti-industrial and in that sense reactionary. Rather than being exposed to the attitudes and values that might aid his orientation toward the skills necessary for urban life, he becomes a "mass man" and a potential participant in movements whose extreme violence threatens any solution of the problems involved.

Another characteristic problem of labor supply in the period of mass urban migration in newly industrializing areas is the siphoning off of large portions of the supply into what might be termed "primitive" tertiary industries. The new urban migrant lacks not only general social skills, but also the specific labor skills desirable for factory employment. Thus while he moves to the city to seek factory employment, he is likely to encounter the greatest difficulty precisely in finding such a job. One result of his poor position in the labor market is a drift toward employment in "nonmarket" urban services. This is exemplified in the exaggerated and inefficient proliferations of small (stationary or "mobile") retail outlets, the large numbers of marginal workers connected with tourism, etc. Such labor is generally unproductive in that it does not add to the economy.[16]

[16] Simon Rottenberg, "Note on Economic Progress and Occupational Distribution," *Review of Economics and Statistics*, 35:168–170 (May 1953).

In a sense the development of such services can be characterized as an insane kind of superspecialization. Many of these jobs are created by arbitrary splitting of tasks. No criterion other than the creation of as many jobs as possible is involved in such specialization. There may be one servant to do the marketing, another to carry goods from the store, another to sweep, another to cook, etc., or one bearer for every piece of luggage.

More important, such arrangements are frequently institutionalized and thus permanently built into the culture. The migrant's access to training that would allow him to improve his labor market position is not likely to increase with the length of time spent in the urban environment. The expansion of educational institutions necessary for the wholesale retraining of the migrant population is a slow and arduous process. The emphasis here on mobility as an essential feature of labor market development is, therefore, something more than the requirement for "bodies." Movement into the market sector is itself problematical and still leaves uncertain the further performance of appropriate kind and quality that characterizes a developed labor market.

Norms of the Labor Market

The norms appropriate to the labor market are perhaps not so commonly understood as are the performance requirements. Commitment entails acceptance of the norms of affective neutrality or impersonality, ethical universalism, functional specificity, and achievement orientations. Part of these are summarized by the concept of "contract," and all are likely to be novel elements in the social structure of underdeveloped areas, particularly as applied to the performance of services (labor).[17] Moreover, as implied earlier, their institutionalization is probably never complete, and not likely to be so, in the most thoroughly industrialized systems.

Job loyalties. Commitment to the labor market as a system is inevitably filtered through the demands and expectations appropriate to specific positions—jobs or occupations. We find, therefore, that the norms applicable to the financially rewarded exchange of services are always tempered by specific loyalties to the occupational group, to the generalized status of which it is a part, to the client or employer, or to the productive organization. The loyalties, as well as general labor market norms, are presumably symmetrical and thus apply, for ex-

[17] K. N. Llewellyn, "Contract: Institutional Aspects," *Encyclopaedia of the Social Sciences* (New York: Macmillan Company, 1931), Vol. 4, pp. 331–332.

ample, to both the buyer and the seller of services. Even if the loyalties are regarded as nominally temporary because of the presumption of potential mobility, they do not necessarily coincide with general market norms. The situation is further complicated by the circumstance that the claims to loyalty are often conflicting, as the total supply of positive affect is likely to be regarded as limited and possibly indivisible. The *actual* specialization of roles and corresponding commitments is always fragile and incomplete, thus leaving a residue of dynamic tension in any labor market system. This tension does not appear to be resolved in any known or theoretical socialist scheme, or in any approximation to administratively organized production of goods and services.

The argument may be restated in terms of the phenomena of commitment to a labor market in newly developing areas. Involvement in new kinds of social relations requires not only the sacrifice or rejection of traditionally accepted norms of conduct, but also the acceptance of a normative order that is itself not perfectly "integrated."

Rewards for work. The discussion to this point has neglected an important aspect of the normative order of labor markets—the question of rewards. In the "pure" labor market the rewards are financial and presumably proportional to merit, which is a function of the scarcity and functional importance of the services rendered. From this general formulation there may be derived a number of normative orientations, including competitive occupational placement, the requirements of learning about and rational appraisal of alternative opportunities, the "cult of talent," the expectation of bargaining, and notions of "reasonable" performance or a "fair day's work." (The norms appropriate to independent, and possibly all, professional practice are especially interesting in the extent to which explicitly commercial considerations are minimized or nominally prohibited.) [18]

Much of the literature in labor economics, industrial psychology, and industrial sociology is concerned with various impurities in labor markets—particularly in the form of motivational complexity and the alleged competition between financial and nonfinancial rewards.[19] The

[18] William J. Goode, "Community Within a Community: The Professions," *American Sociological Review*, 22:196–198 (April 1957); Parsons and Smelser, *op. cit.*, pp. 151–156.

[19] Robert L. Kahn and Nancy C. Morse, "The Relation of Productivity to Morale," in Industrial Relations Research Association, *Proceedings of the Fourth Annual Meeting, 1951*, pp. 69–79; Richard A. Lester, *Labor and Industrial Relations* (New York: Macmillan Company, 1951), Chapter 2; Moore, *Industrialization and Labor,*

fact of motivational complexity and the partial unreality of the model of the economic man in the labor market may be admitted without rejecting the functional importance of a labor market. We may note two kinds of interpretation that are in apparent contradiction. One maintains that the closest approximation to the model of economic man in the labor market is likely to occur in the early stages of industrialization. The reason for this relative purity of relation between performance and financial reward is that other incentives (occupational prestige and esteem, security, pleasant working conditions, appropriate status and situs symbols, etc.) are likely not to be operating or to be operating negatively. The other interpretation is that financial incentives are likely to be of increasing importance through time, because of the steady expansion in the number and proportion of goods and services moving through the market and therefore available only by monetary outlays.

There is a resolution to this theoretical conflict. Work incentives are always partial in the total range of the individual's aspirations. The less extensive and intensive the individual's commitment to a full-scale industrial social system, the more sharply defined and limited may be his performance and involvement. He may indeed be working for money, and so for the limited range of goods and services that money will buy and that fit his relevant standards. Thus financial and nonfinancial incentives or rewards may increase simultaneously by extension of the importance of work in total life patterns.[20]

It appears, then, that both interpretations are correct, and that much of the theoretical dispute about labor motivation has been sterile in its neglect of variable contexts of work orientations.[21] The perception that money is especially important if you do not have it has significance in both cross-sectional and temporal dimensions. In both there is likely to be a high correlation between financial and nonfinancial rewards.

---

pp. 153–177; Ross Stagner, *Psychology of Industrial Relations* (New York: John Wiley & Sons, 1956), especially Chapters 4 and 5.

[20] Allison Davis, "The Motivation of the Underprivileged Worker," in William F. Whyte, ed., *Industry and Society* (New York: McGraw-Hill Book Company, 1946); William H. Form, "Toward an Occupational Social Psychology," *Journal of Social Psychology*, 24:85–99 (August 1946); Wilbert E. Moore, *Industrial Relations and the Social Order* (New York: Macmillan Company, 1951), pp. 253–258; Lloyd G. Reynolds and Joseph Shister, *Job Horizons: A Study of Job Satisfactions and Labor Mobility* (New York: Harper & Brothers, 1949), especially Chapter 6.

[21] Moore, *Economy and Society,* pp. 16–18.

Agencies of Commitment

The conditions and agencies that are likely to be involved in achieving and maintaining commitment to the labor market as a system may be briefly noted. The following discussion is confined to the elements of the general social structure that have intrinsic relevance to this particular locus, although *any* locus of commitment is theoretically a potential agency for effecting involvement in all others. (The family as a primary agency of affective socialization is an important illustration of this principle.)

The conditions in the preindustrial social system that may aid the development of a labor market include rational work organizations and, especially, the existence of specifically bartered services. The intimate connection between labor markets and commodity markets should also be emphasized, if for no other reason than the history of misinterpretations concerning the nonexistent or limited interest in wages or profit opportunities in situations where few if any "wants" could be satisfied by purchase.

Haphazard Westernization. Any contemporary preindustrial or "underdeveloped" society is in concrete terms rarely if ever uninfluenced by political, religious, commercial, ideological, and educational contacts with the "West." (A society that is now instantaneously undergoing the simultaneous impact of all phases of an alien and industrial culture exists only in the imagination of social scientists who phrase their analyses in those terms.) The prior introduction of colonial administration, public or missionary schools, and even beads and calico may be conducive to the development of a labor market. Sheer location and exposure therefore become relevant, as does the hypothesis of "intervening opportunities." [22] Because of the uneven introduction of Western patterns, as exemplified in educational developments without employment opportunities, one may frequently encounter the phenomenon of "precommitment" and "overcommitment" as applied to individuals. On the other hand, many workers may still be more "pushed" than "pulled" into the labor market. The "pushes" include deteriorating ratios of men to land, owing to rapid population growth, and the displacement of handicraft producers by the introduction of cheap manufactured goods.[23]

[22] Samuel A. Stouffer, "Intervening Opportunities: A Theory Relating Mobility and Distance," *American Sociological Review,* 5:845–867 (December 1940).

[23] Moore, *Industrialization and Labor,* pp. 304–305.

Transitional agencies. To the transitional agencies in the socialization process that have already been indicated should be added several agencies principally relevant for cognitive socialization: employment exchanges and labor recruiters, various communications media, informational services and standards of unions and professional societies, and vocational education and counseling. Co-workers and other peer and reference groups may contribute to affective socialization, the acceptance of the norms appropriate to labor market participation. Paradoxical as it may seem, the *personal* influence of teachers, employers, and supervisors may be the source of the individual's gradual internalization of normative standards that include impersonality.

The transitional agencies may in turn serve to *maintain* commitment, but maintenance is also likely to depend on widening kinds of participation and possibly of protest or occupational protection, and the institutionalization of the system of rewards. Otherwise the recruit is likely to withdraw from the market if the opportunity arises. A work ethic, supported not only by financial and other rewards but also by the positive approval of meaningful others, is an element in self-maintenance of labor market systems that is likely to develop very slowly in the process of industrialization.

COMMODITY MARKET

Our concern here is with the exchange of physical goods and various property rights in them. (A limiting case is the "money market" as such, which is included.) The commodity market system itself may be relatively simple or complex. Its complexity may relate, on the one hand, to the number and variety of goods exchanged, and to the number and variety of "steps" in the distribution process, on the other.

Market Diversity

Markets may be classified by various criteria and degrees of detail. The patterns of relations and appropriate norms of conduct appear to be sufficiently different to warrant the following distinctions:

1. The individual and household consumer, including the structure of distribution;

2. The business consumer, including distribution of end-use products, components, and capital equipment;

3. The governmental consumer, including distribution of end-use goods, and weapons;

4. Factor markets, including transfers of capital and property in raw materials and primary commodities.

All these market structures are presumably subject to various controls in terms of public policy: consumer protection, preservation or limitation of competition, economic development strategies, military and foreign-relations policies, and concern for public welfare, collective or distributive. The nature and extent of controls therefore will vary in the degree of centralized planning and in implemented political ideologies.

The present discussion is oversimplified by distinguishing only two market structures: consumer goods and "business" relations. This distinction is fairly fundamental in terms of the conceptual organization used here. The market behaviors appropriate for the financier or investor, the entrepreneur, the distributor or salesman, all involve work roles in the technical sense, and therefore might have been discussed in Chapter 2 as "intrinsic work factors." Their treatment here, instead, is justified by our conviction that market or exchange relations may be thought of as a single locus of commitment at some level of generalization. The logic of the organization is neater with respect to consumer behavior as such.

Criteria of Performance

The minimum characteristics demonstrating involvement in markets for capital and components are transfer of property (at least *control* and *use*) rights and rational cost calculation and accounting.[24] Whatever the form and degree of state control, mobility of the factors of production and capital accumulation appear to be essential for economic development. The actual mechanisms of course depend heavily on the degree of administrative regulation and control.

The sensible consumer. For the individual or household consumer, a classically "pure" market vests "sovereign" choice of goods in the buyer, subject to limits on total economic capacity and to lags introduced by the response of buyers and sellers to shifts in preferences expressed in prices. Without here arguing the various intrinsic and empirical limitations on market operation, it appears that consumers will make budgetary decisions, exercise some minimum choice among available alternatives, and base that choice on such considerations as "needs," prices, and qualities. The choice may be implemented by shop-

[24] Weber, *op. cit.*, pp. 267–268.

ping and possibly bargaining behavior. A planned or socialist economy presumably radically reduces the range of such preference behavior, and indeed may establish various noncompeting markets. The point of present interest is that any substantial form or degree of industrialization is likely to require a consumers' market in which monetary trading and some choice is operative. Since such behavior may be novel to early participants, commitment again becomes a problematical component in economic development.

The norms appropriate to business transactions require little comment. The institutions of property and contract are crucial, involving a "free" market resting on nominally complete transferability and divisibility of property rights and virtually complete freedom of contractual negotiation. (No viable social system could permit the complete absence of controls "in the public interest," if for no other reason than the prevention of force and fraud for the maintenance of order.) The norms, however, also include rationality of cost and profit calculation (with or without the "profit motive") and the accountability of fiduciaries.

Associated with the conduct of "business" are many interesting problems concerning the functions and ideologies of entrepreneurs, public or private; behavior and norms with reference to risk taking; and the influence of nonmarket or nonprofit considerations in business decisions.[25] These cannot be pursued here, but their relevance for any analysis of factors in economic development should be noted. For example, has the rapidity of growth in the American economy rested in part on the unjustified optimism of risk takers, who thus paved the way in technical or other innovations for subsequent successful production? Will planned rapid expansions in production in newly developing areas succeed despite "sound economic principles," perhaps because of "sacrifices" and goal innovations not possible with gradual growth?

For the ultimate consumer the norms of conduct in the market are only partially those applicable to business transactions. The relevant standards include such norms as impersonality, functional specificity, and universalism ("money talks"). Honesty, credit integrity, reliability, and notions of fair dealing are likely to become institutionalized and thus sanctioned in a developed market system. Contrary assumptions

[25] Reinhard Bendix, *Work and Authority in Industry: Ideologies of Management in the Course of Industrialization* (New York: John Wiley & Sons, 1956); Francis X. Sutton and others, *The American Business Creed* (Cambridge: Harvard University Press, 1956).

are not only likely to undermine the commitment of consumers to the market system, but also to threaten the system in other ways. "Unlimited" competition is a contradiction, and the principle of *caveat emptor* has early limits as a mode of market orientation.

The committed consumer should show a rising level of demand, both because of the increased proportion of goods moving through the market and because of a rising *standard* of living (crudely summarized as acquisitiveness). Consumer behavior, however, is also guided by the norms of the "needs" of the consuming unit (say, the household) collectively and individually, and these are rarely determined by market principles. The act of purchase therefore implements and symbolizes the relationship of the family (and other social units) to the economy. Thus the appropriate norms include the acquisition of relevant *situs* and *status* symbols.[26]

Dynamics of market purity. The norms of the consumers' goods market and of the labor market are always threatened by outright violation—fraud, manipulation, captive clienteles—and also by the intrusion of personal, diffuse, and particularistic relations. It seems probable that such intrusions increase with the persistence of relations among particular participants. (A function of "shopping" is precisely to minimize such tendencies.) It also seems probable that there are sequences of normative structure somewhat analogous to those hypothesized for the labor market. The functionally diffuse preindustrial system of exchange gets transformed into a functionally specific, "rational economic" market, which operates especially at low absolute levels of demand. An increase in "discretionary income" may introduce considerations not only of "service," convenience, "snob appeal," etc., but also of stable, particularistic loyalties between buyer and seller. Thus, the model of "rational" consumer behavior is most applicable in the early development of impersonal markets, and precisely then at greatest variance with previous expectations.

Market organization favors a highly general principle of change, namely, the *degradation of status symbols*. The speed of such degradation is greatly accelerated by conditions of a free market and the related expectation of status mobility. The socialized consumer will be expected, therefore, to change his buying preferences from time to time.

[26] Harvey Leibenstein, "Bandwagon, Snob, and Veblen Effects in the Theory of Consumers' Demand," *Quarterly Journal of Economics*, 64:183–207 (May 1950); Thorstein Veblen, *The Theory of the Leisure Class* (New York: B. W. Huebsch, 1899), especially pp. 24–34.

The course of industrialization leads to competing status systems and their distinguishing symbols. Subsequent diversification of noncompeting occupational groups may lead to a relative increase of *situs* symbols and styles of life.[27] Consumer behavior commonly identified as fads and fashions appears to be governed by these two general principles. The norms involve identification with and loyalty to particular reference groups, and correlative distinction from others.

Agencies of Commitment

In discussion of the processes of achieving and maintaining commitment to a commodity market system, keeping the distinction between consumers' goods and business relations seem appropriate. In analysis of business transactions, one must consider those structural elements and processes that form the principal content of the literature on economic development—for example, returns on investment, risk taking, the attempt to rationalize operations and procedures. In analysis of consumers' markets, one must look at phenomena that are only modestly represented in analyses of the behavior of *any* market system—family needs and desires, the manner and role of expansion in wants.

The conditions for business operation. From the literature on economic development, particularly that on industrial and business entrepreneurship, a few hypotheses may be presented concerning the development of markets in capital and producers' goods, and commercialized distribution. The focus here, it may be emphasized, is the commitment process and not the entire process of economic growth. For simplicity, the problem may be posed as that of the social production of the "businessman" as a type, with the understanding that this neglects the "bureaucrat" as a type important in both public and private economic enterprise.

For commitment of the businessman, certain prerequisite and predisposing conditions may be identified: (1) Political order is essential to protect fixed capital from civil disorder, to permit the physical transit of the factors of production and of finished goods, to maintain stable credit relations, and to provide reasonable certainty in the effectiveness of the laws of property and contract. (2) National economic integration is helpful, if not absolutely necessary, and is particularly important in currency, banking, and financial organization, as well as in the size of markets and the elimination of barriers to trade. (3) Negatively, it ap-

[27] Benoit-Smullyan, *op. cit.;* Paul K. Hatt, "Occupation and Social Stratification," *American Journal of Sociology,* 55:538–543 (May 1950).

pears that businessmen may seek new opportunities when faced with diminishing returns in commercialized agriculture or preindustrial commerce,[28] or when opportunities for acquisition of status are blocked in the traditional structure—for example, the inaccessibility of landed estates because of nontransferability or limits on size of holdings.[29]

The transitional agencies in the encouragement of businessmen include many "standard" economic prescriptions—more attractive investment possibilities, returns proportional to risks, security of returns that encourage long-term investments, as well as commercial codes and credit ratings. Organizations, such as trade associations, may not only serve common economic interests but also act as "primary" peer groups for the new class of entrepreneurs. The emergence of a new and competing status system that gives prestige to an entrepreneurial elite and to commercial success may also help destroy the monopoly of an alien or ethnically distinct trading class.[30] The whole notion of business leadership rests on recognition and prestige, as well as on financial rewards.

The maintenance agencies appropriate for the committed businessmen are again partly economic, partly social. The rating of business success requires the development of short-term and long-term profitability or efficiency.[31] In a competitive system relative "market position" may serve as an additional rating device. In developed economic systems a complex pattern of adult socialization encourages a large measure of identification between individual and organizational success, particularly among business administrators. Thus the nonowning manager is still rewarded both psychically and materially for business success, although his activities decreasingly resemble the risk-taking entrepreneur. Within "free enterprise" systems there appears to be a trend toward the broadening of participation in capital markets, reducing the distinctiveness of businesslike investment without diminishing the prestige attached to the position of manager.

Because the standard model of business markets is one of impersonal competition, little thought or research has been devoted to the affective relations that would implement the internalization of market

28 Alexander J. Morin, "Editorial," *Economic Development and Cultural Change,* 1:3–7 (March 1952).

29 Everett E. Hagen, "The Process of Economic Development," *Economic Development and Cultural Change,* 5:209–210 (April 1957); Marion J. Levy, Jr., "Contrasting Factors in the Modernization of China and Japan," *ibid.,* 2:161–197 (October 1953).

30 Yale Brozen, *op. cit.*

31 Bert F. Hoselitz, "Non-Economic Barriers to Economic Development," *Economic Development and Cultural Change,* 1:13–14 (March 1952).

norms. The classical or Schumpeterian concept of the entrepreneur implies too lonely a character to fit other knowledge of patterned social conduct. Weber's Protestant was at least committed to God.

Consumer commitment. The development of consumer commitment or the general principles of consumer behavior have shaky theoretical foundations in social science literature. Various forms of preference analysis, including "indifference curves," have been developed as analytical models in economics, but it is perhaps not unfair to say that the models have virtually no empirical foundation. On the other hand, sociologists have gone little beyond Veblen's "conspicuous consumption": emphasis on status symbols, orientation toward peer groups, and household budget allocations as indicative of relative position and "needs" within the family.

These theoretical difficulties are encountered when one asks what conditions would predispose persons in an underdeveloped area to accept a commodity market system. Many economists assume virtually unlimited wants, which would make the acceptance of buying opportunities automatic (although limited means would still require the analysis of relative values of particular products). Many sociologists, on the contrary, would assume strictly limited wants, largely supplied by particularistic exchanges, and in any event conditioned by the standards of consumption appropriate to relatively fixed social positions. Some middle course is no doubt more nearly correct. It almost appears that the sociologists have a sounder theoretical position by inference from known principles of social behavior; the economists have crude empirical confirmation in the rapid expansion of "materialistic" standards.

However this controversy may be resolved, it appears that acceptability of "consumer" orientations (in the technical sense) will be relative to the degree and form of prior exchange relations. Thus a functionally specific barter system, money-mediated barter, or even limited monetary markets will predispose to market expansion and commercialization, whereas a purely village-bound form of particularistic exchanges will not. Descriptive studies of newly developing areas reveal many interesting transitional forms, such as the commercial purchase of cattle for the bride-price. Clearly a major predisposing condition for commercial exchange is the transformation of agricultural and handicraft producers into wage employments. As employees they are virtually barred from traditional barter arrangements, and virtually forced into the technical role of consumers. Thus the industrial worker, whose commitment is a primary concern here, may himself be a major agency in the development of "consumership." It may also be assumed that recognized but unsatisfied material wants or needs and any prior acquisitive orientations will precondition the development of market commitment.

Formal education and urban migration clearly constitute major elements in exposure and cognitive socialization toward the market system. But in the market itself one finds advertising in the broadest sense, as information and persuasion, appeals to real or alleged needs, wants, and aspirations that are status appropriate. Since status *is* partially symbolic, symbol manipulation may be used to enhance status.

In this particular connection the family is not external to the market in the same sense that education and urban residence are; the family is the typical unit of consumption and of buying decisions. Thus it serves not only as a primary agent of cognitive and affective socialization, but as a major source of maintenance of motivation. The family's budgetary and market behavior is in turn oriented to its reference groups (both *situs* and *status*) and to those of its individual members (which may differ markedly in a rapidly changing social system), as well as to collective and individual needs more internal to the family unit. Indeed, the changing kinship structure accompanying economic development often poses tensions and value conflicts precisely with reference to budgets and consumption patterns, including the obligations of breadwinners for support of others. Intergenerational conflict on these issues is very common, and marital conflict by no means unknown. It cannot be said that the relation of the family as consumer to other familial economic and social functions has been clearly settled in any industrialized society. It appears probable that it is the *importance* of family functions, including budgetary ones, and the tensions surrounding them, rather than the "loss" of functions, that accounts for family instability in industrial societies. Certainly for the socialization, including adult socialization, appropriate to market commitment in a newly developing area, the structure of the family is as critical as the influence of marketing practices themselves.

4 THE SOCIETY

Arnold S. Feldman
Wilbert E. Moore

To the extent that an industrial system may be viewed as functionally integrated, involvement in industrial work and a market economy leads sooner or later to involvement in a variety of other groups and aspects of society that are novel in comparison with the social structure of preindustrial societies. The organization of the following discussion implies "broadening spheres" of social activity extending outward from the work place. This is a possible pattern in both causal and sequential terms, although not the only observed sequence of involvement. Thus any simple theory of economically determined change is rejected, whether on the grand scale of institutional dominance or the small scale of adult socialization via work. Yet the temporal patterns are certainly not random.

MAJOR INSTITUTIONAL COMPLEXES

Attention is centered here on the institutional order of society, and particularly on certain major functional complexes, their associated norms, and various common orientations and integrative norms. Groups are treated primarily as concrete structures that are predominantly related to a major functional complex. For example, kinship systems comprise families as well as other patterned social relationships; social stratification is partly manifested in unions and other occupational groups and partially implemented by educational systems; political systems comprise, among other things, governmental structures and parties; common orientations in social systems are implemented by education, religious affiliation, and many other agencies of socialization.

The organization used here tends to understate the possible importance of some voluntary and some recreational and ephemeral associations. One reason for the neglect is that their action patterns hypothetically are of a low order of requirement in the social structure and in the "full" commitment of the social participant, although of course some such groups—and indeed any group, pattern of action, or value orientation—may be of high or virtually exclusive salience for some participants. Such "distortions" cannot be generalized, however, without gross social imbalance.

The typological actor is ordinarily oriented primarily toward concrete structures, with a low order of cognition or recognized commitment to the broader institutional framework. However, in the transitional process that is our primary analytic concern, underlying values and norms are likely to become overt, precisely because their translation into action patterns reveals the conflict between the new and the traditional beliefs and practices.

Structural Interdependence

The problems and processes of commitment provide a consistent frame of reference for many aspects of changes in social systems associated with economic transformation. If functional interdependence of social systems is again assumed, the thread may be traced through the entire fabric. The paths so pursued are likely to be tedious, however, and considerable parts of the design may be seen in overly minute perspective. It seems preferable to note that important changes in social structure are essentially left out of account by our concern with commitment. Thus various ecological, demographic, and even technological and economic factors are viewed as "conditions" from this limiting viewpoint. The justification for this exclusion may be restated: these variables rarely operate directly with reference to occupational acts and norms, except possibly at policy-forming political and administrative levels. A few illustrations of indirect influence will suffice both to establish the connectedness of social systems and the minor importance of various "conditions" from the perspective of commitment:

When ecological patterns refer to urbanization or the city, it is clear that the latter may be the *site* of social transformation, but also possibly even an agency of socialization or locus of commitment, as noted in Chapter 3 with reference to labor markets. More commonly, however, relevance is situational rather than central.

Demographic changes are probably of primary importance in connection with allocation of resources, that is, the standard "problem" of the relation of population size and growth to the means for support. However, mortality conditions may affect the attractiveness of occupations in terms of both risks and vacancies. Likewise, low upper-class fertility rates may augment the accessibility of privileged positions.

Technological changes patently alter general occupational structures, particular employment opportunities, and demands for various skills. Economic patterns and policies such as currency stability, interest rates, and tariffs affect investors and managers and, indirectly, the conditions and opportunities affecting employment throughout the economy.

In sum, consideration of social structure as a locus of commitment is limited here both by the selection of particular segments of social systems for attention and by the concern with the actor in transitional situations, but there is no implication of abandonment of concern with changes in societies as systems. Rather, in the treatment of major functional complexes, the emphasis is precisely on the interrelations of the various specific loci of commitment. Thus, it is the general function of the institutional order of societies to provide norms of conduct in specific contexts, and consistent both with general values and with the appropriate claims of other social structures. Economic, political, social status, and kinship structures intersect with reference to common values, by rules governing the relations among substructures of societies, and by virtue of common membership, which in turn requires appropriate role behavior on the part of the individual.

Reinforcement of Activities

There are two conflicting hypotheses concerning differential commitment and participation. The commonly accepted one may be summarized as the principle of "frustration and diverted activity." According to this principle, the frustrations inherent in specialized work and possibly other roles lead to the search for alternative modes of expression, representation of interest, or reform. The second is the doctrine of "differential level of positive affect," according to which both dissatisfactions and satisfactions are mutually reinforcing, and thus individuals' levels of participation and involvement are generalized rather than compensatory. Although this second view is rarely expressed in the literature, it is represented in the aphorism that "Nothing succeeds like success," which implies the corollary that "Nothing fails like failure." If this position is correct, it has clear implications for the interdependence of roles in social systems.

We believe that commitments to the several contexts are mutually reinforcing and thus that the loci must be interrelated appropriately for the successful development of an industrial society. This means that the commitment process involves learning and performing the acts and norms that constitute the relations among the loci as much as it involves learning and performing the acts and norms specific to the individual loci. In the ideal typical case the individual thus becomes committed to the system as well as to its parts. Although individuals, particularly in transitional situations, may not traverse the entire social territory so encompassed, the industrialized system does traverse it, and the failure of some or many individuals to do so is itself a theoretically significant phenomenon.

Economic development under totalitarian controls presumably minimizes the various leads and lags typical of more haphazard social transformation, and similarly maximizes the stark contrast between the old and the new. The integration of liberal and democratic orders is looser by several tests: the partial autonomy permitted to substructures, the areas of choice permitted the social actor, and the consequent lack of precise synchronization of evolutionary and deliberate change.

Yet it may be insisted that a viable society requires some integration in both the structural and the temporal sense. This means, in terms of the typological actor in a social system undergoing economic transformation, that as his area of involvement begins to spread, the process of commitment includes learning and performing acts and norms that relate the new areas of involvement to the older ones. The important point is that in a transitional society the integrating principles are learned by many relatively late in life, and normally after some other involvement. They may be viewed as tardy and uncertain generalizations from particular contexts of action. Once the transitional period is over, however, the unifying acts and norms become the foundations for learning more specific kinds of behavior, rather than the results of them. The integrating principles are inculcated earlier in life, before participation in the labor force.

This sequence is important for any attempt to understand the transitional phase of commitment in currently industrializing societies. It emphasizes the sociological obstacles to development, in that initial exposures to the new forms are limited to specific contexts. Thus even when commitment to a specific context occurs, there is no guarantee that over-all commitment to an industrial social organization can be achieved more easily; the opposite may be true. In the earliest period of transition partial commitment may present fewer difficulties than the type of commitment characteristic of the later stages of transition. The transitional phase culminates in the involvement of the individual in all the loci. At this point commitment requires rejection of the most basic values, and a greater extent of substitution of new integrating principles than at any previous point. Thus the process of commitment may be easily started, but the culmination may present the greatest difficulties yet encountered.

KINSHIP

Many problems of social change are sharply highlighted in kinship systems. Since kinship is a fundamental and universal structural feature of all societies, and one maximally surrounded by sentiments and values, it is a major potential barrier to social transformation, as well as a principal source of individual orientations to life. So fundamental, indeed, is the position of the family with its several interdependent functions that by one extreme interpretation it should make *attitudinal* change virtually impossible. By emphasis on the family's primary responsibility for early socialization, and a possibly exaggerated emphasis on subconscious motivation as part of that socialization, it is possible to view the preindustrial family as a critical barrier to social transformation.[1] This position tends to neglect the phenomena of adult socialization, repeatedly stressed here as critical in the transitional stages of economic development. It also tends to understate the importance of the family and possibly of extended kin ties as sources of emotional security and adult affectivity and thus as potential agencies of change. The historical transformation of Western family systems that has accompanied industrialization appears to have increased the functional importance of the family in these respects, while other functions (economic, educational, religious, etc.) were being weakened.

It appears that there is generally a pronounced strain between individual mobility and traditional kinship obligations. A partial exception in Japan appears to have been related primarily to small-shop production, and may be a transitional phenomenon deriving from interest in minimizing conflict, rather than a durable association of industrialism with an extended kinship system.[2] The commonly noted tendency of economic modernization to be subversive of extended kinship systems has been limited by Hoselitz (Chapter 12) to household units and by Nash (Chapter 17) to "corporate" kinship structures. Nevertheless, the

---

[1] Everett E. Hagen, "The Process of Economic Development," *Economic Development and Cultural Change,* 5:209–210 (April 1957); David C. McClelland, "Community Development and the Nature of Human Motivation: Some Implications of Recent Research," mimeographed paper prepared for a conference sponsored by the Center for International Studies, Massachusetts Institute of Technology, December 1957.

[2] See Wilbert E. Moore, *Industrialization and Labor,* pp. 30–31, 74–75, 194.

"conjugal family," emphasizing the marital tie and the two-generation familial unit to the virtual exclusion of other kinship obligations among adults, clearly increases the mobility potential of the breadwinner.[3] However, the persistent strains between family and economy, especially the hardy survival of kinship reciprocities between adult generations and siblings even in American society, cast doubt on the simple view that extended kinship cannot survive the onslaught of industrialism.

Commitment requires at the minimum a rejection of such kinship obligations as at the extreme would prevent involvement in new occupational roles or grossly impede responsiveness to occupational opportunities. At the maximum, commitment to new norms involves orientation toward career mobility and improvement of objective "life chances" for children, coupled with their socialization in terms of "achievement." This maximum commitment almost certainly depends on maintenance of a small-family system, by minimization of extended kinship and by deliberate controls on fertility.

The new, industrially oriented kinship system is quite unlikely to be in a "lead" position in social change, and commitment to modern family norms and actions is likely to follow the individual's entry into a transformed social system. Indeed, the socialization function of the family in this respect entails a generational lag. Whatever future research may demonstrate concerning the nuances of structural relations, the dynamic sequence will involve a lag in novel kinship norms and actions, although there are some indications that ideal family size and aspirations on behalf of children change early in the process of economic modernization.

STRATIFICATION

The newly recruited worker may gain or lose social status. The relevant judgment *on comparable bases* is most likely to be mixed and in any event difficult. The reason is simple: the transitional worker moves between competing stratification systems. Moore has said of the historical experience in industrialization:

. . . The presumed initial "downgrading" of industrial recruits is debatable. No doubt some craftsmen had their skills downgraded in specialized but relatively unskilled factory employments, and some of them and of agricultural workers may have been "expropriated" from ownership of the tools of pro-

[3] See Talcott Parsons, *Essays in Sociological Theory* (Glencoe: Free Press, 1949), Chapter 11.

duction. Generally, however, the transition involved a radically different *mode* of productive organization, with little legitimate basis for comparison of skill or status and common scale.[4]

Commitment with reference to social stratification is accordingly dual, involving acceptance both of new types of social differentiation and of the individual's place in the system. In transitional situations the two aspects may well become confused, and the disgruntled worker will view the preindustrial system with nostalgia. Since the new worker is likely to be *both* unskilled and uncommitted to industrial specialization and accompanying status distinctions, the confusion is understandable. As the economic transformation continues and expands, the confusion may be reduced with or without concomitant commitment to the new status system.

The coherence of the industrial system of social stratification is likely to be at a maximum precisely when substantial displacement of the preindustrial system has been achieved. At that juncture the older modes of social placement and various rewards may be regarded as anachronistic, and something approximating a single, clear-cut scale of social inequality becomes evident. Subsequent upgrading and diversification of the occupational structure is likely to increase "situs" distinctions and reduce the intercorrelations with income. In other words, an advanced industrial society combines detailed status distinctions within large administrative organizations and other contexts of differential position, with relatively unreliable translations of these in general terms of status in the community and particularly in the society as a whole. Notions of general status or class position rest on meager criteria, such as income, that can be generalized for the population. These criteria have low predictive value for social placement in any particular context.

Any system of stratification, even a complex multidimensional one, raises questions of equity. If social stratification (unequal rewards for social performance) rests on differential functional importance of positions and differential talent of persons,[5] existing systems tend to trans-

---

[4] Wilbert E. Moore, "Technological Change and Industrial Organization," paper prepared for International Social Science Council Conference, Paris, March 1959, to be published in a symposium edited by Georges Balandier for the Council. See also Moore, *Industrialization and Labor*, pp. 21–44, 99–102; and Feldman, "Men and Machines," *Challenge*, 7(3):62–66 (December 1958).

[5] See Kingsley Davis and Wilbert E. Moore, "Some Principles of Stratification," *American Sociological Review*, 10:242–249 (April 1945).

form inequality of position into inequality of opportunity.[6] Thus commitment to a system of rewards based on merit, and of mobility consistent with talent and training, may still require the participant to attempt to alter the system as well as his place in it. These questions partially account for interest groups oriented toward status, and for the importance of education as an agency of social placement. Comments on these aspects of social stratification are therefore in order, to supplement our earlier consideration of differentiation at the work place and in the market.

Unions and Occupational Groups

Interests, including economic interests, deriving from position in the productive system are predictably the basis of group formation. The interests, however, are not simple, and all attempts to make them appear so are misleading. The individual's identification may be with the productive organization, the occupation or occupational type, his status in the organization, or in the general system; and the types so derived can be designated roughly as the "loyal employee," the craft unionist or member of a professional body, the industrial unionist or member of a management association, and the class-oriented political partisan. These possibly competing bases of loyalty and identification are omnipresent and thus not mutually exclusive. Organizations formed on one basis do not thereby dispel other claims, which are sources of continuing tension and structural change in industrial societies.

In the long-term process of economic development there is some hypothetical basis for predicting the following sequence of primary identification by the individual: with the productive organization, with his status in it, and with his occupation. Thus, acute status identification and interstatus hostility of the Marxist or neo-Marxist variety are likely to occur at early, but not the earliest, stages of industrialization. It also appears that whether unions and other occupational groups are strongly or weakly political (i.e., with reference to legal codes and the role of the state in the economy) is partially a function of the existence of alternative means of political expression and influence.

Unions and other occupational groups, whatever their initial primary emphases, will tend through time to broaden their bases of affiliation and their services to members and thus their relations with other groups. In this way, "competing jurisdictions" develop, not only with

[6] See Melvin M. Tumin, "Some Principles of Stratification: A Critical Analysis," *American Sociological Review*, 18:387–394 (August 1953).

other groups similarly constituted, but with other forms of social affiliation that are nominally functionally distinct. For example, unions may act as employment agencies, insurance companies and credit unions, community centers, and providers of supervised recreation.

Because of the importance of participation and a sense of participation in the commitment process, unions and similar groups may stimulate as well as possibly impede the rate of economic transformation. The actions indicative of commitment are, of course, those appropriate to the orientation of the group in question. Specifically, joining and maintaining membership and participation in common or assigned activities are problematical and thus interesting. The actions are also those appropriate to the specific job, the occupation, and the occupational status. (In reverse order, the physician acts as a professional, a practitioner of his particular specialty, and a competent performer for his patients or employer.)

The appropriate norms prominently include loyalty—which is, however, both divisible and possibly competitive, as noted—ethical codes for the occupation and status, and thus identification with group interests and welfare.

In the preindustrial West, craft and professional groups were common and so constituted a possible model for new organizations, even though the particular organizations often performed conservative or reactionary roles. Apparently little attention has been paid to the elements of preindustrial social structures that might precondition the new industrial worker or manager for identification with occupational groups. Belshaw's discussion in Chapter 6 is a noteworthy exception.

The process of commitment to an occupational group such as a union has the indirect consequence of involving the transitional worker in the industrial way of life, even if the specific group orientation is one of conflict. The paradox deepens when any occupational interest group competes or bargains with other groups, for success reduces the chance of rejection of the system as a whole, or even of radical changes in its structure.

The rewards and controls that serve to maintain commitment to occupational interest groups are variable, but include the standard principles applicable to peer and reference groups. One range of variation can be crudely designated in terms of the number of interests served by group membership. Here we may characterize the extremes as "the union as a commodity," an economic service bought with membership dues; and "the union as a community," the organization as a

focus of many life activities, in possible substitution for more traditional structures.

If, with successful industrialization, social stratification loses some
of its coherence as a single rectilinear system, it follows that groups
oriented toward the status system are likely also to exhibit the strains
of intersecting interests. Coalitions based on common status may become increasingly fragile and temporary, subject to realignment on particular issues rather than remaining durably inclusive of many related
issues. The divergent interests of various occupations are likely to
become increasingly troublesome to inclusive labor organizations. The
attempt in totalitarian systems to discourage both status groups and
competing interest groups may achieve greater commitment to the
system as such, but it is doubtful that this removes the underlying
uncertainties or strains concerning questions of equity.

Education

Schools manifestly serve as agencies of socialization, especially with
regard to general and specialized cognitive orientations. Our interest
is in the school as an agency of status mobility and possibly as a functional and symbolic focus for social action and reform. In the latter
connection the educational system may provide both a locus of commitment in itself, and an "equitable" basis for a general system of social
differentiation.[7]

An extensive educational system makes possible different levels of
educational attainment and also different kinds of attainment, in the
sense of occupational specialization. The critical questions with respect
to commitment are several: the "goodness of fit" between the educational curricula and the needs of an industrial order; the accessibility of
educational opportunities; and the extent to which formal education
results in normative socialization with regard to new values as compared with mere information.

It may be noted that the strategy of educational development in
transitional societies may be distorted by undue emphasis on "high-
level manpower," although this is incidental to the present discussion.
The training of technical and administrative elites is particularly important in highly industrialized societies where a broad and expanding
"mass" educational base has been established. Given limited resources,

7 See Melvin M. Tumin and Arnold S. Feldman, "Status, Perspective and Achievement: Education and the Class Structure in Puerto Rico," *American Sociological
Review*, 21:464–472 (August 1956).

which are acutely restricted in underdeveloped areas, an emphasis on training of elites can only widen the gap between technicians and the labor force in general. The appealing notion that limited resources should be devoted to excellence is a special form of the entrepreneurial determinism noted in the discussion of the labor market (page 45 supra). It is incorrect on both technical and motivational grounds.

The enthusiasm with which educational expansion is undertaken in newly developing areas is obviously explained by the needs for skilled manpower and the opportunities for greater participation in community and national life. It also appears probable that schools provide a potential bridge from preindustrial to industrial status systems, and an acceptable means for allocating status in the new systems. The transitional worker may be induced to accept the new conditions of life, even in an unfamiliar and disadvantaged position, if by so doing he can improve opportunities for his children. His willingness to make sacrifices for such opportunities, although seemingly consistent with traditional kinship virtues, is more realistically viewed as acceptance of a system of intergenerational mobility that is rare in nonindustrial societies. Such acceptance implies commitment to new forms of social stratification and also of kinship responsibilities and illustrates the interdependence of such institutional complexes.

POLITICAL SYSTEMS

History and the contemporary world exhibit a wide variety of structural forms of the state associated with economic growth. This variety is not unimportant for analysis of the rate of growth and the precise structures of national economies.[8] In the areas now emerging from colonialism, still additional political relationships are likely to develop (see Apter's discussion in Chapter 18). Here the variations in political systems are largely neglected, and attention is focused on some common problems and features of political organization.

It is commonly, and probably correctly, assumed that wherever economic development becomes a matter of public policy (and that is nearly everywhere), the state plays an active role at least where critical barriers appear. Although the economic activity of the state in the historic laissez-faire economies should not be understated,[9] there is ample

[8] See Hugh G. J. Aitken, ed., *The State and Economic Growth* (New York: Social Science Research Council, 1959).

[9] See Joseph J. Spengler, "Laissez Faire and Intervention: A Potential Source of Historical Error," *Journal of Political Economy*, 57:438–441 (October 1949).

reason to assume that the contemporary state figures more largely as an agent of growth than was true in the past.[10] Questions of political loyalty and participation therefore assume an importance directly relevant to labor commitment, in addition to the structural position of the state as the focus of national integration and identity and as the ultimate agency for enforcement of social codes.

The repeated association between deliberate economic development and extreme nationalism is surely not accidental. Nationalism presents an essentially nonrational unifying force that may ease and rationalize the hardships of personal change. The importance of this explicitly common locus of commitment increases to the degree that rapid economic transition undermines various intermediate social structures that have shared or even captured loyalties in the preindustrial social system.[11] Yet nationalism should also be viewed in the context of actions as well as values, and specifically with reference to political associations.

Political Associations

The fully committed industrial worker, in whatever occupation, will become involved in political associations. These may be unions, occupational groups, other voluntary associations, even residential groups; but specialized political associations are likely to be organized also. The principal totalitarian states have attempted to integrate organizations "at the top," but these have been specialized at the level of rank and file membership. State enterprises, unions, and the party differ in organization, membership, and local leadership.

An inferential corollary is that economic development is accompanied by specifically political participation by a growing proportion of the population, and that many participants may become deeply involved. Changes in internal and external power relations are indeed so critical in the developmental process that political involvement may be the initial activating form of personal transition. The type of organization may vary from the formal party to the "spontaneous" street mob. At either extreme there is provided an agency of leverage and protest, which may have direct consequences for the social system or only the indirect effect of draining off dissident energies.

[10] See Bert F. Hoselitz, "Economic Policy and Economic Development," in Aitken, op. cit., pp. 325–352; Felicia V. Deyrup, "Limits of Government Activity in Underdeveloped Countries," Social Research, 24:191–201 (Summer 1957).

[11] See David E. Apter, The Gold Coast in Transition (Princeton: Princeton University Press, 1955), pp. 322–323.

To say that political participation is appropriate for committed workers is not very helpful. The questions remain: In what form, and to what ends? Political participation exemplifies the sociological principle that the internal cohesion of groups increases with external competition or conflict.[12] Political partisanship is therefore likely to increase commitment to particular political groups, and concern shifts to the stability (including orderly change) of the state as a whole. Presumably eufunctional political commitment in this situation requires acceptance of democratic procedures for resolving conflicts, and of the state as a more general locus than any party. The complementary generalization for totalitarian states is not novel but is theoretically valid: such states require external enemies, whether real or mythical.[13]

The norms governing political participation vary at least along the range from partisan to totalitarian. At any place along the range apathy is presumably a principal shortcoming, but political organizations and their leaders may have more trouble with overcommitted individuals than with either dissidents or nonparticipants.

There is a common assumption that "rational" or "realistic" political affiliation corresponds closely with economic interests. However, this represents an ideological doctrine, the accuracy of which depends on narrowly restrictive conditions. These include the existence of unresolved normative issues of high salience, chiefly issues of general economic policy and of the equity of differentials in income and power. (The interdependence of institutions is thus again illustrated.) Although such issues are probably never completely resolved, they appear to have high salience in those situations of rapid institutional change typical of contemporary or historical industrialization. In other situations the doctrine must rest on one of two untenable assumptions: (1) a crude "static" economic determinism in the sense of the primacy of "economic motives," which is nonsensical; (2) a radical "functionalism" in the sense that any central interest or value will define all others, which is both theoretically and empirically false. It follows that one-party or two-party systems represent heroic compromises of the heterogeneous interests of party members. The theoretical alternative is not only a multiparty system, but a multitude of splinter associations, each oriented toward a particular stand on a particular issue. Coalitions for political efficacy may then represent compromises of short duration.

[12] See Kingsley Davis, *Human Society* (New York: Macmillan Company, 1949), pp. 161–162.
[13] This is implied in *ibid.*, pp. 504–505.

The Politics of Development

The preindustrial forms of political organization are at least as variable as the potential forms of the modern state. The most reliable generalization is that most of the newly developing political entities are or have been under some form of external rule. This preindustrial political organization has had several standard patterns significant for commitment to political groups: (1) The establishment of imported educational systems somewhat independent of placement opportunities has usually produced an oversupply of prospective civil servants; these unemployed intellectuals commonly form the nucleus of new political associations. (2) Even "indirect rule" results in the political education of native intermediaries along modern lines, while the loyalty of their followers is generally maintained along traditional or quasi-traditional lines.[14] (3) Native leaders often have encouraged active and even violent political participation directed toward nationalistic ends; this not uncommonly is subsequently a source of embarrassment to the same post-independence leaders. (4) Historical imperialistic competition and modern ideological competition among the more developed areas have resulted in political penetration and activation of the backward or "uncommitted" areas.

Because the nature of the adult (or any) socialization process requires emotional involvement for internalization of norms, it is not surprising that transitional forms of political involvement are commonly characterized by "charismatic" authority. The Latin American concepts of *caudillismo* and *personalismo* are outstanding cases in point. The general principle of the "routinization of charisma" may be expected to apply, but this may be a slow and uneven process that does not bar the possibility that the maintenance of commitment to political groups may entail a succession of civil disorders inimical to economic development. In other words, institutionalization of political participation may be very slow, unless accomplished by totalitarian organization.

COMMON ORIENTATIONS

One of the most frequently noted features of industrial societies is their internal diversification. A complex division of economic function is integrated through the impersonal operation of the market or the

[14] See Apter, *op. cit.;* Lloyd A. Fallers, *Bantu Bureaucracy* (Cambridge, England: W. Heffer and Sons, for East African Institute of Social Research, n.d.).

quasi-impersonal discipline of administrative organizations. Urbanization and other forms of geographic mobility potentially bring together people of highly diverse backgrounds. Income and status differences result in variable styles of living. A multitude of associations vie for members, whether to press economic and political interests or simply to represent expressive and recreational affinities. Behind such diversity there are three principal common orientations: a minimal cognitive consensus; an acquiescence in, if not positive acceptance of, a normative order without which coordination could not emerge from specialization; and a minimal consensus on ultimate values.[15]

The importance of the educational system in providing common cognitive orientations has been noted. Many less formal agencies of socialization contribute to the same end—at work, in the market, in urban neighborhoods. Also, mass communication media are used increasingly for the quick dissemination of information, for propaganda, and for persuasion. The person in transitional situations must learn a multitude of facts and skills, from survival tactics in urban traffic to the arbitrary divisions of life's activities into temporal units.

The normative order has been a central concern throughout this discussion and needs little further comment. The fully committed individual has internalized the appropriate norms, and thereafter needs little help from external sanctions. By nature rules are specific and therefore arise in particular action contexts. More general normative orientations appear to operate pervasively. Promptness and a rational orientation toward decisions are two examples of such generalized norms in industrial systems. The transferability of such norms from one action pattern to another aids role playing by individuals and indirectly serves to maintain the systemic character of highly specialized substructures.

Finally, a value consensus is a theoretical necessity of a viable society. Not only is the normative order usually referable to common values; but such values may be directly explicated and thus serve as incentives to appropriate action. Standards of equity and justice, the allocation of wealth, power, and position, and the maintenance of institutional balance, all serve as value premises for particular sets of rules. In addition, political and religious ideologies may provide goals as well as standards of conduct.

The debate over the importance of Protestantism in the rise of capi-

[15] Marion J. Levy, Jr., *The Structure of Society* (Princeton: Princeton University Press, 1952), pp. 168–197.

talism is now largely academic, but the general problem of ultimate values is not. The mystical elements in nationalism, the transformation of "scientific socialism" into a religious doctrine, and the very acceptance of economic development as a goal serve as warnings that common ultimate values cannot be dismissed as inconsequential for policies and patterns of action. Conventional sociological analysis puts value questions last, as they are placed here. In the last analysis, they may be first.

5 PREINDUSTRIAL FORMS
OF ORGANIZED WORK

Stanley H. Udy, Jr.

The collective organization of productive effort is, as a general phenomenon, probably universal to all human societies. It may, of course, assume varied forms both technologically and organizationally. Often, however, types of organized productive effort that appear on the surface to be quite different prove on closer examination to possess many important similarities. Some knowledge of the principal similarities and differences between nonindustrial and industrial production systems, in particular, seems fairly crucial to an understanding of the problems involved in industrial development. The purpose of this paper, then, is to examine the major ways in which technological processes are socially organized in nonindustrial societies, with a view toward discovering some major organizational similarities and differences between nonindustrial and industrial systems, and isolating certain organizational problems of industrial development that seem likely to be widespread.

Any organization manifestly engaged in the production of some material good is a *production organization*. All such organizations, whether industrial or not, are subject to structural limitations both technological and social in character. The nature of any technological process sets limits on the kinds of organization by which it can be carried out, and the social setting limits the kinds of organization institutionally possible in the society concerned. These limiting mechanisms affect at least four structural variables of any production organization: its permanence or impermanence, specificity or diffuseness, use of achievement or ascription as the basis of rewards for work, and social or territorial recruitment of personnel. A production organization is here designated as *permanent* if its structure is expected to outlast the job spans of its members, and *impermanent* if not. If its objectives are explicitly limited to material productive ends, the organization is deemed *specific*; it is *diffuse* to the extent that other ends are involved or if its objectives are obscure. When rewards for work depend in any respect at all on the amount of work done or effort expended, *achievement* is considered to be emphasized; when rewards are consistently allocated independently of work or effort, evaluation of performance is said to be

78

based on *ascription*. Recruitment is based on *social* grounds if membership in the organization depends on prior membership in some other social group within the society concerned; recruitment is *territorial* if the criteria are solely spatial.[1]

The structure of any industrial enterprise is typically characterized by permanence, if only because of the considerable fixed capital outlay involved. Specificity of objectives tends to be requisite to industrial production, owing at least to the necessity of coordinating diverse technological operations. Similarly, some modicum of achievement must be emphasized, since highly specialized skills are ordinarily relied on for successful production. And recruitment must be territorial insofar as reliance is placed on a potentially mobile labor force, irrespective of traditional social ties.[2] Industrialization, then, implies a commitment to this peculiar combination of organizational attributes. Such commitment is by no means automatic, for indigenous forms of nonindustrial production are often likely to involve quite different organizational characteristics. However, if any society is to become industrialized, institutionalized commitment to this particular pattern must be possible.

Major Types of Nonindustrial Production Organization

In analysis of the structure of any production system, recruitment is a crucial variable, for it has reference to both organizational and general social structure. The social or territorial aspect may be further broken down on the basis of the obligation to participate. Examination of available data has suggested four general types of recruitment: familial, custodial, contractual, and voluntary. The first two types are predominantly social; the latter two, predominantly territorial.

A production organization is *familial* if the obligation to participate is based on ascribed kinship status. Personnel are drawn from some kind of kinship group; the group may range in scope from a nuclear family to a ramified set of extended kin affiliations. Membership is compulsory in the sense that sanctions of whatever sort relative to the maintenance of kinship solidarity are operative. Other institutional content may reinforce kinship obligations, but not necessarily.

[1] See Talcott Parsons and Edward A. Shils, *Toward a General Theory of Action* (Cambridge: Harvard University Press, 1951), pp. 80–84, for a discussion of specificity and diffuseness and of achievement and ascription. See also Marion J. Levy, Jr., *The Structure of Society* (Princeton: Princeton University Press, 1952), pp. 240–298.

[2] See Chapter 2 supra; Levy, *loc. cit.;* and Wilbert E. Moore, *Industrialization and Labor* (Ithaca: Cornell University Press, 1951), pp. 106–139.

In *custodial* production organization, the obligation to participate is based on differential ascribed power, with kinship status secondary, if operative at all. Personnel are drawn from some group defined in predominantly political terms. Membership is compulsory in that participation may be legitimately forced, if necessary. Again, reinforcing institutional content may or may not be present.

Contractual production organization differs quite radically from both of the preceding forms. The obligation to participate is determined at some point by the conclusion of a voluntary contract between two or more parties, i.e., an agreement to behave in a specified way for a specified time in the future.[3] Once the contract has been concluded, participation in accordance with its terms is generally compulsory, but the specific means of enforcement is highly variable. The basis of recruitment tends to be territorial, inasmuch as there is no invariable social obligation to conclude any agreement in the first place, but social elements do enter into such agreements. Their organizational variations generally assume one of three types: In the first, the source of personnel is some relatively small group which is neither predominantly familial nor political in nature, such as a military society or mutual aid association. A voluntary contract is concluded between someone who needs workers, on the one hand, and this group or its legitimate representative, on the other. The group then does the work, with participation compulsory in terms of the agreement. In the second type, a number of individuals conclude an agreement to work together for some common productive purpose. Participation is again compulsory in accordance with the agreement, but the methods of enforcement often appear quite weak. The third type is like the second except that the agreement is between a number of individuals, on the one hand, and the person desiring work to be done in his own interest, on the other.

In *voluntary* production organization, membership is expected to be based on self-defined self-interest, and no purely social sanctions are manifestly attached to nonparticipation. This does not mean that severe personal deprivations cannot result from failure to participate, but only that there is no social mechanism to compel membership. Recruitment is territorially based, in the sense that anyone who can do the work and who happens to be in the vicinity may join.

Viewed in slightly different perspective, these four types indicate four different ways in which members of a labor force may be committed to production organization. In this light, contractual and vol-

[3] Kingsley Davis, *Human Society* (New York: Macmillan Company, 1949), p. 470.

untary organizations bear marked resemblances to industrial forms, while custodial and familial types do not. Furthermore, these similarities are not restricted to recruitment but extend to other aspects of organization as well, owing to certain interrelations among the four structural variables.

COMPARATIVE ANALYSIS OF A SAMPLE OF NONINDUSTRIAL ORGANIZATIONS

In this context a comparative analysis was made of 150 nonindustrial production organizations.[4] Three working hypotheses governed the analysis:

1. The structure of any production organization is partly determined by the nature of the technological process carried on, and partly by the social setting.

2. The four variables of organization structure are functionally interrelated in that they do not vary at random in relation to one another.

3. Some forms of technology may be organizationally impossible in any given social setting.

Sample and Methodology

Any comparative social analysis relying on secondary sources immediately encounters two rather difficult problems of method. The first is the question of independence of the units of observation, inasmuch as diffusion is often an unknown quantity. Each of the 150 organizations studied was drawn from a separate society, on the assumption—not entirely realistic, to be sure—that production organizations in different societies constitute independent entities, while those in the same society do not. The second problem is the difficulty of securing a sample known to be unbiased. It is obviously impossible to select societies at random, owing to the unevenness in ethnographic data. The expedient of consciously selecting societies distributed as evenly as possible over world culture areas was therefore resorted to, using the selection criteria set forth by Murdock. A roughly equal number of societies was chosen from each of the six major culture areas that he delineates.[5]

To obtain something approaching an even distribution within each

---

[4] The present report draws from portions of the author's unpublished doctoral dissertation, "The Organization of Production in Nonindustrial Culture," Princeton University, 1958.

[5] G. P. Murdock, "World Ethnographic Sample," *American Anthropologist,* 59: 664–687 (August 1957).

area, no fewer than two and no more than four societies were used from each subarea. Beyond this, the societies chosen were those on which the material available seemed most reliable and complete. The result was a "quota" sample of 150 societies roughly stratified by culture area and distributed as follows:

Culture area	Number of societies
Africa	27
Circum-Mediterranean	18
East Eurasia	26
Insular Pacific	25
North America	32
South America	22
Total	150

From ethnographic sources on each of the societies, material was then abstracted on every production organization clearly described. Through this procedure, 426 cases of production organization were collected, from which one case was drawn at random from each society, with the exception that the sample was stratified so as to include an approximately equal number of organizations of each of seven major technological types (for definitions of these types see pages 84–86 infra).[6]

Structural Characteristics

A cross-classification of the sample organizations by the four organizational types distinguished on the basis of social or territorial recruitment, and by two of the other structural attributes, yields some rather striking internal consistencies:

	Specific		Diffuse	
	Permanent	Impermanent	Permanent	Impermanent
Familial	—	—	55	—
Custodial	—	—	30	7
Contractual	17	2	4	—
Voluntary	—	32	—	—

[6] In the abstracting of materials, the Human Relations Area Files were utilized whenever possible. For their nature and scope see G. P. Murdock, C. S. Ford, and others, *Outline of Cultural Materials* (New Haven: Human Relations Area Files, 1950). In all statistical tests of the sample, cases lacking relevant data were dropped; unless otherwise noted, this practice did not result in any radical upset of the over-all distribution by culture area. Chi-square was used to test the existence of association among the variables, and Q (Yule's coefficent of association) to measure the degree of association.

The tabulation indicates that only 4 out of 16 possible combinations occur with any degree of frequency. This finding suggests a number of hypotheses concerned with the interrelations between the structural features of the different organizational types. The following three hypotheses are amply confirmed by the data:

1. *Familial and custodial production organizations tend to be diffuse and permanent:*

	Diffuse and permanent	Other
Familial and custodial	85	7
Contractual and voluntary	4	51
Q = + .98	$x^2 = 100.86$	P < .001

2. *Contractual production organizations tend to be specific and permanent:*

	Specific and permanent	Other
Contractual	17	6
Familial, custodial, and voluntary	0	124
Q = + 1.00	$x^2 = 67.28$	P < .001

3. *Voluntary production organizations tend to be specific and impermanent:*

	Specific and impermanent	Other
Voluntary	32	0
Familial, custodial, and contractual	2	113
Q = + 1.00	$x^2 = 132.78$	P < .001

The relation of the use of achievement or ascription as the basis of rewards for work to the other structural variables is not quite so consistent; furthermore, lack of data made the necessary cross-classification difficult. A fourth relationship, however, may be observed where data are available.[7]

4. *Achievement tends to be emphasized only in contractual and voluntary organizations:*

	Contractual and voluntary	Familial and custodial
Achievement	14	8
Ascription	26	63
Q = + .61	$x^2 = 7.76$	P < .01

[7] South American and Circum-Mediterranean societies are underrepresented among the organizations that could be classified.

These relationships are largely in accord with what one would expect on the basis of structural-functional theory, in that territorial recruitment and specificity of objectives occur together, and achievement is seldom used as the basis of rewards in the absence of the other two attributes.[8] The attribute of permanence or impermanence, however, cuts across this cluster: contractual forms are permanent, voluntary forms are impermanent. It is hardly surprising that organizations having no social sanctions attached to nonparticipation should be impermanent, but it is rather disturbing to note that such a large group of organizations emphasizing "rational" administrative characteristics should be ephemeral. Contractual forms, therefore, most closely resemble industrial types; voluntary forms are similar except that they are not permanent. Familial and custodial forms, on the other hand, are radically different.

It seems reasonable to suppose that the societies in which contractual forms are relatively widespread encounter less organizational difficulty in commitment to industrialization than do societies that do not already possess contractual production organization. Also, societies in which voluntary production organization is widespread do not seem to have far to go in adapting to an industrial mode of organization. However, a predominance of familial or custodial forms suggests a necessity for quite radical organizational reforms if industrialization is to take place. In such cases, commitment to the norms of specificity and achievement apparently cannot be secured without a complete change in the recruitment mechanism. Such a change may not be forthcoming in a nonindustrial situation. The kind of technological processes carried out may be such that existing organizational forms are stable and perfectly adequate; and the social conditions may be such that institutionalization of changes in the direction of territorial recruitment would be difficult.

Technology, Organization, and Social Setting

A *technological process* may be defined as that system of physical operations on raw materials essential to the production of a given product. Seven types of productive process may be differentiated: tillage, hunting, fishing, collection, animal husbandry, construction, and manufacturing. Each of these types has rather obvious distinguishing characteristics and also possesses more subtle attributes that tend to be

---

[8] Levy, *loc. cit.*

structurally reflected in the corresponding production organizations. The result is that the four organizational types are not randomly distributed over the types of technological process. Nonindustrial technological processes appear to fall into two broad categories: those tending to require an emphasis on specificity and achievement but not permanence; and those tending to require permanence, but not specificity or achievement. In no instance does permanence seem to be combined with specificity and achievement in one set of organizational requirements, as is the case in industrial systems.

Technology and organization. Tillage and animal husbandry are closely tied to the seasonal cycle, require relatively long periods of time for their yield, and tend to be continuously repetitive in yearly cycles. Construction is somewhat similar in that it lends itself to work in successive stages over a fairly long period. None of these three processes ordinarily requires the undivided attention of members of the production organization. It is perfectly possible to cultivate a field, tend a herd, or build a house, and be carrying on some other activity during the same period. In fact, in tillage and animal husbandry there are limits beyond which more exclusive attention to the process would in effect be wasted, since at some point there is no alternative but to wait for crops or animals to mature. Similarly, in these three processes, failure of one member of the production organization to perform his role correctly would not ordinarily result in failure of the entire process. What is not done today can be done tomorrow, and what one person fails to do another can do at another time. One would consequently expect a tendency toward permanence in organizations carrying on tillage, animal husbandry, or construction. On the other hand, specificity and achievement would not tend to be required, since success is not dependent on immediate unfailing performance of tasks, and other activities can be carried on also.

The situation of hunting, fishing, and collection is quite different. These processes are of relatively short duration. Members of organizations performing such work cannot ordinarily do anything else at the same time if only because some search procedure is generally necessary. The workers usually must be away from other activities and must be specifically concerned with finding game, fish, or produce. Once the game has been located, undivided attention is often necessary to keep it under control; success frequently depends on every member doing what he is supposed to do competently and effectively. In hunting by drive or surround, for example, failure of one or a few members on the job may result in the breakthrough and escape of the quarry. Permanence tends to be unnecessary in these processes. Specificity and achievement, on the other hand, tend to be emphasized, and success greatly depends on effective role performance by each member, especially in hunting.

These inferences, in combination with the previous findings as to structural consistency of production organization, suggest the following propositions:

5. *Tillage, construction, and animal husbandry tend to be carried on by familial or custodial organizations:*

	Familial or custodial	Other
Tillage, construction, and animal husbandry	64	11
Other	29	46
$Q = +.80$	$x^2 = 32.71$	$P < .001$

6. *Hunting, fishing, and collection tend to be carried on by voluntary organizations:*

	Voluntary	Other
Hunting, fishing, and collection	31	37
Other	2	79
$Q = +.94$	$x^2 = 37.39$	$P < .001$

Contractual organization, as the argument would suggest, is not significantly associated with any particular type of nonindustrial process. Since this form of organization tends toward specificity and achievement, one might expect hunting and fishing to be alternatively organized in this way, particularly in view of the large number of exceptions in the preceding tabulation. Only one of these exceptional cases, however, is contractual; most are custodial:

7. *Hunting and fishing, when not carried on by voluntary organization, tend to be carried on by custodial organization:*

	Custodial	Other except voluntary
Hunting and fishing	20	10
Other	18	69
$Q = +.76$	$x^2 = 19.45$	$P < .001$

Deviations from organizational forms expected on purely technological grounds have been found. In particular, a preponderance of custodial organizations are found where one would expect contractual structures instead. This apparent tendency merits some exploration, inasmuch as industrial development is evidently dependent on the possibility of contractual organization. These findings suggest strong pressures toward custodial rather than contractual forms in nonindustrial contexts, and this in the face of seemingly stringent technological requirements to the contrary.

Production organization and social setting. The populations of the great majority of newly developing areas practice settled agriculture and live under *centralized government,* defined as an ultimate monopoly on the legitimate use of force exercised by a concrete group. Such specialized political organization is unlikely in a society of less than 1,500 persons.[9] In other words, the societies now on the brink of industrialization resemble the "peasant" variety more than the "tribal" or "primitive" sort. Custodial and contractual organizations both seem relatively more likely to occur in "peasant" societies:

8. *Custodial and contractual organizations are both associated with settled agriculture combined with centralized government:*

	Settled agriculture and centralized government	Other
Custodial and contractual	37	21
Other	23	52
$Q = + .59$	$x^2 = 13.18$	$P < .001$

A stable political system, which generally involves some kind of centralized government, has frequently been alleged to be a requisite of contractual relationships.[10] Here, however, custodial forms are involved as well. This might be expected in view of their essentially political basis, but it is particularly significant because custodial forms are quite unsuited to industrialism. Next to the contractual type, the voluntary organizations seem more closely akin to industrialism even though adapting them to industrial use is largely precluded by the fact that they are more characteristic of "tribal" than of "peasant" societies and hence are less likely to be found in newly developing areas:

9. *Voluntary organizations tend to be absent in societies with settled agriculture and centralized government:*

[9] Levy, *op. cit.,* pp. 485–486; Murdock, *op. cit.,* pp. 674–686.
[10] See pp. 58–59 supra.

	Settled agriculture and centralized government	Other
Voluntary	4	27
Other	56	46
Q = − .78	$x^2 = 15.28$	P < .001

Propositions 7 and 9 together imply another:

10. *Under conditions of settled agriculture and centralized government, hunting and fishing tend to be carried on by custodial organization; in the absence of these conditions, they are carried on by voluntary organization:*

	Custodial	Voluntary
Settled agriculture and centralized government	13	4
Other	7	20
Q = + .80	$x^2 = 8.80$	P < .01

Contractual organization does not seem to be significantly associated with any particular type of process. The data imply that settled agriculture and centralized government involve a shift away from voluntary forms and toward custodial organizations, rather than contractual. Although this involves permanent organization rather than impermanent, it also involves a departure from administrative "rationality" in favor of social recruitment, diffuseness, and ascription. Custodial organization, which is generally associated with tillage, construction, and animal husbandry, tends to be generalized to all other types of process, technological suitability notwithstanding. No similar "generalizing" tendency can be shown for contractual structures:

11. *Custodial organization is more likely to occur in more than one type of process in the same society than is contractual organization:*

	More than one type	One type only
Custodial	15	35
Contractual	1	31
Q = + .86	$x^2 = 7.34$	P < .01

Familial forms are also quite likely to occur in more than one type of process in the same society, but not in processes for which they are technologically ill-suited. Furthermore, familial forms cannot be shown to be associated with particular social conditions; they are simply ubiquitous, within technological limitations.

An explanation of the tendency of custodial organization to occur in more than one type of productive process is suggested by various theoretical writers. Production of an agricultural surplus makes support of a specialized political structure possible and implies a decline in the marginal importance of success in hunting and fishing as sources of food supply. Thus the relatively stable land tenure arrangements necessitated by settled agriculture tend to involve a structure of political authority centered around landed property, and to make the society able to afford the "costs" of custodial organization, as opposed to contractual or voluntary. In such circumstances there appears to be a high probability of pre-emption of control over land and other resources by the political authority. One specific mechanism in this connection is described by the "conquest theory of the state." The result is a generalized political system on which custodial organization can be based in all types of production by virtue of the control over resources.[11]

A tendency toward custodial organization does not necessarily imply a tendency toward direct government control of production. All that is required is a structure of differential power ultimately supported by governmental sanction. The group actually carrying out production may or may not be governmental in nature; often it is not. Structural alternatives to direct government control may be found in a context of general social stratification:

12. *Societies with centralized governments are more likely to possess complex hierarchies of general social stratification than are societies without such governments:* [12]

	Complex stratification	Stratification not complex
Centralized government	45	22
No centralized government	8	59
$Q = + .87$	$x^2 = 40.45$	$P < .001$

Why do these tendencies not occur with contractual organization? The relative incidence of contractual forms is higher where centralized

---

[11] See Ralph Linton, *The Study of Man* (New York: D. Appleton-Century Company, 1936), pp. 243–252; Melville J. Herskovits, *The Economic Life of Primitive Peoples* (New York: Alfred A. Knopf, 1940), pp. 372–387; Henry Maine, *Lectures on the Early History of Institutions* (New York: Henry Holt, 1888), pp. 64–97; Maurice R. Davie, *The Evolution of War* (New Haven: Yale University Press, 1929), pp. 160–175; Raymond Firth, *Elements of Social Organization* (New York: Philosophical Library, 1951), pp. 50–57.

[12] *Complex stratification* is considered to be present where "three or more social classes or castes" or "hereditary aristocracy" are reported (Murdock, *op. cit.,* pp. 673, 675–686).

government exists; but the over-all incidence of such forms is rather slight and is not connected with any particular type of production. Furthermore, contractual organizations do not appear in situations for which they are not technologically better adapted than other forms. Centralized government, it appears, simply provides a context within which contractual organization is possible because of the political stability. On the other hand, centralized government provides a direct basis for custodial organization. Additional conditions are evidently necessary for contractual organization.

These findings indicate, then, that settled agriculture and centralized government in nonindustrial societies are likely to set in motion institutional forces that militate against territorial recruitment, specificity, and achievement in production organization. The functions of voluntary organizations appear to be assumed by custodial types, and the development of contractual forms appears to be inhibited.

SUMMARY

While forms of production organization typical of industrialism are by no means absent in nonindustrial contexts, they are not likely to dominate the particular types of society now on the eve of industrialization. Of the four major types of nonindustrial production organization—familial, custodial, contractual, and voluntary—the latter two are closest to industrial requirements. Voluntary organizations, however, tend to be absent in societies with centralized government and settled agriculture, and so drop out of practical consideration as possible models for industrial commitment. Contractual organizations, on the other hand, appear to depend in part on the condition of centralized government.

Centralized government as defined for this analysis, however, does not in itself involve any mechanism directly conducive to contractual forms. In contrast, it provides a direct basis for custodial organization, through consolidated control over resources. It thus appears that, under conditions of settled agriculture and this type of government, custodial organization is more likely to develop on a large scale than is contractual. In fact custodial forms tend to be generalized to any situation, regardless of their technical suitability. Inasmuch as they involve social recruitment, ascription, and diffuseness, they appear in direct opposition to industrial development.

The major locus of this latent opposition to industrialism seems to lie in the political system, either directly or as reflected through social stratification. At the same time, centralized government appears necessary for the ultimate development of contractual forms and is certainly essential to industrialism. It is thus not surprising that many newly developing areas that are in fact developing successfully are characterized by political unrest. The analysis suggests that at some point of development a choice may have to be made between assured political stability, on the one hand, and effective industrialization measures, on the other. If the industrialization measures undermine the political structure too severely, the industrialization effort may collapse. The shift from custodial to contractual bases of organizational commitment thus emerges as a rather crucial test for newly developing areas.

6 ADAPTATION OF PERSONNEL POLICIES IN SOCIAL CONTEXT

Cyril S. Belshaw

This paper is not concerned with the industrial psychology that the management of large firms in developing countries may use to keep their employees working and happy. It is doubtful that enough studies of this subject have been made to permit us to draw very clear conclusions, although there is considerable interest in current studies of such enterprises as the larger Japanese industries, the Indian cotton factories, and the Middle East oil companies. Furthermore, the emphasis here is on newly developing areas, which almost by definition implies a lack of either large capitalist or state enterprises. How, then, can we speak of personnel policies at all?

By "policy" in this context we mean the principles that apply to the actions of persons in authority; and the relevant aspect of policy deals with the use of labor ("personnel"). The newly developing areas considered in this paper are units of state operation (countries, colonies) that have important sectors (a) entering the world market for the first time or (b) changing from a stationary economy to one characterized by increases in per capita production or consumption. The number and scope of units of organization corresponding to our Western idea of the firm are increasing rapidly in such areas; yet the existence of conventional firms cannot be assumed as a prior or necessary condition of growth. In theory at least, and in some cases in fact, organizations that mobilize labor in modified traditional ways can be responsible for entry into a world market or for an expansion of the volume of production. When we bring small entrepreneurs, homestead units, and village cooperatives into our purview the topic under examination is broadened. It can be rephrased as "the ways in which persons wishing to use labor devise means of obtaining a supply, or rewarding it, and of using it productively, with special reference to the influence of modified traditional institutions upon their decisions." [1]

---

[1] Cf. Cyril S. Belshaw, *Changing Melanesia: Social Economics of Culture Contact* (Melbourne: Oxford University Press, 1954), Chapter 10.

TRADITIONAL SOCIETY AND ITS MOVEMENT

The Static Model

Let us assume, first, the existence of a small community isolated from the world market, in a stationary economy. This implies a stationary culture, since it can be demonstrated that alterations in cultural values and forms involve adjustments in the use of resources (including time, knowledge, and organization) and in the ways in which they are related to goals. Let us assume that society and culture are "traditional," a term we shall use arbitrarily, indicating that exchange and political control are based on considerations of social structure rather than on an impersonal market and legislation. Also, the culture is relatively homogeneous rather than large scale and heterogeneous: although deviance is possible and conflict or culturally prescribed competition may be of great significance, the range of behavior that the people perceive to be possible is severely limited. In such a society acts of the same kind will be repeated indefinitely, and the supply of labor will develop in the same way and in response to the same motivations.

In a strict sense the stationary economic state is not found in the real world, and the analysis of its model is uninteresting. Aboriginal societies are often characterized as stationary, but they are so only in a special and relative sense and do not correspond to the model. A full list of sources of disturbance is not needed here; one only has to think of warfare, demographic change, physical cataclysms, power shifts between rival groups, or variations in health and hunting luck, for each such factor is a source of adjustment and change. We can no longer assume that religious practice is customary in the sense of unchanging: there is now considerable evidence of experimental, thoughtful, and dramatic alteration in cults, mythology, ritual and the like, all of which must have repercussions in the culture involving modified ways of using time and other resources.[2]

Theories of Sequential Change

Leach, in his account of Highland Burma,[3] has suggested that it is sometimes possible for one set of social institutions, *A*, to contain within

---

[2] Melanesian rituals may be interpreted in this manner, and syncretist religious movements such as cargo cult are frequently the expression of experiments with the supernatural. For the impact of such religious change, see P. M. Worsley, *The Trumpet Shall Sound* (London: McGibbon and Kee, 1957).

[3] Edmund R. Leach, *Political Systems of Highland Burma* (Cambridge: Harvard University Press, 1954).

themselves determining factors which direct change, when it comes, to a contrary set of social institutions, *B*; and as *B* is the obverse of *A*, it too contains factors that lead back to *A*. Such cyclical equilibrium must be extremely rare in history, since its continuance would depend upon the isolation of the system from the disrupting factors mentioned above. Similarly, the beautiful self-contained marriage exchange models erected by Lévi-Strauss and others [4] and even Malinowski's account of the ceremonial exchange rings of the Trobriand Islands [5] imply that regulated systematic adjustment between persons in a defined spatial and social relation cannot persist unless the institutions involved are insulated from the sources of change. This may be done by deliberate protection or by devices that permit change to be absorbed elsewhere in the culture. Both considerations suggest that cyclical or continuous models cannot apply to total economies.

Older theories of social evolution suggested that when change is initiated *A must* tend to become *B,* which then *must* tend to become *C,* and that human progress is summed up in the series *A, B, C* . . ., which could never become *A, F, X, G* . . . Such theories have been thoroughly discredited, but recently Steward has given technical support to a theory of multilinear evolution,[6] which permits *A* to become *B, C,* or *D,* depending upon the factors of change, but not to become *E, F,* or *G* (though, in time, *B* may reverse to become *A* again). This looks a little better, since our supposition that the second stage in change must bear some relationship to the first is supported, while greater flexibility is introduced. But even this is not enough. What happens to *A* depends on numerous factors that are beyond the scope of this paper. Suffice it to say that *A* is composed of a large number of parts (institutions, beliefs, techniques, resources, etc.). Factors of change are also numerous and of varying influence. Each factor will affect each part differently; the number of parts affected will vary; and the ramifying effects of a change in one part upon another part will also be variable. Even at the simple level of numbers of parts affected, the possibilities are little short of infinite, even were we to exclude (as we must) many changes as logically impossible. We cannot assume historically that *A* will become *B,*

---

[4] C. Lévi-Strauss, *Les Structures Elementaires de la Parente* (Paris: Presses Universitaires de France, 1949).

[5] B. Malinowski, *Argonauts of the Western Pacific* (London: G. Routledge & Sons, 1922).

[6] Julian Steward, *Theory of Culture Change* (Urbana: University of Illinois Press, 1955).

C, or *D.* Forecasting is historical and empirical, and hence subject to tremendous variety and error. However, we can abstract certain characteristics for theoretical examination.

Neotraditional Equilibrium

We can state, for example, that one type of change that occurs from the base of traditional stationary economies is a change into another stationary economy. In other words, in neither *A* nor *B* is a characteristic increase in per capita consumption or production associated with existing social processes. Most of the changes between *A* and *B* have been concerned with kind or quality, or the ways in which resources are used. It is of course unlikely that such change will not involve quantity—of satisfactions obtained, or of this resource used as against that. It is a one-step operation, with an equilibrium achieved at *B* such that no further steps need be taken until new, inescapable factors of change come on the scene.

To examine why some changes are of this step-by-step nature, and others dynamic, would lead us too far afield. A vast number of the changes taking place throughout the newly developing world are of this step-by-step nature. Accounts of the "new conservatives" in modified traditional society are legion. There are, for example, the Northwest Coast Indian or New Guinea villagers living according to patterns set as a response to Victorian missionary culture, and the Melanesian village communities supplying migrant plantation labor instead of becoming peasant proprietors.

It appears that for many newly developing economies the movement from one stationary equilibrium to another constitutes the first stage. For this reason entering the market was distinguished from per capita increase in our opening definitions. In New Guinea it is possible to distinguish several distinct levels of equilibrium, each involving a different kind of relation to the market economy.[7] At each point of change a new culture is formed, with new quantities and kinds of consumption and production. But the quantities alter only at the time of change, and not during the sometimes lengthy period when equilibrium has been established.

During the period of change the individual producer must decide at what point and to what degree he will follow the trend. Although

---

7 Cyril S. Belshaw, *In Search of Wealth: A Study of the Emergence of Commercial Operations in the Melanesian Society of Southeastern Papua,* American Anthropological Association Memoir No. 80 (February 1955).

considerable variation is possible, we are still dealing with a homogeneous traditional society, and the producer must act on the assumption of shared values. His personnel policy must be entirely congruent with this modified traditional culture. Once the change has been completed, it is possible to describe in static, repetitive, and predictive terms what each producer will do. We do not (or should not) expect the peasant copra producer in such a society to employ wage labor, maximize monetary profit, and reinvest capital as would the Western industrialist. We would expect that the labor supply would relate to kinship obligation and be rewarded by feasting or reciprocal duty, and that many laborers would also be entrepreneurs, since the two roles would be interchangeable during the course of the season.

Transition to Continuous Change

The state of society that is most significant for economic growth is one in which the step-by-step process has been left behind, and production or consumption increase shows a continuous, though perhaps fluctuating, progression. It seems likely that the most significant difference is that in the growing economy the entrepreneur has a new attitude toward the size of his organization. He is interested in doing more with what he has, in moving into new fields of endeavor, in expanding his land, his plant, and his labor supply. There is some reason to believe that this interest in physical and organizational growth is an especially important incentive in itself and an intellectual challenge to the entrepreneur. Such growth is probably a function of capital reinvestment, which may in part be interpreted as an increased demand for labor productivity.

Viewed in this way, labor commitment is a cultural phenomenon, and its development is a process of culture change. It has been indicated that the forms of economic growth can be multifarious and can be predicted only if we know the specific limiting conditions in each case. Statements such as "Societies of Type A will develop labor commitment and take off into economic growth more readily than societies of Type B" are of dubious value, since the structure of society is only one among a number of sets of variables. Instead, we must seek variables that apply to social and economic change in general; this implies the need for analysis of changes in the nature of rewards and punishments and human reactions to them, of the cultural content of goals and aspirations, of ways in which the costs of change are assessed, of ability to use resources, and of alteration and stability in human relations.

The temptation is to believe that growth behavior in all significant respects must be the same as growth behavior in our own society. The argument would run that the entrepreneur must hire and fire freely and impersonally, must translate rewards into money wages, must provide material and social services at his plant in order to add to the income of labor in accordance with its demands, must be prepared to see the growth of labor organizations parallel that of industrial organization, and so on. The entrepreneur must come to terms with labor to get the most out of it in productivity and profit. However, it may also be argued that these are not necessary conditions of growth, and that we may conceive of alternative institutional patterns that are compatible with growth. If analysts such as W. A. Lewis are correct, the rate of capital investment is the factor that governs growth.[8] We may then ask to what extent institutional changes have to take place to permit capital investment at the required rate? And this leads to the central question of this paper: What are the likely or necessary labor adjustments?

ENTREPRENEURIAL AND LABOR ROLES

In many *newly* developing areas, units of production such as the factory or the firm have yet to make their appearance or else are still a relatively small part of the total productive economy. The commitment of labor to improvements in agriculture or to work with small productive units that, while expanding, have not achieved a fully "rationalized" work organization should be borne in mind throughout the discussion.

Types of Entrepreneurs

The entrepreneur committed to growth through productive expansion and capital investment can be thought of as occupying a variety of social roles. He may be a cultivator producing new crops and using more land, labor, and equipment. He may be a proprietor operating a taxi service or constructing cane furniture. He may be a go-between, marketing produce for persons who feel unable to cope with commercial techniques. He may be a village official or cooperative leader guiding a community enterprise, or a state politician heading a ministry of public works. The entrepreneur's interest in labor and the way in which he conceives of its manipulation are obviously highly variable, even

8 W. A. Lewis, *The Theory of Economic Growth* (London: Allen and Unwin, 1955).

within the same society. Each role poses many similar questions, but the answers differ.[9]

The first questions might be: What is his need for labor, and how does it relate to his goals? The entrepreneur who is simply seeking and acquiring greater control over more and more labor is not contributing to economic growth in general, although he is increasing the size of his own establishment. He is just concentrating existing work under his own management. Such expansion is seldom a completely isolated factor. Increases in size often suggest new economies and methods. To the extent that the entrepreneur attempts to put labor to new uses, to rearrange or regroup it in more productive organization, or to enable it to use new and more productive techniques, he may be said to be investing in increased productivity and contributing to growth. Thus it may be concluded that the entrepreneur committed to growth must be interested in committing his labor force (a) to work for an employer, (b) to work for him instead of for someone else, and (c) to contribute to economic growth through adjustable productivity. Each of these points may be examined in turn.

Commitment of Labor to Work

Working for an "employer." The most overlooked element in motivating labor to work for an employer probably has been the continuance of modified traditional rewards and organization—so much so that the very existence of an "employer" can be obscured. In South Eastern New Guinea, for example, there are men who mobilize labor for boat-building, copra production, or commercial agriculture by holding out promises of nonmonetary rewards and work in a traditional organization. Men offer their labor in return for a feast, or a distribution of trade goods, or because they have access to the stores and hospitality of the "employer." Where the entrepreneur is not too specialized and a significant number of persons in the community can perform his functions, the old principle of reciprocity in sharing labor through work teams sometimes continues as an effective method of getting agricultural work done. Even where there are relatively few "managers" in a community—say, one executive for each lineage—it is quite likely that they will be operating not on their own account, but as coopera-

---

[9] An analysis of the relationship of the entrepreneur to society in newly developing economies is contained in Cyril S. Belshaw, "The Social Milieu of the Entrepreneur: A Critical Essay," *Explorations in Entrepreneurial History,* 7:146–163 (February 1955).

tive leaders for their kinsmen. In such a case, semitraditional organization is used to focus individual production, and what to the outsider might appear as a firm using labor is in reality a cooperative group of peasants delegating managerial responsibilities to one of their number.

Working for wages. One does not have to go far into the literature to realize that the operation of wage rates as a force securing the commitment of labor is an elusive variable. The point has been made that where the variety of things that money can do is limited, the marketing of products (including labor) can reach a point at which the income earned can be distributed not only with optimum marginal satisfaction but with maximum total satisfaction, so far as money use is concerned. In other words, the attractiveness of earning more money is negligible. This I believe to have been the case throughout Melanesia up to World War II, and it carries the implication that monetary inducements to increase labor supply and productivity are not likely to be successful. These particular premises of course are not the only ones leading to such a conclusion. One merely has to assume the more common condition that even with a wide variety of uses of money, the disutility of work is such that the elasticity of the supply of labor is very great.

The statement that labor works for wages conceals the whole range of things for which wages are wanted. Here economic analysis and cultural analysis come into sharp contact. In the old days the demand for money was enforced through taxation. Today money has percolated throughout traditional cultures, so that it can be used for traditional purposes such as marriage exchange, potlatching, purchasing foods for feasts, setting up a household, and even rewarding the diviner or sorcerer.[10] The definition of limitations on the uses of money is almost entirely cultural, although in some cases the organization of the supply of goods is involved. Thus, one Melanesian community limits itself to the goods available in the trade store; another community only a few miles away has developed uses for bicycles, has learned about cameras, and, being literate, demands pen, paper, and books. One Northwest Coast Indian group, despite the fact that mail-order resources are available in all their plentitude, limits its demand to basic foodstuffs, clothing, and trapping equipment. Some distance away another community has learned to invest in mechanical equipment, domestic lighting, and

10 Cyril S. Belshaw, *The Great Village: The Economic and Social Welfare of Hanaubada, an Urban Community in Papua* (London: Routledge & Kegan Paul, 1958).

encyclopaedias. Such variables affect the demand for cash, of course, and are one element in the commitment of labor to work.

Unstable involvements. A common method of organizing the supply of labor is represented by migrant labor in Africa and Melanesia, and even in the Orient and among North American Indians. Here we have a dramatic symbolization of many of the factors involved. On the one hand, there is the pull of traditional attachments, with the heart of the culture geographically removed from the place of employment. Labor is committed to work for a period which depends in part on the speed with which monetary objectives can be achieved, and these depend on the limitations of its conception of monetary use; and in part, on the degree to which money *cannot* be used to satisfy valid traditional goals. (For example, there is in migrant labor a dilemma which is seldom resolved: Going wage rates do not normally support village families, hence the industry is as it were subsidized by village labor; yet there comes a point at which potential laborers must remain at home in order to maintain the village production, which in turn is subsidizing the migrant-consuming industries.) And of course, both the quantity of labor supply and the period for which it is available are responsive to the positive nonmonetary advantages of migration. The commitment will vary according to the intensity of those pressures that may force the migrant from his home, according to the expectation that migration is a major educative or initiatory experience providing a man with status on his assumed return home, and according to whether the excitement of the new world arouses strong hopes for continuous, urban, monetary demands.

Although these factors are most strongly dramatized in migrant labor, they are present to some degree wherever there is a contrast between the values of employment and those of home life. In urban New Guinea, where working for wages is the order of the day, there are still the decisions to be made: Shall I throw up my job to participate in the competitive feast and dance series? Shall I break into continuous conspicuous consumption, or stop work when I have earned enough to buy groceries and pay for my child's wedding?

MOBILITY AND COMMITMENT

If we examine commitment to different kinds of work, rather than to work in general, some of these points become clearer. This can be of great importance to the employer or organizer, since in many cases he can affect the kind of work that is offered.

Mobility versus Commitment

To operate effectively, a social system must ensure both a steady supply of committed labor and its commitment to the particular *kinds* of work that the culture demands. In a rapidly changing society, such as ours, a great problem is to ensure the mobility of the labor supply between different industries, and techniques within industries, to match changing economic and technological conditions, which themselves reflect a continuously expanding cultural demand for material goods. But underlying this mobility, and constituting something of a dilemma, is the necessity for continuous commitment. Unless enough workers stay with a job for at least some minimum period of time, the economic benefits from their training cannot be derived, and the industry does not have an established base of technological aptitude on which to build its next move. Too much turnover is commonly regarded as wasteful and an index of unsatisfactory personnel policies.

Without exact data relating to industrial turnover in newly developing countries, a reasonable impression is that in many countries there is a high rate, which constitutes a major limitation on technical training and economic operation. The worker must choose between occupations. He knows he wants money and he senses his technical and social limitations in the new world. His knowledge of the range of potential occupations and industries is limited not only to those present in his country, but to the few that employ his acquaintances. Thus he offers only his generalized human abilities to the market; his special potential skills are not, and may never be, fully developed. Without precise knowledge about man's sensitivity to his underemployment, it is possible to observe enough of it in military situations, in bureaucracies, and in colonial territories, to recognize it as a major source of frustration and a stimulus to experimental change.

Mobility as an Instrument of Commitment

Because of lack of knowledge or of opportunity or both, employees seem to tend to seek new employers rather than new occupations. An interesting hypothesis would be that in a newly developing economy the workers most committed to particular occupations or firms are either (a) those who by good fortune have been in a position to develop talents, exercise authority, and attain prestige, or (b) in the majority, those who lack sensitivity and enterprise. Despite its uneconomic effects for the individual firm, such mobility is to be encouraged in order to keep the newly developing economy moving and alert to satisfactory paths of development.

If custom is destroyed, however, it tends to be reformed in new ways. In colonial territories unwritten agreements of employers are common; these provide that workers will not be rehired if they have left previous employment on their own initiative. In New Guinea, governmental departments customarily refuse applications for transfer. By such means the less enterprising are discouraged, and the enterprising are forced to be objectionable in order to be dismissed. In the Canadian Indian reservations, enterprise is limited to members of the band that resides there. Since occupational opportunities are largely geographically determined—only coastal Indians are deep sea fishermen, only interior Indians can be pastoralists—an Indian cannot seek employment with other Indians if he does not have the aptitude for the occupation characteristic of his reserve.[11] In an urban New Guinea community the people first entered the market as wage earners; for fifty years they remained unaware of the possibilities of their own private enterprise.

The considerable pain and cost attached to experimentation that is associated with negative learning progressively reduce the probability of continuing the experimentation unless some positive opportunities for breakthrough appear. This applies most dramatically to the choice between commitment to wage earning for government, large firms, or established (mainly European) employers, and commitment to independent individual enterprise or partnership with a native entrepreneur. In many countries, at least until recently, the former choice had the benefit of security, whereas the second raised all the frightening complications of risk taking. If there is no break-through after a generation or two, it is possible to speak of a strong tradition of dependent wage earning or limited occupational distribution. Such a tradition, like all others, may be challenged and destroyed, but it can be a definite hindrance to enterprise and movement. For this reason the urban workers of Port Moresby in New Guinea or the Indians of British Columbia will find it much more difficult to alter their limited commitments than, say, the peoples of West Africa who hope they have the world before them.

Since many units of production are small and undifferentiated, labor need not be committed to "skill dilution" within the productive unit to enable initial steps toward growth to take place. Certainly, there

[11] H. B. Hawthorn, C. S. Belshaw, and S. Jamieson, *The Indians of British Columbia* (Toronto: University of Toronto Press, 1958).

must be a gradually increasing specialization of production between geographical areas, communities, or forms, with its concomitant increase in the circulation of wealth; but the practical implications of this can be minor at the village level. Significant growth can take place with very small production units, so that the work teams involved in copra making, fishing, rubber growing and tapping, or furniture making *need* not involve much greater division of labor than before. This may be true even when, for technical reasons, particular *operations* become more differentiated, for the effect of operational differentiation on dilution of skills may be significantly reduced by labor mobility between operations. In chairmaking or prefabricated housebuilding, for example, the group involved may be forced to rationalize its methods to achieve greater and steadier production. But (1) workers may interchange their roles frequently, and (2) they may organize their calendar of factory work so that their domestic agriculture or fishing suffers minimally. There is less dilution of skills and perhaps greater commitment of labor under some such circumstances, which is one reason for the popularity of village industry with some theorists.

The preceding remarks have been predicated largely on the assumption that wage earning in some form has become a tradition before small-scale or peasant indigenous industry has had a chance to get started. This is not always the case, and some of my examples (such as the Northwest Coast Indian) have shown conservatism against wage earning across the cultural boundary. In this case all the factors affecting commitment to particular occupations (peasant agriculture, fishing cooperation) are still operative, but in addition community, lineage, and family ties provide not only an organization but also a strong sentimental attachment to the way of life. The development and communication of technological and procedural ideas under such circumstances are major problems in policy.

ADAPTATION AND CONTINUOUS CHANGE

We may now consider the commitment of labor to economic growth. For our purposes, this may be thought of as willingness to go along with expansive investment through technical adaptability and the support of efficient production.

Personnel Selection and Occupational Choice

Factors of mobility, occupational opportunity, and occupational interest affect commitment to specific industries, interest in tasks, and the willingness to master them. In other words, personnel policies will be more effective in promoting investment and growth if the right men can be placed in the right jobs. At one end of the continuum of economic change, the principle has been generalized and sometimes applied in the form: tasks should relate as closely as possible to those for which labor has traditionally shown an aptitude and interest. For example, in a community traditionally composed of deep-sea canoe fishermen, the inhabitants could develop naturally as commercial fishermen, shell divers, or seamen, but they would lack aptitude for and interest in becoming pastoralists. Similarly, peoples who have been hunters, gatherers, and woodsmen should make better berrypickers and lumbermen than agriculturalists.

The support for such an argument is based largely on the haphazard historical developments in communities with minimal commercial variety, or where efforts to change a community's way of life have been associated with political or religious policies that have aroused antagonism or promoted paternal dependence with lack of administrative imagination. For a more positive formulation, stating that traditional techniques may be used as a basis of interest, rather than that development should be limited to traditional techniques, there is good theoretical support. If it is true that learning is best based on accepted experience, the new money-making goals will tend to be achieved when they can be related to existing techniques and organization. Persons may be introduced to economic growth very effectively if lineages and similar traditional groups can be persuaded to perform tasks similar to those they already know. But this is so *only* because experience is limited and the perception of alternatives is very slight. Even where alternatives are perceived, unless they can be associated with rewarding experience, they must appear dubious, if not even frightening. Once they *are* rewardingly experienced by members of a community, their occupational interest may change almost over night, and they may commit themselves to performing the new tasks with vigor and initiative. Examples are legion—the high-level Iroquois construction workers of Caughnawaga and the rubber growers of Southeast Asia are outstanding. Growth of experience more typically leads to variety of personal commitment and enables individuals to choose from a greater offering of occupations.

When such a stage has been reached, the possibility of mobility contributes significantly to efficiency, in the long run. Allocation to rewarding occupation (in its broadest sense) can only be effective when information or evidence is presented to the worker, enabling him to make the choice properly, and he can only decide whether he has made the right choice on the basis of comparative trial and error. Mobility, in the first generations encountering change, will give the population as a whole greater experience in the varieties of employment and improve the possibility that the right man will be available for the right job. This is particularly so since aptitude and interest tests have very little validity in such situations, and labor exchanges, however well organized, can contribute only so much by way of advice. Mobility, of course, has its own costs. It would be interesting to know the optimum balance between the costs and advantages of job change.

Broadening the Bases of Development

The advantages of training and education, whether traditional or novel, cannot be realized unless the main elements are put to social use. Mobility will cost less if it can be confined to occupations requiring similar training. When an electronic utopia is attained, it may well be that labor can be assigned to quite different productive processes that use similar techniques of control. But the achievements of productive mobility are at the cost of occupational variety. If we limit persons to jobs for which they are trained and train them against their aptitudes and interests, we are no further ahead. A tremendous responsibility for the effective commitment of the labor force in newly developing areas thus clearly rests with the humanity and intelligence of the system of vocational education.

Other factors than aptitude for and interest in technique, *qua* technique, are involved. The prestige and power rewards of supervision may be as important as pride in artisanship. The mine or plantation foreman can be acutely conscious of his superior knowledge of the environment that is so strange to his village cousins. His example can spur others to emulate and compete with him. This sometimes creates its own difficulties, as when workers of differing cultures are brought under one occupational or legal jurisdiction. Some employers keep men of different cultures separate, counting on the stimulus of rivalry. Others mix them, contending that group rivalry can be misdirected and that individual rivalry is a more effective stimulus.

Traditional societies are so highly interdependent that some theorists have characterized them as being held together by the bonds of reciprocity that have marked relations to productive incentives and effective organization. Such bonds should not be exaggerated, but they can be of great assistance in giving labor a sense of security and personal control over events during the first stages of economic growth. Indeed, a false emphasis on individualism and impersonality in policy can do great harm to the cause of growth. Such a condition cannot last, however. When specialization and productive relations lose contact with coherent external social bonds, such as those indicated by a lineage system, interdependence exists schematically but is difficult to translate into belief and motivation. The worker is hardly able to define a purpose common to himself and his employer; he works perforce, with little interest in the product. He is likely to be influenced by his desire to support his fellow worker, but this may take the form of being against management and for minimal production. The concept of "affective neutrality" seems to by-pass the issue that, other things being equal, production is likely to be greater if the working force has a sense of positive identification with the prosperity of the work organization itself. Support for the fellow worker is a necessary part of such an attitude, but the reverse is not always true.

The effect of union and political objectives on commitment to efficiency and growth should be mentioned also, for the sake of completeness. Clearly, personnel policy will have a simpler task if the developing unions adopt policies directed toward sharing the rewards of increased production. Although this implies increased attachment of profits, it also implies a common interest in production. Such clear-cut unity of interest is seldom achieved, and it is likely that the prevailing political philosophy in newly developing countries will be an increased demand for wealth and social services. These will compete with investment in productive capital. In such circumstances employers, like governments, may be expected to provide rewards in terms of job and personal security as well as wages.

Does this mean that the dilution of individualistic profit-making with cultural or welfare goals is necessarily detrimental to investment in productive capital? At the national level, investment in hospitals, for example, clearly uses funds which might otherwise be employed in developing skills or factories; but at the level of individual or firm enterprise, it is not always easy to analyze what happens. Much depends on how the entrepreneur conceives of his relations with his labor force, and how it uses its monetary rewards. In one New Guinea community, for example, the entrepreneur rewarded his labor force by feasting and by gifts of food and of money.[12] To the casual observer, he was

12 Belshaw, *In Search of Wealth.*

being ruined by the continuous and temperamental demands of relatives. In fact, he was able to devote a fair amount of his expenditures to
capital improvement, and his labor-force relatives sometimes supplied
him with equipment and funds when he needed them. Furthermore,
many of his relatives had ambitions to run enterprises of their own,
devoted some of the income they received from him to improving their
own stock of tools, and had plans for the education of their children.
A village leader may have the social improvement of his village at the
forefront of his mind when he initiates a cooperative form of production. It does not necessarily follow that a cooperative with social objectives will be unable to reinvest significant amounts of income. Even if
a large proportion of income is distributed to the workers as personal
dividends, capital investment may still be made through the expenditure of increased incomes and the raising of new share capital. In such
cases of welfare or community-oriented production, much depends on
administrative and personal allocations of income.

General Viewpoint and Conclusion

Patterns of behavior in cultures or subcultures are based on regularities in individual behavior. Individual behavior is not composed of
mutually independent units, but is strongly influenced by physical,
social, and cultural factors. From this viewpoint, every person or subculture (defined as possessing behavioral uniformities) operates with
ideas, concepts, and subconscious influences that are more or less sys-
tematized. These mental images or influences set ends that may be
translated into real action, or remain as potential. The ends may be
variously interpreted as goals, wants, desires, drives, values; there
should be no necessary psychological assumption that they are rational.
At the cultural level, determining influences on the ends are many,
the most important being related to the socialization process, the growth
of perception, the effects of learning through experience, and the integration of such processes through personality.

The ranking of ends in terms of the worth-whileness of acting them
out may be regarded as valuation, and one may assume with the economist that scales of preference will be present. These need not be highly
organized, conscious, or rational. Their presence is a necessary consequence of our being unable to do everything we would like to do at
once. What persons actually decide to do may be regarded as resulting
from the assignment of an end to a priority, when the circumstances

of the moment and the resources, difficulties, and costs of achievement are taken into account. Uniformities in such decisions constitute tradition and culture; exceptional decisions represent deviance, eccentricity, or idiosyncracy; cultural change and innovation, as Linton made quite clear, represent alterations in these judgments. For example, the creation of new hierarchies involves deference patterns composed of numerous elements. By abstracting work authority out of these elements, we are not left with forms of deference based only on a technical interpretation of work skill. The worker's concepts of what constitutes skill and knowledge are significantly formed by considerations external to the organization. It is doubtful whether he would be significantly attracted by the skill of his neighbor if he were hostile to the product. A laborer's assessment of his neighbor's work skill would not be unaffected by the fact that his neighbor was a chief, or a close and trusted relative.

Personnel policy is essentially the manipulation of such factors by employers who are acting both as the subjects and the objects of change. It aims at securing an appropriate division of labor, organizational bonds, and motivation for effective production as the entrepreneur sees it. Although the firm may be thought of as a microcosm of society, the data with which it deals are already partially formed and set by the wider social processes. Every act of an entrepreneur attempting to influence the patterns of behavior of his personnel is, almost by definition, an act aimed at cultural change. Its result, in terms of commitment or any other goal, must thus be interpreted in a varied and complex framework

7 MANAGEMENT IN ECONOMIC TRANSITION

Peter B. Hammond

In many technologically underdeveloped areas a dominant foreign managerial group is charged with directing the productive behavior of a dependent indigenous labor force. Cultural differences separating the two groups frequently result in failure of managerial activities designed to achieve and maintain labor commitment. These same cultural differences often prevent management from accurately perceiving the cause of this failure and correcting it. Two sets of variables appear significant for understanding this problem: (1) the managerial activities most crucial to the attainment of labor commitment; and (2) the cultural differences between management and labor most likely to impede successful implementation of the former's plans.

Requisite Managerial Activities

Certain activities appear basic to the administrative or managerial process regardless of the specific nature of the enterprise or its context. They have been identified as: decision making, programming, communicating, controlling, and reappraising.[1] The effective implementation of all these activities is important for the achievement and maintenance of labor commitment, but two of them appear crucial. Communication seems vital to the achievement of labor commitment; and reappraisal appears essential to its maintenance.

Communication

The importance of communication in achieving labor commitment within an enterprise increases in inverse ratio to the degree of consensus among its members; for labor commitment results from comprehension and acceptance of organizational goals and of the role of labor in attaining them. When the usual social and economic differences separating management and labor are complicated by cultural differences

---

[1] Edward H. Litchfield, "Notes on a General Theory of Administration," *Administrative Science Quarterly*, 1:12 (June 1956).

between the two groups, the likelihood of their failing to perceive organizational goals in the same way increases.

Even within the managerial group itself, social and economic differences between those in high positions and their subordinates may result in diverse perception and evaluation of the organization's goals. In a cross-cultural situation the security of those occupying superior positions in the managerial hierarchy is less likely to be threatened by the social or economic advancement of the indigenous labor force. As a result their evaluation and communication of managerial goals related to advancement of the workers is likely to be quite objective. However, those occupying subordinate positions in the managerial group are the first to be threatened by the social and economic encroachment of the indigenous laborers and so tend to modify those directives that are perceived as a potential menace to their own security.

Language differences and the concept of the proper use of speech in social interaction are additional factors likely to complicate the problem of communication. Because of the social distance between the two groups, conflict in perception resulting from these cultural differences is not likely to be alleviated by the development of channels for informal communication. Thus, if labor commitment is to be achieved, formal communication channels must be established. They must assure communication downward from management to the labor force, upward from the labor force to management, and horizontally among all those in the enterprise whose roles are interdependent.

Reappraisal

The importance of reappraisal for maintaining labor commitment refers to the necessity of revising managerial decisions as rapidly as change occurs. As an indigenous labor force gradually adapts itself to a new economic organization, it develops new wants that must be provided for promptly. Many of the managerial techniques originally designed to control laborers—the method of recruitment, the delegation of authority, and the distribution of rewards and punishments—must be altered as commitment grows; for if a lag develops between the emergence of new wants and management's ability to satisfy them, the newly won commitment of the labor force may not be sustained.

The initial response laborers make to a new enterprise and to the new economic behavior required of them is largely determined by their previous cultural conditioning. In an unfamiliar setting they seek analogues to traditional institutions and usages and attempt to react to them in familiar ways. From the new work organization, the laborer anticipates the satisfactions that he has been conditioned to derive from the indigenous economic system. He makes familiar motor responses to new tools, expects accustomed emotional rewards from new companions, and relies on traditional social usages in new relationships. He may even try to use traditional religious observances to control this relation to the new "supernatural" environment.

Management, in turn, interprets the laborer's response to the new work situation in terms of its own cultural conditioning. It may not understand that initial inefficiency at new tasks is the inevitable result of an unsuccessful attempt to adapt previous learning to the solution of new problems. It is far more likely to attribute this inefficiency to stupidity and slothfulness than to the dynamics of relearning. Consequently, when some managerial activity designed to achieve commitment fails because of the cultural differences separating management and labor, the cause of the failure is likely to be misperceived.

THE MOSSI: OBJECTS OF DELIBERATE CHANGE

Analysis of the interrelations between these two sets of variables—managerial activities, and cultural differences between management and labor—may be clarified by examination of some of the problems of economic transition at the Niger Irrigation Project in the Sudanic Republic. The Project was established in 1932, to irrigate and place under cultivation the potentially rich alluvial plain of the central Niger delta. More than 20,000 African laborers have been resettled on the newly developed lands. Under the direction of European managers these workers apply modern agricultural techniques to the production of rice and cotton. Within this indigenous labor force are some 5,000 Mossi from the neighboring Upper Volta kingdom of Yatenga.[2]

The traditional way of life of the Mossi has been relatively undisturbed by European cultural influences. They are millet farmers. With the assistance of their kinsmen, they cultivate the lands assigned to them by their lineage elders. Work in the fields begins with the first rains in early May and lasts through the harvests in September. The long months of the dry season are devoted to trading and migratory labor in other countries, as well as the repair of houses and equipment, and small crafts.

[2] D. Zahan, "Les Mossis du Delta Central Nigerien," unpublished manuscript (Segou, Soudan Francais, 1954), p. 3.

Authority in Yatenga is divided between the representatives of social and of supernatural power. Political authority in the highly centralized state is distributed by the king among his ministers, provincial lords, and village chiefs. Authority within the Mossi kinship unit is delegated to the eldest male in the patrilineage, who also serves as intermediary with the ancestral spirits. Control over the supernatural forces of the environment is the prerogative of Earth Custodians belonging to lineages descended from the original inhabitants of the region.

The Mossi is conditioned to perceive the maintenance of his own social, economic, and supernatural welfare as dependent on maintaining good relations with these various loci of social and supernatural power. This requires social, economic, and ceremonial cooperation with his kinsmen, his chief, and the local Earth Custodian. Although such cooperation sometimes results in neglect of his own personal economic endeavor, maintenance of balance in this intricate web of relations is both the focus of the Mossi's intellectual and emotional energies and the source of his greatest satisfactions.

As a consequence of the previous cultural conditioning of the Mossi, their resettlement at the Niger Project creates problems of readjustment with implications beyond mere technological adaptation. The workers must not only learn new skills; they must overcome previous conditioning and learn to respond to new sources of social, emotional, and supernatural security and satisfaction.

So far, the managerial activities designed to achieve the commitment of the Mossi labor force have failed. The goals of the Project are not understood by the workers; they perform the new tasks assigned them mechanically and without understanding the underlying rationale. Maintaining balance in their relations with their kinsmen and communities at home continues to be perceived as the activity most important to their own well-being. Management has responded by increasing punitive sanctions against the workers and by increasing mechanization that will take many important tasks out of the hands of the indigenous labor force.[3]

The reasons for this failure to achieve commitment of the Mossi workers can best be analyzed by examining the effects that the cultural differences separating them from management have had on its relevant activities.

3 "Les Realisations de l'Office du Niger," *L'Equipment de l'AOF* (Paris: Notes et Etudes Documentaires, 1951), p. 16.

ANALYSIS OF THE FAILURE TO ACHIEVE COMMITMENT
OF THE MOSSI LABOR FORCE

The cycle of managerial activities affecting the achievement of labor force commitment begins with decision making. The first managerial decision likely to affect labor commitment relates to the kind of labor force to be recruited. At the Niger Project management had the choice between a migrant labor force and a permanently settled one. It chose the latter, and the Mossi were selected for permanent resettlement on the newly developed lands.

Settlement of the Labor Force

There is a long tradition of migratory labor in West Africa. Ever since the establishment of intertribal peace, following the European conquest, young men from the Voltaic and Sudanic regions have left their villages after the harvest to seek work at either local commercial centers or on the plantations of Ghana and the Ivory Coast. Workers from the same region have formed associations that serve both to orient newly arrived laborers and to provide a substitute for the kinship affiliations they have previously relied on for support. Some work for a single season; others stay for years, accumulating sufficient cash to make a triumphant return to the homeland with new clothes, a bicycle, and enough other goods to begin negotiations for a bride. During this period of separation they maintain contact with their villages by means of presents and messages sent back and forth through other migrant workers. Although most such workers ultimately return to their villages, recently a few who have become well adapted to the alternative satisfactions offered by their new environment have remained as permanent settlers.

Since the beginning of this century young Mossi have journeyed to the cities of Bamako, Bobo-Dioulasso, Kumasi, and Abidjan, as well as to the plantation areas, to seek work. These journeys have become institutionalized as part of a young man's initiation into full adulthood. Even those who stay away for years send their kinsmen money and other gifts frequently as a sort of insurance that their interests in lineage affairs will be looked out for and that their ancestral spirits will not forget them. Thus if the migrants should fail at their new endeavors, they are assured of a secure position in their homeland. Most Mossi migrant workers verbalize their intention ultimately to return to their fathers' households, even though they may not do so. They do not have a tradition of permanent resettlement outside the

Yatenga. Historically they have left their homelands permanently only as the result of ostracism or warfare. Thus permanent resettlement may be interpreted as punishment by the individual and by the community.

When the management of the Niger Project decided to resettle the Mossi as a permanent labor force rather than to rely on migratory labor, it failed to perceive the cultural aspects of the alternatives from which it had to choose. The result was a decision least likely to achieve labor commitment and most likely to create resistance among a people profoundly attached to the land and community of their kinsmen and ancestors.

Forced Recruitment

Programming, the translation of a managerial decision into action, follows in the cycle of activities affecting the achievement of labor commitment. In implementing the decision to establish the Mossi as a permanently settled community of workers, management again had two alternatives. It could develop a program of voluntary recruitment or it could rely on an existing tradition of *forced* labor. Again failing to perceive the cultural aspects involved in the choice, it chose the latter. The first Mossi resettled at the Project were forcibly recruited.

Recruitment of a voluntary labor force requires persuasion and the offering of attractive alternatives to accustomed rewards. Reliance on force makes other means of persuasion unnecessary. Ever since the conquest of French West Africa the colonial administration had used forced labor; by the time the Niger Project was established the practice had gained an evil reputation among West Africans forced to work on the roads and buildings belonging to the colonial administration and on the European-owned plantations of the Ivory Coast. When the Commandant at Ouahigouya, the capital of the Yatenga, ordered the village chiefs to select men for labor at the Niger Project, some of the workers who were chosen fled. All those selected were to be transported to the Project with their wives and children, and were made to understand that they would not be permitted to return to their homeland. Those who did not escape stoically accepted resettlement as a punishment.

When forced labor was abolished throughout the French Union in 1944, many of the Mossi workers left the Project to return to their homes in the Yatenga. Others stayed on because they were in debt or because they had become adjusted to the satisfactions offered by life at the Project. But, in most instances, commitment was achieved despite the worker's original resentment of forced recruitment.

Artificial Village Replication

Programming was also required for organization of the villages in which the Mossi workers were to be resettled. Here some attention was given to their traditional culture: management tried to reproduce the structural appearance of Mossi villages in the Yatenga, where the compound residence of each lineage is enclosed by a wall and located at a distance from the others. At the Niger Project these compound dwellings each contain a dozen or so houses and are separated from one another by wide avenues and a central square. In contrast with the Yatenga, however, the workers living within these dwellings are unrelated. Laborers coming from different parts of the country find themselves housed with strangers, as if they were kinsmen.

In the Yatenga the system of authority within such a compound dwelling is based on kinship. The eldest member of the lineage directs the economic endeavor of the group and arbitrates its conflicts. At the Niger Project the potential for conflict exists in such a residence, but the means of arbitration, reliance on the authority of the eldest male within the kinship unit, does not exist. In the absence of spatial separation as a means of avoiding conflict, the Mossi workers rely on social and emotional separation as a substitute. To avoid conflict for which they have no culturally sanctioned method of resolution, laborers and their families seek to minimize interaction with their neighbors.

In their homeland social withdrawal of this sort means that a man has failed in his most important social responsibility, the maintenance of good relations with his kinsmen. At the Niger Project this withdrawal is less serious because neighbors are not kin. Nonetheless, it is indicative of the workers' dissatisfaction with management's reproduction of their traditional pattern of residence without regard for the kinship affiliations that provide related social and emotional rewards.

Artificial Maintenance of Traditional Authority

In establishing an authority system for the Mossi villages at the Project, management again tried to reproduce a traditional Mossi institution without regard for its cultural meaning. Each village at the Project has a chief. These chiefs are usually selected because of their successful adaptation to life at the Project and their willingness to cooperate with management. In some instances those chosen are members of noble lineages whose rank entitles them to chieftainship, but this criterion appears secondary to their cooperativeness. The man selected as Paramount Chief of all the Mossi villages belongs to a lineage whose traditional religious role proscribes the exercise of political authority by its members.

All chiefs at the Niger Project are equipped by management with the formal accoutrements of chieftainship, but these forms are meaningless in the absence of the necessary traditional sanctions. Lacking these traditional sanctions for their authority, the chiefs receive little support from the Mossi villagers and are almost entirely dependent on the support of management. As a result, the chiefs often fail as arbitrators between management and the Mossi labor force. Thus, in every aspect of programming the cultural differences separating the two groups resulted in failure.

Barriers and Distortions in Communication

Communication comes next in the cycle of managerial activities, and has already been identified as one of the two activities most crucial to the attainment of labor force commitment. At the Niger Project the director and those immediately subordinate to him are highly trained and widely experienced administrators whose social and economic security would not be disturbed by the advancement of the African workers. The experience and status of these managers would help them obtain positions in other parts of the French Community or in France. Thus, there is little potential conflict between their interest in their own security and the Project's goal of establishing a permanent and efficient African labor force. In initiating downward communication, they seem to seek the best method of achieving this goal.

In contrast, those in subordinate managerial positions tend to reinterpret the goals of the organization in order to protect their own security. These are the semiskilled European technicians who work directly with the African labor force. Some teach the Mossi the new agricultural techniques they are required to use; some are foremen in the shops where agricultural equipment is repaired; others supervise the mechanized aspects of the harvesting and the processing and transport of the crop. Their lack of highly specialized skills and their low status within the managerial organization place them in a social and economic position not greatly superior to that of the indigenous labor force. And it is the limited skills of these technicians that the African workers might acquire most easily. The number of other positions that such technicians might find within the French Community is decreasing, and taking positions in France probably would entail some loss of status. Consequently, they tend to modify their communication with the workers in order to assure the security of their own economic and social positions.

These supervisors fail to explain to the Mossi the rationale behind the new skills they teach them. The tasks the Africans perform are broken down so as to assure the continued need of European supervision. The Mossi are simply shown a series of responses or motions and required to repeat them until they have been "learned." Those who work where agricultural equipment is repaired are confined to a part of the shop where only one aspect of the total operation is performed. African farmers are discouraged from trying to learn to operate the equipment used in cultivation. As the Mossi participate in and comprehend nearly all the activities of which their traditional economy is comprised, lack of understanding of the rationale of their new tasks lessens their satisfaction and results in mechanical, disinterested, and frequently inefficient performance.

The language difference separating management from the laborers at the Project is a further obstacle to communication. Nearly all members of the managerial group are French-speaking Europeans. The Mossi speak *möré;* only a few speak sufficient French to communicate successfully. Scarcely any Europeans at the Project are able to speak to the Africans in their own language. This absence of a common language strengthens the tendency of the European supervisors to give orders rather than explanations.

The two groups also differ in their conception of the proper use of speech in social interaction. The system of communication indigenous to the Mossi is characterized by indirection—by circuitousness in the approach to both the subject of communication and its object. In contrast, the system of communication imposed by management is based on the European tradition of directness. The previous cultural conditioning of the Mossi workers leaves them poorly prepared to adjust to this; and their reticence is interpreted by management as indifference.

When the Niger Project was first established, cooperative agricultural societies were organized for the purpose of facilitating upward communication from the indigenous labor force. But there was nothing in the previous cultural experience of the Mossi to prepare them for participation in such democratic organizations. On the contrary, they had been taught never to question directly those in authority. Because of the strong negative sanction placed by their culture on directness in communication, they did not use these cooperatives to express their grievances and to protect their interests. Ignorant of the cultural conditioning that leaves the Mossi unprepared to participate in such organizations, management interpreted their behavior as apathy. Those cooperatives that have not been abandoned altogether have been turned into mechanisms for the automatic ratification of managerial policy.

Thus the cultural differences separating management and labor at the Niger Project have impeded communication, one of the managerial activities most crucial to the attainment of labor commitment. Direct action, resulting from frustration, has taken the place of communication. Those in subordinate managerial positions limit their communication with the workers to orders unaccompanied by explanation. The workers are fined if they do not comply. Failing to comprehend either the goals of the enterprise or the rationale of their assigned tasks, the Mossi workers defect emotionally, refusing to commit themselves to the goals of an enterprise they do not understand.

Rewards and Punishments

Control, the setting of standards and their enforcement, has its place in the cycle of managerial activities important to the achievement of labor commitment. Given a set of goals defined by management, a system of rewards and punishments must also be established in order to motivate the labor force to achieve these goals. Identifying rewards to which the labor force will be responsive obviously depends on a knowledge of its culturally derived value system, but this is ignored at the Niger Project. Increased cash payments for larger yields are the principal rewards offered to the labor force. This creates a difficult budgetary problem for the individual worker.

In the Yatenga a large part of the harvest is stored in granaries to provide food during the long dry season. The contents of a man's granaries and those of his kinsmen form the basis of his economic security. After this security is assured, any surplus may be sold for cash. This small money income is supplemented by that from whatever dry season occupation a man undertakes: the weaving of cloth, the importation and sale of kola nuts, or day labor for the Europeans. Money earned in this way is used for the satisfaction of personal, non-subsistence wants: for the purchase of European clothing, jewelry for his wives and lovers, or a bicycle or wrist watch for himself. Careful budgeting of this cash income is not important to his basic economic security.

The worker is thus ill-prepared to solve the budgetary problem he faces at the Niger Project. In the rice-growing sector of the Project the Mossi keep part of the harvest for their own consumption; the rest is sold to the Project management. In the cotton-growing areas the entire harvest is converted into cash, which must be used for the purchase of subsistence goods and for satisfaction of the personal wants of the farmer and his family. Because his previous experience has not taught him to manage cash to meet subsistence wants, he is inefficient in the budgeting of this money. This is frustrating both to him and to the members of his household for whom he is expected to provide. The younger members of the family are frequently resentful at receiving what they consider unequal shares of the profits from their endeavor.

Thus cash offered by management as an inducement to greater production and deeper commitment frequently has the opposite effect. Frustration over the problems of budgeting, combined with other dissatisfactions with life at the Project, actually discourages labor commitment. The acquisition and accumulation of money merely speed the day when the laborers can leave the Project permanently, to return to the surer satisfactions of life in the Yatenga.

Fines are imposed on the farmers for a number of offenses. If they have not kept their dikes mended or fertilized their fields properly, money is withheld from the payment they receive for their crops. As the workers are frequently not aware that they have committed any violation until harvest time, the system does not motivate them to improve. It only discourages them further from trying to comprehend management's behavior. In the absence of explanations for the fines imposed, the Mossi perceive them as just another indication of the inscrutability of the European manager's mind.

By ten years of successful debt-free cultivation a Mossi farmer may earn the right to permanent proprietorship of his land. This might serve as a more effective inducement to the laborers if they understood the requirements. But the system of charges for mechanized cultivation, for seed, and for the transport and processing of their crop, combined with the system of fines, is confusing to them. Frequently they are deeply in debt without being aware of it.

Many farmers do not understand why they have not been granted proprietorship to their lands and are resentful. Others who believed they had received this right have been removed from their land without explanation. This of course has increased their frustration in trying to secure their economic well-being within a system they do not comprehend. In response, the frustrated Mossi farmers tend to refocus their interest on the traditional source of their economic security, the maintenance of good relations with their kinsmen in the Yatenga. Management's failure to understand the cultural origin of this further impediment to labor commitment is indicated by its increased reliance on negative or punitive sanctions in order to control the productive behavior of the Mossi labor force.

Experience without Learning

Reappraisal is last in the cycle of managerial activities important to the achievement of labor commitment and is the second of the two activities that appear most crucial to it. Managerial reappraisal in this context implies recognition that labor commitment is achieved gradually and must be maintained. At the Niger Project management has consistently failed to reappraise accurately its original decisions about the indigenous labor force. Those few policy changes that have been made involve greater reliance on punitive sanctions and mechanization, and have not resulted from accurate perception of the cultural reasons for earlier failures. The inefficient performance of the workers has been attributed to their ineptitude rather than to their lack of comprehension of what was required.

Change in the Mossi workers' response to an aspect of their traditional authority system provides an example of what may occur when cultural differences between management and labor prevent accurate reappraisal of managerial decisions. When the Mossi were first resettled at the Niger Irrigation Project, authority within each household was vested in its eldest male member in accordance with Mossi tradition. With time, however, the younger members of households, especially those born at the Niger Project, have grown restive under this control. They are more efficient than their elders, both in learning the new techniques required and in communicating with the French-speaking managers, and consequently believe they should be granted land of their own and given freedom from economic dependence on their elders. Adherence to the original authority system, explicitly recognized and supported by management, requires the younger members to cooperate with their elders in maintaining good relations with their kinsmen in the Yatenga. To assure that the names of all Mossi at the Project will be remembered and that they will be represented when sacrifices are made to their ancestral spirits, they must send to the Yatenga a portion of the payment they receive for their crop. Many young people at the Project have not been conditioned to regard their elders in the Yatenga as the principal source of security, and therefore resent the system that requires them to share their earnings with kinsmen whom they may never have seen.

Management does not understand that this system of authority is no longer functional. By continuing to delegate authority to the eldest, least adaptive, members of the Mossi community, management fails to satisfy the younger workers' emergent desire for a larger share in the control of their own economic destiny. Because of the artificial maintenance of the traditional system of authority, many young men become discouraged about making a permanent identification with the Project. They are frustrated and, like their elders, refocus their interest on their lineage in the Yatenga as the more reliable source of social and economic well-being. Consequently, they also come to make increasingly mechanical responses to their assigned tasks. Their real interest is diverted to preparation for the time when they too can "return" to the homeland.

Conclusion

For the purposes of this brief analysis, the managerial activities that appear most relevant to the achievement of labor commitment have been described as if they occurred in a single cycle. Obviously this is an oversimplification. In any organization many such cycles of activity are going on at the same time. Although it has been stated that certain of these managerial activities appear more crucial than others in attaining labor commitment, the successful functioning of each is likely to depend largely on the successful implementation of the activity that precedes it. When action results from a misperception of reality, every succeeding action is likely to compound the original error. This gives further support to the contention that communication and reappraisal are the two activities most crucial to the attainment of labor commitment. By the successful establishment and maintenance of communication, a mistaken action ultimately can be reappraised and rectified.

In newly developing areas the most significant cultural difference separating management from the labor force is frequently nothing less profound than the differing sources from which the two groups derive their basic social, economic, and supernatural security. Each expects the other to behave as if it shared in the perception of the proper source of this security, and is frustrated to the extent that this is not so. Management must recognize this difference, not so that it may alter the satisfactions it offers the workers, but in order to comprehend the cultural aspects of the problem of relearning involved in achieving labor commitment.

It is not realistic to expect management to refrain from action until it has examined all the cultural differences between it and the labor force, but management should accept the possibility of their existence and maintain adequate channels of communication so that the nature of the differences may become known. Once they are identified, reappraisal—derived from and dependent on organizational flexibility—provides the means of responding to them.

To achieve labor commitment, management ultimately must provide the indigenous labor force with a substitute for their traditional sources of security. This cannot be done by the successful teaching of new skills, nor by physical adaptation to a new habitat. The problem is one of reassurance, of positive demonstration that the new enterprise offers the labor force an equally certain source of security. Communication and reappraisal appear crucial to the achievement of this reassurance and its continued reinforcement as commitment grows.

8 THE ORGANIZATION OF WORK

Melville J. Herskovits

When we project the problems with which this volume is concerned against the backdrop of the total field of economic growth, we find that they can be resolved into two principal categories, the institutional and the human. These categories may also be thought of as sociological and cultural or, from another point of view, as comprising the observable aspects of behavior, on the one hand, and the underlying sanctions that motivate responses, on the other. In the totality of a developmental situation we thus set up a continuum on which particular points of interest can be abstracted and isolated for analysis, and which extends from the technological through the social to the cultural. Although there is a certain strategic advantage to be gained from focusing on the middle position, it is essential that the polarities be not disregarded.

For this reason the present discussion of the general implications of the three preceding papers on the organization of work is principally concerned with the motivational, cognitive, and other non-institutional aspects of the place of labor in developing areas. Since the institutional, structural approach tends inevitably, in a situation of change, to lay stress on the problems faced by the agents from outside the area who act to stimulate development, we hold entrepreneurial and managerial problems in the background. Our focus is on the traditional attitudes and the values that the indigenous worker brings to the new setting to which he must adapt.

CULTURAL DYNAMICS

Form and Process

The problems we are studying may be thought of as lying in the general field of cultural dynamics. The analysis of questions of this nature involves balancing the factors of conservatism and change. It is the interplay between these factors that makes for the adjustments toward a desired end or brings about the defeat of attempts to introduce innovations—in this case, in the patterns of work and the drives to achieve given objectives that underlie them. This approach indicates a way out of the dilemma posed, by implication at least, by Feldman

123

and Moore at the outset of their theoretical formulation. There they speak of cultural relativism as the "ultimate refuge" of the social scientist who despairs of resolving the complexities of the means-and-end dichotomy they sketch. This, they suggest, is a way out for the theoretically faint of heart, since it "essentially denies the possibility of any repeated relations or predictive propositions."

This statement expresses a misunderstanding that is commonly encountered. The relativist's search for universals in the light of the varied manifestations of behavioral phenomena is too often submerged in the undue emphasis, by critics of relativism, on his recognition of these differences. In a sense this misunderstanding is a reflection of the approach that, in stressing analysis, relegates dynamics to a subsidiary place, identifying the search for general principles with the first and associating the second with the relativistic position. When we go into the matter, however, we find that insofar as "a generalized theoretical system" of dynamics is concerned, the methodological implications of cultural relativism involve a recognition of the difference between *form* and *process* if the principles advanced are to attain any degree of validity. It is patent from any point of view that a problem carrying the label "development" must be dynamic. We must then give full weight to the position that holds a given form to be the end result of a historical process whose character as a universal is to be induced from its manifestations in unique historical sequences.

In their phrasing Feldman and Moore seem to be saying something not much different from this. What else could they mean when they assert that "the elements of social behavior associated with productive systems are not randomly variable. The possible sequences of change are substantially short of infinite in their variety"? Their interpretation of relativism appears even stranger in the light of their incisive comments on the means-and-end aspect of development.

From the point of view of a dynamic approach to this constellation, "development" is to be thought of as a process whose mode of operation (means) and results (ends) represent the working out, in a given place and at a given time, of an impinging force whose identity in various places and at various times has been established. The categories of *form* Feldman and Moore have abstracted are thus to be thought of as variations in the conditions under which the common *process,* subsumed in the phrase "economic and technological development," may be expected to bring about comparable results. This point is perfectly exemplified in Belshaw's paper. He advances the proposition that "one type of change that occurs from the base of traditional stationary economies is a change into another stationary economy," a process which, as he makes clear, can result in varied manifest forms.

The Base Line of Change

The three preceding papers, which treat the organization of work in newly developing areas, fit the model that shapes the approach to the problem in terms of cultural dynamics. To consider change, in any of its phases, there must be a base line against which a situation under study is projected. This permits the student to have a grasp of the rate and extensiveness of change and of its intensity, as revealed by the psychocultural adaptations that have been reached. This base line is suggested by Udy (Chapter 5) who employs a technique that is essentially comparative. This is not the place to discuss his method as such. The advisability of setting up a system of categories, such as one based on the degree to which the organizations that function in producing goods are to be differentiated, might be questioned. The diffuseness of institutions and the relatively slight degree of specialization in non-literate groups that are small and isolated, and that have a relatively simple technique, make it hazardous to equate their organization with that of technologically oriented societies. The *caveats* in his paper imply recognition of this reservation. In any case, the relationships Udy derives from the statistical manipulation of his data represent promising leads for intensive study of societies in which new technologies have made for a reorientation of social configurations to conform with a new system of production.

Hammond's exposition of the response of the Mossi to the system of agricultural production in the Niger Project (Chapter 7) lies at the other end of the scale of specific reference. It is in the long-established tradition of cross-cultural field investigation that certain general principles and methods developed out of the study of a given phenomenon in one culture are tested by ascertaining their cogency in another. In this, Hammond is contributing toward establishing that "wider empirical frame of reference" that Kuznets called for to achieve "the critical re-examination of concepts, established relations, and analytical models" [1] needed in analyzing economic growth.

Hammond has demonstrated that, despite the attention given by the

---

[1] Simon Kuznets, Wilbert E. Moore, and Joseph J. Spengler, eds., *Economic Growth: Brazil, India, Japan* (Durham: Duke University Press, 1955), p. 28.

Niger Project leaders to reproducing the physical setting of Mossi life in the Yatenga, failure to take into account the values and beliefs that underlie Mossi motivation to work operated to vitiate the effectiveness of the undertaking. In this negative sense we have a demonstration of the importance of the psychocultural approach in a specific case where its use was essential to the success of a development project. The questions that, by implication, are posed by Hammond reveal certain logical leads for research in situations of this kind. What are the antecedent systems of social structure and interaction that obtain? What values associated with land and labor are connected with these systems? To what extent has this total complex figured in the observed results?

To the point here is the comment by Bauer and Yamey, that economic growth may bring "a clash between security or stability and progress." [2] It is quite true, as these students observe, that "the security of the status quo may be wholly illusory," and that the process of change may, and often does, substitute "one set of risks for another set." But unless this is apparent to those who are subjected to the changing economic order, especially in regard to the substitution of new values and new social orientations for old, change will have little meaning and will be accepted only passively, where active resistance is not engendered. In this case the advantages of the new way of life were not made apparent to the Mossi.

The Impact of the New

Belshaw (Chapter 6) underscores another principle stated earlier in this discussion, the need to look at both sides of the picture—the precontact patterns as well as those introduced by industrialization—in theorizing about the processes of economic and technological change in newly developing areas. The points he makes are critical: his stress on the need to understand the adaptation of pre-established motivation to the changed situation; his designation of wage rates as "an elusive variable" in furthering the commitment of labor; and in the case of migrant labor, his recognition of "the degree to which money *cannot* be used to satisfy traditional goals." All these indicate the need for full consideration of the factors that are too often obscured by what, from the point of view of Euro-American society, are subsidiary questions.

Belshaw's observations on the reason for the high rate of industrial turnover found in many newly developing countries take on added

2 Peter T. Bauer and Basil S. Yamey, *The Economics of Under-developed Countries* (Cambridge, England: Cambridge University Press, 1957), p. 180.

significance from the ubiquity of the frustrations he suggests. In a similar context, for example, lies the industrial color-bar. This phrase may be used here as a general term applicable to any situation where the rewards of commitment are out of line with opportunity of advancement, whether the discrimination is based on racial affiliation, as in Africa and the Far East, or on nationality, as in South America. There can be little doubt of the effectiveness of discrimination in inducing the "stimulus to experimental change" in developing countries, to say nothing of its role in inducing the response that takes the form of "rejecting new opportunity" and "reverting to tribalism." A conversation reported from the Belgian Congo between an agricultural officer and an African who were discussing private ownership of land as against the traditional communal system is to the point: "Will I be able to sell my land?" asked the African. "Yes." "Can I take the money and buy better land?" "No."

NONINDUSTRIAL DEVELOPMENT

We may turn to another point that needs clarification. One gains the impression that the phrase "newly developing areas" is frequently held to be synonymous with "newly industrialized areas." Yet is the introduction of a machine technology—particularly through the instrumentality of a factory or a firm—all that is meant when the word "development" is used? Belshaw's analysis, for example, is not so limited.

If we consider the case of Sub-Saharan Africa, the area from which the documentation of this paper is drawn, such an identification of terms would touch only a small aspect of the total developmental picture, and this is true of other tropical regions. In Africa, even if we take into account the growth of mechanized industry in the Union of South Africa and Southern Rhodesia, at the Jinja dam in Uganda, or in Leopoldville or Abidjan or Dakar, even considering the enterprises for the exploitation of mineral resources in the Copper Belt of Northern Rhodesia and in the Katanga, on the Jos plateau of Nigeria or in the Bomi Hills district of Liberia, these are of far less importance in the total economy of the continent than agriculture. And by this is not meant large-scale agricultural enterprises such as the Gezira scheme in the Sudan, the Niger Irrigation Project, the banana plantations of the Cameroons Development Corporation, the palm-oil groves operated in the former Belgian Congo by the Leverhulme Company, the Cassequel sugar-growing estates in Angola, or the farms of the white settlers in Kenya and Tanganyika. To ignore the humbler, less dramatic dissemination of new agricultural techniques to individual African farmers distorts the picture and hinders effective analysis of the totality of development.

To be explicit, it is suggested that "development" be defined as having to do with the diffusion of that complex of technological, economic, political and sociopsychological elements, historically grounded in European and American practice, that in their totality bring hitherto isolated areas into the stream of world-wide currents of contact and change. Under this formulation the introduction of the plow and the various improvement schemes to consolidate the scattered patches of land traditionally cultivated by a farmer into a single more economic unit, or to induce Africans to employ fertilizer and better seed, are as much a part of the process as the erection of a canning factory, a weaving establishment, or a steel plant. Taken as a whole, these agricultural improvements have more far-reaching effects in terms of total productivity and total contribution to the world market.

Money and Markets

It would seem that what we are facing here is the tendency to fix on the more dramatic aspects of a situation and to take for granted those things that seem to exist in the nature of the case. As an example, we may consider the role that has been played by a development that rarely receives more than passing mention, the introduction of money. Considerable evidence supports the proposition that one important factor contributing to the difference in reactions to the total developmental complex in Western Africa and in Eastern Africa, especially in reactions that influence attitudes of Africans toward wage labor, is the presence or absence of pre-existing least common denominators of value and instruments for effecting the exchanges of the market place. The difference between the cowrie shell or the bar of salt or the cruciform iron, on the one hand, and the shilling or franc, on the other, is one of degree, not of kind. Selling cocoa on the world market makes sense in traditional terms to the Ghana farmer, who lives in a culture where for generations commodities have been produced for sale in local markets as well as for consumption by the producer.

It is true that, in the eastern parts of the continent, Africans have learned that in the changing situation they can benefit by producing a cash crop, as is demonstrated by the Chagga coffee-growers of Tanganyika or the Acholi cotton-producers of Uganda. The movements to produce cocoa in Ghana and palm oil in Nigeria were self-generating, while in East Africa the shift was achieved in the instances cited through persuasion, and in still other cases through pressure. European administrative officers in East, Central, and South Africa, almost without exception, complain about the difficulty of changing the antecedent African attitudes toward cattle, from those generated by patterns of prestige based on the possession of a large herd, to a recognition of the economic returns that can be obtained by selling even a part of one's holdings.

Disorganization and Reorganization

When the cross-cultural factor enters the study of change, we must emphasize the importance of the initial step within which the structural framework of the psychosocial processes of readjustment is established. We can then consider the underlying values and beliefs attached to sanctioned modes of behavior in the nonindustrialized setting and proceed to determine their role in shaping reactions to the new order. Do these values either undergo reinterpretation, in which established sanctions become associated with forms not present in earlier patterns, or do they set up resistances that necessitate the revision of plans for development? Even where adjustment seems most satisfactory, analysis in depth tends to reveal tensions that arise from failure to adjust behavior required by the new system of life to standards that have grown out of a nonindustrial way of life.

It is unrealistic, however, to consider these adjustments only in their negative sense, as is so frequently done. It is not difficult to see how this tendency arises. Perhaps, more than we realize, we are enculturated to patterns of interest set by our organs of communication and publicity, whereby only situations of crisis are held to merit attention. In pointing this out, the utility of studying the instances where a plan has failed or has produced tensions that minimize the efficiency of the operation is in no way denied. Such study has given us many valuable insights and can continue to do so. Nonetheless, more attention should be paid to the cases of minimum friction in achieving adjustment to innovation, whether the latter be large or small. In other words, the many studies of social disorganization made in newly developing countries could be supplemented to advantage by equally intensive and extensive studies of social reorganization. Emphasis on structure in such studies should not preclude analysis of the adjustment of characteristic response patterns of individuals, as well as the realignments of the institutional framework.

CULTURAL BASES OF LABOR COMMITMENT

The adjustment of individuals as well as institutions would seem to be particularly relevant in considering the commitment of labor to new economic and technical orientations, since it is here that acute problems of psychocultural adjustment often occur. No study of economic development has given serious attention to the precontact patterns of mobilizing labor, such as have been indicated by Udy, so as to provide a grasp of their mode of adaptation under the *new* order. Of particular significance in this context is Udy's conclusion that forms of production organization typical of industrialism are by no means absent in nonindustrial contexts. The point is stressed with full cognizance of his reservations concerning this conclusion—reservations which derive from assumptions of a technical anthropological character and which lie outside the terms of this work.

Continuing to use Africa as a source of examples, let us ask about some of the positive elements in the indigenous cultures of the continent in the way of institutions, susceptible of reinterpretation, that have been operative in shaping the commitment of Africans to participation in economic development.

Cooperation and Authority

A basic African pattern of mobilizing the labor force comes from the stress laid on cooperative effort. This varies from the formalized work societies of West Africa to the family groupings that perform tasks, such as housebuilding, that would be difficult for the individual to execute by himself. It is not suggested that such work is comparable to that in the industrialized plant, where in the nature of the case it would be difficult to organize the labor of any but a small proportion of the workers on this model. One reason for this difficulty, pointed out in other papers, is that such work groups are in most cases formed on an *ad hoc* basis, certainly as far as their objectives are concerned; and this is quite different from the sustained effort required in mechanized industries, whether these be agricultural, mining, or manufacturing.

Yet while the tradition of the cooperative work-group is difficult to translate in terms of industrial labor needs, there is one important aspect of it that could undoubtedly function to good effect under in-

dustrialization. This has to do with the patterns of authority in groupings of this kind. From the time of the early travelers in Africa, the
functioning of these patterns in the organization of labor has been
noted. In the early days of European penetration the comments of
travelers had to do with the problems to be faced in managing porters.
Later writers described how the cooperative principle aided them in
dealing with the workers who enlarged foot trails into roads and performed other labor required by the administrative authorities. Such
work may be thought of as comprising the initial steps toward later
economic developments.

The principle that invariably comes out of these accounts is how
ineffective direct control proved to be, and how efficiency could be
achieved only when clear lines of authority that moved through a
member of the work group who was recognized as its leader had been
laid down. A group directed by an outsider was continuously beset by
quarrels, but one that had a responsible African headman, through
whom orders were transmitted, worked without friction. Le Herissé,
one of the early governors of Dahomey, tells of the difficulties he experienced with the young boys who pushed the carts loaded with water
containers, until he designated one of their number to head the gang
and held him responsible for whatever was done. But there is a corollary
to this pattern of authority. The responsible head is held to account
for the performance of his group; by the same token, nothing is more
likely to introduce discord than for the one who has named him to
deal directly himself with the individual workers over whom authority
has been assigned.

This pattern was operative in the administrative practices of pre-
conquest kingdoms in various parts of the continent; it was operative
in the early dealings between Europeans and Africans on plantations
and farms; it is as living a tradition today as it was in earlier times.
The possibilities, in terms of a smooth functioning of labor in industry,
are not difficult to envisage and are actually employed in European
and American industrial plants. The difference is that the kind of
leader accepted by the African workers is not the same as the leader in
industrialized countries, often being essentially tribal representatives.

Some Peculiarities in Labor Unions

There can be little question that the inner disciplines that maintain
the socioeconomic structures of African society have significantly influenced the form and functioning of labor organizations. This point

merits some attention here as an important element in the series of cultural reinterpretations that are evident in the commitment of labor under economic development. The apparently contradictory facts that the African is amenable to organizational discipline, but that he operationally distorts the traditional forms of Euro-American trade unions has considerably puzzled European labor leaders who must deal with the problem of forming unions in Africa.

For one thing, the scope of trade unions in Africa tends to include matters that, from the American point of view, are quite unrelated to the primary concerns of labor unions. Hodgkin points out that the Sudanese unions included in their original aims "mutual help in times of illness, death and unemployment; the establishment of savings schemes and cooperative societies; the organization of 'literary and scientific lectures.' " He also quotes as one of the aims of the Iwo Carpenters' Union in Western Nigeria, "To make merriment with each other in joy and to sympathize with those in sorrow." [3] Trade union activities of this sort can be thought of broadly as an expression of the unities of life that derive from the relatively lesser degree of specialization under tribal conditions or, as applied in West Africa, as continuing the many nonkinship associations that characterize the cultures of this area. Nor do such activities, extraneous by American definition, seem to hinder these African organizations from functioning efficiently in the traditional role of trade unions, as is indicated by the numerous instances where they have prevailed in disputes with management.

A member of the British Labor Party recently pointed out that in the industrialized Copper Belt of Northern Rhodesia, where Africans have a union whose strength has been proved in many tests, it is difficult even to find the union headquarters. The number of dues-paying, card-carrying members is very small in comparison with the number that can be mobilized when a strike is called; bookkeeping methods are rudimentary, and the money received is handled casually. Yet one can but contrast this picture with the account given me in 1953, in Luanshya, of a little-known strike that took place in February of that year at the Roan Antelope Mine. After a strike vote had been taken, some 10,000 workers and their families, totaling perhaps 30,000 persons, overnight left the mine compounds and camped quietly in the bush for three weeks, until their demands were conceded.

[3] Thomas Hodgkin, *Nationalism in Colonial Africa* (London: Frederick Muller, 1956), p. 127.

The attitude of the African workers toward their leaders is what seems most to puzzle Europeans who study or deal with African trade unions. The same British Labor Party member, describing what he felt to be the irresponsibility of African union officials in handling union funds, cited facts that came out in the inquiry into the conduct of the 1949 strike at the Enugu collieries in Eastern Nigeria. Unquestionably the leader of this strike had used union funds to purchase for himself a house, a car, and other things. This was quite freely admitted by him when he gave evidence. Yet worker after worker who testified stated that he had no criticism of this conduct; on the contrary, all felt that their leader, whose efforts had obtained for them the wage increase they were demanding, merited everything he had been given, or had taken. The British Labor Party member said, "They treated him just as though he had been one of their chiefs!"

Labor and the Mechanism of Cultural Reinterpretation

Cultural reinterpretation is powerful in assuring an adequate African labor force in the mines and factories of industrialized South Africa. Going to work in the cities there is reinterpreted in terms of a preexisting tradition which held that a boy must establish his status as an adult by going to war. Today, in the Portuguese territories of Mozambique and Angola, in the Rhodesias and the High Commission Territories of Bechuanaland, Swaziland and Basutoland, as well as among the Zulu, Xhosa, and Sotho peoples of the Union itself, going to work in the mines or the factories is the socioeconomic and cultural, if not the moral, equivalent of going to war. This is well known to labor recruiters and is played on by them when they attempt to induce Africans to sign on for a term of work. As in the period before European control was established, this proof of manhood is demanded before a marriage may be consummated. In terms of the continuity of a tradition, it is worth noting that most of the members of a Xhosa group of young men, visited in the seclusion of their circumcision hut, said that they had worked in the cities of the Union before returning to satisfy this other cultural imperative in achieving full status as adults.

Another aspect of this complex functions significantly in the industrial scene. One of the most widespread elements in the marriage patterns of Eastern and Southern Africa is the requirement that an earnest of the capability of the bridegroom to fulfill his obligations as a husband be given by him or by his family to the father of the bride. This earnest—known as *lobola* or bride-wealth or, under the misleading term used in the earlier literature, as "bride-price"—has traditionally taken the form of cattle, which thus symbolize the legitimacy of the mating. Under earlier conditions these cattle were made available to the suitor by his father or uncles, and this is still the case among peoples who are living in a relatively unacculturated state. But in far more cases *lobola* today must be earned by the young man himself. Among many urbanized Africans, the complete transition from cattle to money has been made. Outside the cities, however, the change is more in the mode of acquiring cattle than in their use for this purpose. Cattle now are frequently bought with money a man has earned himself. Thus, the Swiss owner of a large farm (in the Kivu highlands) devoted entirely to raising cattle stated that his sales are mainly to Africans for use as bride-wealth. The importance of this tradition as a factor in accessibility to the potential labor force is obvious, although it merely provides an initial impulse to undertake wage labor and does not lead to the kind of permanent commitment that is essential for a smoothly running industrial establishment employing skilled labor.

In some instances continuous outside pressure has succeeded in holding Africans to the performance of tasks that, in terms of earlier conventions, were not accepted until the processes of re-enculturation to new values brought about the desired adjustment. We see this in the insistence of the Belgian Government, which a decade ago decreed that each African farmer in the Ruanda-Urundi hills maintain a plot devoted to growing coffee, the trees to be planted in squares of eight by eight. Until these trees began to bear, the Banyarwanda resisted the enforcement of this order in every way they could. When the crops from the mature trees started to come in, however, voluntary planting, even to the extent of doing everything possible to obtain extra seedlings, became the rule.

Unintended Reactions

Responses of this kind do not always follow attempts to enforce changes. In the same territory the ditching of hillsides to halt erosion is carried out only under supervision and compulsion. In the more strictly industrial sphere, we have a demonstration of how a plan can be oversold to the Africans, so to speak. In the Katanga, where for a generation or more pressures had to be exerted to obtain workers for the mines and smelters, acceptance of the new way of life created other problems. Social scientists were called from one of the Belgian universities to study and prescribe ways of lowering surplus African urban population, by inducing Africans to return as farmers to the villages from which they had migrated.

De Schlippe, summarizing the results of moves initiated some years ago by the British Administration in the Southern Sudan to improve Azande agricultural techniques and practices, indicates how pressure to mobilize labor so as to achieve a particular result does not always work out as intended. "Neither early burning nor abstinence from cultivating river valleys, nor resettlement nor cotton growing would survive the withdrawal of administrative pressure," he states. "On the other hand, inconspicuous reforms, such as local food markets, may survive and mark an epoch in Zande history." However, as to "the unexpected changes which, due to cultural linkages, took place as a consequence of intentional changes introduced administratively, it must be stated that in every case these changes were deleterious and undesirable." [4]

CONCLUSION

From the three papers considered, as from the formulation presented here, it must be clear that study of the commitment of the labor force demands as full knowledge of the traditional sanctions to work in a given society as of the technological, economic, and institutional factors that are introduced into the society. It would seem that something of a reorientation, more fully taking into account the theory of cultural dynamics, is called for. The methodological importance in research of this kind of seeing that changes in the social structures are exhaustively analyzed, and that the generalizations to be drawn from repetitive manifestations of institutional change in different situations are studied to the fullest, is self-evident. Beyond this lie the concepts of cultural theory, based on principles derived from recognition that culture is a learned phenomenon, concepts which lead us to the study of change under development in terms of the observable retentions and reinterpretations. We may thereby reach a deeper understanding of how the people involved in the new situation adapt pre-existing patterns to newly oriented modes of behavior, and how they achieve new psychological sets that make for an equitable adjustment to the broader resources that economic growth can make available to them.

[4] Pierre De Schlippe, *Shifting Cultivation in Africa* (London: Routledge & Kegan Paul, 1956), pp. 254–255.

9 THE LABOR MARKET
IN PUERTO RICO

Peter Gregory

An efficient labor market is one of the most important requirements of large-scale modern industrialization. Efficiency of the market is a function of the responsiveness of a labor supply to monetary and other incentives to enter and remain in the market and of the effectiveness of differentials in guiding the movements of workers within it. In some industrializing societies the development of labor markets has encountered serious obstacles in the form of limited interest in material incentives among the potential labor supply, considerations of status and security based on the traditional community that conflict with the organization of the new industrial work community, or inability of workers to adapt to the discipline and working conditions of modern factory employment.

The evolution of an industrial labor market can be traced from the initial entry of workers in response to the appearance of new employment opportunities, through a transitional period during which new patterns of behavior and responses develop, to the eventually mature and stable market performing its allocative functions smoothly and efficiently. These stages provide logical foci for analyzing the process of achieving commitment, as illustrated by the parallel sequences of prerequisites, transition, and maintenance, defined by Feldman and Moore. Their framework follows the temporal sequence of the development process and delineates the stages and facilitating factors in the passage to full commitment. That this framework is readily adaptable to empirical studies can be demonstrated by analysis of the development of the industrial labor market in Puerto Rico.

Modern and accelerated industrialization in Puerto Rico is a postwar phenomenon dating mainly from 1948. With the exception of rum distillation and raw sugar processing, earlier industrial activity was limited largely to handicraft and needlework. Most of the latter was hardly done under modern conditions; industrial discipline was not highly developed, productive efficiency and wages were low, and management was unschooled in modern rational methods of production.

In contrast, a large majority of the new factories have been established as branch plants of continental United States firms, and North American standards and practices have been introduced. Since output is destined almost wholly for the mainland market, a very rapid attainment of production competitive in both quality and cost has been demanded.

It is true that Puerto Rico, even before the recently intensified drive to industrialize, had been characterized by relatively advanced development, and therefore is atypical of most underdeveloped areas. However, the higher level from which the current industrialization has developed should not obscure the distance that had to be traversed in order to make the Puerto Rican effort a success. In most developing societies the sheltering of the home market and the prevailing wage levels often permit or tolerate relatively great inefficiency or only gradually rising efficiency. In contrast, the level of efficiency required of the new Puerto Rican industry has been defined by mainland United States standards; and speed in the realization of a close approximation of these standards has been crucial to the incipient development program. Thus, the pressures exerted on the industrial labor force to adapt to the more demanding conditions of factory employment in Puerto Rico may be about equal to those felt by new factory workers in other industrializing societies, although the short-run absolute objective in terms of worker performance in the latter is likely to lie considerably below that required of the Puerto Rican worker. Given an approximate equality in the relative degree of change required in the performance of workers, their responses may also prove to be comparable. Credence is lent to this possibility by the high frequency of reports by factory managements of the types of work force problems—high instability, limited consciousness of quality, indifference to financial incentives, and undisciplined work habits—that are typical of all industrializing areas.

The data on which the present discussion is based were obtained in an empirical study of the Puerto Rican labor market during 1953–56. Both sides of the market were intensively studied. The recruitment, training, and employment practices and experiences of some 85 employers were reviewed during a sample survey of plants. On the supply side, formal interviews were held with a sample of 1,045 industrial workers, in which we explored work histories, income and occupational aspirations, as well as attitudes toward factory employment, discipline, and wage incentives. The sample was drawn from three areas: the San Juan Metropolitan area; the second largest city, Ponce, which is also considered to be among the most "traditional" centers; and a northern coastal area of small urban communities and open agricultural country. One intensive plant study was also undertaken, in which both formal questionnaires and participant observation were employed.[1]

ORIGINS AND INVOLVEMENT OF WORKERS
IN THE INDUSTRIAL LABOR MARKET

The emergence of a labor market as an allocative institution depends on the concurrence in time of several conditions. First and most obvious, on the demand side, the emergence of a market implies the appearance of new employment opportunities offering rewards not obtainable in others. On the supply side, its operation depends on the existence of forces motivating entry and participation by the potential labor supply or on responsiveness to the rewards proffered. Intervening are conditions or institutions that facilitate entry and employment. The speed with which a reasonably efficient market becomes established is a function of the ease with which involvement becomes regularized and permanent. In this section we are concerned with the variables that govern, characterize, and facilitate entry and involvement.

Entry and Continuity in the Market

The appearance of employment opportunities, of course, will not assure the appearance of an adequate labor supply; there must also be some motivation or stimulus impelling or inducing workers to enter the market as active participants. Perhaps the most compelling force is a dire need for cash income for current consumption or for discharging debts or other obligations in an environment offering no other adequate sources of cash. Second, entry to the market may follow a rational evaluation of available opportunities and a decision that factory employment maximizes the worker's utilities. Finally, entry may be motivated by a spirit of adventure or a desire to escape the narrow confines of a traditional environment. Which of these motives actually governs a worker's entry into the market may be expected to have important implications for the probable ease with which commitment will be achieved.

Given the opportunities and a potential labor supply, a number of

[1] Space limitations preclude a detailed exposition of the scope and methods of the study. For these, readers are referred to the forthcoming volume by Lloyd G. Reynolds and the present author. The study was sponsored by the Social Science Research Center of the University of Puerto Rico.

intervening conditions and institutions may be considered facilitating variables since they link the two sides of the market. For example, active participation in the market is more easily secured, the wider the knowledge or awareness of the job opportunities. Obviously no market can hope to function in the absence of some such knowledge. The more generally knowledge is dispersed, the more likely it is that the attractions of employment will come to the attention of those most disposed to seek and accept industrial employment. Entry also requires at least a rudimentary understanding of the operating principles of the market. Such an understanding usually derives from prior exposure to a market economy, although not necessarily from direct participation in that economy. Of course, entry occurs more readily, the greater the proximity to or involvement in a modern sector of the economy either through residence near an urban center or the sometime wage employment of family or community members. Education, which gives a greater awareness of alternatives to the current situation and which stimulates new wants, is similarly likely to facilitate entry to the modern market. An example of an institution that serves a facilitating function is the labor exchange, which is a source of job information and matches workers with jobs.

For the long-run efficiency of the market and of the new industrial sector, it becomes crucial whether entry is soon followed by withdrawal or whether permanence in and commitment to the new sector characterize the behavior of the new labor supply. Many factors influence the probability and speed of achievement of commitment. Among the most important of these are the immediacy of the goals motivating entry, the speed with which these are fulfilled and new ones are adopted, and the relative weights assigned to the rewards and costs that result from participation. One may hypothesize about the implications for commitment of these factors under each of the conditions motivating entry which were enumerated above. A dire need for cash, for example, may be the motive that is least favorable to commitment. If the need is immediate but can be satisfied quickly, the participation may be short-lived. The period of involvement may be too brief to develop new wants or to overcome the initial resistance to industrial discipline. If the need is continuous because of the inadequacy of other sources of income, commitment may be achieved gradually as a new value system encroaches on and eventually replaces the old. On the other hand, an individual's behavior may approach that of a committed worker in terms of stability and permanence within the industrial labor market, but commitment in the full sense may still be lacking. While forced to accept the discipline of industrial employment, the worker may yet resist adoption of the associated values or fail to respond fully to the incentives such employment may provide.

When the decision to enter the market is the product of a desire for adventure or of rational economic calculation, commitment may be easier to achieve than under conditions of "forced participation," but this cannot be assumed. Resistance to the values and incentives of the industrial sector should be lower, to be sure. Satisfaction of immediate wants is less likely to lead to withdrawal, as these are constantly replaced by new wants. However, the conflicts attendant on sustained participation and the actual adjustments demanded by it may prove too great a price for the rewards it yields.

Motives and Facilitators of Entry

In the light of the framework outlined above, let us examine data obtained from our sample of interviewed workers to see what forces motivated their entry to the labor market and what conditions may have been important in developing a predisposition toward entry and commitment. Why did the workers interviewed enter the industrial labor force? To what extent did there already exist an industrial tradition or other condition predisposing workers to enter? How did these workers respond to the industrial work situation once they had become involved?

In Table 1 a number of characteristics of the sample labor force are classified as favorable or unfavorable to involvement in the industrial labor market; the percentages of respondents in these categories give some indication of the degree of prior exposure to an industrial tradition or of the existence of other predisposing conditions such as education. The backgrounds of these workers suggest in a striking way the absence of an industrial tradition. Both the pattern of residence prior to industrial employment and the infrequent employment of fathers in factories point in this direction. Partial offsets are to be found in the exposure of most workers to some formal education and the currently high incidence of urban residence. However, it is likely that urban residence was either concurrent with or followed entry into the industrial labor market and so cannot be considered a predisposing factor, even though it may be favorable to eventual commitment.

It is not easy to disentangle the various elements involved in the conditions motivating entry, although it appears that escape from a life

TABLE 1. PERCENTAGE OF RESPONDENTS IN CONDITIONS CONSIDERED FAVORABLE OR UNFAVORABLE TO INVOLVEMENT IN THE INDUSTRIAL LABOR MARKET

Characteristics of workers	Favorable		Unfavorable	
	Category	Percent	Category	Percent
Residence prior to first job	Urban	30	Rural	70
Current residence	Urban	73	Rural	27
Industry of father's job at the time of respondent's first job	Manufacturing	5	Agriculture	52
Industry of respondent's first job				
Men	Manufacturing	22	Agriculture	43
Women	Manufacturing	55	Home handicrafts	26
			Domestic	12
Years of school completed				
Men	5 or more	63	4 or less	37
Women	5 or more	69	4 or less	31

of mere subsistence was not an impelling factor. A combination of desires to maximize income and to seek change for its own sake appears to have been more important. Yet it is not entirely correct to speak of these factors as impelling active participation in the factory labor market. An awareness of possible gains contributes to receptivity to factory employment and introduces some rationality in a decision to accept such employment, but is not immediately translatable into purposeful effort to find a factory job. More often than not, participation results from the presentation to an individual of a specific job opportunity. This is reflected in the means by which workers obtained their first factory jobs (Table 2). A large majority of the respondents landed their first factory jobs as a result of referrals by persons or by the Employment Service or of unsolicited job offers. Only a small group found their first factory jobs on their own initiative by direct application at the gate. Thus, a large measure of chance would appear to govern the original involvement of workers.

Whatever information the respondents had about industrial employment conditions before they accepted their first factory jobs appears to have increased their receptivity to job opportunities when these were presented. There were few major differences between men and women in the mention of those employment conditions that were the basis of their favorable anticipations (Table 3). Wages, the opportunity to see and learn new things, and the physical effort involved in factory work

TABLE 2. MEANS OF OBTAINING FIRST FACTORY JOB

	Number of respondents		Percent of respondents	
Means	Men	Women	Men	Women
Referral				
By Employment Service	20	52	3.7	10.3
By person knowing of vacancy	360	334	66.8	66.0
Unsolicited job offer	43	22	8.0	4.3
Application				
In response to advertisement	18	34	3.3	6.7
On own initiative	89	55	16.5	10.9
Other	8	9	1.5	1.8
No answer	1	—	.2	—
Total	539	506	100.0	100.0

were the three factors most frequently mentioned by both sexes. Stability of employment and opportunities for advancement were mentioned twice as often by men as by women, perhaps reflecting the men's breadwinning role and greater concern for career opportunities. Few reported an anticipated dislike of particular conditions, although there was some apprehension on the part of respondents about their ability to learn the jobs to which they would be assigned. In short, the responses provide evidence of rational economic calculation underlying decisions to enter the industrial labor market. It would seem from the frequency with which "opportunity to see and learn new things" was advanced, however, that a desire for adventure was not altogether lacking as a motive.

A large majority of the respondents expected to like factory work "very much" even before they had taken their first factory jobs. Only 7 percent said that they had expected to like it "very little" or "not at all," although this figure may understate the facts since the respondents were speaking from hindsight. It would appear that the favorable expectations were generally realized, for fewer than 3 percent of the workers reported a dislike of factory work at the time of the interviews, and 80 percent affirmed that they liked it "very much." More workers had found they liked the work better than they had expected, than had found it disappointing (Table 4).

Several variables were analyzed for association with disappointment

TABLE 3. FREQUENCY OF MENTION BY RESPONDENTS OF FACTORY CONDITIONS THEY EXPECTED TO LIKE

| | Respondents mentioning | | | |
| | Number | | Percent | |
Conditions workers expected to like	Men	Women	Men	Women
Wages	256	273	47	54
Opportunity to see and learn new things	264	203	49	40
Physical effort required	172	206	32	41
Stability of employment	161	72	30	14
Opportunities for advancement	140	65	26	13
Physical conditions of job and plant	68	31	13	6
Type of work or task	14	32	3	6
Hours of work	8	30	1	6
Unknown or no answer	48	24	9	5
Total number of respondents	*539*	*506*	—	—

in factory work. For both sexes there was a highly significant relation between a decline in liking the work and the level of weekly earnings. Earning levels of those whose liking had declined were significantly lower than were those of respondents whose attitudes had not changed or whose liking for factory work had increased. Among men, the small

TABLE 4. RESPONDENTS' ANTICIPATED AND CURRENT LIKING OF FACTORY JOBS

| | Workers anticipating specified degree, prior to first job | | Workers reporting current degree of liking | |
Degree of liking	Number	Percent	Number	Percent
Very much	764	73.1	837	80.1
Moderately well	156	14.9	178	17.0
Very little or not at all	70	6.7	28	2.7
Unknown or no answer	55	5.3	2	.2
Total	1,045	100.0	1,045	100.0

minority working on an incentive basis reported a much greater relative frequency of decline than did men working on an hourly basis. Among women, where piece work is more common, no significant relationship was found. The Chi-square test was applied to other variables, such as length of urban residence and factory employment, education, agricultural experience, level of skill, and age, but the results were generally not significant. However, a decline in liking was significantly associated with poorer job performance, in quantity and quality of production, as evaluated by the individual workers' supervisors.

Former Agricultural Workers

A more extensive inquiry was made into the reasons for the involvement in the industrial labor market of workers with agricultural experience. Their intentions to remain in the market were tested more fully than those of other workers, on the assumption that agricultural employment and rural culture represent sharp contrasts with industrial work conditions and that commitment represents a greater feat for rural workers than for those raised in an essentially urban environment. Interestingly enough, to date the commitment of the former does not seem to have been impeded greatly by their past.

The outstanding characteristic of the sample workers with agricultural experience is the absence of ties to the land in the form of land ownership. Of the 291 male respondents with agricultural experience, all but 9 had been landless wage laborers in their last farm employment. As such, they were well integrated into a market economy. Unfamiliarity with the market mechanism, therefore, cannot be advanced either as an obstacle to entry and assimilation into the industrial sector or as a condition differentiating the Puerto Rican rural and urban labor forces. If any differences exist in the predisposition of rural and urban workers to enter the industrial sector and to become committed to it, these must be sought in other cultural or environmental characteristics, such as levels of material aspirations, leisure preferences, family cohesiveness, and customary work patterns. Our data do not show such differences in predisposition and adaptation to industrial employment.

Indeed, the predisposition of the rural workers to seek industrial jobs appears to have been enhanced by the low estate in which a rural wage-earning status held them. It is probably fair to say that the workers who left agriculture were those who had the least to lose in terms of security or status. They enjoyed none of the social prestige associated with landownership. With the almost complete conversion of agricul-

tural employment relations to a purely cash and increasingly impersonal basis, reciprocal obligations or personal relations that once might
have tied workers to employers were no longer at stake. Thus, the chief
obstacles to integration and assimilation into the industrial sector have
probably been the difficulties of adapting to the rhythm and discipline
of the factory, not the ties to the traditional sector.

On the other hand, it is noteworthy that the economic forces pushing
these workers out of agriculture were not as strong as one might expect.
Those who left agriculture were not forced to do so to escape a marginal
existence. Indeed, our sample workers appear to have been among the
elite in the agricultural wage labor force; for over two thirds of the
291 men said they had been employed throughout the year in the last
farm job held—a proportion almost 2.5 times greater than that prevailing for the agricultural labor force as a whole in 1952. In other words,
these were among the most employable of the agricultural workers, not
those marginal to that work force.

Further evidence that dire economic need was not the force compelling these men to abandon agriculture is found in their specific
reasons for quitting (Table 5). Only 15 percent of the group said they
left primarily because of unemployment or irregularity of employment.
The hope for greater earnings in industry or, conversely, the loss of
hope for an improvement in the future outlook for agricultural workers
was of much greater significance. Eliminating multiple responses within
these two categories, 70 percent of the workers gave one of these two
reasons as either a primary or supplementary reason for leaving. The

TABLE 5. REASONS GIVEN BY 291 MALE WORKERS FOR HAVING QUIT AGRICULTURE

Reasons given	Workers reporting reason as primary		Workers reporting reason as supplementary	
	Number	Percent	Number	Percent
Hope of higher earnings	135	46.4	68	23.4
Dislike of agricultural work	37	12.7	70	24.1
No future in agriculture	38	13.1	68	23.4
Irregularity of employment	22	7.6	8	2.7
Unemployed	23	7.9	5	1.7
Desire to live in the city	2	.7	20	6.9
Other	30	10.3	22	7.6
No reason given	5	1.7	107	36.8

emphasis on hope of an improvement in economic status again suggests a rational economic approach to entering the industrial labor market.

The men with agricultural experience appear to have become integrated into factory employment without serious resistance. Their anticipated liking of factory work was consistently greater than that expressed by workers who had no experience in agriculture, although only the differences in the Ponce area were statistically significant. At the time of the study only 6 percent of the 291 men indicated that they liked factory work less than agricultural work, while 90 percent said they liked it better. Their job histories after they left agriculture show that the break was a permanent one for most of them. Only a small minority indicated that they had either returned to the farm after they had left it without intentions of returning, or continued to cultivate land to the present (Table 6).

TABLE 6. RETURNS TO AGRICULTURAL EMPLOYMENT REPORTED BY TWO GROUPS OF MALE WORKERS

| | Men reporting | | | |
| | Return | | No return | |
Group	Number	Percent	Number	Percent
Men employed in agriculture after 1945 and with complete job histories	27	15.7	145	84.3
Men employed in agriculture before 1945 and with complete job histories since 1945	0	0	119	100

As a further test of the commitment of these workers to industrial employment, those who had expressed a greater liking for factory work than for farm work were asked under what conditions they would return to agriculture. As can be seen from Table 7, 60 percent of the 274 men in this group indicated that they would not return under any condition; 73 men or 27 percent said they would return if they could own farms. In order to correct for diverse expectations of income from farm ownership and to test preferences at the margin, the 73 men were asked whether they would return to agriculture even if they would be able to earn no more than they were currently making; 51 affirmed that they would still do so, whereas the other 22 would return only if land ownership would yield a larger income.

TABLE 7. FREQUENCY OF MENTION OF CONDITIONS UNDER WHICH 274 MEN EXPRESSING GREATER LIKING FOR FACTORY THAN FOR FARM WORK WOULD RETURN TO AGRICULTURE

Conditions under which respondent would return	Respondents mentioning	
	Number	Percent
Under no condition	165	60.2
Farm ownership	73	26.6
Only if earnings greater than at present	22	8.0
Even if earnings no greater than at present	51	18.6
Employment as foreman or *mayordomo*	5	1.8
Higher wages than currently earned in factory	22	8.0
Other	16	5.8
No answer	3	1.1

The men willing to return to agriculture as landowners at their current incomes were distinguishable from the other former agricultural workers in several respects. The 51 men were a significantly older group (most were over 40) and they were currently at the upper end of the income distribution of former agricultural workers. They also reported relatively longer years of agricultural employment, generally over 11 years. Presumably many of these men were not looking upon a return to agriculture as an active career. Rather, a return to the land was probably viewed with a measure of nostalgia or as a sort of partial retirement wherein the bulk of the labor would be performed by hired hands.

A further observation about the organization of agricultural production and its possible influence on landowning attitudes may be made. A distribution of these men by the crop produced in the last agricultural employment reveals significant differences in the relative frequency of current interest in return. The greatest interest in return at current income levels was found not among the former sugar and plantation workers, but among the former workers on minor fruit and vegetable crops which are cultivated largely on small independent holdings. This is a reasonable finding. The former sugar workers constituted a real rural proletariat possessing very narrow skills and experience. It is likely that they would be quite incapable of independent cultivation. The versatile workers formerly employed on small productive units might more reasonably be expected to aspire to proprietary positions.

While the agricultural background of the older and better paid workers appeared to be associated with their attitudes toward farm ownership, this relationship was not significant for other groups. There was a general disinterest in farm ownership among the younger workers and particularly the lower-wage workers. One might expect that at low industrial wages the traditional agricultural sector would seem attractive or, conversely, that the adjustment to industrial discipline would not be adequately compensated. However, even if the lowest industrial wage rates did not compare favorably with some agricultural wage rates, annual incomes probably did. Moreover, the heavy preference of the lowest-wage workers for industrial employment may be grounded in the realistic belief that industry holds greater promise for future increases in income than it is possible to foresee in agriculture. It would appear that land ownership, in itself, is viewed as only a limited source of social prestige and certainly as no effective substitute for income. Such a finding in a society that has traditionally associated status with landownership, and in which wealth has been accumulated in that form, should be of considerable interest.

The men who originally stated that they would not return to agriculture under any condition generally persisted in this view under further questioning. When asked whether they would return to agriculture if they could be assured of maintaining their current level of earnings, only about a fourth of them said they would do so. However, the difference between the incomes of this subgroup and of the workers who persisted in their refusal to consider a return to agriculture was not statistically significant.

Within the group of men with agricultural experience, then, about 42 percent either expressed a greater liking for agriculture than for industrial employment or volunteered an interest in returning to agriculture under some specific income or other status condition, whereas 57 percent initially said they would return under no condition. An examination of the characteristics of these two groups of workers showed that there were no significant differences in their levels of education, levels of weekly income, years of urban residence or factory experience, or levels of skill in their current employment. Only two variables were significantly associated with interest in returning to agriculture. The Chi-square test showed an association with age significant at the 2 percent level. The greatest deviations of actual from expected frequencies were found at the two extremities of the age distribution; the men under 23 years of age took a decidedly dim view of returning to agriculture, while those over 40 were most receptive.

Length of agricultural work experience showed an association significant at the 10 percent level; those who had spent 11 or more years in agriculture showed the greatest interest in returning. The factors that were operative in the workers' interest in returning to agriculture under conditions of landownership may also be reflected in this larger group of former agricultural workers.

While receptiveness to the idea of return was fairly widespread among the sample workers, this should not be interpreted as indicative of an intention or of active planning to return. At another point in the interview the sample workers were asked what kind of work they would like to be doing five years hence. Among the men with previous agricultural experience only 6 percent of those who indicated any occupational preference chose to return to agriculture, while 60 percent indicated that they would like to be employed in factory work. Thus, even those who might reconsider agricultural employment, given certain income and property conditions, do not seem to be actively hoping or planning to return to agriculture. Shifts from agriculture to industrial employment appear to be followed by a commitment to permanent participation in the industrial labor market more often than not.

Permanence of Involvement in Industrial Employment

The conclusion just reported for the 291 former agricultural workers also seems to hold for the total sample of male workers. We found considerable evidence that the bulk of the 539 men regarded their involvement in the industrial labor market as permanent. For example, they did not often report subsequent nonindustrial jobs once they had entered industrial employment. Among the men with complete job histories, only 17 percent reported nonindustrial employment following their first factory jobs; of those whose histories were incomplete, 72 percent showed no nonindustrial employment at least since 1945. Their occupational aspirations also indicated that they expected to continue being employed in factories. When asked what kind of work they would like to be doing five years hence, over two thirds of those men who indicated a positive choice for some employment chose factory work, as can be seen in Table 8. The most frequently indicated alternative for men was self-employment, either as artisans or as small merchants.

The level of education of the respondents in the Ponce and coastal areas does not appear to make a significant difference in the choice between factory and nonfactory work. In San Juan, there is a significant

TABLE 8. OCCUPATIONAL ASPIRATIONS EXPRESSED BY 1,045 SAMPLE WORKERS

Kind of work desired 5 years hence	Number		Percent	
	Men	Women	Men	Women
Factory work	286	257	53.1	50.8
Same work as at present	157	138	29.1	27.3
Supervisor in a factory	27	22	5.0	4.3
Other job	102	97	18.9	19.2
Nonfactory work	135	129	25.0	25.5
Own business	83	38	15.4	7.5
Semiprofessional	12	37	2.2	7.3
Clerical or sales	21	54	3.9	10.7
Agriculture	19	—	3.5	—
Unknown or never considered	81	87	15.0	17.2
Retirement from labor force	12	23	2.2	4.5
Other	25	10	4.6	2.0
Total	539	506	99.9	100.0

tendency for higher education to be associated with choice of non-factory occupations. This tendency is consistent with the existence of more numerous and varied employment opportunities in the San Juan area. However, it is interesting that the more educated groups in the other areas did not at least express a preference for white collar or other more prestigeful employment. The disregard in which manual labor is held in most Latin cultures, including Puerto Rico, would lead one to expect many more workers to express hope for escape into occupations carrying greater status. The failure to do so may be a sign of realism in appraising the probable employment opportunities. Alternatively, the pattern of choice may indicate a belief that factory employment in itself is a significant advance over earlier expectations or previous employment, so that satisfaction with the current status is experienced and further advances are not considered likely.

Participation of Women in the Industrial Labor Market

It might be argued that the participation of women in industrial employment is of only marginal interest since they are more likely to enter the market as supplementary wage earners rather than as bread-winners, their involvement is likely to be temporary, and therefore they are less likely to develop a commitment to the market. However, the radical change in the economic status of women and their reactions to the opportunities that have appeared justify some elaboration.

We have noted that the appearance of factory employment opportunities was directly responsible for drawing a majority of the women in our sample into the active labor force. The significance of this response to the expanding opportunities is considerable, in view of the cultural obstacles to full labor force participation by women. In Latin societies woman's place has traditionally been in the home, where she can perform the duties of her sex and where she remains sheltered from the worldly eye of the community at large. It is not surprising that at the earliest stages of the expansion, and particularly in the smaller and less cosmopolitan towns, the new employment opportunities were regarded with some suspicion by the conservative elders and husbands. Some employers reported that before women were permitted to take jobs in their plants, the morality of the factory and the management had to be established. Furthermore, once women had taken such jobs, it was a familiar sight to see an unmarried daughter escorted to and from the factory by another family member, in order to protect her reputation and honor. This practice appears to have been abandoned quite soon after factory employment of women had become a more common phenomenon, however.

A greater obstacle to the entry and commitment of women to the industrial labor market has been the inherent threat to the customary role of husbands and other male family members. The disparate income levels in manufacturing and other activities meant that women factory workers' incomes often exceeded those of the male breadwinners by a considerable margin. In a society in which the male role is a strongly dominant one, this reversal of income roles has sometimes resulted in tensions. In some cases husbands or fiancés have insisted that the woman quit her job, demonstrating a preference for foregoing income in order to re-establish the man's dominant role as the principal source of household support. While some women have acceded to such demands, it also seems that there has been a large measure of successful resistance. In our plant study, during which we were able to discuss the subject more fully with women, we found that some men had reacted to women's resistance by demanding that the women either quit their jobs or assume the main burden of financial support of the household. If the women persisted, the men then felt free to withdraw a substantial part of their earnings from the family budget and to use these for their own personal ends, generally entertainment, in an assertion of male prerogatives. The fact that women resist pressures to conform to their traditional role is significant and indicates their determination to retain the gains employment has brought them.

We do not have to look far for an explanation of the women's persistent involvement in the market. Economic reasons rank foremost, although only about 20 percent of the women, primarily divorcées or widows, were reported to be the sole support of their households. Another strong push toward entering and remaining in the market is the desire to escape the tedium of the home. In contrast to the restricted social opportunities available to most women who remain at home, the factory provides a social experience of great value, which reinforces the pull of an augmented income. Indeed, this social experience has sometimes been valued so highly that women have preferred to work even though their personal monetary gains have been small or the net effects of their contributions to family income have been limited by the men's diverting part of their earnings from the household budget. Finally, women have gained a new feeling of independence which, for some, has been important. These factors combine to provide positive motivation for continued involvement and commitment to an active labor force status. It was surprising to find the extent to which the women expressed a desire to continue working. Significantly, the desire was almost equally strong among all women, regardless of marital status. About 90 percent of the single women and 85 percent of the others expressed positive interest in continuing to work indefinitely.

In terms of their attitudes toward industrial employment, women seemed to be no less committed than men. They liked factory work with equal intensity and generally foresaw their continued employment in industry. Of the women expressing an occupational choice for a time five years in the future, almost two thirds indicated some class of factory work (Table 8). However, there were sharper differences within the female sample based on education than there were among the men. Women who had completed more than 9 years of school showed strong preferences for clerical or other nonfactory occupations that were considered more prestigeful.

WORKERS' MARKET BEHAVIOR AND OTHER INDEXES OF THE LEVEL OF COMMITMENT

A modern and mature industrial labor market is characterized by both mobility and stability. Stability derives from the fact that workers do not generally move in irregular fashion between the industrial and nonindustrial sectors of the economy; nor is there constant and large-scale exit from and re-entry into the labor force. At the same time there is mobility within the market as workers tend to move in response to differentials in wages and working conditions toward jobs that promise to maximize job utilities. The immature industrial labor market, on the other hand, may be characterized by frequent changes in workers' labor force status, as well as by an extremely high degree of movement among jobs within the market. Indeed, extreme job mobility in newly developing industrial labor markets is often believed to be indiscriminate or irrational, in an economic sense, and to be evidence of an inability of workers to adapt to the working conditions and discipline of factory employment.

Stability

In the preceding section we characterized our sample industrial labor force as one that appeared to be substantially committed to continued involvement in the industrial labor market. In this sense it fulfilled one requirement of a stable labor force. An additional basis for stability was the infrequency of repeated voluntary withdrawal from and re-entry into the labor force. These sources of stability, however, do not ensure stability within the industrial sector or within individual firms, as can be demonstrated by the extreme variations in labor turnover among the firms surveyed. Their net turnover in 1953, computed as the ratio of replacements to the average number of production workers employed during the year, ranged from as low as 5 percent to well over 400 percent of the average number of production workers employed in the plant. While the high rates may suggest a singular absence of adaptation and commitment, the lower rates suggest precisely the reverse.

The incidence of high turnover is not random among firms or industries. We believe that rational explanations of the diversity in turnover reported by firms can be found in their characteristics and management practices, as well as in the ends workers seek to realize by their interplant movements.

We found considerable evidence that workers' movements were influenced and guided by the structure of wage differentials. For 67 of the 85 plants we visited, adequate data were available for measuring and analyzing employment stability. Dividing these firms into three groups according to level of turnover, we found a striking inverse rela-

TABLE 9. SAMPLE OF MANUFACTURING PLANTS IN PUERTO RICO, DISTRIBUTED BY TURNOVER, ABSENTEEISM, AND WAGE RATES, 1953

Net turnover as percent of average plant employment*	No. of plants	Median turnover rate	Absenteeism†			Average straight-time hourly earnings in cents			
			Low 0-4%	Moderate 4.1-7%	High over 7%	25-39	40-49	50-59	60 and over
0-40	24	23.3	11	3	9	3	8	3	10
41-75	19	52.2	4	6	5	4	9	5	1
Over 75	24	183.6	4	6	13	10	10	2	2
Total	67		19	15	27	17	27	10	13

* Replacements as percent of the average number of production workers employed during 1953 (average number employed on the first day of each month). Firms whose turnover rates range through 40 percent are considered stable; those with rates of 41 to 75 percent, moderately stable; and those over 75 percent, unstable.

† Man-days lost for all reasons as percent of man-days scheduled (weekly average for 4 weeks in August 1953). Absenteeism rates could not be computed for 6 firms due to inadequate records.

tion between the wage level and the level of stability (Table 9). Nor could the differences in stability be attributed to such other factors as age of the firm, its size, or the sex composition of the work force. When the influence of wages was held constant, these factors showed a statistically insignificant association with turnover levels. When the firms were combined into ten industry groups, the inverse relationship between the group average wage and turnover levels was discernible in a rank correlation of —.66. It is notable that, as wage levels have risen in firms and industries characterized by high turnover, stability and sometimes productivity have increased in spite of employers' expectations that leisure preferences would lead to greater absenteeism and the effectiveness of discipline would be weakened.

Like high turnover, high absenteeism may be attributable to undisciplined work habits or an inability to adapt to the requirements of factory work. Rates of absenteeism (man-days lost for all reasons) varied widely among the sample firms, ranging from less than 2 percent to almost 20 percent of scheduled man-days. Furthermore, like turnover, the level of absenteeism appeared to be inversely associated with plant wage levels, although not as closely as in the case of turnover. Thus, generally, high turnover and absenteeism tended to be found together.

Interviewed employers offered evidence of a subjective nature that workers move from the lower-wage industries to the higher. For example, in the relatively high-wage electrical goods industry some of the metropolitan plants that opened after 1953 were able to begin operations with a large proportion of industrially experienced women in their work forces. It was often asserted that the plant could easily have been converted into a brassière or other garment plant because of the number of women with needle-trade experience. This was true despite the rapid expansion currently taking place in the garment industry.

Within the garment industry itself, plant managers reported considerable movement of women from the lower-wage native section of the industry to the newer producers for the mainland market, who paid higher wages set under federal regulation. This movement is of particular interest since the native sector was by far the more "traditional" in the imposition of discipline, in output and quality requirements, in the relations between owners and workers, and in other conditions of employment. By moving to plants managed by continentals, the workers generally exposed themselves to much more severe discipline, higher production and quality requirements, and more impersonal, though less authoritarian, relations. The starting wage differential of 30 percent or more, however, seemed adequate to overcome any preference workers may have had for the more tolerant and traditional climate of the native sector. At the time of our survey this sector was rapidly becoming a training ground for the higher-wage sector of the industry.

Management employment practices themselves must be credited with part of the responsibility for great instability where it has persisted over time. For example, very high turnover rates in the sample plants were sometimes found to be associated with inefficient recruiting and hiring practices. Many firms hired workers before they screened them; those who did not show rapid progress would then be discouraged from remaining. Training personnel and methods were often found to be inadequate and not conducive to early achievement of the high output standards that were demanded, so that, again, frustration and turnover were encouraged. Some firms dismissed absenteeism as endemic to the Puerto Rican work force and made no attempts to reduce it even though it could be demonstrated that excessive absenteeism was successfully being curbed by other firms. Of course, high turnover and absenteeism also reflected some resistance on the part of workers to the discipline of factory employment, but it appeared that resistance could be greatly softened under appropriate training and wage conditions. Under optimum conditions, labor force stability could be achieved in a plant employing a moderately low order of skills in as short a time as one to two years.

The association of stability with wages, however, should not be attributed solely to workers' responses to higher wages. We noted that rising minimum wages also had an impact on management practices. Many practices that may be economic at low wage levels are not economic when wages rise. Managements' desire to restrain labor cost leads to more careful hiring and training procedures, more vigorous measures to combat absenteeism, and a tightening of production standards. Thus, higher wages not only reduce workers' incentive to move but also force a rationalization of management practices. This may have the further effect of minimizing the frustrations to which workers would otherwise be exposed.

Interplant Mobility

In exploring the pattern and reasons for past job changes and workers' attitudes toward their current jobs, we found that wages were an important underlying factor. We have already noted that workers' expectations of higher wages were heavily emphasized as a force encouraging their original interest in industrial employment and drawing them into the market. Once involvement is achieved, both actual and potential mobility seem to be guided or influenced by wage differences. For example, dissatisfaction with earnings, because of either low wage rates or irregular work, was by far the most frequently given reason for voluntary separations by workers in their postinvolvement period. Evidence that mobility has not been irrational in a wage sense is provided by the earning records accompanying the employment histories of our sample workers.

Our data show that among male and female workers who had made between one and three job changes since 1945, about two thirds of the moves were accompanied by increases in earnings; among workers with over four job changes, a smaller proportion of moves—one half among men and 40 percent among women—was accompanied by increases in earnings. However, it must be noted that these figures include all moves, both voluntary and involuntary, and some that preceded entry into the industrial labor force, and that they probably reflect the greater seasonality of nonfactory employment. Thus the high proportion of reported increases in earnings is even more impressive. There need be nothing irrational, of course, about movement among plants that offer identical minimum wages within a particular industrial sector. For example, the high rate of movement of women among brassière and other garment plants was often motivated not so much by hope of an immediate increase in income, as by hopes that instruction or supervision would be better or that output standards would be easier to meet. Part of this movement should be viewed as a process of developing standards for judging the desirability of particular employments, rather than as an indiscriminate or irrational movement, which most employers thought it was.

A stress on wage factors in other contexts suggested their importance for motivating possible future moves as well as past moves. Among the sample workers, a higher degree of dissatisfaction with the current job or employment situation was expressed by the lowest-wage workers than by any other group, and they cited wages as the principal reason for their dissatisfaction. Workers interested in other jobs in the plant, workers who did not expect to remain in their current places of employment, and workers who expressed a preference for employment in some other factory all had wages below the average of the sample as a whole and mentioned wages as a primary reason for desiring a change.

Occupational Mobility and Aspirations

If our view of the labor market were restricted to the area of inter-industry and interfirm mobility, the Puerto Rican industrial worker would appear to be firmly integrated into the industrial labor market and his behavior consistent with that of a committed industrial worker. An extension of our area of reference, however, reveals other respects in which the development of an industrial society is incomplete. One of the most conspicuous is the current occupational structure of the industrial labor market; the workers' view of its vertical dimension and of their potential mobility within it is limited.

As an allocative institution, it is not enough that the labor market draw workers into the industrial sector and induce them to remain there. Simultaneously the market must serve as an efficient mechanism for allocating workers throughout the occupational hierarchy. At an early stage of industrialization, this distribution may be achieved by purely administrative job assignments with little consideration of preferences of employees, which may be neutral in any case. As development proceeds, however, and labor requirements become increasingly diverse, the market must be concerned with the hierarchy of jobs and skills and the adequacy of the incentives offered to workers. Alternatively it can be argued that the development of an occupational hierarchy and opportunities for mobility are essential for gaining full commitment of the labor force. Unless opportunities are consistent with workers' aspirations, commitment is likely to be uncertain or temporary. Thus, the requirements of both sustained economic development and commitment point to the extension of the labor market and the formalization and impersonalization of the allocative process.

Under what conditions does a consciousness of mobility develop among workers? When do their aspirations for advancement actually become effective determinants of their behavior or a standard against which their satisfaction with industrial employment can be measured? In the Puerto Rican study we found that workers were very much aware of the substantial gains in income and status that their initial involvement in factory employment had given them. On the other hand, they displayed only a vague awareness of possibilities for further advancement within the industrial system. It is not surprising, therefore, that there was also a notable lack of aspiration to advance to skilled or more responsible positions.

For example, only about a third of the men indicated a preference for a different job in the plant in which they were currently employed

(Table 10). Of these barely half expressed interest in a job at a higher skill or supervisory level. Interest in skilled jobs was expressed by only a third of the men making a choice, but a substantial number of these were already skilled workers interested in other skilled jobs. Unskilled workers chose unskilled and semiskilled jobs much more often than they chose skilled ones. The most striking characteristic of those indicating some other job preference was their earning level, which was significantly lower than that of the other workers at the same level of skill.

The reasons given for the indicated choices are suggestive (Table 11). Wage differentials were relatively more important than physical effort in choosing skilled and supervisory jobs; physical effort was relatively more important than any other factor in the choice of unskilled jobs, and of considerable influence in the choice of semiskilled. In other words, the choices of the lower skill levels were made with an eye to minimizing effort as well as to maximizing income. That this is not an unreasonable economic choice will be indicated shortly. Prestige appears important only in the choice of supervisory posts; skilled positions were not chosen for reasons of prestige any more often than were semiskilled jobs.

The demonstrated patterns of aspirations cannot be dismissed simply as informed choices in the face of unlimited opportunity. Indeed, other factors, including the technological nature of the industrialization to date and many employers' policies restricting the number of opportunities for advancement, make the choices appear quite understandable.

The majority of the new manufacturing firms in Puerto Rico at the time of the study were light industries which employed largely low-level skills, except in plant maintenance. A well-developed occupational hierarchy within a plant was the exception rather than the rule. In the more common case the wide gulf, in terms of skill, that separated production from maintenance jobs removed the latter from an occupational line of progression. Since employment as a skilled mechanic usually presumed the possession of the skill qualifications, workers may justifiably have viewed the possibilities of qualifying as very remote.

In general, our data suggest that aspirations for more highly skilled jobs in the plant are a function of the skill composition of its work force. Among the industries that employed men, the three having the highest proportions of skilled workers included two of the three industries within which the largest proportion of workers who expressed preferences for another job chose skilled jobs. Conversely, in the in-

TABLE 10. JOB PREFERENCE WITHIN THE PLANT OF CURRENT EMPLOYMENT OF 539 MEN, BY LEVEL OF SKILL OF CURRENT JOB

Preferred job	Total		Current job						Unclassified
			Unskilled		Semiskilled		Skilled		
	No.	Percent	No.	Percent	No.	Percent	No.	Percent	No.
Skilled	58	10.8	11	5.8	27	15.0	19	11.5	1
Semiskilled	62	11.5	30	15.9	23	12.8	9	5.5	—
Unskilled	25	4.6	21	11.1	3	1.7	1	.6	—
Inspection, etc.	19	3.5	10	5.3	7	3.9	2	1.2	—
Supervisory	14	2.6	5	2.6	4	2.2	5	3.0	—
Office work	5	.9	2	1.1	2	1.1	1	.6	—
Subtotal	183	34.0	79	41.8	66	36.7	37	22.4	1
No preference expressed	356	66.0	110	58.2	114	63.3	128	77.6	4
Total	539	100.0	189	100.0	180	100.0	165	100.0	5

TABLE 11. FREQUENCY OF MENTION OF FACTORS INFLUENCING JOB PREFERENCES WITHIN PLANT OF CURRENT EMPLOYMENT OF 183 MEN

Factors influencing preference	Job preferred										
	Skilled		Semiskilled		Unskilled		Inspection		Supervision		Office work
	No.	Percent	No.	Percent	No.	Percent	No.	Percent	No.	Percent	No.
Higher wages	48	82.8	35	56.5	6	24.0	7	36.8	12	85.7	4
Less physical effort	18	31.0	26	41.9	17	68.0	10	52.6	9	64.3	4
Cleaner work	7	12.1	17	27.4	6	24.0	7	36.8	4	28.6	3
More prestigeful	10	17.2	10	16.1	2	8.0	1	5.3	7	50.0	3
Desire to learn new things	10	17.2	16	25.8	—		2	10.5	—		—
Opportunity for advancement	2	3.4	1	1.6	1	4.0	—		—		—
Independence from supervision	2	3.4	4	6.4	3	12.0	2	10.5	3	21.4	—
Liking for task	6	10.3	1	1.6	—		—		1	7.1	1
No. of men	58		62		25		19		14		5

dustries with the smallest proportion of skilled workers, least interest in skilled jobs was shown by those workers who indicated alternative job preferences. This suggests the common-sense observation that the level of aspirations is a function of the proximity to and awareness of opportunities in skilled positions and of their advantages. However, while the *level* of aspirations in the industries with higher ratios of skilled to unskilled workers was higher than in the predominantly low-skill industries, there were no significant differences in the proportion of all the workers employed in these industries who made some choice, except in the textile industry. Not only was its proportion of workers aspiring to skilled positions among the highest, but it was the only industry in which a majority of the sampled workers expressed some alternative job preference. This may be explained by the existence in this industry of a more formal ladder of job progression on a step-by-step basis, which makes qualification for advancement seem feasible and therefore gives rise to greater expectations.

Even where diverse skills are employed, however, managerial policies often militate against the early development of active aspirations for advancement among workers. We found that many firms sharply limited the opportunities for advancement within the work force by filling the more skilled positions from the outside. This may be understandable in the case of maintenance positions where the possession of a skill may be prerequisite for employment, but it is less understandable in the case of skilled production operations that are staffed with raw recruits. Employers justified their procedure on the grounds that internal progression aggravated the problems of instability and inefficiency of the work force and created training problems, since both the promoted worker and his replacement would have to be trained. Furthermore, it was contended by some that Puerto Ricans were not interested in advancement either because of a disinterest in increasing their incomes or out of abhorrence for the responsibility that often accompanied more highly skilled jobs. Even where internal recruitment for more skilled positions was practiced, some managements preferred not to encourage aspiration to promotion lest they lose control over the selection of the workers to be advanced.

Wage policies likewise often militate against the development of aspirations for advancement. It is common to find no formal wage structures in factories; the bulk of the production workers are all paid at the same rate or within a very narrow range of rates. Since differences in job content do exist but are not reflected in the wage rates, it is not unreasonable that workers' job preferences reflect desires to minimize effort, dirtiness, or other elements of disutility in jobs. There is generally a sizable wage differential between production and maintenance jobs, but workers do not seem to aspire directly to the latter; perhaps the jump seems too great to be feasible.

The wish to minimize elements of disutility in jobs does not mean that this course would ordinarily be preferred to an opportunity to increase income if one were available. Our plant survey showed that where opportunities for advancement existed and a job hierarchy was paralleled by a structure of wage rates, the response of workers was always sufficient to fill job openings. True enough, managers reported cases of workers who hesitated or refused proffered promotions to more skilled and responsible jobs. Such hesitancy flows in part from the high disutility that is assigned to responsibility, and in part from insecurity, the worker's feeling that he may not be able to learn to perform the new operation satisfactorily. He overlooks the fact that learning is a continuous process and that he is better equipped to learn a new operation after some industrial experience than he was when he learned his first factory job. Employers reported that such hesitancy could usually be overcome with a little persuasion and encouragement.

The partial and transitional character of commitment among the sample workers is discernible in other ways as well. There has yet to emerge among the new factory workers a separate identity as a group or class. Most factory workers undoubtedly still think of themselves as belonging to the lower working class, although a cut above most other manual laborers. However, one does not sense a strong feeling of common interests or of identity in the work group. The lives of factory workers appear to be organized about two separate poles, the factory and the home, and the two rarely have anything in common. Once the worker leaves the plant, his activities appear to be oriented toward his residential neighborhood much more than toward the work group. His friendships in the plant are separate from his associations outside.

In the plant there may be cooperation in getting out the work, and various informal controls may operate within the work group. On the other hand, group action to rectify grievances has not been common among the newer industrial workers. One notices a rather strong residue of values and expectations associated with the traditional paternalistic relationship between *patrono* and *obrero*. Workers were commonly found to identify with the employer as a person and to desire recognition directly from him. At the same time, the employer was expected to be the arbiter of the worker's job problems, if not his personal problems as well. Thus workers tended to look to the employer for the dispensation of "justice." Assuredly, "justice" was not always forthcoming, but this did not appear to stimulate formal moves for common forms of action. Beyond the employer, workers tended to look to the government, as personified by a charismatic governor, as the protector of their interests. While there are trade union organizations in many of the old native industries, there is a notable paucity of organization in the newer sectors as well as some resistance to organization. Where unions have been organized, they are generally weak and ineffective.

Individual workers emerge as composites of the traditional and the modern industrial man. We had expected, perhaps naïvely, that there would be distinguishable "types" among the sample workers—those who would be very "traditional" and those who would be "modern" in their attitudes and values. Furthermore, we had hoped that these "types" might be distinguishable by certain characteristics. This expectation was not fulfilled; no sharply defined "types" emerged from our analysis. There were workers who, by their expressed aspirations for higher income and stress on the importance of opportunities for advancement, appeared on balance to have an outlook more characteristic of workers in a dynamic industrial society. However, interspersed with their "modern" values were those of the traditional culture, such as an emphasis on the importance of the quality of the personal relations between the employers and the workers.

We compared the characteristics of workers with a configuration of their job values and personal aspirations and found that the level of weekly earnings was the variable most closely associated with differences in workers' outlooks. The lower the earnings, the greater the emphasis on money as the important source of job satisfaction, and the more desirous the workers were to seek other employment or another job in the same plant. When the influence of earnings was held constant, the marginal effect of most of the other variables tested (agricultural experience, age, years of urban residence, years of factory experience, job mobility rate, etc.) was statistically insignificant. The exception was education: among men, higher education was significantly associated with higher income and job aspirations.

The importance that workers ascribed to wages throughout our interviews was impressive. We do not wish to imply that noneconomic bases of motivation or satisfaction either do not exist or are unimportant, but our data suggest that at absolutely low wage levels economic considerations far outweigh the noneconomic in determining the level of a worker's satisfaction with his job and his movements between jobs. Further weight is lent to the relative importance of wages by the rather narrow range of noneconomic factors to which most workers currently assign high positive value. For example, job factors that rank high among continental American workers—independence from supervision, inherent interest in the job, job prestige, or opportunities for advancement—are very infrequently mentioned as bases of worker satisfaction or mobility within the industrial sector. The noneconomic considerations that were mentioned most frequently included a generalized desire to be "treated well," good personal relations with other workers and the employer, and the distance from home to the factory (which is unrelated to the job situation).

These various attitudes of workers indicate that our sample work force was still in a transitional stage in the development of a new system of meaningful ends and values within the industrial environment. It is reasonable to expect that, with time and a continued expansion of industrial employment opportunities, new values and aspirations will emerge and will tend to offset the immediate importance of purely material ends. Support for such an expectation was found among our highest wage workers, who tended to assign more weight to nonwage factors as reasons for satisfaction with a particular employment situation and for lack of interest in changing jobs.

FACTORS FACILITATING COMMITMENT

The degree of commitment observed in the sample work force was surely incomplete, but it was sufficiently advanced to permit a relatively efficient level of manufacturing operations. Indeed, an observer of the Puerto Rican scene could not help but be impressed with the rapidity with which plants under experienced and capable managements were reaching profitable levels of operations.

It is gratifying that the performance of Puerto Rican industry does not appear to have been achieved at the cost of great physical or psychological strain on the workers. We found the level of over-all satisfaction with factory work surprisingly high. Questions concerning workers' attitudes toward their tasks and their current places of employment generally yielded positive responses and little overt evidence of dissatisfaction, although the desire for higher wages was widespread. In the intensive plant study, we again found workers readily adaptable to plant conditions without developing either resentments or distaste for their jobs. This does not mean, of course, that particular grievances did not arise among workers, but only that more often than not these did not seem to arise from a fundamental resistance to the discipline and work conditions imposed by the factory.

A number of factors have contributed to the adaptation and commitment of workers to industry. First, the organization of factory production does not represent a radical change from preindustrial patterns. The industrial labor market has much in common with some of the preindustrial markets, particularly with the plantation labor market, in the impersonalization of employment relations and in the organization of production. Thus, the development of factory employment opportunities has meant merely the extension of the boundaries of the labor market for many male workers, rather than a transition from a nonmarket system of allocation. The nature of the employment relationship has changed more for those formerly employed in small productive units, but more in detail than in basic character.

Clear Opportunity for Improved Position

The characteristics of the labor force must be considered a second factor favorable to commitment. We have noted that the workers who have been drawn into the industrial labor market are those with the least to risk in either economic or status terms. Among those in agriculture, the wage laborers, not the peasant farmers, entered the factory. As wage laborers in a society that had formalized the exchange of services almost entirely on a money basis, they had nothing to lose in terms of perquisites, obligations, or security of employment. Already at the bottom of the social hierarchy, they had no social position to lose. The higher income and better working conditions of industry could only enhance their social status.

In even stronger terms we may say that the Puerto Rican rural proletariat has adapted to the industrial order so readily because it did not feel a prior commitment to any other order. If commitment to industrial life had required the loss of commitment to some preindustrial living pattern, the process of adaptation could have been expected to be slower and to have encountered many more critical obstacles.

Other characteristics of the labor force have eased the process of involvement and adaptation. The sample work force exhibited a moderate amount of education, although a majority of the workers reported less than 8 years of formal schooling. This level of education is quite insufficient to qualify them for white collar positions, which may be more highly coveted for their prestige value than are factory jobs. The only alternative to factory work is largely unskilled manual labor, which requires little or no education. Industry offers the employment that demands the most in terms of educational qualifications and often at a higher wage than that available in more prestigeful occupations. The demands of alternative employments either greatly underemploy the capacities of workers or disqualify them. Thus, the association of some educational requirements and higher income with factory employment has accorded it a status level recognized as above that of the alternatives realistically available to most factory workers. Education also facilitates adaptation by developing an appreciation of order, discipline, and preciseness, as well as by stimulating greater material and social aspirations.

Limited Initial Aspirations

That workers have entered the industrial labor force with only limited immediate objectives—higher wages or increased employment stability—is a third factor favorable to commitment. These goals have generally been susceptible to early satisfaction in industry. As material aspirations continue to rise under the impact of increasing contact with the United States and exposure to its information media, workers can look forward to gradually rising incomes with which to satisfy these wants. The ready availability of consumers' goods, of course, has insured the realization of the utilities potentially derivable from higher money incomes.

The legal procedures for determining minimum wages have contributed to the effectiveness of industrial wage levels in encouraging commitment. Given extensive and chronic unemployment and the free play of market forces, an industrial labor force probably could be recruited at wage levels close to those prevailing in nonindustrial employment. However, while industrial employment may not need to offer a gain in real income in order to involve workers in the industrial labor market, the offer of gain may surely be necessary to secure their commitment. In Puerto Rico a substantial wage differential in favor of industrial employment has resulted from legal minimum wages, which are determined largely by the criterion of industry profitability rather than by market supply conditions. In our view the existence of this differential and the expectation that wages will continue to rise steadily, if not rapidly, have been of vital significance in securing the permanent involvement of workers in the industrial labor force and in facilitating the level of commitment that currently characterizes the sample work force.

Absence of Visible Disorganization

Fourth, industrial employment has not resulted in visible large-scale social and family disorganization, although considerable reorganization is readily observable. For many of the industrial workers, their integration into industrial employment has not meant a complete uprooting of community or family ties. There has been considerable migration to urban centers, but most of this is family migration, so that homes are not disrupted and individuals are not left isolated in new environments for long. The wider dispersal of factories throughout the island promises to permit more workers to accept factory employment without severing their ties to their residential communities, thus preserving one source of security and familiarity for the new industrial recruits. The desirability of retaining close ties to the community of origin may be open to question in many societies, since that community may be the locus of conservative forces that impede commitment to the new industrial culture. In Puerto Rico, however, such ties do not appear to have been inhibiting.

It is to be expected that some family relations will undergo significant change under the impact of economic development, as indeed they have. Industrial discipline has accelerated the already weakening traditional ties to the extended family. Obligations and responsibilities are being increasingly restricted to the immediate family. Furthermore, the expansion of industrial employment opportunities for women has been forcing a redefinition of the role and status of women within the family. Thus, while the adjustment of family relationships seems to be proceeding without widespread family disintegration, some of the demands of industrial employment may still provide a potential basis for conflict. It should also be acknowledged, on the other hand, that the disruptive effects of industrialization may be either partially or completely offset by the concomitant contribution it makes to family stability in the form of increased economic security.

Quality of Management

Finally, substantial credit for the successful integration of workers into industry must lie with the over-all quality and the employment practices of the new industrial management. By its control over the organization of the productive process, its proximity to workers, and its power to determine working conditions, management is in a unique position to ease the physical integration of workers into the process, to interpret the new order to them, and to make it possible for them to realize some of their goals and aspirations. In brief, it is largely up to management to make adaptation appear worth the cost. This requires skill in training workers so that they may reach high levels of technical proficiency as quickly and painlessly as possible, and the availability of rewards commensurate with increases in proficiency.

Since most of the expansion in Puerto Rico has been in the form of branch plants of mainland firms, there has been a readier availability of skilled managerial personnel for new plants than may be the case in developing areas that must rely more heavily on internal sources. The quality of management has not always been uniformly high, however. Particularly at the earlier stages of the industrial expansion, mainland investors, misled by the low level of wages prevailing in Puerto Rico, sent completely inexperienced or otherwise unqualified men to start and manage operations that required managerial skills of the highest and most diverse order. Profiting from the difficulties and failures encountered in many of these earlier ventures, recently established plants have generally been entrusted to managements of vastly improved quality. The fact that these plants are managed by others than Puerto Ricans, that communication between workers and management is often limited by language barriers, and that standards of output and conduct are higher and more exacting than in previous jobs does not appear to have engendered serious resentment or resistance on the part of workers. On the contrary, they appear to be adapting to the new environment satisfactorily, to show a rather sophisticated understanding of the needs and problems facing managements, and a surprising awareness of the varying abilities of management personnel.

While plant personnel policies still leave much to be desired, the atmosphere does not appear to be oppressive, and relations between workers and managements are generally cordial. Workers often do express a wish for closer personal relations with employers. On the other hand, they have been responsive and appreciative of the greater impartiality, the less authoritarian approach, and the greater evidence of managerial skill that most of the new managerial force has brought to its task. And managements, anxious to facilitate the adjustment of workers to modern factory conditions, in many cases have successfully adopted selected paternalistic practices, which help to increase workers' feelings of security without compromising plant efficiency.

These factors and conditions help to explain the relatively early achievement of a level of commitment consistent with the immediate requirements of the new industrial sector. While the level of commitment proved to be greater than casual observation of Puerto Rican industrialization would have suggested, full commitment has yet to be attained. The process of commitment is clearly in an evolutionary stage during which the current mixture of traditional and modern views of the market, employment relations, and society will give way to a complex of attitudes and associations more consistent both with the new opportunities that industrialization offers and with the limitations it imposes.

CONCLUSION

This account of the development of the Puerto Rican industrial labor market has dealt with three broad aspects of the process—the conditions and motives governing entry into the market, the nature of the adaptation made by workers within the new environment, and some of the possible explanations for the relative ease with which the currently observable level of commitment has been achieved. It seems appropriate to state the significant findings of our study in a number of general propositions and at the same time to indicate some of the questions that remain unanswered:

1. Motivation based on a maximizing rationale for entry into and involvement in the industrial labor market appears to be favorable for the achievement of commitment, when there is a reasonable satisfaction of workers' expectations. Our findings in Puerto Rico are fully consistent with this proposition. It was our hypothesis that under such motivating conditions commitment may be achieved more easily than when entry is impelled by dire need and a complete lack of alternative sources of income. Since need in this sense was not a dominant consideration governing entry of our sample workers to the industrial labor market, we have no clear test of the implications of forced entry for commitment. Whether such need is actually less favorable for commitment than a rational motive of maximization therefore cannot be determined here but must remain in the realm of untested hypotheses.

2. Exposure to and involvement in commodity or labor markets prior to industrialization facilitates entry into, as well as continuity

within, the industrial labor market. Prior exposure not only acquaints the potential industrial worker with the operational mechanism of the market, but it also is likely to be associated with the acquisition of new wants and a greater tendency to base decisions related to one's job on rational economic grounds. Both the achievement of commitment and efficiency in the functioning of the market may thereby be served.

3. Exposure to markets will be reinforced as a facilitating factor where considerable transformation of social and economic relationships has occurred in the preindustrial setting as a result, for example, of the development of large-scale commercial agriculture. Given such a transformation, the further changes necessary to accommodate the demands of industrialization may be achieved without serious and persistent difficulties. The former plantation and other rural wage earners in our sample evidenced no greater difficulty in adapting to industrial employment than did the urbanized workers. The paucity in the sample of workers who had been independent peasants precludes a comparison of their adaptability to industrial conditions with that of others. However, the very scarcity of peasants in the sample may suggest a greater adherence to traditional values and social forms and a correspondingly greater resistance to the incentives and demands of the new industrial sector.

4. Feldman and Moore have advanced the hypothesis that commitment as a means to development is reinforced when the process of change includes the gradual achievement of the ends of development. Our observations in Puerto Rico are consistent with experience elsewhere in confirming this hypothesis. The early realization of tangible benefits from industrial employment, together with fulfillment of expectations of continued gains, has undoubtedly served to minimize the problems of gaining commitment. This observation highlights the importance of providing immediate incentives for overcoming obstacles to an efficient reorganization of production processes and relations.

5. In the case of persons who become industrial workers out of a rational consideration of alternatives, financial incentives may be of decisive importance not only for inducing entry but also for motivating subsequent responses within the market. Since these workers enter the market with a fairly well-developed store of unsatisfied wants and readily acquire new wants, it is reasonable to expect that they will continue to respond to financial incentives, even though nonfinancial incentives gradually assume increasing importance. The effectiveness of financial incentives for motivating behavior beyond initial entry in the

case of workers who seek the satisfaction of limited and immediate needs cannot be determined from our study. These workers may be passive participants without interest in maximizing their income, whose involvement remains perfunctory. On the other hand, with continued exposure such individuals may develop increasing responsiveness to financial incentives as their wants broaden.

6. Efficient performance on the job is neither synonymous with nor dependent on the attainment of full commitment. It suffices that, in Feldman and Moore's terms, commitment be achieved within the loci of intrinsic work factors and the market. These are the loci within which the process of commitment is likely to be most rapid. Our Puerto Rican workers demonstrated the relative ease with which the maintenance stage of commitment could be reached within these two loci, even while commitment in the other loci of social affiliation and social structure remained at a much earlier stage of development.

A final word of caution must be entered concerning these summary statements. They have not been subjected to tests under conditions other than those prevailing in Puerto Rico. On the other hand, they are generally consistent with the hypotheses advanced in Feldman and Moore's conceptualization of the commitment process. Elevation to the status of truly general propositions, however, must await empirical testing in a variety of environmental contexts.

10 THE LABOR MARKET IN INDIA

Morris David Morris *

This paper is devoted to an analysis of certain features associated with the mobilization of a labor force and its commitment in Indian industry. "Commitment," as used here, refers to the participation by workers in industrial employment on some permanent basis as measured by objective behavioral indexes. The paper deals successively with the recruitment of the work force and the degree to which it has become permanent in industry, with the work force's attitudes or ideological responses that bear on commitment, and with the degree to which trade unions have emerged to express these attitudes through formal organization. The data are drawn mainly from research in the Bombay City cotton textile industry and the Tata Iron and Steel Company, Jamshedpur, Bihar.

We shall limit our discussion to that portion of the work force employed as wage labor in organized large-scale industrial units that typically operate throughout the year, and in which capital equipment is powered by inanimate sources of energy. The analysis encompasses those portions of the Indian economy in which the corporate form predominates and where the writ of factory legislation has traditionally run since 1881. To the extent that the conclusions apply to other newly developing regions, their relevance is possibly restricted to regions in which the pressure of population on the land is very heavy.

RECRUITMENT OF AN INDUSTRIAL WORK FORCE

Alleged Labor Shortage

Although there is full agreement that in India today unemployment is widespread in both rural and urban areas, most scholars have assumed, on the basis of the conclusion of the 1929 Royal Commission on

* The research on which this paper is based was made possible by a grant under the Ford Foundation Foreign Area Training Fellowship Program and by a supplemental grant from the American Philosophical Society. The grantors, of course, bear no responsibility for the content of the paper. I owe debts of gratitude for materials and ideas to a great many people in India and in the United States. I cannot name them all, but I must specifically thank the officers and staff of the Tata Iron and Steel Company who made possible the collection of the Jamshedpur data.

Labor, that urban industrial development suffered from an absolute shortage of labor prior to 1925.[1] This purported shortage of labor is supposed to have affected the rate of industrial growth and to have shaped the attitudes and behavior of workers entering industry.[2] No real distinction was made between the shortages of skilled and of unskilled labor in Indian industry. Rapidly developing economies can be expected to be short of the skills and techniques for which they have had no previous need. The lack of skilled labor, however, has been misconceived as a shortage of raw unskilled labor from which other forms of labor could be created.

One view is that, because labor was short in industry, employers had to scramble for their work forces and make all sorts of concessions that weakened their hold on the workers. Because of the absence of effective discipline by employers, employees were able to indulge in the luxury of all too frequent returns to the villages to which they were unyieldingly devoted.[3] The alternative, and entirely contradictory, view recognizes the potential surplus of labor in the cities and argues that, as a consequence of this surplus, employers were able to abuse workers unmercifully and employ them under the most arduous conditions. Since working conditions in the factories were so bad, labor tended to remain in the villages or go back to the land for recuperative purposes.[4]

Whatever the hypothesis, workers retained their rural links. This retention of identification with traditional rural forms of social and economic existence is supposed to have prevented the growth of urban and industrial or proletarian types of behavior, and to explain the purported high rates of absenteeism and turnover and the slow growth of trade

[1] *Report of the Royal Commission on Labour in India* (London: His Majesty's Stationery Office, 1931), p. 21. Cf. Oscar A. Ornati, *Jobs and Workers in India* (Ithaca: Institute of International Industrial and Labor Relations, Cornell University, 1955), p. 35, which refers to "the excess of jobs over job-seekers which typified Indian industries for the period between 1900 and 1935."

[2] *Report of the Royal Commission on Labour in India*, pp. 11–14; D. H. Buchanan, *The Development of Capitalistic Enterprise in India* (New York: Macmillan Company, 1934), pp. 294–295; and Vera Anstey, *The Economic Development of India* (London: Longmans, Green and Co., 1929), p. 56.

[3] *Indian Factory Labour Commission, 1908*, Vol. 1, *Report and Appendices* (Simla: Government of India, Central Press Branch, 1908), pp. 18–19.

[4] G. B. Jathar and S. G. Beri, *Indian Economics*, Vol. 1 (3rd ed.; London: Oxford University Press, 1931), pp. 71–72; D. R. Gadgil, *The Industrial Evolution of India in Recent Times* (4th ed.; London: Oxford University Press, 1942), pp. 127–130; and Charles A. Myers, *Labor Problems in the Industrialization of India* (Cambridge: Harvard University Press, 1958), pp. 43–44.

unions in India. Interestingly enough, there have never been any significant tests of these assumptions. Generally, what has been written has been either tautological in character or deficient in analysis.

Study of historical data suggests that we need to revise orthodox judgments of the behavior of the industrial labor force and the consequences of this behavior. A review of the literature shows that to a great extent large-scale and small-scale industries have been combined in the discussions. The economic and operational characteristics of these two classes of industry are so different, however, that any attempt to derive a single pattern of labor force behavior can only lead to serious confusion. Another source of difficulty has been the lumping together of industries working the year round and those essentially seasonal in character.

Supply of Labor

In 1908 the Tata Iron and Steel Company started construction of a plant in the rather thinly populated Singhbhum district of the Chota Nagpur plateau of eastern India. The area contained a largely tribal population possessed of a few rudimentary agricultural and technical skills. The district did not possess any significant number of "superior artisans." [5] A 1906 survey concluded that "Singhbhum is not to be recommended as a field of recruitment for any industry." [6] Despite the thinly populated character of the district, its distance from any substantial concentrations of population, and the purported pressure on the labor supply in the country at large,[7] the shortage of labor, raw or semiskilled, did not emerge as a difficulty to be considered during the original planning or early stages of the steel project.[8] Moreover, at no time in the 50-year history of the Company has there been any problem in recruiting an adequate supply of labor for training in the requirements of the steel industry.

In the beginning unskilled labor was recruited from among the tribal people in the district. Employed initially in construction, they remained to work in the factory when production began. These people were not strangers to wage labor, for many of them had worked on railroad construction in earlier years. As soon as word of the proposed steel mill

[5] L. S. S. O'Malley, *Bengal District Gazetteers: Singhbhum, Saraikela and Kharsawan* (Calcutta: Bengal Secretariat Book Depot, 1910), p. 132.

[6] Quoted, *ibid.*, p. 133.

[7] P. P. Pillai, *Economic Conditions in India* (George Routledge & Sons, 1925), pp. 240–241.

[8] Tata Iron and Steel Company, "First Statutory General Meeting, 25 February 1908," typescript report in General Manager's office, Jamshedpur.

spread, unskilled labor from surrounding districts, including the Chhat-tisgarh districts of Drug and Raipur more than 300 miles away, began to turn up at the work site. Skilled artisans—notably fitters and riggers with experience in shipbuilding and construction—were recruited partly from Bombay Province and partly from the railway workshops. Some of the Indian administrative and supervisory personnel were bright and ambitious young men, transferred from other Tata enter-prises. The rest were recruited in a rather haphazard fashion. Skilled technicians were brought from the United States, Great Britain, and Germany.[9]

The history of the Tata Iron and Steel Company at Jamshedpur is not an exceptional and isolated case. A study of the supply of labor in the Bombay cotton textile industry also suggests that the prevailing view of the supply of labor is grossly wrong. With the exception of the short period after 1896 when an epidemic of bubonic plague drove a substantial portion of the population out of the city, the Bombay mill industry has never suffered from any limitation on its expansion be-cause of a shortage of raw labor.[10] This is supported by the evidence of wage rates, which remained remarkably stable until 1914.[11]

On the basis of detailed studies of these two industries and examina-tion of data from other centers, it seems safe to say that in India there has never been a shortage of raw labor willing and able to move from rural to urban activities, or from agricultural to industrial employment. This judgment is supported by historical data on urban centers and by the increasing incapacity of the agricultural areas after 1850 to provide income and employment for the rapidly growing population.

Mobility of Labor

The issue is not entirely settled by the evidence that a labor force for new industrial activities has been generally available in India. It has sometimes been argued that Indian workers will not move long dis-tances, that the ideology of the society and its social institutions tend to keep the population near its place of origin. The historical data refute this contention, also.

In the past economic opportunities in Indian society were very lim-

---

[9] John L. Keenan, *A Steel Man in India* (New York: Duell, Sloan & Pearce, 1943).

[10] M. D. Morris, "Some Comments on the Supply of Labour to the Bombay Cotton Textile Industry, 1854–1951," *Indian Economic Journal*, 1:138–152 (October 1953).

[11] S. D. Mehta, *The Indian Cotton Textile Industry: An Economic Analysis* (Bom-bay: Textile Association, 1953), p. 29.

ited; there was no new land to be easily opened to cultivation, and there was no continuous and systematic expansion of an urban industrial economy. In these circumstances steady and large movements of an essentially agricultural population could not have occurred. Nevertheless, where new opportunities of any magnitude were revealed, there were substantial movements of population. This is illustrated by the history of Indian migration to the Assam tea plantations and to the overseas colonies. The total migration out of India between 1834 and 1937, although not comparable to emigration from Europe during the same period, has been estimated by Davis at over thirty million people.[12] Davis says: "We may assume, indeed, that the pressure to migrate, in an economic sense, has always been great enough [in India] to provide a stream of emigrants much larger than the actual stream, given the opportunity. In other words, the demand has been less than the supply." [13]

What Davis has said about overseas migration is equally relevant to internal migration and can be illustrated by the history of the Tata Iron and Steel Company at Jamshedpur, where the population grew from 5,672 in 1911 to 218,162 in 1951.[14] Employment at the works in 1912 totaled some 6,300 persons, including the construction staff. In 1957 the Company employed some 40,000. From its beginning it has drawn its labor from every region of the subcontinent. Table 1 shows that almost three-fifths of the workers hired from 1932 through 1937 came from distances of over 200 miles, and almost a third came from distances greater than 350 miles.

In 1925, when the Company was adding substantially to its labor force, 12,358 people made personal application to its employment bureau. Of that total, more than 21 percent came from provinces at least 350 miles from Jamshedpur. In the same year, according to the files of the Company's Labor Bureau, 867 additional applications were made by mail. This is a substantial number for a society in which literacy, more than thirty years ago, was very low.

In the Bombay cotton mills a large portion of the work force came from long distances, from Uttar Pradesh and the south of India.[15] The

12 Kingsley Davis, *The Population of India and Pakistan* (Princeton: Princeton University Press, 1951), p. 99.

13 *Ibid.*

14 Government of Bihar, *District Census Handbook: Singhbhum* (Patna: Superintendent of Secretariat Press, Bihar, 1956), p. 6.

15 R. G. Gokhale, *The Bombay Cotton Mill Worker* (Bombay: Millowners' Association, 1957), pp. 16–17; *Report of The Royal Commission on Labour in India, Evidence*, Vol. 1, Pt. 1, pp. 385–386.

TABLE 1. PERSONS HIRED BY TATA IRON AND STEEL COMPANY, 1932–37, BY DISTANCES OF PLACES OF ORIGIN *

Distance of district of birth from Jamshedpur in miles	Number of hirings	Percent of hirings
0–100	3,998	28.0
101–200	2,034	14.2
201–350	3,734	26.2
351–500	1,102	7.7
501–750	380	2.7
751 and over	3,021	21.2
	14,269	100.0

* Source: Tata Iron and Steel Company, Ltd., *Answers to the Questionnaire of the Labour Enquiry Committee, Bihar* (Bombay: Tata Iron and Steel Co., 1938), pp. 91–98. The data are inflated by the fact that some of the hiring was of a temporary sort and many persons were hired more than once. However, the work force used for temporary jobs tended to be drawn from certain districts, the Singhbhum district in which Jamshedpur is located, and the Chhattisgarh districts of Drug and Raipur. As a consequence the hirings shown within the 0–100 mile radius and the 201–350 mile radius are somewhat exaggerated.

same story seems to hold for the labor force in Calcutta's industries, although no detailed study provides specific information. It is clear that Indian labor will and does move long distances from rural agricultural occupations into urban industrial ones. This long distance movement of part of the labor force should not be taken to imply any difficulty in recruiting labor from nearby regions; the phenomenon stems from special characteristics of labor market organization, some of which are discussed by Hoselitz in Chapter 12 infra.

ATTITUDES TOWARD INDUSTRIAL EMPLOYMENT

Instability of the Labor Force

Even if the adequacy of the labor supply and its mobility are accepted without argument, another alleged characteristic of the Indian industrial labor force has to be evaluated, namely, its alleged instability, devotion to rural districts of origin, and unwillingness to relinquish ties to them. In other words, it has been said that even labor that has moved into industrial employment regards it as temporary and is unwilling to relinquish rural links for a firm commitment to the urban labor market.

Much of the evidence for this persistent rural loyalty has been adduced from census data showing that in the large industrial towns a substantial portion of the population has been born elsewhere.[16] In itself, this evidence proves nothing about the lack of commitment. In centers where economic opportunity has been growing, the population has tended to increase at a rate greater than the birth rate, the difference representing migration from rural areas. But birth outside the city has no necessary implication for instability of the labor force. Moreover, Indian census data historically have tended for many reasons to understate the population permanently residing in urban areas.[17]

The unbalanced sex ratio in industrial centers (i.e., the very high proportion of males of working age) is typically taken as evidence that workers have retained their rural ties.[18] Having left their wives in the villages, the argument goes, the workers frequently return there. But from what Davis reports, workers migrating from nearby districts probably come with or are followed by their wives; those from greater distances came alone.[19] This generalization seems to fit Bombay specifically. Of all the groups migrating to Bombay, those from the distant United Provinces have the smallest percentage of women resident in the city. Yet it is commonly agreed that in the cotton mills this group is permanently committed to the industry. Even Jamshedpur, an industrial center with a committed work force, has had a persistently high, albeit declining, ratio of males to females. In 1911 there were 147 males per 100 females. In 1921 this ratio rose to 161. Successive censuses have shown a falling ratio, but even in 1951 it was as high as 125.[20] The continued existence of industrial centers with highly masculine populations may tell us a good deal about the lack of housing facilities or the absence of employment opportunities for women, but nothing about the commitment of the work force.

Purported high turnover rates have also been taken as evidence of noncommitment of the work force in India. Apart from the fallacious assumption that labor turnover and return to the village are merely two aspects of the same phenomenon, the available data must be questioned. Mukerjee reports that labor turnover at the Tata Iron and Steel Company was very high in the early years, gradually declined over time,

16 Pillai, *op. cit.*, p. 236.
17 *Report of the Royal Commission on Labour in India, Evidence*, Vol. 1, Pt. 1, p. 4.
18 *Ibid.*, p. 7.
19 Davis, *op. cit.*, p. 141.
20 Government of Bihar, *op. cit.*, p. 6.

but remained at a fairly high level, as shown by the following percentages of the Company's employees who terminated their employment in selected years: [21]

1925	36.6
1926	31.3
1927	24.1
1936	16.5
1937	14.0

However, these data are not correctly representative of labor turnover in the sense we are considering. They include all types of job termination: deaths, discharges for cause, layoffs because of reductions in staff, resignations, and discharges of workers absent without leave. They also include the discharges of the large proportion of workers employed on temporary assignments.

For an analysis of commitment, the percentages should include only terminations by resignation or discharge for absence without leave. These two categories alone represent workers whose attachment to the industry would be questionable. Unfortunately, relevant data are not complete, but the following percentages represent net turnover among monthly paid permanent workers at the Tata Iron and Steel Company during the years indicated: [22]

1932	2.55
1933	2.25
1934	2.43
1935	2.55
1936	1.79

These figures for workers with permanent status eloquently depict a high degree of stability in the work force.

Another view of labor turnover is obtained by inspection of the work force's length of service. The 1948 column in Table 2 understates the tenure of the work force, including as it does large numbers of workers hired during and after World War II. Beginning in 1949 the Company ceased hiring on any significant scale. As a result the average length of service in 1955 shows a marked increase. In fact, the comparison sug-

[21] Radhakamal Mukerjee, *The Indian Working Class* (2nd ed.; Bombay: Hind Kitabs, 1948), p. 39.

[22] Computed from *Report of the Conditions Affecting the Labourers of the Jamshedpur Works of the Tata Iron and Steel Company, Ltd.* (Jamshedpur: Tata Iron and Steel Company, October 1937), p. 27.

gests a rather phenomenal attachment of the work force to its employment. Even as of January 1947, for example, 24.6 percent of the
monthly paid workers had been employed for more than 20 years.

TABLE 2. LENGTH OF SERVICE OF MONTHLY PAID WORKERS AT TATA IRON
AND STEEL COMPANY, 1948 AND 1955 *

| | Percent of monthly paid workers | |
Years of service	January 1948	August 1955
Less than 1	5.3	0.5
1– 5	15.8	9.9
6–10	28.4	19.1
Over 10	50.5	70.5

* Data computed from Tata Iron and Steel Company's Labor Bureau files.

Intense Commitment

The phenomenon of intense commitment is not a recent one, although the relevant statistical data do not go back to the initial stages
of the Company's operations. In recent years this phenomenon has created three critical problems for the Company, problems exactly the
reverse of those supposedly facing the Indian industrial employer. First,
there is a substantial surplus of permanent labor, which cannot be
easily discharged and which will remain surplus in the foreseeable
future because the rate of attrition is so low. The Company is currently
engaged in an expansion program, which in a year or two will double
its output to two million tons of steel. Even with this doubling of output, it is expected that the labor surplus will remain embarrassingly
high for some years. Second, more than 1,000 workers who have been
used as a temporary force for a long period are exerting pressure for
positions on the permanent staff. Third, a large portion of the labor
force when retired at age 61 refuses to return to its places of origin but
seeks to remain in Jamshedpur, adding to what already is a difficult
housing problem.

It can be argued that the case of Jamshedpur is exceptional, but the
evidence suggests that it is not. Even in Bombay the data, although by
no means unambiguous, indicate that similar manifestations of commitment on a fairly large scale came early and have persisted. The am-
biguity of the situation in the textile industry derives from the fact that,
unlike Jamshedpur where there have been only a few large employers,
Bombay has had as many as 90 cotton mills and numerous other em-

ployers of labor. In Bombay commitment has been hidden by the mobility of workers among employers, a phenomenon reflecting not so much the peculiarities of labor force psychology as the impact of employers' policies. For reasons that need not be discussed here it seems historically clear that in Bombay, as in many other centers, employers have not really been concerned with the stability of the unskilled work force. In fact, in a situation in which vast reservoirs of unskilled labor were available, employers were encouraged to keep the labor force unstable. This was true in the Bombay mills.[23] Nevertheless, scattered evidence from as early as 1890 indicates that part of the work force had by that time a permanent attachment to the industry; in later years, an increasing part of the labor force was permanently attached to the cotton mill industry.[24]

The Roles of Caste and of Language

Caste. It has often been argued that the caste system has restrained the growth of an effective labor force. This view was strongly advanced by Banerjea:

The chief economic significance of the system is that it fixes absolutely the supply of any kind of labor. The scope given for the play of competition thus becomes limited, and consequently the law of demand and supply is rendered either inoperative or oppressive in its operation. When there takes place any change in the economic world, labor is unable to adjust itself to the altered circumstances and suffers in consequence, sometimes very heavily. . . . Further, the institution of caste is ill-suited to large-scale production in which minute subdivision of labor is essential and which requires the supply of any kind of labor to immediately respond to the demand for it. Under the caste system the people lose their adaptability to changed circumstances. The system, moreover, has its influence on the character of the individual.[25]

It is interesting that this distinctive institution of caste has been almost entirely ignored in connection with Indian industrialization. No detailed study of the relation of caste to industrial work is available. In the vast array of official investigations into the conditions of industrial labor, virtually the sole reference to caste relates to caste dietary restrictions, which employers claimed prevented them from establishing

23 M. D. Morris, "Labor Discipline, Trade-Unions, and the State in India," *Journal of Political Economy,* 63:295–296 (August 1955).

24 *Report of the Royal Commission on Labour in India, Evidence,* Vol. 1, Pt. 1, p. 14; Gokhale, *op. cit.,* pp. 24, 28.

25 Pramathanath Banerjea, *A Study of Indian Economics* (2nd ed.; London: Macmillan & Co., 1916), pp. 41–42. By permission.

factory canteens. The institution has been treated mainly by anthropologists, and almost entirely in its rural setting. Those who have studied caste have ignored industry, and those who have studied industry have ignored caste.

It has been implied that it is the low-caste workers, mainly untouchables who are economically as well as socially depressed, who have been forced into industrial employment.[26] However, there has been no clear study of the migration and employment of labor in industry on which to base this conclusion. In fact, what studies there are seem to confuse the low-caste and the economically distressed groups.[27]

Data relating to caste composition at the Tata Iron and Steel Company show that a substantial portion of its work force comes from the "twice born" or high castes. High-caste workers are employed in every occupation except that of sweeper or scavenger, although they tend to be concentrated in certain occupations. There is, for example, a clustering of Brahmans and Kayasthas in the clerical and supervisory posts. The reasons do not seem to be associated with caste as such, but with the advantages of literacy and experience possessed by these groups when the plant was established. Although these advantages were historically a function of caste status, the employer was selecting workers on the basis of occupational qualifications and not because of caste affiliation.

These caste concentrations in Jamshedpur have persisted partly because of the Company's policy of hiring relations of those already employed, and partly because these castes have continued to sustain at least a quasi monopoly of literacy and experience. Despite these tendencies, there is striking evidence of Muslims, Christians, tribal people, Sikhs, and high- and low-caste Hindus working side by side in the same occupations. Moreover, one can find low-caste workers directing high-caste workers. Castes do not seem to cling to their traditional occupations even where modern industrial requirements make this possible. For example, there is no evidence that the occupation of mason in the company is dominated by traditional mason castes, for very few of them are involved even though all castes are found doing masonry.

[26] Buchanan, *op. cit.*, pp. 294–298.

[27] P. N. Prabhu, "Bombay: A Study on the Social Effects of Urbanization on Industrial Workers Migrating from Rural Areas to the City of Bombay," in *The Social Implications of Industrialization and Urbanization: Five Studies in Asia* (Calcutta: UNESCO Research Centre on the Social Implications of Industrialization in Southern Asia, 1956), p. 53.

The neglect by scholars of relations between caste and industry does not mean that caste functions so well in modern industry as not to generate problems. Caste has been ignored because it has been administratively irrelevant in creating and disciplining a labor force. This is not intended to suggest that caste does not continue to be important for the individual, but in industrial development it has not proved to be a barrier of any great significance. Apparently it has not impeded either the recruitment of labor or the direction and commitment of labor.

I do not mean to eliminate the significance of caste altogether, for in a few cases it is obviously influential. Brahmans tend to be hired as food handlers in works canteens because all groups are able to accept food from Brahmans. On the other hand, in the Bombay and Jamshedpur factory canteens nobody seems to ask many questions about caste. In the Bombay textile mills, however, untouchables are not often employed in the weaving sheds. The most important evidence of the caste system in industry is the employment of untouchables as sweepers, their traditional occupation. Untouchables have had access to other jobs as well, but to the extent that other groups have been unwilling to accept jobs as sweepers these have been filled by untouchables. The cleaning of cesspools and the removal of carrion and refuse are the jobs most intensely repugnant in the traditional order of values and have no higher status in the industrial situation. In general, the influence of caste in industry persists more through inequalities of education and experience than through mandatory exclusiveness.

Language. The cosmopolitan character of the Indian labor force in the areas being discussed raises another problem, that of language, on which no detailed study has been made. It can be said, however, that language generally has not been a substantial barrier to either recruitment or the establishment of industrial discipline. The evidence is that an occupational lingua franca quickly developed where it was needed. In Jamshedpur it was based on Hindi and English; in Bombay it was a combination of Marathi, Gujarati, and English. In industrial centers in which the work force was drawn from a single linguistic region, there was no need for creating an industrial patois. Thus, without minimizing the general problem of language in India, we may say that it seems not to have been critical in the process of industrialization.

The Myth of "Paradise Lost"

What has been implied so far is that in India the shift from traditional, rural agricultural occupations to modern, urban industrial occupations has not been as difficult as has usually been assumed. Our analysis, which has centered on Bombay and Jamshedpur but has kept other industrial areas in mind, suggests that:

1. The raw labor supply willing and able to move into industry at the pace set by industrial expansion has been adequate for all needs.

2. Members of the labor force have moved long distances when employment opportunities warranted such movement.

3. The industrial labor force has not been particularly unstable; the degree of commitment is largely determined by the way in which the employer uses his labor rather than by the worker's psychology.

4. The caste system has not generally prevented the movement of workers into industry nor their mobility within industry.

These statements do not deny that the breakup of the traditional order in densely populated India has not been painful to individuals; but all that is relevant here is that the task of recruiting and disciplining (committing) a rural population to industrial employment has not been socially difficult. The point has been well made by Mace:

In the restatement of the law of habit, recognition must be accorded to the fact that habits not only condition but are themselves conditioned by social facts. Within the complex situation to which the habitual action is the response, the most potent factors are within the group. To parody McDougall, habits are formed and maintained by the pressure of social expectations. . . . Custom is a social habit, socially reinforced. All this would suggest that it may be easier to educate a group than to educate an individual, to change the custom and the "culture pattern" of the group than to change the standards of value and the habitual modes of behavior of the single member of society. This, at any rate, would seem to be what is actually happening.[28]

There is no doubt that these propositions run counter to generally accepted doctrine, not only for India but for other parts of the underdeveloped world. If this thesis is valid, some explanation is needed of the scholars' reluctance to read the evidence in this way and of their strong stress on the passionate human attachment to the land and the disruptive consequences of movement to urban industrial centers.

Because analysis of the process of commitment of workers to industrial life is of only recent interest, very few relevant data are available. England's economy has been most intensively studied, and the conclusions established there have been transported for application to other

[28] C. A. Mace, "Foreword" to Ferdynand Zweig, *The British Worker* (Harmondsworth: Penguin Books, 1952), p. 12. By permission.

areas. Many scholars were struck by the horrors of urban existence in England and stressed these phenomena in their writings. From their preoccupation emerged the theme of the rural "Paradise Lost," which has been elaborated by social scientists in recent decades. They have stressed the virtues of rural life, the violent changes that industrial life has required, and the grim features of factory discipline and urban existence. But careful study of their material shows it to be mainly logical, the result of certain deductive arguments from the basic assumption that rural life is somehow better than urban industrial life. There is little substantial evidence to support this theme.

Part of the error comes from the tendency to place rural and urban life in sharp contrast and to treat the traditional rural system as a holistic institutional arrangement, entirely consistent within itself and capable of disruption only from outside. It is true that the Indian village system has persisted for many centuries, but it has also been riddled with internal tensions and centrifugal tendencies. This suggests that it has been maintained by the absence of alternatives. When alternative opportunities appear and are bulwarked by legal institutions that make them real opportunities, the village system reveals its internal contradictions and is threatened by collapse from inside. This general idea is implied by Feldman and Moore's statement that "the socialized or committed individual will not necessarily remain so unless the learned actions and ideas and the believed values are more or less consistently buttressed by a system of rewards and expectations" (page 12 supra). This proposition, however, lacks two elements. It relates to existing as well as to developing economic systems; and existing systems are often perpetuated by the lack of alternatives—the absence of choice —so that expectations can be maintained at a very low level.

Although India for millennia has been a traditionally organized agricultural society, this has been a very intricate and sophisticated one, characterized by a complex division of labor and the employment of extensive skills, many of which were transferable to the new industrial pattern. In other words, when modern institutions began to invade India in the nineteenth century, they did not take root in an environment entirely unprepared for them. The elements of literacy for a modern bureaucracy existed, a sophisticated system of banking and commerce was in operation, and there was a substantial tradition of artisanship. As new industries slowly grew during the late nineteenth and twentieth centuries, they found that the ground had been partly prepared. The construction of the cotton mills in Bombay and of the steel mills in Jamshedpur depended in large measure on the reservoir of fitter and rigger talent that derived from the traditional shipbuilding industry of Surat. By the late nineteenth century much traditional iron-working skill had found its way into the railway workshops, and from the railways this modernized skill ultimately was drafted into private industry, as at Jamshedpur.

Flexibility of Industrial Discipline

Students of industrial development have stressed another sharp distinction between rural and industrial life, in the rhythm of the machine process, the consequent necessity of rigid discipline, and the special attitudes that characterize mechanized activity (cf. Chapter 2 supra). For certain purposes neither this stress on the particular discipline of industrial life nor the emphasis on the holistic character of traditional village existence is incorrect, but this dichotomy is a purely logical construct. When such logical devices are applied to situations for which they were not originally designed, the basic issues become confused. In analysis of commitment and work force ideology as a historical process, this is especially true.

In industry there is no "one right way" of organizing machine technology or labor. One can manipulate the whole range of processes and even individual operations, depending on the relative costs of capital and labor. A surprisingly wide range of choice in technical arrangements permits many varied combinations of capital and labor. In most industries developed in India before 1947, capital and labor cost ratios made for the use of far larger proportions of labor per unit of capital than was true in the West.[29] At Jamshedpur men and women carried materials in pans on their heads. Wheelbarrows were sparingly used, and the replacement of human beings by steam shovels and trucks was thoroughly uneconomic. In Bombay the cleaning of cotton in the mills was done by hand until after World War I. The consequences of this substitution of labor for capital have been enormous, but the most important feature for our purpose is that an overwhelming proportion of the labor required for modern factory industry in India has been of the absolutely unskilled sort in which physical strength rather than training is the essential element. Modern industry in the West of course has also used large quantities of unskilled labor, but the point is that proportionately more has been used in similar industrial employments in

[29] S. D. Mehta, *The Cotton Mills of India, 1854–1954* (Bombay: Textile Association, 1954), pp. 121–123.

India because of differences in capital and labor cost ratios. This means that most of the approximately 2,000,000 factory workers have been employed in work indistinguishable from that done in rural areas. They have been the pickers, handlers, carriers, wipers, and sweepers, of which India from ancient times has had so great a supply. The discipline imposed on these people in industrial situations has been no more rigorous than that imposed by rural employers. This somewhat qualifies the implication of the Feldman-Moore proposition about the impact of "machine pacing" on the work force.

It is true that factory employment has imposed on the labor force the discipline of the clock, the need to appear at and leave work at specified time. But for the landless agricultural workers who had eked out an income as a rural proletariat, this change was not as sharp and distinctive as it may seem. In Indian factories, moreover, the length of the workday has almost never been greater than it has been traditionally in the rural occupations and has been substantially shorter during most of the factory era.

For semiskilled and skilled workers, the requirements of factory discipline became progressively more demanding. But routines of those in traditional occupations—carpenters, masons, ironworkers, and the like —probably have been no more drastic in the factory than in other employment. Where the discipline is more demanding, the advantages in terms of money, opportunity, and prestige have eased adjustment to the discipline. Indian industry from its earliest stages has had little difficulty in keeping skilled groups attached permanently to the discipline of the factory.

Consciousness of Scarcity and of Opportunity

In the past one of the distinguishing characteristics of the Indian population has been a lack of concern for achievement, a lack of eagerness to seek out opportunity. This has often been attributed to the ideology and social organization of Indian society;[30] whereas actually the passive sense of no opportunity is a consequence not of ideological and institutional arrangements but of the lack of opportunity in the society. How can choice be made where there is no choice?

The Indian subcontinent, with its combination of fertile soils and monsoon rain patterns in its core regions, encouraged the early establishment of dense concentrations of population. Survival was made possible by the development of an elaborate social economy that did not

[30] Ornati, op. cit., p. 26; Anstey, op. cit., pp. 46–47.

encourage experimentation, and best preserved those who changed least. For the great masses of people margins of survival have been slim, and change and experimentation have involved risks far greater than the visible benefits. The dependence on unyielding custom has been intensified by the large continental area involved, the lack of effective political unification, and the characteristics of an Oriental despotism that rigidly inhibited the roles of private groups. The general tendency in India to view the world as without material opportunity has been the ideological reflection of close observation and conformity to fact. This is the basic complex of attitudes toward opportunity that the mobilized work force initially brings to its industrial employment.

The workers come into the urban industrial environment with a traditional consciousness of scarcity, and this represents a rational adjustment to the environment from which they come. Their traditional attitudes have been strengthened by the failure of opportunity in the rural areas. In addition, they find this traditional sense of scarcity and lack of opportunity relevant to the new environment. Indian industry from its inception has shown no capacity for self-generating and sustained growth. It has lurched forward in sudden bursts, succeeded by relapses into stagnation. The work force has not had a history of sustained growth nor of stability of employment patterns. The growth of the factory labor force has been relatively insignificant, in comparison with the absolute size of the Indian labor force, increasing from 254,000 in 1892 to 2.6 million in 1954.[31] In the absence of great increases of employment opportunity in the villages, there was an increasing tendency for rural folk to press into the urban labor markets. Insecurity of employment and income, especially for the unskilled, has been almost as typical of industry as it has been of other segments of the economy.

This insecurity has kept alive in the industrial environment the traditional sense of scarcity and lack of opportunity. As in the rural environment, once the worker in industry has obtained a job, he seeks to cling to it. He attempts to give it hereditary character, preserving it for his son if possible. This point is also made by Hoselitz in his discussion of the extended family (page 229 infra). Any change of custom in the factory seems to threaten the worker's own hold on the job or his capacity to enhance the hereditary principle. Menaces to these customary social security devices are likely to arouse violent reactions. This feature in part accounts for the rather violent behavior that not infrequently has characterized the Indian industrial work force.

[31] Myers, *op. cit.*, p. 17.

Higher wages will not necessarily reduce these violent reactions. Stability of income is more important than the level of wage rates. Higher wages have frequently been purchased at the cost of jobs. Even when rationalization and higher wages have been coupled with a guarantee that the job of no present worker will be terminated, there has been opposition based on the implicit violation of the hereditary principle. There must be no curtailment of job opportunities for sons and relations on whom will rest the responsibility for the father in his old age. None of this reflects a clinging to special ideological preconceptions; the responses are convincingly congruent with immediate experience and expectation.

The ideological pattern is not as completely monolithic as the discussion has so far suggested. Industrial developments in India, although slow and tentative, have provided some new opportunities during the past century. We therefore find in the work force the development of attitudes at odds with the traditional orientation toward scarcity—attitudes that can be described as oriented toward opportunity. There is a shift from an effort to preserve unchanging work relationships to an acceptance of change and a willingness to attempt to master its possibilities. This consciousness of opportunity is not randomly distributed through the work force. It is least prevalent among unskilled workers and most prevalent among artisans, supervisory groups, and clerical staff. The difference seems to stem from the advancement experienced by members of the latter groups and the promises of advancement they can foresee for the future.

While industrialism generally increases mobility and engenders consciousness of opportunity, in the absence of universal compulsory education in India industrialism has tended to perpetuate traditional social inequalities. The Jamshedpur data show that groups that had the advantages of literacy or skill when the steelworks started have been able to perpetuate their relative advantage. Hindu Brahmans and Kayasthas, Anglo-Indians, and Parsis were among those whose literacy rates were relatively high in India at that time. These groups necessarily furnished the technical, supervisory, and clerical cadres for the new enterprise. Similarly, workers with special craft experience in railway workshops or with skills transferable from the village to industry started with advantages which they were able to maintain. Opportunities for advancement came most easily and frequently to these groups.

The unskilled groups entered the industry's dead-end occupations. With no experience of upward mobility, they see little opportunity for their children and consequently make little effort to educate them even when schools are available. Those with some experience of advancement do sense the importance of education and make greater efforts to see that their children obtain it.

This variation in group attitudes toward opportunity can be seen in another way. As India industrializes, the greatest opportunities for increasing prestige and income are found more and more in mechanical and technical jobs. Clerical posts, the traditional preserve of high-caste Brahmans and Kayasthas, are falling progressively behind in economic and social attractiveness. The Jamshedpur clerical staff, ideally situated to discern the trend and literate enough to understand its meaning, is making every effort to divert its children from clerical to technical training. There seems to be little pride in seeing that the children follow the occupations traditional to the castes from which they come. In fact, considerable pride is taken in the fact that high-caste persons can be flexible in the face of changing conditions. Unskilled workers, on the other hand, to the extent that they have any incentive to better themselves still strive for the formerly prestigious clerical jobs. The groups low in the industrial hierarchy seem to be one or two generations late in their estimates of where prestige and pelf are likely to be found. Ironically, but understandably when access to opportunity is considered, the greatest acceptance of the new order has been and is among those who have done best under the old. Those most reluctant to shed their attachments to the traditional ideology are those who have the least to thank it for and the most to gain by departing from it.

Informal Tradition

As soon as a plant is equipped for operation and the labor force is recruited, its members must develop certain relations set by the character of the machine process and the requirements of the division of labor. The records show no evidence of difficulties in meeting the organizational requirements or establishing new group relations in the factories in the early stages of the Bombay cotton mill industry. Also, one finds only satisfactory reports about the ease with which workers adapted themselves to job requirements during the first decade at Jamshedpur.[32] In both places, within the limits of discipline and efficiency set by the employer, the work force was able to establish the necessary

[32] T. W. Tutwiler, testimony in Indian Industrial Commission, *Minutes of Evidence, 1916–17* (Calcutta: Superintendent of Government Printing of India, 1918), Vol. 2, p. 354.

operational relations to the machine process and to the group. More-over, these formal relations seem to have rapidly become accepted patterns of behavior.

These work group relations also soon proliferated into a complex network of interations that had nothing to do with the formal requirements of factory operation. These new informal relationships had to do with the workers' collective need to control their new environment. Such informal connections may grow more quickly where newly recruited workers already have ties of village, language, or caste, but seem to emerge quickly even where the work force is cosmopolitan and completely new relations have to be forged. Language has not been a substantial bar. Caste seems to have been of limited importance; it is of least consequence where labor has been drawn from many regions because caste relations have operated mainly in the essentially stable village environments. Urban factory relations and tasks that are frequently new make it difficult to maintain the bench marks by which caste has traditionally been defined and enforced.

It is in this context that informal tradition emerges. At the beginning, when the initial work force is recruited, the employer is relatively free to establish work relations as he sees fit. As the force becomes accustomed to the routine of its tasks, it builds up a system of expectations, a sense of what is usual and therefore proper. Once established, new recruits absorb the work group tradition, and changes of routine expectations become difficult. Short of a complete change in personnel, the employer becomes limited in his freedom to manipulate the terms of work.

The development of this informal tradition is obvious at Jamshedpur. One is struck by the extent of the workers' information that is not relevant to the specific work processes in which they are engaged. At all levels there is a constant interchange of information, a sensitivity to new developments and potentialities. There is a systematic informal analysis by work groups of the possible effect of every aspect of the work on the *status quo* of individuals and groups. This occurs among groups in the steel company, also among workers in the several companies in Jamshedpur, and to some vague extent even between workers in Jamshedpur and similar groups elsewhere in the region and the country. Among unskilled workers surprising amounts of information are circulated regarding the objective factors that might affect them.

Not all the information garnered by workers is accurate, of course. Even when the facts are accurate, the meaning is often misinterpreted.

Generally speaking, the higher the work group's level of skill, the more detailed the information and the broader the framework of experience into which it can be fitted. These groups tend to be better able to distinguish between work changes that will substantively affect their status and those that will not. They bitterly oppose the former when they are disadvantageous, but they are not afraid to risk the latter. The unskilled, because of their more limited range of experience, seem to react sharply against all changes, regardless of importance. Here we have one of the differences between work groups that have some consciousness of opportunity and those for whom the orientation toward scarcity is still fundamental. For the latter any change seems risky, carrying implications they are unequipped to analyze or control.

Moreover, the more highly skilled groups tend to act collectively not only against what seem to be adverse decisions by management but also to achieve improvements for themselves. The less skilled seem capable only of defensive action and are less able to act collectively to improve their conditions, partly because they recognize the weak bargaining power they possess in a surplus labor market, and partly because of their limited vision of what can be demanded, i.e., they continue to function with a scarcity mentality.

Significance of Strikes

The tendency for an informal tradition to grow quickly does not mean that work groups immediately become powerful enough to challenge their employer. Nevertheless, strikes seem to be the most important objective evidence of this quickly developing web of custom and cooperation. Commentators have frequently argued that strikes in India have expressed the workers' lack of commitment to the industrial situation. On the contrary, strikes in large-scale Indian industry from its beginning have been an expression of their attachment to the industrial environment rather than an effort to destroy it. Strikes indicate the acceptance of work relationships and are an effort to preserve them. If workers were truly uncommitted and retained their fundamental loyalty to rural life, there would be no strikes, but only frequent flight to the countryside. This has not occurred on any substantial scale.

The records show that as early as 1875, or 20 years after the establishment of the first Bombay cotton mill, there were department-wide strikes in several factories, apparently the result of employers' efforts to modify wage and working conditions. Information for a detailed analysis of this early situation is lacking, but the records for Jamshedpur are more detailed. In 1920, less than a decade after the steel plant started production, a strike shut down the entire operation for one month. The leaders of the strike came from many parts of the country and various departments of the plant. There were Hindu and Sikh fitters from the Punjab, some north Bihar *mistries* (mechanics), some "local men," a few from the United Provinces, and some Anglo-Indians. Although the leaders were skilled workers, money was collected to maintain the unskilled workers during the strike.[33] Although not highly organized, the strike reflected the capacity of informal organization to express itself, spanning provincial and religious lines as well as divisions of skill. The date of this extended strike shows the brief interval needed for the work force to develop a sense of community and a capacity for effective cooperation.

Certain features of these early strikes are worthy of mention. First, they originated within the work force; there is no evidence of "outside" instigation. After 1918, in the larger strikes at least, outsiders did play an important role, directing or at least giving voice to the demands of workers. The appearance of outside middle-class leadership after 1918 is associated with the fact that the National Movement took on the more critical characteristics of a struggle for independence, and the industrial labor force became a political prize of importance. Second, whereas literacy appears to have been a factor in strike leadership in the early period, a more critical element was the level of industrial skill. Skilled workers seem to have been more militant and to have provided the leadership for the less skilled. Generally, clerical groups in industry did not develop a militant attitude until the beginning of World War II, as a consequence of the declining social importance and economic advantages of their occupations. This decline has been manifested in the unequal effects of inflation. Under inflationary circumstances, and where escape is impossible, clerical groups are becoming more prone to collective action of the bellicose sort, once the monopoly of groups more closely connected with the productive process.[34]

THE ROLE OF UNIONS

To what extent has this tradition of informal cooperation, which has grown up in organized industry and has found one expression in

[33] Information taken from daily official reports on the Jamshedpur strike in 1920, prepared by J. C. Scott, Deputy Commissioner, Singhbhum.

[34] Benoy Ghosh, "The Crisis of Bengal Gentility in Calcutta," *Economic Weekly*, 9:821–826 (July 6, 1956).

strikes that require great capacity for endurance, been expressed also in formal and permanent organization for the improvement of working-class life? In other words, to what extent has there been a growth of trade unions?

A glance at statistics of the wage-labor force and trade union membership in India (Table 3) suggests that the latter is a substantial percentage of the former. In March 1954 there were 220,000 workers employed in the Bombay cotton textile mills. The dominant union claimed a membership totaling 22.6 percent of the work force, while all unions in the industry claimed a membership of 40 percent of the workers. The total number of employees at the Tata Iron and Steel Company in March 1954 was 39,500, and the local union claimed a membership totaling 53 percent of the labor force.[35]

TABLE 3. TRADE UNION MEMBERSHIP AND EMPLOYMENT IN MAJOR
INDIAN INDUSTRIES, 1953 *

Industry	Union members	Average no. of daily employees	Percent unionized
	In thousands		
Railways	370	930	40
Cotton textiles	310	660	47
Plantations	160	1,230	13
Food, beverages, tobacco	150	430	35
Coal mining	90	340	26
Jute textiles	86	270	32
Posts and telegraphs	64	240	27
Iron and steel	45	75	60
Chemical products	38	77	49
Wholesale and retail trade	34	960	4
Banking and insurance	28	150	19
Printing and publishing	27	67	40

* Source: Charles A. Myers, *Labor Problems in the Industrialization of India* (Cambridge: Harvard University Press, 1958), p. 70. By permission.

Union Weakness

But whatever the records show, virtually all who are connected with the union movement in India or who have studied it agree that trade

[35] *Bombay Labour Gazette*, 33:1318 (August 1954); *The Indian Labour Year Book 1953–54* (Delhi: Manager of Publications, 1955), pp. 383, 386–387; and Tata Iron and Steel Company Labor Bureau files

unions there are very weak. Whether we measure strength by capacity to achieve wage and welfare gains via collective bargaining, by ability to maintain effective control of plant working conditions, or ability to discipline members into acceptance of decisions made between union leaders and employers, the union as an institution so far has failed to function adequately. The strong informal relationship among industrial workers has not found effective expression in formal organization.[36] To some extent, the weakness of the trade union has been glossed over by the proclivity of scholars to concentrate on the organizational and ideological maneuvers of national federations, although these do not reflect the realities of the local trade union situation.[37]

Analysis of the limited development of trade unions in India has been inadequate. The differences between unions there and in the United States and Great Britain have been attributed to illiteracy, poverty, rural attachments, and linguistic differences. The character of the labor force and its psychology have been assumed to explain the slowness and feebleness of the unions' development. It has generally been implied that there is an ideal type of union development from which all deviation represents a "distortion." Within certain limits this judgment has validity. Modern industry and its concomitant, an industrial labor force, inevitably give rise to a capacity for collective action and a search for some formal expression thereof. But comparative analysis need not be inflexible. It must be recognized that Indian industrial development is proceeding at a different pace and in a different domestic and international environment than existed during the callow stages of Western industrial development, although similar general responses may be expected. It is unlikely that Indian unions at this phase of the nation's economic development would have the current outlook and character of unions in the developed Anglo-Saxon economies.

In terms of stages, India at the time of gaining her independence was at a level of industrial development somewhat comparable to Great Britain in 1820 and the United States in 1850. In neither country were unions stable or effective then. The same elements used to explain the

[36] On the failure of unions to make wage and welfare gains without the aid of government action, see M. D. Morris, "Labor Discipline, Trade Unions, and the State in India," *Journal of Political Economy*, 63:293–308 (August 1955); on the inability of unions to establish effective relations in the plant, Van Dusen Kennedy, "The Role of the Union in the Plant in India," in Industrial Relations Research Association, *Proceedings of the Eighth Annual Meeting* (Publication No. 16, 1956), pp. 249–264.

[37] Ornati, *op. cit.*

weakness of Western unions in the first half of the nineteenth century can be used to explain the feebleness of the Indian unions to the first half of the twentieth century. If the beginnings of modern industrialism can be set at about 1780 in England and at about 1830 in the United States, modern unionism began to be effective in both countries only after a half century of struggle and experimentation, and then only in the craft unions. Efforts to create industrial unions were not successful in either of the "model" countries for more than a century. If this "stage theory" of historical development is used, one can say that Indian union growth, by comparison with "normal" developments in the West, is on time or perhaps even ahead of schedule.

This statement, however, does not tell us anything about specific features that can inhibit the translation of informal collective action into formal organization. What characteristics have inhibited the development of formal union structure?

It has frequently been observed that Indian society lacks any voluntarist tradition of group self-help on a nonparochial basis. This lack, it is argued, has meant that collective action was extremely unlikely to develop on a formal basis. It is true that until slightly more than a century ago there had been little experience transcending family or subcaste bounds, but this was essentially because of lack of opportunity. Nevertheless, the Indian village is itself an expression of the capacity for collaborative endeavor, and the expeditious manifestation of the informal tradition in modern industry throws doubt on the observation. At least one observer had similar doubts half a century ago:

I will even venture to make a prediction which may appear extravagant to those who cannot easily imagine the growth of new forces. The Indian people possess, as the caste system proves, a marvelous power of acting in groups, where they are held together by the class sentiment due to employment in the same occupation. This is just the condition needed for the development of trade unions. I have no doubt that as soon as a distinct factory population has been evolved in this land—a process which has already begun—there will arise trade unions of peculiar tenacity and strength.[38]

Whatever else may be involved, the critical feature is the learning through experience of the techniques by which trade unions are organized and perpetuated. This is a task that baffled British and American organizers for decades. In India the problem is made manifestly more

[38] H. B. Lees-Smith, *Studies in Indian Economy* (London: Constable and Co., 1909), p. 11. By permission.

difficult by one special feature of industrial development suggested by Singer (Chapter 14 infra). In the West, unions developed first along craft lines; the administrative techniques were transferred to the industrial unions at a later stage. In India, by contrast, industrial development has not lent itself to craft forms of organization. Borrowing directly from the West, modern industry has tended to be large-scale right from its inception. The logical form of union organization in such an environment of primarily unskilled and semiskilled workers was inevitably industrial in character. If it took British and American workers a century to solve the administrative problems of sustaining industrial unions, it may be that this *expertise* will take almost as long to develop in India.

Political Orientation of Unions, and Influence of the State

Observers have emphasized the political orientation evident both at the national federation level and that of the local union. This is partly explained by the simultaneous emergence of working group action on a widespread basis and the national movement for independence. No group, whatever its character, could keep clear of the most important issue of the period. Moreover, individual unions frequently obtained leadership, financing, and tactical direction from sources with political objectives. But while the national federations were almost entirely occupied with political maneuverings, in the concerns of individual unions the political stresses as a rule merely gave color to fundamental industrial grievances. There is evidence that leaders in local unions have been forced in recent years to reduce the degree of attachment to objectives of national political parties. Too much should not be made of this development, however, for certain characteristics inherent in the industrial union strengthen the tendency toward political involvement.

When British and American unions were predominantly craft unions, involvement in politics was kept at a minimum because craft unions were financially and organizationally powerful enough to finance most of their own social welfare requirements. But when industrial unions organized the lower paid and less skilled workers, those workers were not able to provide the benefits made available by craft unions. Industrial unions quickly recognized that these benefits could be obtained for their members only through state action. Consequently, in Great Britain and America the emergence of industrial unions was marked by increasing pressure on the state for social welfare benefits. Indian unions, inevitably industrial in form, similarly possess a strong bias toward political action that will not disappear because of the triumph of the independence movement.

By the time Indian industrialization began in the 1850's, relatively late by comparison with the West, the social impact of industrialization in the West had already evoked a strong humanitarian response that was being expressed in industrial welfare regulations. For reasons too complex to explore here, the liberal humanitarian tradition of the West was transported to India more quickly than were the industrial institutions that gave it rise. This social welfare bias has become stronger with national independence. An elaborate industrial welfare code has been laid down largely in advance of strong efforts by the working class. The legal devices that were set up and their humanistic bias have tended, paradoxically, to make the organization, management, and growth of virile, self-administering trade unions more difficult than in the West.

Two other features are likely to differentiate the formal expression of the informal tradition of cooperation among workers in India and in the West. The decision to develop the Indian economy along planned lines has reduced the state's willingness to permit sharp and free conflicts between workers and their employers. A planned economy cannot afford such luxuries. In addition, the concentration of industrial workers with a strong sense of collective loyalty in relatively circumscribed geographical areas makes them a political prize of great importance and a political menace of great potentiality. Guided by its concern for political stability, the state is attempting to minimize the disruption that voluntary collective bargaining might cause, by itself assuming responsibility for the main wage and welfare decisions in the economy.[39]

SUMMARY

Historical evidence indicates that the transformation of a rural, traditionally organized population into a committed industrial labor force has not been socially difficult in India. The desperate poverty of the countryside made available a large labor supply that was eager to move into industry as opportunity appeared. Once employed in the factories, the workers on the whole rather readily adjusted to the disciplinary requirements of mechanized industry. Early in the history of the steel company at Jamshedpur an intensely committed labor force emerged.

[39] Morris, "Labor Discipline, Trade Unions, and the State in India," *op. cit.*, pp. 302–308; Myers, *op. cit.*, pp. 139 ff.

In Bombay, although the evidence is somewhat less conclusive, commitment to industrial employment was not difficult to achieve. Neither the multiplicity of languages nor the institution of caste seriously affected employers' ability to obtain a labor force committed to the factory system.

The labor force brought into industry certain ideological preconceptions typical of the scarcity-ridden countryside. The transplanting of the scarcity orientation into industry can be seen in the efforts by workers to freeze industrial employment relationships into a quasi-hereditary system reminiscent of the village systems. These attitudes have been perpetuated by the instability and insignificant growth of industrial employment opportunities during the past century. But the very effort of workers to stabilize work relations, to give them a traditional character, is in itself strong evidence of commitment.

Despite the varied regional and social origins of the textile workers of Bombay and the steel workers of Jamshedpur, there were strikes early in the history of both industries. These strikes revealed the workers' capacity quickly to create informal group relationships, but are themselves evidence of commitment to industrial employment. Whereas strikes and the informal tradition of cooperation among workers came early, its formal expression in trade unions came much later. However, at the time of independence in 1947, Indian unions were ineffectual, as yet incapable of solving the particular administrative problems that beset all industrial unions. Since 1947 strong, independent union growth has been inhibited, perhaps permanently, by the increasing importance of the state in economic matters. Economic development in India is coming too late and under too great political pressure to permit the recapitulation of British and American trade union history.

The growth of an industrial system depends not only on the commitment of workers to factory employment but ultimately on their flexible acceptance of continually changing work requirements. Here, it is important to recognize that consciousness of scarcity has not been a ubiquitous feature of the Indian industrial labor force. Among those groups whose jobs provided prestige and experience with advancement, the sense of scarcity was quickly supplanted by consciousness of opportunity. It is quite clear that the development of a disciplined industrial labor force, flexible as well as committed, depends not on the psychology of the rural population from which the workers come, but on the rate of expansion of industrial employment opportunities.

11 CHANGING DEMAND AND CONSUMPTION

Richard H. Holton

The literature on the economic development of low income countries offers surprisingly little comment on the role of consumption expenditures in the process of commitment of the labor force. In the aggregate these expenditures have been examined at considerable length, generally as a by-product of the discussion of capital formation, but their *composition* has been grossly neglected. This paper indicates that the composition of consumption expenditures may have much more to do with the development process than has yet been recognized.

The consumption of specific goods has frequently been discussed, for invariably the development plans for an economy include some consideration of the local demand for various goods that might be produced locally. Peripheral comments about the small size of the local market, the possibility that consumers have a preference for imported goods, etc. are generally injected; but no one appears to have projected beyond the immediate future the pattern of consumers' wants in developing areas. Such projections would seem to be worth while since these wants will influence not only the degree of commitment but also the structure of production, foreign trade, and employment distribution in the country.

Just what factors determine the percentage of income that a community will spend on the various categories of goods and services? The relative prices of goods and the level and distribution of income come to mind immediately. The influence of the age distribution of the population and that of the degree of urbanization are also generally recognized. Of particular relevance for the argument of this paper, however, are the effects of three other factors, namely, the extent of contact with other societies, the cultural background of the population, and the nature of the goods and services that are available. In today's awakening countries these last three factors are vastly different than they were in the wealthy countries before they became so wealthy. If these three factors are of real consequence, the allocation of consumption expenditures among various goods and services in the newly developing areas will surely not parallel that in the industrialized countries. We must look, then, for the differences in the nature of economic development that may follow as a consequence.

The process of commitment of the labor force to industrialization is likely to give rise to a pattern of consumption that is in some measure inconsistent with industrialization. The development process may be characterized by expansion of the primary and tertiary sectors of the economy, while the growth of the manufacturing sector is retarded by, among other forces, the limited demand for locally manufactured goods as compared with services and imported goods. Public policy can be designed to alter what many would call this "unbalanced" development; but, in the absence of an appropriate public policy, manufacturing may be discouraged and tertiary production encouraged by the process of commitment more than has been generally recognized. A stunted manufacturing sector in an area with a low but rising per capita income may be not only common but readily explainable. This does not mean that in the typical case there is little or no development of manufacturing, but that relative to the rest of the economy the manufacturing sector may remain quite small simply because of the pattern of consumption expenditures.

There are countless reasons why the manufacturing sector of a developing economy grows very slowly. Among these is the famously high marginal propensity to consume, which leaves little income for capital formation. The impact of this level of aggregate consumption expenditures is well-known; but their composition quite independently of their *level* may also do much to discourage domestic manufacturing.

The rationale of this argument, shorn of details and of some important qualifications, can be shown in a simplified model. Suppose that the industrialization of a country begins with some raw material processing industries employing previously idle members of the society, who are drawn from both urban and rural areas. The slightly greater degree of urbanization and the slightly higher incomes lead to some imitative consumption, i.e., the living standards and consumption patterns of higher income countries are copied to some extent. This means that the developing area is consuming more durables and more services per capita than did the high income countries when their income per capita was at a comparable level. The high income countries have such a comparative advantage in the production of the durables that the developing area will choose to import them for reasons of economy as well as prestige. Services, on the other hand, must be produced at the point of consumption, so they are produced in the developing country. Consequently its pattern of demand will lead to the production of more services and fewer manufactured goods than was the case in the presently industrialized countries.

In this process two forces are especially powerful in shaping consumption. First, the awareness of higher living standards elsewhere causes a certain amount of what has been called "imitative consumption." [1] This awareness makes for a high marginal propensity to consume—the demonstration effect operates across international boundaries, as suggested by Nurkse [2]—and causes the low income countries to want specific goods and services. Thus imitative consumption involves more than the demonstration effect. Imitative consumption can appear without a change in income, whereas the demonstration effect, strictly defined, is limited to the effect of changes in income.

The second major force in changing consumption patterns is urbanization; it shapes consumption in two ways. Urbanization can help bring about imitative consumption since the immigrant to the city learns of the consumption standards of other countries as well as his own. But some changes in consumption would be expected even in the absence of imitative consumption, or of an increase in income, merely because urban living is a different way of life.

The effect of population growth, changes in the age distribution, and changes in the distribution of income are largely ignored in this paper. These factors certainly affect consumption expenditures, but it is more rewarding to emphasize the effect of changing preferences at the level of the individual consumer.

EXPANSION OF WANTS VIA CULTURAL CONTACT

The "theory of want development" is in an embryonic stage and enables us to say very little of a positive nature about the path that such development is likely to take as all the changes associated with economic development occur.[3] The many case studies of acculturation and cultural change apparently have not substantially improved our ability to

---

[1] Norman S. Buchanan and Howard S. Ellis, *Approaches to Economic Development* (New York: Twentieth Century Fund, 1955), p. 385.

[2] Ragnar Nurkse, *Problems of Capital Formation in Underdeveloped Countries* (Oxford: Basil Blackwell, 1953), Chapter 3.

[3] See Elizabeth E. Hoyt, "Want Development in Underdeveloped Areas," *Journal of Political Economy*, 59:194–202 (June 1951). Apparently Ralph Linton would not agree. He has said that "if we know what a society's culture is . . . we can predict

predict whether a want for a specific good will develop in a society. Thanks to these studies we are familiar with the proposition that a want will develop only if it is consistent with the culture of the society in question,[4] but this is a necessary rather than a sufficient condition. The fabled difficulty of selling iceboxes to the Eskimos had been recognized long before the anthropologists became seriously interested in "culture contact." There is, however, still great uncertainty about what one *can* sell to the Eskimos. Most of the knowledge of want development seems to be of this negative sort, i.e., one can predict what will not be wanted more easily than what will be wanted.

Wants for specific goods and services will develop only if they have some favorable association. The African has identified the United States and the Western European nations as the economically and politically powerful countries and so wants to copy our material standard of living.[5] Thus, cultural contact between the European and the African tribesmen results in the adoption by the latter of certain aspects of European culture but not vice versa. The African frequently wins some prestige among his fellows by this transfer, but the European would lose status in his society if he were to "go native."

It is difficult to proceed beyond these broad principles to discern just what goods will and what goods will not be taken up by a group of consumers not previously exposed to them. Goods may be desired in a community either because of some simple curiosity or because they provide some specific advantage. The advantage may be nothing more than the prestige associated with ownership, or it may be a functional one.[6] At least some items of Western clothing, for example, are adopted only for prestige reasons, while pots and pans and firearms are clearly

---

with a fairly high degree of probability whether the bulk of its members will welcome or assist a particular innovation."—"Cultural and Personality Factors Affecting Economic Growth," in Bert F. Hoselitz, ed., *The Progress of Underdeveloped Areas* (Chicago: University of Chicago Press, 1952), p. 74. But Linton seems to be in a minority. See Edward M. Bruner, "Cultural Transmission and Cultural Change," *Southwestern Journal of Anthropology*, 12:191 (Summer 1956); and Melville J. Herskovits, "The African Cultural Background in the Modern Scene," in C. Grove Haines, ed., *Africa Today* (Baltimore: Johns Hopkins University Press, 1955), p. 39.

[4] See Hoyt, *op. cit.*, pp. 195 ff.; Ralph Linton, "Acculturation and the Processes of Culture Change," in *Acculturation in Seven American Indian Tribes* (New York: Appleton-Century Company, 1940), pp. 466 ff.; and Herskovits, *op. cit.*, p. 40.

[5] W. A. Lewis, "The Economic Development of Africa," in Calvin W. Stillman, ed., *Africa in the Modern World* (Chicago: University of Chicago Press, 1955), p. 98.

[6] Linton, "Acculturation and the Processes of Culture Change," *ibid.*, and Herskovits, *ibid.*

superior in performance to the indigenous equipment. Yet functional advantage by no means assures adoption. Herskovits has reported that the natives of southern Mozambique accepted the plow while other Africans did not, even though draft animals were available.[7]

Meager though our knowledge of the development of wants may be, observations of cultural change permit us to draw at least three fairly significant conclusions as to the transmission of consumption patterns to low income countries. First, it is clear that imitative consumption will be practiced most by the industrial labor force, since industrialization, to the extent that it is associated with urbanization, leads to more frequent and intense contact with higher standards of living.[8] Second, the goods and services bought with the new income may be desired less for their functional value than for the prestige associated with them. Perhaps the most important conclusion that can be drawn from our knowledge of acculturation is that imitative consumption can be self-reinforcing. If a community takes on some elements of the consumption pattern of a more affluent culture, it will probably be easier to adopt additional elements of that pattern. In other words, acculturation apparently proceeds more rapidly as the differences between the two cultures are narrowed. One can expect to find, then, that the consumption standards of the committed labor force in newly developing areas may change at an accelerating pace, even though the rate of increase in income and the degree of "culture contact" remain stable.[9]

COMPOSITION OF CONSUMPTION EXPENDITURES

Food

Food consumption may be altered by the industrialization process in several ways. The economist looks at once for the effect of the increase in income that presumably is associated with industrialization. Houthakker has recently computed the expenditure elasticity of demand for food from various budget studies; he found expenditure elasticities ranging from .344 to .731, thus supporting Engel's Law.[10] We expect

[7] Herskovits, *ibid.*, p. 39.

[8] See Ralph Linton, *The Study of Man* (New York: D. Appleton-Century Company, 1936), p. 328.

[9] Yet occasionally cultural contact with a higher income community may not affect the consumption pattern. See Sol Tax, "Changing Consumption in Indian Guatemala," *Economic Development and Cultural Change*, 5:147–158 (January 1957).

[10] H. S. Houthakker, "An International Comparison of Household Expenditure Patterns, Commemorating the Centenary of Engel's Law," *Econometrica*, 25:532–551 (October 1957).

the increase in food expenditures to be less than proportional to the increase in income; history leads us to anticipate also a shift away from the cereals producing energy and toward the protective foods, such as meat, vegetables, fruit, and fish.[11] Expenditure or income elasticity estimates are not particularly illuminating in the context of industrialization, however, since so many determinants of consumption other than income are also changing. It is entirely possible that these other determinants are more important than the change in income. For example, urbanization in at least one instance was associated with an increase in the demand for meat products in spite of a fall in real income.[12] Diets may be altered even in the absence of income change, as imitative consumption shifts expenditures toward prestigeful foods, including processed or other foods that are less nutritious than those in the original diet.[13]

A study in Puerto Rico provides a few pertinent insights because it distinguishes between the urban and the rural worker.[14] However, since families are classified by money income rather than by real income (money income plus income in kind), it is not possible to identify corresponding rural and urban real-income groups. Nevertheless, at least one set of comparisons is illuminating. In urban families earning less than $500 annually, each member consumed 40 percent more milk, about 50 percent more fat, 12 percent more rice, and slightly more codfish (the main protein source) than did the rural families in the same income class.[15] Since the urban families were probably earning less than their rural counterparts in terms of real income, this may be a case of urbanization associated with increased food consumption.

The effect of urbanization on consumers' tastes may be reflected, too, in the difference between urban and rural attitudes toward imported

[11] P. K. Chang, *Agriculture and Industrialization* (Cambridge: Harvard University Press, 1949), Chapter 2; W. S. and E. S. Woytinsky, *World Population and Production* (New York: Twentieth Century Fund, 1953), pp. 297–306.

[12] Naum Jasny, *The Socialized Agriculture of the U.S.S.R.* (Stanford: Stanford University Press, 1949), pp. 91–92, 98–99.

[13] Margaret Mead, ed., *Cultural Patterns and Technical Change* (Paris: UNESCO, 1953), p. 260.

[14] Lydia J. Roberts and Rosa Luisa Stefani, *Patterns of Living in Puerto Rican Families* (Rio Piedras: University of Puerto Rico, 1949); the recent *Survey of Ceylon's Consumer Finances* (Colombo: Central Bank of Ceylon, 1954) distinguishes between estate and nonestate sectors, but these are not synonymous with rural and urban sectors.

[15] Roberts and Stefani, *op. cit.*, pp. 357, 366, 368, and 386.

canned fruits. These fruits were preferred over native fruits by 81 percent of the urban families but by only 63 percent of the rural families.[16] This difference held for all income groups. Such a difference in preferences probably cannot be completely explained by differences in relative prices in the rural and urban markets. Exposure to higher living standards, to more advertising, and to more accessible retail stocks of the imported fruits must be part of the cause. The effect of this change of preference is of course a decline in the demand for domestic agricultural produce. The imitative consumption which may characterize urbanization can be brought about by what must be called imitative production—local manufacturers or processors may also imitate.

The domestic demand for locally produced foodstuffs might be reduced with urbanization not only because of the insertion of processing margins and the shift toward imported foods, but because of a reduction in the money income available for food. Typically the urban migrant must pay much more for housing than he had to pay in the country. So it is possible for a worker to go to the city for a higher money wage that leaves him with less income, after he pays for housing. This puts pressure on his food expenditures.

All this points to the possibility that urbanization may require quite a substantial increase in the migrating workers' incomes if a depressing effect on the agricultural sector is to be avoided. But another pressure operates in this direction; industrialization with its consequent centralization of population requires more elaborate marketing channels for that portion of agricultural output consumed domestically as food. The impact of this can be substantial. Suppose the distributive margin is 33 percent of the farm value of the food item.[17] If a wage earner moves to the city and buys in the store the same products he once bought directly from the farm, he must spend one third more. The food expenditures of such workers must rise by at least one third as they move to the city unless the demand curve is to shift (ignore for the moment possible change in preferences caused by urbanization).

Population growth and the increase in incomes may be sufficient in any given case to affect the forces outlined here, but the problem of the

[16] *Ibid.*, p. 383.

[17] Margins of this size are probably not unrealistic. See K. C. Abercrombie, "Marketing Margins for Foodstuffs," *Monthly Bulletin of Agricultural Economics and Statistics*, 3:1–8 (November 1, 1954); and John K. Galbraith and Richard H. Holton, *Marketing Efficiency in Puerto Rico* (Cambridge: Harvard University Press, 1955), especially Chapters 3–4.

marketing margins may be especially significant. Perhaps this underlies the observation by the Economic Commission for Latin America that urbanization and the shift of manpower out of agriculture were "not accompanied by appropriate improvements in the standard of living of the greater part of the population, both rural and urban, and to a considerable extent produced merely a redistribution of incomes." [18] This result occurred in the face of a ratio of gross product per capita in the nonagricultural population to gross product per capita in the agricultural population of 3.6.[19]

The urbanization movement increases the size of the marketing sector relative to the rest of the economy. Although there may be an ample labor supply for industrialization, the capital syphoned off into trade is foreclosed from aiding industrialization; and trade is favored as an investment since it provides liquidity, quick turnover, and minimum risk.[20] Thus urbanization may retard the commitment of the labor force to industrialization in the sense that urbanization brings about certain employment opportunities that compete with the manufacturing sector for both labor and capital. However, the imitative consumption of food products creates opportunities for investment in the food processing industries. In underdeveloped countries those industries are usually among the simplest to establish. Urbanization, the extension of the marketing sector, and imitative consumption all encourage such industrialization.

Clothing

Imitative consumption generally operates to alter the demand for clothing very early in a period of "culture contact." Industrialization and urbanization seem merely to accelerate this change in consumption.[21] But changes in style of dress would seem to have only limited effects on industry and agriculture. The greater effect lies in the shift in demand toward the synthetic fibers that have been developed in the high income countries. So far, only rayon seems to have been of any sig-

---

[18] Economic Bulletin for Latin America, 2:18 (February 1957).

[19] Ibid., p. 28.

[20] See Henry G. Aubrey, "Investment Decisions in Underdeveloped Countries," in National Bureau of Economic Research, Universities – National Bureau Committee for Economic Research, Capital Formation and Economic Growth (Princeton: Princeton University Press, 1955), p. 409.

[21] Pandharinath Prabhu, "Social Effects of Urbanization on Industrial Workers in Bombay," Sociological Bulletin, 6:14–33 (March 1957); and Audrey I. Richards, Land, Labor and Diet in Northern Rhodesia (London: Oxford University Press, 1939), p. 216.

nificance in this regard. The fact that rayon looks like silk and lends itself to bright colors recommends its use in several low income societies. The results of this diffusion of consumers' taste from the developed to the developing countries are to depress the demand for the natural fibers, to insert greater processing charges between the producer of raw material and the consumer, and to encourage imports. This change in demand presents an opportunity for investment since the cellulose base for rayon can be derived from ubiquitous materials, but it must be remembered that consumers' preferences for rayon can cross international boundaries with far greater ease than can the techniques for producing rayon.

The demand for shoes, which is commonly identified with urbanization, has a happier result than does the demand for rayon. Shoe manufacturing is relatively simple to establish and the raw materials involved are seldom a problem. In this instance urbanization because of its effect on demand is an unmistakable catalyst in the industrialization process.

The Westernization of clothing apparently leads to a related demand for services, e.g., shoe repairing and tailoring, and thus provides some additional employment opportunities.[22] These may facilitate industrialization by expanding the supply of experienced craftsmen.

Durable Goods

It is particularly intriguing to trace the consequences of urbanization and imitative consumption as they operate on the demand for durable goods. One can exaggerate the difficulties that these demands may cause, since so few people are likely to have incomes large enough to afford durables. Yet to the extent that economic development succeeds in raising incomes, a demand for durables is likely to arise. Even in the early stages of cultural contact with higher income societies, imported kitchen utensils, for example, are substituted for those formerly made in the home.[23]

Consumers' durables were developed in the high income countries in part to permit the substitution of capital for labor. The automobile reduced the time and effort involved in personal travel; the washing machine reduced the drudgery in laundering; and the modern stove required less tending. These were not, of course, the *only* reasons for

[22] Richards, *ibid.*
[23] See Margaret Mead, "Native Standards of Living and African Culture Change," *Africa,* 11(Supplement):21–24 (1938).

development of these durables. The radio seems to have no labor-saving feature whatsoever. Certainly in the case of the refrigerator and the automobile, one objective was to produce a *better* service as well as one requiring less labor input. But economizing the consumer's labor seems to have been at least a prominent causal factor in the development of such products. Their adoption, then, was motivated in part by the chronic labor shortage and the adequate supply of consumers' capital in the countries of origin.

Now the low income countries, through contact with those with high income, may acquire preferences for these durables. But these preferences will be selective; the durables that perform a new service, such as radios and television sets, will be adopted much more readily than those that are essentially labor saving. Why buy a washing machine or vacuum cleaner when domestic help is so cheap? In a society in which physical labor and especially housework are identified with the lower classes, buying a vacuum cleaner implies that one is doing one's own cleaning. The radio, the refrigerator, and the automobile provide the preferred new services, and also bring a certain amount of prestige to the owner.

We are familiar with the point that the underdeveloped areas enjoy an advantage in their prospects for development because the latest production techniques of the high income countries can be taken over; the developing countries are spared the cost of innovation and need only imitate.[24] Similarly it is easy for a low income country to adopt the consumers' durables of the high income countries. Again they need only imitate. In some instances the introduction of durables is accelerated, because secondhand models can be brought in from the high income countries at prices below the cost of new models. So the demand for durables in a low income country is likely to be greater than its stage of development would seem to warrant. The cost of development of durables is borne by other countries; the secondhand market may provide an element of subsidized consumption; and the durable goods may bring prestige to the owners.

This demand for durable goods has some serious repercussions that

[24] This is true even though the difficulties of transferring technology are manifold. See Samuel P. Hayes, Jr., "Personality and Culture Problems of Point IV," in Bert F. Hoselitz, ed., *The Progress of Underdeveloped Areas* (Chicago: University of Chicago Press, 1952), pp. 203–229; and Yale Brozen, "Entrepreneurship and Technical Change," in H. F. Williamson and John A. Buttrick, eds., *Economic Development: Principles and Patterns* (New York: Prentice-Hall, 1954), pp. 196–236.

affect the prospects for development in several ways and to various degrees. Difficulties in foreign exchange are likely to arise, since the durables are commonly produced abroad rather than domestically. Even more serious repercussions are likely to be felt because of all the related goods and services that are introduced with the durable goods. It is the impact of the related demand that must be stressed. Suppose that there is a demonstrated demand for refrigerators among the workers and entrepreneurs whose incomes have increased because of industrialization. The stores established to sell refrigerators are likely to offer radios and other appliances as well, thus stimulating demand for appliances. To the extent that increases in income are used to buy durables, the demand for other goods and services is less than it would otherwise be unless the rate of saving bears the impact. The mere existence of durables may cause the income elasticity for agricultural commodities and other domestically produced goods to be lower than would otherwise be the case. It seems entirely possible that imitative consumption, working within the community, might cause demand to shift toward imported durables even among families whose incomes do not increase.

One of the more distressing repercussions of the introduction of durables involves the allocation of the country's capital. The distribution of these durables must be financed; thus scarce capital is attracted into trade. But the resulting installment credit may have even greater impact. The very high interest rates on such investments make it especially appealing for capital, some of which might otherwise be enticed into the industrialization program. Managerial talent is also drawn into the distribution and financing of the durables; thus the talent available for manufacturing is reduced, and the commitment of the managerial labor force to industrialization is retarded.

There is likely to be a related demand for other goods and services as well. More widespread ownership of refrigerators may affect patterns of food consumption. Once radios are owned, the effectiveness of advertising is enhanced and consumption patterns are presumably altered accordingly. The spread of television to the major cities in low income countries will have a similar effect; importers are likely to reap the major benefit from the new advertising media. They are better supplied with working capital to finance advertising than are the struggling domestic manufacturers, and are likely to be more sophisticated advertisers because of their contacts with the exporting countries. Phonographs generate a demand for records, especially with the music-loving

Latin Americans. The demand for automobiles creates a demand for roads, service stations and garages, and gasoline and oil. The purchase of these related goods may involve the expenditure of foreign exchange funds or create an outlet for the investment of local funds. The trade and services sector of the low income economy may develop considerably faster and may absorb more capital than would have been the case if the economy had not had the opportunity of adopting the consumption standards of the higher income countries.

At least two results of the demand for consumers' durables are beneficial to the local economy. First, because the durable goods require servicing, a body of service mechanics is developed. This small pool of skilled workers is desirable both because they are more readily committed to industrialization and because their existence stimulates others to acquire the same skills. The mechanic is accorded considerable prestige in the industrializing community. The demand for skilled mechanics in the servicing of durables, however, creates a market outside manufacturing for skilled talent, so some of the "committed" labor force may flow into the services sector of the economy. Second, to the extent that consumers' durables epitomize the higher standards of living to which the members of the work force aspire, they are motivated in the direction of the industrialization program. Want development is in part a function of what is available, and the availability of goods creates wants. Furthermore, installment credit in a low income community is probably an excellent disciplinarian. If the worker realizes that absence from work next week means repossession of his radio, he is likely to appear for work. To a considerable extent then, the existence of durables tends to aid commitment of the labor force to industrialization and to "maintain" commitment in the sense in which Feldman and Moore use the term.

In summary, the availability of durables may operate to raise the demand for imports, to depress the demand for domestically produced goods, and to attract labor and capital into the trade and services sector. On the other hand, the existence of these goods on the market may stimulate greater productivity, improve industrial discipline, and hence accelerate commitment of the labor force to industrialization.

Leisure

Imitative consumption may be associated with the demand for leisure. The industrialization of underdeveloped countries does not now involve the 12-, 14-, and 16-hour working days of early industrial development in England and the United States. Although the 40-hour week may not be the rule in the plants of developing countries, the length of their work weeks is tempered by the frequency of the 40-hour week in the United States.

Just as the demand for durable goods introduces a complex of demands for related goods and services, so the demand for leisure involves a concomitant demand for the goods and services one might buy to enjoy leisure. These, like the durables, may be borrowed from the high income countries. India's moving picture industry is an outgrowth of this kind of demand. Also, if foreign movies are in demand, foreign exchange difficulties are accentuated. Foreign movies themselves are of course very effective means of demonstrating to other countries the living standards of high income countries or of people with high incomes in low income countries. In some instances leisure time has resulted in notable increases in gambling, drinking, and prostitution, suggesting that new goods *should* be introduced so that workers might have available more beneficial uses for their increasing incomes.[25] The demand for some durables can be traced in part to leisure; the ubiquitous jukebox in Latin America is an illustration. Similarly, the demand for transportation (and the derived demand for equipment and facilities) is in part a function of available leisure time. The possible magnitude of all these expenditures is indicated by a recent study of Indians in Bombay who had migrated from rural areas. These Indians reported that movies, radio, games, athletics, and dramatics are their main diversions and that one seventh of their income was spent on these items.[26] This figure may be an exaggeration, but is impressive even if discounted heavily.

Government Services

If we consider government expenditures for social services as consumption in the sense that such outlays are for *community* consumption, then imitative consumption is common. The awakening countries are aware of the welfare programs of the wealthy countries and have chosen to use part of their own national income to provide public health and education, old age benefits, luxurious public buildings, modern boulevards, subsidized housing, and so on. Government expenditures therefore command a larger share of the gross national product than would be the case if economic development were to

[25] Hoyt, *op. cit.*, p. 200.
[26] Pandharinath Prabhu, *op. cit.*

occur in isolation. A certain amount of imitation not justified on the basis of any analyses of costs and benefits is also found in some government investment projects. The commonly observed urge to have a steel mill is of this sort, although perhaps this should be called imitative production rather than imitative consumption.

Government's role in development is also inflated by consumers' demands for some other goods and services. A demand for radios is a demand for electric power. A demand for automobiles and trucks is a demand for highways. A demand for leisure may generate a demand for public transportation. A demand for better health and longer lives is a demand for insecticides and vaccine programs provided by the government, and so on. So imitative consumption applies to a wide range of goods and services. The introduction of a major consumers' good may lead to a whole complex of changes in consumption patterns just as the establishment of a new industry may lead to a complex of changes in production.

CONCLUSION

The newly developing areas are undergoing industrialization in a world quite different from that in which the high income countries were industrialized. One of many differences lies in the much greater number of ways one can spend one's income. Improved communications have made the world aware of the alternatives. The goods and services that the urban worker in, say, Latin America may know about and aspire to are far more numerous than they were in the wealthy countries when these had the income levels now common in Latin America.

A review of the changing patterns of consumption in developing areas shows that consumption expenditures, especially of the industrial labor force, in such areas cannot be forecast accurately on the basis of historical experience. The use of income reflects not only its level and income elasticities, but also the goods and services available. The chronological order in which specific goods and services were developed and introduced into the high income countries was not the order of diminishing marginal utility. We had automobiles and vacuum cleaners before the Salk vaccine not because we wanted better transportation or easier housecleaning more than we wanted to be rid of poliomyelitis, but because we knew how to produce the automobile and the vacuum cleaner before we knew how to produce the Salk vaccine. The developing areas, then, are certain to have quite a different history of want development.

The preceding discussion has indicated how the range of goods and services now available makes it possible that the service component of higher living standards in the low income areas may be quite large. The demand for government services is likely to be great; there is considerable complementarity between the demand for services, on the one hand, and that for goods and leisure on the other. The demand for services will also be tempered by the location of so many of the low income countries in the tropics or subtropics, where clothing and housing requirements generally call for smaller expenditures.

If a country's production resources are geared to domestic demands, the consumption expenditure pattern will affect the whole fabric of economic growth. To the degree that the expansion of consumption departs from the pattern followed in the now wealthy countries, we can expect departures in the pattern of growth of production and trade. The development of the manufacturing sector may be stunted because the labor force is likely to adopt a set of consumption standards somewhat inconsistent with the industrialization process. Once the process of commitment begins, urbanization and imitative consumption generate demands for imported goods, for certain durables, and for a wide array of services. The agricultural sector may shift production slightly away from subsistence crops and toward cash crops in order to increase money income and to be able to buy more goods in the towns. Foreign clothing is introduced and imported cloth may be substituted for local goods. Durable goods are imported initially at least and give rise to related services. The mere availability of other services may draw additional purchasing power away from locally manufactured goods. Meanwhile the demand for government services may result in a tax program that may limit consumption expenditures for other goods and services. The effects of this type of growth can well be: (1) a large increase in the services sector of the economy, since the production of services is oriented toward the market; (2) a decline in manufacturing if homecrafts are included as such, since the high income countries have a comparative advantage in the production of so many manufactured goods; and (3) a commercialization of agriculture. There is evidence that these have been happening in Latin America.

The Economic Commission for Latin America, reporting on the distribution of the population and work force between 1945 and 1955, noted that with respect to employment structure Latin America was close to Southern Europe, "with the substantial difference that industrial development, instead of preceding the development of services, definitely lags behind." [27] This rapid growth in employment in the services sector is not an accurate index of the relative growth in the demand for services, since output per worker rose much more slowly than in the area as a whole. But the Commission's report concludes that the production of physical goods did not keep pace with the production of services.[28]

We should entertain the possibility that the low income countries will see the growth of their manufacturing sector stunted while domestic resources are concentrated in primary and tertiary production. The pattern of consumers' demand leads to this conclusion, and the forces shaping world trade operate to bring about this result. Primary production, being based on resources, and services, being oriented to the market, will characterize the economy of the low income country. The manufactured goods are likely to be produced by those countries that have the comparative advantage in such goods, namely, the industrialized countries.

Public policy can operate to forestall the unbalanced growth suggested here. Tariffs and quotas on certain durables can limit the demand for the complementary services, for example. Budgetary restrictions might limit government services, and so on. But the pattern of development of demands should be added to the factors that can inhibit industrial development of the low income countries.

[27] "Changes in Employment Structure in Latin America, 1945–1955," *Economic Bulletin for Latin America,* 2:20 (February 1957).

[28] *Ibid.,* p. 41.

12 THE MARKET MATRIX

Bert F. Hoselitz

In a celebrated passage in the *Wealth of Nations,* Adam Smith asserts that one of the universal propensities of mankind is to truck and barter. Although this observation is based on empirical materials drawn mostly from the societies of Western Europe, Smith correctly points out that in societies in which there is some division of labor, some arrangement for the mutual interchange of goods and services must be made, and that the market is the most advanced and efficient form of such an exchange mechanism. On the basis of modern ethnographic and cultural anthropological findings, Smith's proposition would be restated so as not to postulate a universal inherent propensity to truck and barter, but rather to distinguish between systems of distribution that differ between cultures. This view has recently been presented with special emphasis by Polanyi, Arensberg, and associates, who not only stress the fact that market exchange is only one form of exchange, but also that even in systems in which market mechanisms exist, different commodities may be subject to different forms of exchange.[1]

MARKETS AND ECONOMIC DEVELOPMENT

From the generally accepted proposition that the most highly developed and, in some ways, the most efficient means of exchange is a market, there might be derived the further proposition that the general level of a society's economic advancement is associated with the over-all extension of markets and the array of goods and services thus exchanged. Such a proposition seems plausible on the basis of superficial observation of various societies at different levels of economic advancement, and is perhaps strengthened by the fact that even in communist countries, which at first attempted to dispense with markets as instruments of allocation, the market mechanism was adopted progressively as the societies developed more complex forms of production.

If we observe a rather close correlation between the prevalence of market exchange and the level of economic development, a further

[1] Karl Polanyi, Conrad M. Arensberg, and Harry W. Pearson, *Trade and Market in the Early Empires* (Glencoe: Free Press, 1957).

problem is immediately raised as to the mutual causal relation between the two phenomena. Is the development of markets a "cause" or a "result" of economic development? What causal connections may be found in the growth of the institution of markets and the raising of the level of economic performance in general? Adam Smith apparently held that markets are one of the causes of economic advancement, for in the passage cited he seems to suggest that markets develop as a result of the propensity to truck and barter and that they in turn provide an impetus for economic specialization and hence greater productivity of resources. On the other hand, it may be maintained that in the Soviet Union, during the period of the New Economic Policy (NEP), for example, the development of markets was a consequence of the greater diversity and efficiency of production, and that the gradual relaxation of policies of physical allocation under the later Five Year Plans and their replacement by allocation through the market occurred in response to similar trends.

The Two Faces of a Market

We are concerned here with the relationship between market mechanisms of exchange and the level of economic advancement and, in particular, with the role of markets in the commitment of an industrialized labor force. To approach this problem more closely, we must distinguish between the market (1) as a mechanism in the process of allocation of resources and (2) as a social institution. The main feature of the former aspect of markets is their efficiency in transferring goods and services from uses that make lower marginal contributions to productive or consumptive objectives, to uses that make higher contributions. It is in this connection that we speak of the objectivity of the market, and it is from this standpoint that we measure the effectiveness of a market mechanism by associating it with degrees of openness and freedom from obstacles to the smooth allocation of resources among competing uses.

Although analysis of the market mechanism in its purely economic aspect is of paramount importance if we are concerned with allocation of resources, in the study of commitment the institutional facets of a market economy are of much greater significance. We are not concerned primarily with the effectiveness of the market in achieving certain distributive or allocative objectives, but with the role that market exchanges play in the minds of persons using the market. The outward physical appearance of a market is immaterial from the standpoint of its purely economic function, but is very important from that of its institutional role. Who meets whom, under what conditions, in what surroundings, for what kinds of contractual arrangements? These questions appear paramount in the institutional analysis of the market. And even more important, what commodities are customarily traded on the market, and what prohibitions or impediments interfere with the market's mediation of certain exchanges? How universalistic are market criteria, with respect to commodities exchanged and with respect to persons transacting business on a market? Are there goods and services that are not subject to market exchange, and are there certain persons who may not use the market at all, or who may use it only under prescribed conditions and for specific forms of transactions?

Although we concentrate in this paper on the institutional aspects of the market, we do not exclude consideration of the economic criteria of the market mechanism, for even from the institutional standpoint the efficiency of resource allocation and the real or alleged impersonality and objectivity of the market have significance.

MARKETS AND OTHER EXCHANGES

Nonintersecting Exchanges

There exist today, and have existed in the past, many societies in which certain commodities can normally be acquired only through purchase on the market, whereas other goods are normally acquired by free distribution, by membership in an extended family or tribe, or by ceremonial gift or exchange. In fact, in some rather primitive societies men still distinguish between goods that are acquired as a matter of course (i.e., without recognition that any special effort is required for their availability), those that may be acquired only through certain forms of ceremonial exchange, and those that have a price and for which other goods must be traded. These three classes of objects are sometimes conceived as belonging in three tight compartments; the transference of objects designated as "free goods," or "ceremonial goods," to that of "priced goods" is outside the realm of what is possible. In more advanced societies the separation between goods that can be traded and those that cannot be is less sharp; and in certain circumstances commodities that normally are acquired by gift or tribute may become priced goods. For example, commonly consumed foodstuffs, which in many simpler societies are normally regarded as commodities not subject to trade, may be traded in a period of shortage or famine; but such situations are temporary, and the application of market exchange to these commodities ceases as soon as the emergency is over.

In superficial observation of societies in which market exchange exists with other forms of distribution, we usually find that the market is first established for "foreign" or "luxury" goods, rather than for the necessities of life or for labor. By luxury goods we mean commodities that normally do not enter the consumption pattern of the masses, but that are reserved for certain, usually privileged, classes of the population. A system exhibiting these features roughly resembles the form of economic organization and the role of the market in the ancient world and medieval Europe; this form persisted in India until the very recent past and still persists in some isolated regions of that country. Such a system even allows certain social groups or classes or certain localities to specialize in trade. In other words, trading centers like Athens and trading castes like the Banyas in India are quite compatible with a social system in which trade and markets are rigorously restricted to certain commodities or certain kinds of contracts. The important consequence of this situation is that as long as markets remain mechanisms for specialized kinds of exchange, the market as such cannot operate as an instrument of commitment; for, although at some stage in his life every member of a society may come into contact with the market and even procure a substantial part of his subsistence through market exchange, the market always remains a special institution with its own rules. These are quite separate from the more common traditional rules determining a man's social position and economic role in the system.

This relationship is confirmed indirectly by Gregory, Morris, and Holton (Chapters 9, 10, 11 supra). They deal with markets in which the process of commitment is already well under way. In the situations they describe, the labor force has become accustomed to deriving its entire livelihood (or to obtaining its entire income from employment) through exchange contracts typically performed on a market. The workers whom they describe live in a social context in which gaining one's livelihood and obtaining wage employment have become completely subject to intervention of the market.

Polar Types of Exchange

The contrasts that have been discussed so far permit us to postulate a pair of dichotomous ideal types, each representing a system of exchange relations with different degrees of access to markets and of labor commitment to an industrial way of life. These two extreme systems should be understood as genuine ideal types, not found in reality; the real systems lie somewhere on a continuum connecting these two ideal types. Use of this methodological device in our analysis of the role of markets in labor commitment may point up some important problems that are at least suggestive of the connections between markets, especially labor markets and the degree of commitment, and thus indicate strategic factors on which further research should be focused.

To describe these ideal types further, we may say that one extreme is a social system in which the acquisition of one's livelihood—the procurement both of consumption goods and of employment—depends on contracts characteristically made on a market. Thus the markets for such goods and particularly the labor market take on predominant significance. The labor market, through which men are brought together with their work, tends to assume a decisive role in a society that is fully market-oriented. (See Chapter 3 supra.)

At the other extreme is a society in which the procurement of one's livelihood is typically independent of contractual relations that are mediated by a market; other systems of distributing consumers' goods and economic roles mediate between specialists in production. In such societies tasks may be distributed not merely on the basis of professional specialization, but on the basis of age, sex, or membership in particular social subgroups. It is probable that economic roles are distributed on the basis of ascription.

The distinction made in this paper between societies that are market-oriented and those that are not is not identical with either Tönnies' difference between *Gemeinschaft* and *Gesellschaft*,[2] or Maine's difference between societies based on status and on contract.[3] It is not asserted that an over-all classification of social systems is possible, nor is this implied by the dichotomous ideal types. The stress here is on the degree of involvement in the market matrix, particularly with respect to the everyday needs, i.e., procurement of an economic role mediated by a labor market and of one's means of subsistence. A society that is not market-oriented is not necessarily devoid of markets or market-like features or of contractual relations, nor is it necessarily a society without a fairly complex social structure. What markets exist are normally devoted to the exchange of certain specialties characteristically con-

[2] Ferdinand Tönnies, *Fundamental Concepts of Sociology (Gemeinschaft und Gesellschaft)*, trans. by C. P. Loomis (New York: American Book Co., 1940).

[3] Sir Henry Sumner Maine, *Ancient Law*, ed. by Sir Frederick Pollock (New York: Henry Holt and Company, 1906), especially pp. 161–165, 422–425.

sumed by only certain social strata or classes and typically frequented by a specialized personnel. It is for these reasons that the societies of the ancient world, medieval Europe, medieval and early modern India, and imperial China may be counted among the societies that are not market-oriented.

CHANGE OF A SOCIETY TO MARKET ORIENTATION

The problem we wish to study more exhaustively is now brought into sharper focus. How does a society that is not market-oriented become so oriented? And in what way is this process of transformation associated with the process of commitment of an industrial labor force, or rather a wage-earning labor force? The first question may be explored by the historical method, for there are societies in which this transition has taken place. In a sense, the history of European capitalism is a history of this transformation. In view of Polanyi's examination of this process, in *The Great Transformation*,[4] this analysis need not be repeated here. We are more interested in analyzing this process of transformation in developing countries. There it is apparently left only in part to the uncontrolled forces of social dynamics; in part it is consciously fostered through induced economic development.

Urbanization

From the evidence available in India and other developing countries, we may identify several factors that tend to widen the sway of markets in the economy. The first, and perhaps the most important, is the process of urbanization. Here emphasis should be placed not so much on the process of "rationalization," which is often associated with urbanization, as on the common man's divorcement from the land from which he previously derived his livelihood. Instead of tilling his own field to procure his subsistence directly, he must derive it by earning an income which in turn allows him access to the market for consumers' goods. However, the process of urbanization does not automatically produce a market for industrial labor. People in Indian cities, for example, are involved in the labor market in very different degrees, although all are involved to a rather extensive degree in the commodity market for consumers' goods.

Relation of commodity and labor markets. In more concrete terms

[4] Karl Polanyi, *The Great Transformation* (New York: Farrar and Rinehart, 1944), pp. 51ff.

we may classify the urban population of India, with regard to its involvement in the labor market, in three classes. First, there are the independent craftsmen who are engaged in so-called cottage industries. These persons do not employ any workers outside their family circle, and they, in turn, are independent operators of their own minute enterprises. In this class are the small craftsmen and artisans and a multitude of individuals engaged in service industries, e.g., washermen, taxi drivers, rickshaw drivers, milkmen, bicycle repair men. Second, there are the persons employed in small-scale industries, i.e., shops and "factories" employing up to about 20 workers. As a rule, jobs are obtained in these shops not through supply and demand on the labor market, but through informal personal relations. A man is hired because he knows the owner of such a firm or someone who knows the owner, or because he is recommended by a member of his family, his extended kin group, or the village in which he originally resided. Sometimes workers, chiefly those with fairly scarce skills are hired through the labor market, but this is the exception and is counterbalanced by the fact that even in quite sizable plants workers are often procured from a pool of acquaintances or relatives rather than through the market. Finally, large enterprises often employ several hundreds or thousands of workers (such as those described by Morris), who are recruited largely through the labor market. But even here frequent exceptions occur; the market does not function well. Unemployed laborers may register with the official labor exchange, but more often than not they also rely on various informal contacts and frequently find that the latter are more effective in the procurement of a job than the regular labor market.

All three classes of workers are dependent on the market for consumers' goods, but only the third class and the second to a very slight extent are dependent on the labor market. These persons are, therefore, partially involved in market relations which are vital to them but still rely on nonmarket processes for some very important aspects of their lives. How and to what extent have these individuals become committed to an industrial way of life by their participation in the predominantly market-oriented matrix of the urban environment?

Commitment to a labor market. A person has become committed to a new way of life if he has adjusted his own life expectations to include the new way of life and if he does not attempt to return to the old way. A good empirical test of whether the members of a group have become committed to a new way of life is to ask them about their preferences for future work and ways of making a living, or about their hopes and expectations for their children. The most convincing evidence given by Gregory as to the high degree of commitment of Puerto Rican workers is in his discussion of their job preferences and expectations of future employment. These workers differ from those in many Indian cities, where people still highly value agriculture as a way of life and where many of the new industrial workers still resist full absorption into the industrial proletariat. It should be noted, however, that the Indian cities—notably the large cities—are undergoing a process of transition and that the industrial and other nonagricultural labor force, with as yet relatively weak commitment to industrialization, is gradually losing its attachment to agriculture. It is difficult to envisage a situation in which these transitional processes could be studied more exhaustively than in some large cities of India.

It may be possible to stipulate a functional relation between the development of markets, especially markets for consumers' goods and labor markets, and the process of commitment to a nonagricultural, nonrural way of life. If a person must secure the goods that serve for his own and his family's sustenance by purchase on the market, if he must obtain employment by offering his services on a labor market, he becomes involved in a market matrix which controls his very existence. There is a jest about a Western city child who, when shown a cow, wondered how milk was transferred from bottles into the animal. For the sake of the joke, the situation is put in an absurd form, but it is merely an extreme description of a situation in which the main access to economic goods of all sorts is through the market. The urban population in almost all underdeveloped countries has become involved in the market in procuring livelihood, but involved in the market only partially in procuring employment or, more broadly, in the determination of the economic role of the individual.

Differential Access to Markets

Market differentiation. Next to urbanization, the factor most profoundly affecting the process of commitment is the difference in access to various markets. The more direct impact of this difference in access to the market on the ordinary urban dweller is manifested in two ways. First, the urban worker is confronted, on the one hand, with markets that are fairly open and free and, on the other, with highly imperfect markets. For example, the market through which consumers' goods are acquired is a fairly well-functioning one in which price considerations determine consumers' choices between different sellers and different allocations of their own income. But there are also rigorously restricted markets in which price plays an insignificant role. The loan market—for all but the largest entrepreneurs—is one instance; the labor market is another.

Noncompeting groups. The second manifestation of differential access to markets is in the labor market, to which different workers have different degrees of access so that noncompeting groups are created. In the classical concept of noncompeting groups, the boundaries between groups of workers were drawn chiefly along lines of skill, but in some underdeveloped countries, notably in the urban areas of India, these are drawn along lines of membership in different social groups. In other words, workers with identical skills may have access to different markets, or some may have access to reasonably well-organized markets and others may not.[5] Moreover, the wages that are attainable on different markets vary and wages on the better-organized markets, generally speaking, are higher than on the imperfect markets. The monopsony power of employers on imperfect markets is great. Since the persons who supply their services through these restricted markets have no alternatives—or believe they have none—their incomes stay well below those of workers who have access to more highly organized markets.

The consequence of these market imperfections are twofold. First, quite wide differentials in wages frequently persist among localities and types of work place, even within the same city; and there are even greater variations in conditions of work, length of workday, and various fringe benefits that make up part of the real earnings of workers. These differences persist in the face of contrary governmental regulations but in part are a consequence of factory legislation, which often applies only to establishments employing more than a certain minimum number of workers. (This discussion of market imperfections and noncompeting groups in the market in part corresponds to, and in part deviates from, the views expressed by Feldman and Moore. In both discussions the importance of mobility and the absence of impediments to free access to the labor market are emphasized. They are more concerned with imperfections originating in the general value system and the ensuing status structure of a society; here we stress the impedi-

[5] For a similar discussion of noncompeting groups with special reference to the rural-urban dichotomy see B. N. Ganguli, *Rethinking on Indian Economics*, Presidential Address to the 38th Annual Conference of the Indian Economic Association, Poona, December 26, 1955.

ments arising from the lack of homogeneity within the market structure as a whole and particularly within the labor market.)

The second consequence of market imperfections is that there is scarcely any relation between wages and productivity of labor. For example, in an as yet unpublished study of Delhi it was found that wages in similar firms—of similar size, producing similar products, located in the same quarter of the city—sometimes varied inversely with the productivity of labor in the different plants. Although the productivity of labor increased with the introduction of power-driven machinery, wages showed no parallel increase. In the end, factories producing the same kind of goods exhibited the somewhat paradoxical picture of higher wages in the nonmechanized plants with lower productivity of labor, and lower wages in the mechanized plants with much higher productivity of labor. A tentative explanation of this persistence of a pattern that is so patently opposed to "economic laws" may be that the traditional evaluation of handicraft work puts it on a higher level than machine labor, even though the latter proves to be much more productive. A situation like this results not merely from the operation of monopsony on the labor market, but also from the real or believed restriction of competitive access by workers with similar skills to the same labor market. In a society in which the supply of labor continuously tends to outstrip the demand for it, as in India, some mechanism must operate to prevent some individuals from having access to the organized labor market if higher than "equilibrium" wage rates are to be maintained there.

This situation is not peculiar to India or other underdeveloped countries with overly dense populations. It was apparently a familiar feature of England during the 1780's and 1790's. The solution evolved there was the temporary rule of the Speenhamland system, which has been described fully by Polanyi.[6] The relations he describes apply *mutatis mutandis* to present-day India: rising factory wages are associated with increasing misery and unemployment among the less privileged; and the government entertains an ambivalent attitude, encouraging the formation of a labor market and, at the same time, initiating various subsidy schemes designed to keep the economically less productive persons from any real access to the labor market. The "ideal" solution to this paradoxical and wasteful system is the creation of a uniform labor market, even though this may bring severe temporary hardships for a sizable number of persons.

[6] Polanyi, *The Great Transformation*, pp. 77–85.

There are, however, two important differences between the British economy of Speenhamland and the modern economies of India and some other underdeveloped countries: (1) Speenhamland was an arbitrary quasi-legal convention, which could be removed relatively easily by legislation; in modern underdeveloped countries the maintenance of differentials in access to the labor market is based on deep-seated traditional structural features of the society. (2) The British economy of the early nineteenth century, in spite of unemployment and low real wages, was essentially one in which labor was scarce, and in which capital formation proceeded at a pace to provide employment for increasing numbers of workers at slowly rising levels of living. In India and other densely populated poor countries, the prospect that the increase of capital and other nonhuman resources will outstrip population growth are remote. We have to envisage labor-abundant economies in these countries for a long time to come. They already have "built-in" mechanisms preventing free social mobility and, consequent upon it, generalized access to the labor market; and even with increasing industrialization these mechanisms are not likely to be reduced in importance, but rather maintained.

Family and Kinship

The maintenance of a system characterized by strong particularistic cleavages in its social structure is associated with the persistence of certain supporting features. Chief among them is the role of the family and kinship in general, and its function in the allocation of economic roles and social status. This is the third factor—in addition to urbanization and differential access to the market—that strongly influences the process of commitment. In our analysis of this factor we again rely primarily on Indian data, but it is not argued that the propositions made about the family and its changes may be generalized to other underdeveloped countries, for India may represent a special case in respect to family relationships. Whatever the ultimate verdict on the possibilities of generalization, we may at least examine a typical situation in a country in which serious efforts are made toward economic development and the improvement of living standards.

Industrialization and the joint family. Many discussions of the changing role of the family in India begin with the statement that industrialization and urbanization tend to destroy the joint family and to put the nuclear family in its place. This very broad formulation hides a host of ambiguities. First, no distinction is made between corporate kin groups and joint or extended families, which are more loosely structured. It is not denied that industrialization and the participation in wage labor by members of corporate kin groups have had the effect of destroying these groups. Nash has shown why this process takes place (see Chapter 17). However, as he points out, there are many societies in which familial units have not adopted jural or corporate character, and we are here concerned with these joint families. We can observe many aspects of the "jointness" of a family, relating to characteristics of residence, to actual or potential commensality, to mutual economic interdependence, and to rules of endogamy and exogamy. Of chief interest to us in the present context is the economic interdependence of family members: a joint family is one in which the members have certain claims on one another for support and other economic assistance and, at the same time, have responsibilities for contributing in prescribed ways to the common patrimony or common support of the members of the whole family. Looking at the joint family in this way, however, we find little reason to support the proposition that urbanization and industrialization have made serious inroads on the tightness of a social organization based on joint families or, more correctly, on extended families.

There does not seem to be conclusive evidence that the extended family has become strengthened, or that it has been weakened, by industrialization. Further research on this question should be most profitable. The following argument therefore is not based on "hard data," but on general impressions. Before discussing these impressions in detail, it is necessary to explain why the demise of the joint family has been so widely attributed to the extension of urbanization and industrialization. This judgment is probably a consequence of diminished "jointness" in commensality and residence, rather than of diminution of joint economic commitment to the extended family. It is true that migration to the cities has torn apart families that used to live in the same household, but it has scarcely diminished their feeling responsible for contributing to a joint patrimony and to each member's subsistence. In fact, the circumstance that some members of extended families have acquired relatively remunerative jobs in the cities has often strengthened the economic tie between the members. The income of the better-paid family members has helped to keep in the possession of a family many a piece of land which otherwise would have had to be sold. Whether one reads the fictional literature on modern urban India, such as the novels of Jhabvala,[7] or visits the homes of Indian friends, one is always impressed by the very strong cohesion of the extended family in its economic, social security, and joint patrimony aspects.

This preservation of the extended family in the economic realm acts as a strong preservative of particularistic attachments in the distribution of economic roles and hence prevents the rapid development of an open, generally accessible labor market. As long as the extended family has an interest in protecting and aiding its members, and as long as this tendency is coupled with an overabundant labor supply, the procurement of many jobs will continue to be influenced by informal and personal relationships rather than by the impersonal standards of a well-functioning market. This conclusion may appear contrary to the commonly accepted theory that the process of industrialization is a powerful means of destroying the extended family and replacing it by the small nuclear family, as seems to have been the case in Western countries. Feldman and Moore appear to subscribe to this view; Nash, on the other hand, admits that in certain circumstances, family units can continue to function as they did before industrialization and that the family is a passive agent in the commitment to working for wages—and hence presumably also to the emergence of a labor market (cf. pages 316, 324).

This conflict raises an important theoretical issue which cannot be discussed in detail here. It may be that the extended family has remained strong in India, and promises to remain so, because India has made only partial progress toward full industrialization. In other words, our conclusions concerning India may be based on a merely transitional phenomenon. On the other hand, one could argue that the exception to the rule is not India, but the West. How destructive of the extended family system was industrialization there? How strong and widespread was the extended family in Western Europe on the eve of the industrial revolution?

From descriptions of peasant life in medieval Western Europe, we may conclude that the nuclear family was a widespread institution, both in its economic and commensal aspects, as early as the time of Charlemagne, and certainly in England in the thirteenth century.[8] The

[7] E.g., R. Prawar Jhabvala, *To Whom She Will* (London: George Allen & Unwin, 1955).

[8] See, for example, the description of the family life of Bodo, a Frankish peasant at the time of Charlemagne, in Eileen Power, *Medieval People* (Boston: Houghton Mifflin Company, 1925), pp. 1–23; and that of English peasant families in the later

intervening centuries, up to the onset of the industrial revolution, can scarcely have strengthened an institution that was weak when urban life was in its infancy. If we compare this situation with the vigor displayed even today by certain extended kin groups in underdeveloped countries, we may be led to regard the case of India as the more typical, and that of Western Europe as exceptional. The historical and cross-cultural aspects of this whole problem might well be examined further.

Caste and communalism. Superimposed on the strength of the extended family in India is that of another factor, namely, the role of caste or, rather, of communalism in its wider aspects. Here, again, we note the frequent assertion that urbanization and industrialization have broken down the rigidity of caste lines; and communalism in its various manifestations has even been declared unconstitutional. It is true that, at various steps in the scale of employment, caste has lost much of its importance, as Morris indicates. There are Harijan Members of Parliament, and ministers who belong to castes that until recently were counted among the untouchables. But, although caste has lost much ground in the large plant and the heavily mechanized industrial sector, a multitude of manifestations of communalism still interfere with the smooth functioning of an open labor market. Members of several communities may be employed in the same plant, but various types of jobs normally are distributed in such a way that members of the same community—linguistic, religious, or geographical—work in close contact. It is not unusual to be told that workers in certain less prestigeful lines in a factory are all, say, Muslims or Biharis, and that some of the more prestigeful jobs are reserved for, say, Bengalis. Whatever may be the ultimate fate of these tendencies, there is little doubt that at present they add to the particularistic forces impinging on the labor market and markets in general, and will do so in the near future.

A Continuum of Change

There are, doubtless, still other factors besides the process of urbanization, the differentiation of access to markets, and the roles of caste, community, and kinship, that influence the interaction between the development of markets and the process of commitment in underdeveloped countries. Their governmental policies are often ambiguous; and despite many high-sounding principles in favor of equality and

Middle Ages by H. S. Bennett, *Life on the English Manor* (Cambridge, England: Cambridge University Press, 1938), pp. 237–256.

nondiscrimination, which abound in the constitutions and other formal documents of the new countries, officials are often under pressure from general opinion to maintain and even to strengthen tendencies that prevent the development of either open markets or conditions favorable to widespread self-commitment of an industrial working class. It appears that the independent, "autonomous" operation of private initiative carries the societies closer to that goal than does public policy. This is because public policy, like several other factors—e.g., patterns of consumption, including food habits and forms of dress, standards of education, and intellectual intercourse—is influenced by the major factors of urbanization and family structure and, in general, only reinforces the tendencies initiated by the main processes of change.

Let us now try to envisage a society characterized by the features described in the preceding paragraphs, which is located on the continuum between a fully market-oriented and a nonmarket-oriented type of social organization. Obviously, the society falls somewhere between these two extremes, but we may say further that different social groups in it exhibit different degrees of commitment to the market and to a market-oriented society. Yet there are conflicting factors at work. Urbanization tends to push the society into a situation in which the market matrix and its allocating function take on a dominating position, whereas the manifold elements of monopoly and the tenaciousness of the extended family and various communalist survivals tend to keep the market from operating smoothly and from fulfilling its allocative function. The particular place of any one society on our continuum appears to depend on the relative strength of these conflicting factors and on the political and social power of the classes that harbor ideologies favorable to one or the other tendency.

In India, in spite of the apparent political dominance of a class with a strong "rationalistic" secular ideology, the issue is not at all clear; and Indian society maintains a most precarious balance between forces that foster the institutionalization of a universalist, open, essentially egalitarian social system and forces that foster one based on strong particularistic, monopoly ridden, anti-egalitarian norms. This uneasy balance manifests itself in the conflict over language, in the continual cropping up of forms of communalist action, in the influence of caste on the political life of the nation (so clearly described by Srinivas [9]), and even in the fact that the leadership of Congress is due more to the dissension

[9] M. N. Srinivas, "Caste in Modern India," *Journal of Asian Studies*, 16:529–548 (August 1957).

among potential opposition and the essentially charismatic character of Nehru's leadership, than to any rational appeal of policies.

Puerto Rico, as described by Holton and Gregory, is considerably closer to a society that is market-oriented. There the degree of commitment on the part of the industrial labor force is much greater than in India. To a large extent this appears to be a consequence of the rather far-reaching breakdown of particularistic forces and institutions, a process doubtless helped along by the openness of the labor market (i.e., the relative facility with which emigration to the continental United States could take place). This has reduced the relative overabundance of labor supply and has diminished monopsony power on the part of entrepreneurs. Similarly, the strength of the extended family (which was never so strong in Puerto Rico as in India) has been unable to withstand the combined effect of rapid urban growth and gradual infusion of the American ideology of achievement, especially since the extended family in Puerto Rico had been partially undermined over the centuries by the impact of European values. Thus, in some ways the development of Puerto Rico—and of some other Latin American countries—must be regarded as a special case whose features are suitable for comparison with other underveloped countries only on the level of very general analysis.

The Market as a Mechanism of Growth

Role of Cash Crops

A final point to which some attention should be given is the case in which the main factors in the economic development of a society are the market and the society's involvement in the market matrix. An excellent example has been described by Neumark, who summarized his argument in these words:

The general assumption that the colonists at the American and South African frontiers were entirely self-sufficient seems to have led to false lines of reasoning and false conclusions. Admittedly, the self-sufficiency of the frontier households everywhere was a matter of degree . . . However, with regard to frontier expansion, what has to be stressed is not so much the extent of self-sufficiency as the significance of the exchange with the outside world.[10]

Neumark later describes how the South African economy developed between the middle of the seventeenth century and the first quarter

[10] S. Daniel Neumark, *Economic Influences on the South African Frontier, 1652–1836* (Stanford: Stanford University Press, 1957), p. 4.

of the nineteenth chiefly in response to the growing markets, first for grain, and then for meat and other animal products. In that situation the market was a necessary precondition for economic growth. Without the involvement of the South African frontier in the world market, development would not have taken place, or at least would have been delayed until much later. A similar situation prevailed in other countries that underwent what may be called an expansionist, as against an intrinsic, pattern of economic growth.[11]

It might be argued that this analysis, whatever its merits for countries like South Africa, Australia, Canada, and the United States, has little significance for the underdeveloped countries that follow predominantly an intrinsic, rather than an expansionist, pattern of economic growth. This argument is of questionable validity, since the phenomena described by Neumark play an important role even in countries with intrinsic patterns of growth. For example, Bauer has shown that one of the important elements of economic growth in Nigeria and Ghana is the cash crops, which are produced by many small farmers and collected for shipment to other parts of the country or abroad.[12] Specialization of production is begun in this way, but its further strengthening depends on the continued growth and extension of markets and the involvement of persons using these exchange mechanisms in a market-oriented system. Similar developments are reported from other underdeveloped countries, e.g., from Malaya and Ceylon—and more recently Liberia—where the production and marketing of rubber have brought many formerly self-sufficient farmers into the market matrix; from East Africa where cotton and coffee play this role; and from parts of India, where certain fruits or oil-bearing plants are grown as cash crops on many farms and marketed for shipment to quite distant places.

The social situations created by these developments and the general growth of cash crops of all kinds make the market a major factor in economic growth. Were it not for a market mechanism of exchange, these commodities would not be produced on the present scale. It may be argued that the development of such cash crops could be fostered by other means, e.g., the requirement of forced deliveries of these crops in lieu of taxes, or the establishment of collective farms, or some other

[11] On the concepts of "expansionist" and "intrinsic" growth patterns, see Bert F. Hoselitz, "Patterns of Economic Growth," *Canadian Journal of Economics and Political Science,* 21:418–420 (November 1955).

[12] P. T. Bauer, *West African Trade* (Cambridge, England: Cambridge University Press, 1954), especially pp. 382ff.

direct regulation. But from all experiments with collectivization in agriculture and direct regulation of agricultural production we may conclude that they are clumsy and ineffective means of fostering economic growth, in comparison with the creation and enhancement of markets for cash crops. In other words, the market itself in certain circumstances may become the most effective means of supporting the forces of economic development.

There is a difference between these markets for cash crops or rural handicrafts that are sold for cash and the urban markets for consumption goods or labor markets. Markets of the two latter kinds become an institution made necessary by the urban situation; the former are both an outflow and an initiator of the process of economic growth itself. In the city the environment is the primary influence in the adaptation of men to a new situation—one in which persons with peasant backgrounds become accustomed to the market because of their separation from immediate control over the means of production; in the development of cash crops the market strengthens the meaning of their control over the means of production and, in fact, acts as a barometer inducing them to employ these means more rationally and efficiently. In the city the market has primarily an institutional impact and only secondarily has meaning as a mechanism of resource allocation; its primary function in the case of cash crops is economic, and its primary impact is on economic behavior rather than on social norms.

Development of Entrepreneurs

Thus the development of cash crops—which at first may be marginal crops destined for consumption by special classes but which gradually may come to include even the staple foods and fibers consumed on a mass basis—creates a pattern of economic development that is market-oriented but different from that discussed earlier (pages 220ff. supra). How does involvement in the matrix of the market, especially in the economic aspects of the market mechanism, affect men's general outlook, behavior, and attitudes toward production, consumption, and investment? The history of the South African, Australian, or American frontier is not fully relevant, for there the frontiersmen—for all their indebtedness to the market for aiding their economic advancement—came from a society in which they had been accustomed to market exchange. The crucial difference between a settler on the frontier in Canada or Australia and a farmer in Nigeria or Malaya specializing in production of cash crops is that the former came to the frontier with full knowledge of and familiarity with the market, whereas the latter must change from participating in an economy based essentially on local self-sufficiency to one based on exchange mediated through the market. While the Nigerian or Malayan makes this transition, he also learns how he can improve his economic status and prospects by making use of fluctuations in price, by speculation, by adaptation of his resources to the changing conditions offered him on the market. In other words, the increasing involvement of the cash crop farmer in the market mechanism tends to make him an "entrepreneur."

This conclusion should not be interpreted as solving all problems of economic development. To be sure, some have regarded the growth of an entrepreneurial class as the main stimulus to economic growth. But the cash crop farmer is an entrepreneur only in a very qualified sense; although he may take the market as a guide in his decisions about production, he is by no means fully committed to becoming a nascent capitalist. To begin with, he can always fall back on subsistence farming if some vagary of the market should make his cash crop unsalable, or salable only at a great loss. Second, he remains a small man, and probably his savings are rarely large enough to allow him to expand his activities on any sizable scale. Finally, he remains an agriculturalist, and the more he prospers as a cash crop farmer, the less incentive he has to become a wage earner or even an industrialist. This means that, although the development of a market for cash crops may alter substantially the conditions of resource allocation and production in agriculture, it does not contribute directly to the commitment of industrial workers. It is not denied that such a situation may create a market orientation on the part of many persons of small means, and may make their acceptance of an industrial way of life easier if for some reason farming seems to hold no future for them. There is some suggestion that this process has taken place in Puerto Rico, if this conclusion may be read into Gregory's paper. But the actual process by which the widespread availability of a market for cash crops contributes to the formation of an industrial proletariat has been too little explored to permit any reasonably firm statements about it.

Some writers have implied that the development of a market orientation leads almost automatically to the kinds of social behavior characteristic of the more highly developed economies of Western Europe. One cannot agree with this proposition without much more evidence than is available. It is granted that increasing numbers of market-oriented individuals in a society may provide a strong stimulus to economic growth, but whether strong enough to overcome the impeding factors in the social structure and perhaps in the ecology of a society is difficult to say. At this stage of our knowledge we can say only that although the growth of markets for cash crops or the products of artisans may create conditions favorable to economic growth, further examination of kinship relations, the processes of urban growth, and actual and prospective social structures is needed before we can generalize further. Only then may we be able to say whether the process of commitment by which the peasant is divorced from his land and forced to find a way of subsisting in the city and the alternative process by which he is induced to use his land more rationally and efficiently mutually reinforce or contradict one another.

SUMMARY

The main contents of this paper may be summarized in the following propositions:

1. The general level of economic advancement is highly correlated with the ubiquity of markets as institutions mediating between classes of persons in the social division of labor.

2. From a purely economic point of view, and on the assumption that tastes, the state of technology, and the distribution of income are given, the market mechanism presents the most efficient means of allocation of resources.

3. From an institutional point of view, the importance of markets lies not in their efficiency in allocation of resources, but in the manner and extent of use of the market as against other institutions mediating the exchange of goods and services.

4. In many nonindustrial societies numerous exchanges take place without the use of a market mechanism, and many commodities and usually all service transactions are excluded from market exchange.

5. Thus it is possible to establish a pair of polar types of exchange systems. At one pole is a social system in which virtually everything is subject to transfer on a market; at the other pole is a social system in which, ideally, market transactions are restricted to foreign imports or other "exotic" and rarely consumed objects, and in which services are not subject to market exchange at all.

6. One of the most significant features of an expanding economy is the development of a market for labor. Breadth and openness of the labor market indicate a high level of economic advancement; such a

labor market is also instrumental in the process of commitment of non-industrial workers to an industrial way of life.

7. Among the social institutions that positively or negatively affect the growth of a labor market are the growth of urban centers, the distribution of status positions that determine differential access to the labor market, and the forms of family or kinship organization.

8. Whereas the growth of urbanism affects the development of labor markets, and hence the commitment process, positively in virtually all cases, differential access to the labor market leads to noncompeting groups on the supply side of labor and manifold other features of market imperfection, and so may often have an adverse effect on commitment.

9. Although it is commonly held that the development of industrialism and the growth of a labor market tend to destroy the extended family, there is some evidence that this process has not yet taken place in several developing economies. The interrelations between forms of familial organization and commitment to an industrial way of life are unclear and await further research.

10. In certain societies, notably those undergoing an expansionist pattern of growth, the market for cash crops has been one of the primary mechanisms supporting economic development. Cash crops and the markets on which they are traded have also been developed, however, in societies with an intrinsic pattern of growth.

11. The influence of the gradual evolution of cash crops on the process of commitment to industrialization is unclear. On the one hand, cash crops tend to reinforce the attachment to agriculture; on the other, they tend to develop a rationalistic profit orientation that may support the commitment process.

13 THE MOBILITY OF LABOR

Walter Elkan
Lloyd A. Fallers

Types of economic and social organization that are generally referred to as Western are spreading throughout the world. To call them Western is probably a mistake because they have more to do with time than place; but the label, if treated as such and not as a definition, is convenient.

Conspicuous aspects of Western economic organization are the existence and use of wages and of wage *laborers*. The two are distinct, of course. Wages, which are regular payments for the performance of certain kinds of service, are an economic category comparable with profits and rent, which are payments for other kinds of services. Wage laborers, or proletarians, are a sociological rather than an economic category. They are people whose lives and livelihoods closely depend on wages, generally from birth to death. They may have other sources of income but these are subsidiary or supplementary to wages.

WAGE LABOR IN HISTORICAL PERSPECTIVE

In this paper we examine the place that wages and wage laborers have come to occupy in the economy and social structure of the East African territory of Uganda during the less than 100 years since it came into contact with the West. We first glance briefly at the pattern of development of wage labor in England, and then note some important differences between that country in the eighteenth century and Uganda today as contexts. In Uganda, circumstances have made possible a certain type of industrial development, but it has not been accompanied by a distinct urban industrial status system of the sort that has commonly accompanied industrial development in the West. Instead, the Uganda labor force has consisted of persons who have maintained fundamental ties with rural agricultural society, participating only partially and sporadically in urban wage labor. The result, we argue, is a relatively stable compromise. Although the situation no doubt will permit considerable quantitative expansion in a certain type of industry, we see no reason to expect an early successful expansion into other types that require a more fully committed labor force.

Town Laborers in England

In England wage laborers were a minority of the population before the eighteenth century, and ever since have been a majority. Wages, however, have affected the majority since long before that century. Before then men commonly spent part of their time in working for a wage, but only a minority were dependent on wages throughout their lives. Wage labor itself was often quite different from the kinds of work we now tend to associate with that term. The most common form of wage work was done at home; employers sent jobs to their employees, lent or leased them the necessary tools, and supplied them with raw materials. When the product was done, the employer collected it and paid for it by the piece. This kind of wage work is now uncommon in the West, but persists in a few minor trades.

The late eighteenth century in England saw another important change: the growth of those industrial towns that owed their origins to industry. Industrial towns were not new, and many of them did not owe their origins to industry. It grew up in them because they were the centers of trade. What was new in the eighteenth and nineteenth centuries was the great growth of towns that did owe their origins to industry and that came to be entirely divorced from the countryside. Town and country previously had shared a common life to some extent, and this had been perpetuated by a good deal of two-way mobility. The emergence of wage laborers into a majority position and the development of a marked wage differential between town and country made the towns decidedly more attractive than the country. The laborers came to be a majority as a result of both agrarian and industrial changes. The agrarian changes tended to reduce mobility between the status of wage laborer and that of farmer; those who had hitherto moved freely and frequently between the two became simply wage laborers. Moreover, farms were becoming larger (except during the Napoleonic Wars) so that the smallest farmers could no longer compete with those who were using more capital and consequently producing at lower cost. Many of the small farmers emigrated, some became industrial entrepreneurs, and others took up wage labor.

Since wages in the towns were higher than in the countryside and since there were more opportunities for employment in the towns, a movement in that direction resulted. It was a movement of wage laborers and not, as has sometimes been contended, of peasants displaced from the land. The importance of this distinction emerges later, when we compare what happened in England with what is happening in East Africa. Furthermore the movement was mainly of families. The balance of sexes, if not their age distributions in the industrial towns, was broadly similar to that in the country as a whole.

Is the Experience Repeated?

In East Africa, wages, wage laborers, and town industry were unknown phenomena until very recent times. This statement, however, prejudges the issue because we want to discuss whether these terms, when applied to what we find in East Africa, have the same connotations as in Europe, America, Japan, and Australia. In other words, does the "wage laborer" as defined in the modern Western sociological category exist in East Africa, or is he likely to exist there in the near future? There is certainly no reason to expect Western experience to be repeated in this connection.

The growth of a body of wage laborers permanently settled in industrial towns has apparently had advantages for England, and all employers in Africa wish that the same might happen there. England now has an industrial labor force in its third or fourth generation, a labor force adjusted to the exigencies and demands of industry, and with a peculiarly urban and industrial culture. By the time a young man takes his first job, he can read and write, he knows a good deal about mechanical contrivances, he has been taught to regard punctuality and regularity as virtues, and he has absorbed a host of suitable maxims, such as "If a job is worth doing, it is worth doing well," and "What the boss says goes." The hope or expectation that this pattern will develop in East Africa, however, may be mere wishful thinking on the part of entrepreneurs and planners.

We assume that a body of persons committed to urban living and wage labor will develop whenever an urban industrial situation as a socioeconomic whole offers greater rewards than does another way of life. The rewards offered must include both greater money incomes and a social status system in which money may be spent in socially satisfying ways. We also assume that there are many degrees of commitment to the urban industrial life, and to this extent our earlier question about the existence of the "wage laborer" in East Africa was not realistic. Certainly within the Western world there has been great variation in the content of this category.

The Economy of Uganda

Of the three East African territories, only Uganda has no seacoast. Extending from the northern and western shores of Lake Victoria, to the west of both Kenya and Tanganyika, Uganda has a link with the coast over 800 miles of railway track through Kenya. Uganda has much in common with both Kenya and Tanganyika and shares with them a tariff, a postal authority, a railway, and a number of other common services, such as university education. But the likeness is superficial.

Unlike Kenya and Tanganyika, Uganda has virtually no white settlers; its population of some 5,000,000 is almost wholly African. There are a few European and a larger number of Indian businesses and plantations, but the amount of land given over to plantations is insignificant in relation to the total cultivated area. Some 3,000 adult European males residing in Uganda are civil servants or missionaries. Indians comprise a larger minority; there are thought to be some 20,000 adult Indian males in the population.

The Indians tend to be regarded as a "problem." In contrast with the Europeans, many of the Indians consider Uganda their home and are concentrated in occupations that arouse the "envy of the multitude." They are prominent in trade and in fact handle a major share of the retail business. They own a great deal of the visible capital of the country—office buildings, shops, factories, and workshops, as well as the only two large farming estates that are not owned by Africans. The Indians are also prominent in the professions, or at least in those that are not connected with the government. Nearly all of those who are employed by others have good jobs as skilled workers in industry or the building trades, as senior clerks, or bookkeepers.

The multitude of Africans, however, are by no means an undifferentiated proletariat or poverty-stricken peasantry. Nowhere in Uganda is there poverty like that found in India, China, or Egypt; land is plentiful and, in most parts, reasonably fertile. Uganda is a backward country, but not a very poor one.

Uganda is predominantly a country of small farmers; a few of its people are pure pastoralists, but the majority combine tillage and pasture farming in varying proportions. The size of farm seldom exceeds 10 acres; each farm provides the staple food for the household and, in many areas, a surplus for sale. The marketed farm products may be surplus staple food, cattle, or a crop grown especially for sale. Much of the cash income of farmers is in fact from crops grown for sale, particularly cotton and coffee. In 1956 the income derived from cotton and coffee accounted for some 60 percent of farmers' incomes.[1]

Farm incomes account for the greater share of the income of all Africans and of the estimated national income. Almost every activity other than farming is in a sense dependent on or subservient to it. When farmers have bad harvests or receive low prices for their crops, commerce and industry are at once affected. Industry has been encouraged in postwar years in an attempt to make the country less vulnerable to the changing fortunes of agriculture, but so far the income derived from industry has been too small to provide any significant degree of stability; every change in the income of farmers is immediately reflected in the sales of industry.

Before World War II almost the only industries in Uganda were those that processed cotton and coffee, the export crops. Cotton ginneries and coffee hulling plants were dispersed throughout the growing districts and were open only at harvest time. The two principal towns, Kampala and Jinja, were commercial centers, not industrial ones; they owed their existence to their functions as centers for collecting and forwarding the country's produce and for distributing its imports. Since the War these towns have grown and have changed their character to some extent, by absorbing new functions. Although they are still primarily commercial centers, they are also centers of industry. Some new industry has resulted directly from the official policy of encouraging its development. Until the Uganda Government, acting through a statutory development corporation, offered to participate in providing capital, no one had thought it safe to invest in a Jinja textile mill. This mill is not typical of Uganda's industry, however; most of the industry that has developed since 1946 must be regarded as a spontaneous response to a growing home market. Like other countries whose major source of income is the sale of primary products, Uganda has recently enjoyed great prosperity. This has encouraged the establishment of factories and workshops that serve a purely local market. They produce beer, furniture, biscuits, cooking oil, soft drinks, and packets of tea, and provide a variety of services centered mainly in the maintenance of motor vehicles.

Most of these ventures have been started by local Indian capitalists and are financed and managed largely by Indians. A few concerns are owned and managed by Europeans; nearly all of these plants belong to large international organizations like the British American Tobacco

[1] Uganda Protectorate, *Geographical Income of Uganda, 1950–56* (Entebbe: Government Printer, 1957).

Co. Ltd. Some Indian concerns employ a few Europeans who have special technical qualifications.

Factories and workshops of this kind are almost always small; only a few—a tobacco factory, the textile mill, a brewery, and the central workshop of the Government's Public Works Department—employ over 250 people. Industrial employment thus does not account for more than a small proportion of all employment in the towns. The public and municipal services—hospitals, maintenance of roads and sewers, street cleaning, refuse collection—employ large numbers of workers; something like a quarter of all employees in Kampala work for public authorities. Large numbers are also employed in commerce, in transport, and as domestic servants. Such employees work mostly alone or in pairs or, at most, in dozens. The total number of employees in Uganda is about 300,000; of these, not more than one third work in the two principal towns of Jinja and Kampala.

Mobility and Type of Job

Since we are concerned with mobility, we classify jobs in two ways: according to the permanence or temporariness of jobs; and according to the proportion of jobs specific to particular firms or industries in relation to the over-all proportion. One would expect mobility of workers to be highest where all work is seasonal and unskilled and where, because it is unskilled, a man may as easily work for one employer as for any other. The mobility of railway signalmen tends to be low in any country, because their jobs are permanent and their skill is worthless outside railway employment.

In the towns of Uganda all but a small proportion of the workers are employed either in unskilled jobs or as clerks and artisans, in a variety of industries and firms. Hence the workers are able to move freely between industries, firms, and jobs. It is in factory employment that there are the largest numbers of semiskilled workers, such as machine operators, whose skill appertains to a particular process. However, the factories employ only a small proportion of all workers, and much of the work there is either highly skilled or unskilled because, with labor cheap and machines expensive, most manufacturers mechanize as little as possible.

The greatest disturbance in the labor market is created by the high proportion of jobs that are temporary and casual or in industries subject to seasonal fluctuations. Nearly a third of the workers are engaged in building and construction; they are hired on the site for particular jobs and when those are finished must find new jobs. Many workers are hired for a few days when a new consignment of goods has to be moved from the railway to a warehouse or from warehouse to shops. All this is probably true in the towns in most of the low income territories of Africa and Asia and contributes to the high mobility that is featured in the literature on labor problems in the underdeveloped areas. The contribution of such jobs to mobility of labor has received less recognition than it might, although they were an important element in labor mobility in England as little as 50 years ago.[2]

Migration and Turnover

A type of labor mobility that has received much more attention—because it is unusual and poses unusual problems—is short-term migration.[3] Labor migration in Africa is often very short-term and involves a very large proportion of the employed workers. This is true of those who work on plantations or estates and, to a greater or lesser extent, of those who work in the towns. In other countries migration often has involved families, whose heads move permanently to new jobs in new places; in Africa often only the men move, sooner or later returning to their families at home. According to Benson this pattern was nearly universal in Africa in 1938: "The vast majority of migrants are males many of whom return home after periods often no longer than one or two years so that the shortness of the stay in employment accentuates the volume of movement." [4]

Twenty years later, short-term migration is still a dominant feature of the African labor market,[5] for several reasons. One is that in some parts of Africa, particularly in the Union of South Africa, governments or private firms have deliberately discouraged the settlement of people in the areas of employment. A second reason is that in many areas short-term migration is the way men maximize their incomes; in the words of the East African Royal Commission, "it appears as the most economic choice which the African can make." [6] It has sometimes been

---

[2] W. H. Beveridge, *Unemployment: A Problem of Industry* (London: Longmans, Green and Co., 1909).

[3] See, for instance, W. Benson, "Some International Features of African Labour Problems," *International Labour Review*, 39:34–45 (January 1939).

[4] *Ibid.*, p. 35.

[5] See "Wage Economy in Tropical Africa," *International Labour Review*, 74: 239–258 (September 1956).

[6] United Kingdom, *East African Royal Commission 1953–1955 Report* (London: His Majesty's Stationery Office, 1955), p. 154.

argued that men are reluctant to commit themselves permanently to a life of wage labor because there is no security in employment against the hazards of sickness, old age, and unemployment, and because conditions of life in the towns are not sufficiently attractive. There is truth in this reasoning but it does not take into account man's unwillingness to sever absolutely his ties with the countryside. The income of the migrant worker and his family does not consist solely of his wages; proceeds in cash and in kind from his family farm are included. The latter accrue only so long as he or his family continue to occupy the farm; once they leave it, their right to its proceeds lapses and they generally receive no compensation.

With some exceptions, farms in Uganda are not bought and sold. This means that, however attractive the towns, and however high wages may be, a man's total income can always be greater than his wages if he does not give up his farm. The proportion of his income that is derived from his farm depends, of course, on the relation between wages and farm income. Where land is fairly plentiful and fertile, as in some parts of East Africa, farm income provides a substantial proportion of the whole, even for persons whose wages are above the minimum. In areas like Kikuyuland and parts of Tanganyika, where farms have become very small and the land yields little, farm incomes are a less significant proportion of the wage earner's total income. This explains why the populations have been more stable in some towns of Kenya and Tanganyika than in Uganda.

Men in Uganda are likely to continue to move to and fro between work on their farms and work for an employer as long as they cannot compound the expected future yield of their farms by selling them. Increases in wages designed to make it possible for men to support families are likely to be of little avail. The increase in wages is much more likely to be regarded as a welcome addition to real wages than as an inducement to give up the family farms, and is therefore not likely to have any marked influence on mobility between employment and "peasant" farming. A recent survey of budgets of unskilled workers in Kampala shows that between 1953 and 1957 those living with dependents had increased slightly, from 26 to 33 percent. During this period real wages had more than doubled.[7] A larger increase in the proportion

---

[7] East African Statistical Department, *Patterns of Income, Expenditure and Consumption of African Unskilled Workers in Kampala* (Nairobi: Government Printer, 1957), p. 17; and *Index of Retail Prices in African Markets: Kampala* (Nairobi: Government Printer, 1957), p. 9. The change in the proportion living with dependents

of workers living with dependents would be expected if it were true that only low wages kept workers from bringing their families to town.

One other aspect of mobility should be mentioned. Nothing that we have said so far explains why a man should not continue to move, at least until he is too old, between wage employment and his homestead. But apparently this does not happen; the Kampala labor force continues to be composed very largely of young men. The average age of employees in Kampala in 1954 was about 26.5 years; those over 30 comprised only about one fifth of the total labor force.[8] Only among the "elite" workers (one tenth of the total, whose earnings were highest) was there a substantial number (one half) over 30 years old. Evidence from the age structure is not conclusive, of course, but is the best we have at present. An official budget survey of 178 unskilled workers showed that one third claimed to have first come to Kampala at least five years before, but that only about one half of these had remained there continuously since they first arrived.[9]

LABOR STABILITY WITHOUT COMMITMENT

We have described the Uganda labor force as highly mobile, i.e., one that on the whole is not deeply committed to urban wage labor. We have suggested some economic reasons for the weak and transitory lure of the town, but from the viewpoint of the potential town worker the choice is not purely economic. It is not simply a matter of maximizing wages. His motivation to enter and remain in urban employment is a function of the total social situation in which he finds himself and by which his personal aspirations are molded. Those who make up the actual and potential labor force are not, of course, homogeneous in these respects; both social situation and personal aspirations differ among the various tribal groups.

It may be useful to examine two groups for which these factors, combined in rather different ways, produce *relative stability* in urban employment. Neither the Baganda nor the Luo in the towns are com-

---

is more reliable than the proportion itself; a large number of dependents were probably mistresses or "town wives." Real wages in 1953 were lower than they had been in 1952.

8 These figures are derived from a sample survey of 130 employees, made in 1954 by A. W. Southall as part of the Kampala Survey that he directed for the East African Institute of Social Research.

9 East African Statistical Department, *Patterns of Income, Expenditure and Consumption of African Unskilled Workers in Kampala.*

mitted urban, industrial proletarians in anything like the modern Western sense, but they are more committed than most members of other tribes. Analysis of their situations may throw some light on the prospects for greater labor stability.

Labor Stability by Compromise: The Baganda

Of all the peoples of Uganda, only the Baganda are able to join the urban labor force without leaving home, for the major centers of employment lie within their tribal territory. Kampala has grown up adjacent to Mengo, the traditional capital of the Buganda Kingdom, while Jinja is on the Nile, the kingdom's eastern boundary.[10]

The European explorers, missionaries, and empire builders who penetrated the Lake Victoria region after the middle of the nineteenth century found in Buganda the political center for the entire region. Like the other peoples of the Interlacustrine Bantu group, the Baganda were organized, on the one hand, into patrilineal clans and lineages and, on the other, into a hierarchical state headed by a hereditary ruler, the *Kabaka*. In Buganda more than the neighboring kingdoms, however, the balance of power had shifted rather more toward the monarchical state and away from the unilineal kinship groups. This no doubt helps to explain the fact that Buganda was actively expanding at the expense of her neighbors. Her pivotal political position in the region attracted Europeans interested in establishing a foothold there.

Anglican and Roman Catholic missionaries brought Christianity, literacy, and education, both "liberal" and "technical." By the time the British Protectorate was declared in 1894, there was a substantial group of literate, Christian chiefs as well as a growing body of artisans and "clerks." As neighboring areas were brought under the Protectorate through the joint exertions of British officers and Baganda military leaders, Baganda chiefs were installed and Baganda clergy sent to

---

10 In the Bantu languages of this region, words are formed by adding class prefixes to roots. Thus, the kingdom of which we are speaking is called Buganda and its people Baganda (singular: Muganda), and their language is Luganda. The Protectorate as a whole, which includes both this kingdom and a group of neighboring peoples, is Uganda.

The implication that only the Baganda have major industry within their own country is not quite accurate. Actually, Jinja lies on the boundary between Buganda and Busoga, so that the Basoga also can work in town without leaving home. Basoga, however, are culturally extremely similar to Baganda and their participation in the labor market follows a similar pattern. For simplicity's sake, therefore, we here ignore the Basoga.

spread the Gospel. Under the terms of the Agreement of 1900 between Her Majesty's Government and the senior chiefs who were serving as regents for the then infant *Kabaka,* the Buganda Kingdom retained within the framework of the Protectorate a greater degree of autonomy than did neighboring states and tribal groups.

Thus, in comparison with their neighbors, the Baganda had two initial advantages: a head start in opportunities for the acquisition of Western ideas, techniques, and goods; and a privileged political position which enabled them to regard the British as teachers and allies rather than as conquerors. Large areas of Western culture could be accepted without loss of self-esteem because the essential structure of Buganda society remained intact. In general, the Baganda have retained their lead during six decades of British administration.

A major factor supporting the Baganda's leading position has been the relatively prosperous agriculture which developed after 1900. Traditionally the staple food crop was plantain, which in the fertile and well-watered soil produced a reliable and abundant source of food with a modicum of labor, mostly supplied by women and children. A variety of other crops, such as millet, sweet potatoes, and maize, as well as meat from cattle, sheep, goats, and chickens supplemented the diet. Cotton was introduced soon after 1900 and, after an initial period of resistance, rapidly spread as a cash crop. Since the 1930's the cultivation of coffee has also become widespread.

With an abundance of good land available, Baganda farmers have been able to remain self-sufficient in basic food supplies and, at the same time, to acquire substantial cash incomes. Over the past several decades Buganda has absorbed immigrants from other tribes to the point that between one third and one half of the kingdom's population is foreign born; yet population density is only 75 per square mile and "there is land to spare for expansion of the human population." [11] Furthermore, an unusual (for Africa) pattern of land tenure has enabled agricultural enterprise to go beyond the simple peasant level. As part of the 1900 Agreement, the better half of the land of the kingdom was distributed in freehold to chiefs and members of the royal family. Over the years these estates have been subdivided, sold and resold, so that land has played a part in economic development—usually impossible in Africa because of traditional restrictions on the free transfer of land. On the one hand, rights in land have been alienated to raise

[11] Uganda Protectorate, *Report of the Agricultural Productivity Committee* (Entebbe: Government Printer, 1954), p. 13.

capital for nonagricultural enterprises; on the other, substantial farms have been built up and cultivated with hired immigrant labor.

In view of all this agricultural prosperity, it is understandable that the Baganda are reluctant to commit themselves permanently to urban employment, particularly at the less well-paid levels. Even though most opportunities for wage labor lie within Buganda, by far the greater part of the unskilled labor is performed by immigrants. Baganda tend to join the labor force mainly at the skilled and white collar levels and even there they seldom become permanent wage workers in the Western sense. More commonly they work in town until they have saved sufficient money to buy a substantial piece of land or to start a business of some kind, usually in a rural area. Wage work in town tends to be a phase rather than a way of life, and ties with the countryside are continuously maintained during this phase. Many Baganda town workers "commute" daily from rural holdings, where their wives cultivate both food and cash crops. Others maintain an urban lodging for use during the week but return every weekend to a rural home many dozens of miles away. Thus town and country are not differentiated culturally or socially.

Modern and traditional mobility. Underlying this modern pattern of urban-rural circulation is a tendency toward mobility, both spatial and social, that is indigenous to Buganda society. The capital itself, with its hundreds of beehive-shaped thatched buildings, traditionally was moved at the beginning of every reign or oftener; and, more important, it was the center of a highly fluid political hierarchy. During the latter part of the nineteenth century, power appears to have become increasingly concentrated in the hands of the *Kabaka*. The unilineal kinship groups declined in political importance, and most of the crucial chieftainships came to be held by personal clients of the *Kabaka*. This fostered both social and spatial mobility; new appointees, who became more frequent as the regime became more despotic, tended to be accompanied by crowds of kinsmen and hangers-on so that whole village populations shifted with each change in the *Kabaka's* favor.

Apart from such politically induced changes in status and place of residence, the Baganda seem always to have been great visitors. Clans and lineages were dispersed, rather than locally concentrated (perhaps due to processes of the sort just described), so that keeping up kinship ties meant frequent journeys. Although kinship groups declined *politically* in the sense that major chieftainships ceased to be held within them, they retained, and retain to this day, important jural functions *vis-à-vis* their members, particularly in regard to inheritance of property. Almost every adult Muganda seems at any given moment to be involved in a "case" of this kind, and the result is constant coming and going. Today a network of graded roads, bus lines, and the frequent possession of bicycles and motorcars facilitate this process, but even traditionally the maintenance of roads was a recognized function of the state. Traditional Buganda was a dense and highly fluid sort of rural society.

Although the Muganda moves easily between town and country, he does not like the town because it is dominated by Europeans and Indians, whom he resents, and is in large part populated by immigrant Africans, whom he despises. But he feels no need to choose between town and country as *alternatives*. Town work can easily be fitted into his pursuit of socioeconomic advancement within the *Buganda* social system. If he owns or has the money to purchase a plot of land within bus- or bicycle-range of the town, he may commute daily to an urban job, thus combining the best of both environments. Having achieved this highly satisfactory compromise, he may well remain in one job for some years. Thus Baganda form the more stable part of the labor force and consequently rise higher in the wage and occupational structure. They have, to be sure, the added advantage of greater educational opportunities. As wages rise, the incentive to give up employment in town decreases. However, sooner or later the break is made. Baganda always assume that eventually they will become "self-employed," either as farmers producing for the market or as shopkeepers, garage proprietors, lorry owners, builders, and so on. There is a good chance that they will succeed, for the opportunities for self-employment are numerous, although they require capital.

The Baganda sometimes face a predicament because this capital generally has to be acquired by saving rather than borrowing. Nurkse has argued that aspirations toward Western patterns of consumption make saving difficult in underdeveloped areas, but Baganda townsmen do not have to look as far as the West.[12] Those whom they regard as their social equals in the countryside enjoy a relatively high level of living because of the high prices they obtain for their cotton, coffee, and other farm products. Geographical and social proximity make it necessary for Baganda townsmen to keep up with their country cousins, but also to provide constant hospitality for them. Kampala, like any market town, has a perpetual stream of visitors from the surrounding

[12] Ragnar Nurkse, *Problems of Capital Formation in Underdeveloped Countries* (Oxford: Basil Blackwell, 1953), pp. 65–70.

countryside, and persons who have made the town their home are expected to keep open house. Moreover, townsmen are constantly called upon for loans and gifts as well as entertainment. All this makes it difficult for them to save and thus, in a sense, delays the day when Baganda town workers can "retire." When some of the larger employers start a provident fund as an insurance against poverty in old age, Baganda welcome it—not as insurance but as a way of saving for independence.

Contrast with short-term migrants. The contrast between the way Baganda relate themselves to wage labor in the towns and the way most immigrant Africans do this is striking. Most of the latter come to town only once and stay for a relatively short period. Their principal motive is to obtain the capital that will enable them to enjoy a higher level of living at home for the rest of their lives. They want money to buy bicycles on which to carry crops to market, for waterproof roofs for their houses, or to pay the bride price of wives who will help grow the crops. In other words, they want money not to pay for recurring purchases, but to equip their farms or homesteads. The regular needs for money—to pay the poll tax, to buy soap or kerosene, and occasionally to buy new clothes—can now be met in most parts of Uganda either by growing crops for sale or by taking sporadic jobs for a month or two near home. The towns, where money wages are high, attract those who want to accumulate larger sums. According to Richards, "In peasant economies a man requires his greatest capital outlay in youth . . . the need for large sums of money gradually diminishes." [13] That is why so few of the immigrant workers in Kampala are over 30 years old.

Long-Term Migrants: The Luo

Next to the Baganda, the Luo are the most stable members of the labor force. Whereas the Baganda form a kind of elite in the labor force as a whole, the Luo are an elite among the immigrants. On the average they earn higher wages for unskilled work than other immigrants and have risen farther in the wage structure. A stratified sample survey of employees in 1954 showed that Luo earned the highest average wage in the lowest stratum, and that more than half of the Luo in the sample were in the middle and upper strata.[14] They apparently earn higher wages for unskilled work because they have stronger

[13] A. I. Richards, *Economic Development and Tribal Change* (Cambridge, England: W. Heffer and Sons, 1954), p. 213.

[14] See note 8, p. 246 supra.

physiques and can do tougher jobs than most other East Africans, but this does not entirely explain their stability and prominence in the upper levels of the wage structure. Unlike the Baganda, the Luo have integrated town labor with their pattern of socioeconomic aspiration in a way that encourages relatively long periods of stable employment.

Unlike the Baganda, the Luo must travel in order to find substantial markets for their labor. Their tribal territory lies at the northeastern corner of Lake Victoria in Nyanza Province of Kenya, roughly midway between Kampala and Nairobi. While Kisumu, the provincial capital, has always provided some employment, it has not offered jobs sufficient for anything like the numbers of Luo seeking them, particularly in recent years. Luoland is not naturally as well-endowed as Buganda, and the former's population is more than twice as dense. Central and South Nyanza, the two main Luo districts, have densities of 185 and 145 persons per square mile, respectively. Cotton and maize have been grown as cash crops, but neither has thrived as cotton and coffee have in Buganda.

For many years large numbers of Luo have traveled to the various labor centers in Kenya or have crossed the lake to Uganda. Unlike most of the immigrant groups, however, they often stay in town for 15 to 20 years. They, better than any other tribe, fit the picture painted by the East African Royal Commission of people who for rather long periods have one foot in the countryside and one in town. They enjoy a higher level of living than complete specialization as either peasant or proletarian could afford.[15]

Another type of compromise. In most tribes, particularly where land is scarce, long absences from the country are unattractive because it is difficult for a man to re-establish himself in tribal society after a long absence. In most areas he would lose his land rights, or at least be given a much less desirable plot upon his return. However, a man may return to his place in the Luo system relatively easily even after a long absence. All Luo remain members of a continuing and cohesive system, even though at any one time many of their number are outside Luoland working for wages. Like the other Nilotic peoples for whom we have reliable information, the Luo have what has been called a "segmentary lineage" system.[16] Status in such systems is governed largely by patri-

15 United Kingdom, *East African Royal Commission 1953–1955 Report*, p. 154.

16 E. E. Evans-Pritchard, "Luo Tribes and Clans," *Rhodes-Livingstone Journal*, 7:24–40 (1949); A. W. Southall, *Lineage Formation among the Luo*, International African Institute Memorandum 26 (London, 1952).

lineal descent; in particular, political and property rights are so determined. A lineage holds such rights corporately, and relations among its members tend to be egalitarian. The social system as a whole consists of an ascending series of more inclusive lineages, from the group of siblings to all the nearly 1,000,000 Luo, who believe themselves to be descended from a common ancestor and thus ultimately to form one great lineage.

This lineage system has important implications for mobility between town and country. Rights in land are determined by lineage membership and are perpetual. According to Wilson's excellent study of Luo land law,

> . . . every member of an *Oganda* [maximal lineage, or "tribe"] has an inalienable right to cultivate a garden within the territory of his *Oganda*. Moreover, he has prior rights to that land over any nonmember of his *Oganda* who is occupying land in it. Every Luo of the Central Nyanza Tribes, therefore, has land in Central Nyanza, the amount of land he is entitled to cultivate depends upon the amount of the tribal area occupied by his *Libamba*, his nuclear lineage.[17]

> . . . [today a] larger number of . . . [Luo] go away to work . . . It is usual in these cases for the worker to allow his land to be used by a member of his *Jokakwaro* [lineage formed by sons of the same grandfather]. In such cases the worker is entitled to his land when he returns to claim it.[18]

The high degree of ethnic self-consciousness of the Luo who live in towns (which is probably due in part to the peculiarly cohesive structure of Luo society and in part to their being surrounded by alien Bantu-speaking peoples) helps them to keep in touch with events in Luoland and thus to keep track of their places in the social system. The Luo Union, an association that combines the functions of a "friendly society" and a political party, has active branches in all the main urban centers and serves as the organizational manifestation of Luo-ness for townsmen, much as ethnic associations have for European immigrants in American cities. Finally, Luo agriculture, emphasizing as it does annual crops which require minimal care during the growing season, allows men to bring members of their families with them to town for at least part of the year, leaving only a skeleton crew to tend the fields. This factor, with the relative cheapness of the boat fare across the lake,

[17] G. Wilson, "Luo Customary Law," unpublished manuscript, East African Institute of Social Research Library, p. 2.
[18] *Ibid.*, p. 57.

allows Luo in Kampala to lead more normal family lives than can most immigrants.

Thus Luo remain for relatively long periods in urban employment. Indeed, large numbers of them *must* go away to work, for the relation between land and population is now such that Luoland could not accommodate all Luo at once, even on the barest subsistence level. For some Luo, then, unlike the Baganda, life in town is a necessity; even so, they are less inclined than the Baganda to regard the town as home. Although the social system and environmental situation of the Luo are very different, they are able like the Baganda to regard wage labor in town purely instrumentally, as an adjunct to a tribal society to which they may return. Relative stability of employment in town, therefore, involves no motivational commitment to a distinct urban social system. In these circumstances, indeed, the latter hardly exists.

The Baganda and the Luo represent two types of compromise with, or partial commitment to, industrial labor. Both types make it possible to spend 10 to 20 years in town work, without the complete commitment to town life that might favor the development of a distinct urban industrial culture. Most other Africans, however, are even more marginally involved in town life. For most of them, conditions at home are such that a long stay in town tends to mean the loss of land rights. In order to maintain a foothold in the countryside, therefore, members of the other tribes tend to migrate only for short periods. Thus, the growth of industry and towns in Uganda has not led to the growth of an urban proletariat; the labor force consists of short-term migrants and of persons who, although they remain longer on the job, nevertheless are only temporary townsmen. The situation has certain implications for Uganda industry and social structure.

LIMITS OF INDUSTRIAL DEVELOPMENT IN UGANDA

We do not need to ask whether industry can develop with a labor force of that kind, for clearly industry *has* developed. However, its course in Uganda has been far from smooth, and only certain types of industry have prospered. First, the industries that have done well have been in some way protected from foreign competition, generally by high transport costs. Thus furniture factories, brickworks, a cement factory, and bottling plants have proved viable. Second, industries whose products must be consumed within a day or two have done well —newspaper presses, bakeries, and until recently an ice-cream factory.

Now even ice cream is imported from England at a price below that at which the local factory can compete. Finally, there are successful service industries and public utilities: engineering workshops, electricity generation, and the like.

Varied though these industries are they have two things in common: nearly all are small concerns and they tend to be of a kind that uses only a small proportion of semiskilled labor peculiar to the particular industry. To clarify the nature of such labor, work can be classified crudely as follows: (1) There is work that requires no particular skill; efficiency in such work is measured by experience and such general industrial attributes as punctuality and regularity. Work of this kind is available in many firms and industries, and a man can easily move from job to job. (2) There is skilled work in the sense of a craft or trade, e.g., the work of carpenters, plumbers, mechanics. In such work efficiency depends primarily on some years of training, in addition to the attributes pertaining to unskilled work. Skilled work is also widely available, and there is therefore no barrier to mobility between firms and industries. (3) In our classification the mobility of the skilled worker largely distinguishes him from the semiskilled. The sense in which we use this term is not qualitative; we do not distinguish, as it were, between semiskilled and skilled carpenters. By semiskilled work we mean work that requires training but that finds application in only one or a few firms and certainly not in more than one industry. A railway signalman was the example we gave earlier.

We are now in a position to see why certain types of industry have proved viable in Uganda despite what appears to be a formidable obstacle, namely, the lack of stability of the labor force. Unskilled labor, although inefficient, is not so much less efficient than in a fully stabilized labor force, and the inefficiency is compensated by low wages and savings in other costs. Skilled workers are mostly Baganda and, as we have seen, they are far more stable in the labor force than most immigrants. Their high wages contribute something toward their stability. Industries that use primarily skilled and unskilled labor are therefore not affected to any marked degree by the inexperience or instability of the labor force, provided they take the known features of the labor force into account.

The real problem arises in industries that have to employ large numbers of semiskilled workers. Because the cost of training them is borne wholly by the employers, a rapid labor turnover among trained semiskilled workers is very costly. Employers must pay attractive wages to the potentially stable element in the labor force, and this makes the average cost of labor high. Industries of this kind are therefore the least viable in Uganda unless they are protected from foreign competition, particularly from the competition of such densely populated countries as India and Japan, where the supply price of labor is low.

Two factories in Uganda employ semiskilled workers in large numbers: a textile mill and a cigarette factory. The textile mill faces heavy competition from India, and high labor costs have caused a loss in the first year of operation of a sum equivalent to one tenth of the capital invested in the firm. The commercial operators have recently decided to liquidate their interest. The cigarette factory pays high wages to its semiskilled workers and therefore has a very low turnover; it can afford to pay such wages because it is largely protected from foreign competition and because it enjoys particular advantages in the market for its raw material. However, the prospects in Uganda do not seem bright for industries that employ large numbers of semiskilled workers trained only for jobs in these industries and therefore sensitive to high mobility.

What, then, are the prospects for the development in Uganda of a more stable urban population with a distinct culture and social system of its own? Such a development does not seem likely in the near future. Unlike England in the eighteenth century, the rural population from which the towns draw workers are not agricultural wage laborers, but peasant farmers with rights of one kind or another in the land. The evidence seems to us to indicate that they will include town labor in the pattern of their lives up to the point where further commitment would involve breaking the tie with the land; further they will not go. It is both economically more rational and socially more rewarding for them to stop at this point. To be sure, the point varies for the various tribes; Luo and Baganda maximize their satisfactions with longer periods in town than do others. The position of these two peoples, however, is fundamentally the same in terms of continued commitment to rural, tribal life. We see no reason for this to change. The various schemes of agricultural development under way in parts of East Africa quite possibly will tip the scales further in the rural, tribal direction.

Another difference between eighteenth century England and Uganda today is worth mentioning. However much the English were divided regionally and by social classes, they were fundamentally one people culturally and linguistically. The African in Uganda who goes to town must offer his labor to an Indian or European with whom he has the greatest difficulty in forming a cultural *rapprochement*. Sheer communication is minimal; neither Baganda nor Luo, for example, speak the broken Kiswahili which is the local lingua franca with any fluency. Neither, for that matter, do many of the European and Indian employers. Still fewer Africans speak English. The linguistic problem will pass as education becomes more widespread; but the towns, particularly their commercial and industrial aspects, will no doubt continue for some time to be dominated by Indians and Europeans. This situation will inhibit the formation of an African urban social system.

The importance of this factor—the cultural attractiveness of town life—is suggested by Weber's study of farm workers in eastern Germany in the late nineteenth century. In explaining the tendency of German workers to leave the Junkers' estates in favor of the cities to the west, Weber stressed the desire to be free of the semifeudal personal dependence on the landowner. Even though life on the estate was more profitable in purely economic terms, urban industrial life was freer and hence more attractive.[19] For Uganda Africans, however, the atmosphere of alien domination in the towns is a negative factor, adding to the economic inducement to maintain rural ties.

[19] Max Weber, *Die Verhaeltnisse der Landarbeiter im ostelbischen Deutschland* (1892), cited by Reinhard Bendix in his *Max Weber: An Intellectual Portrait* (New York: Doubleday & Company, 1960), Chapter 2.

14 CHANGING CRAFT TRADITIONS IN INDIA

Milton Singer *

Recent discussions of economic development have shown a commendable broadening of horizons in the attention given to social, cultural, and psychological factors. In some analyses, however, the assertions about the role of these factors have assumed a definiteness that seems premature in the present state of our knowledge. This is particularly true of analyses that stress the inconsistencies between the values and traditions of preindustrial societies and the requirements of industrial societies. Such analyses are usually based on certain assumptions about traditional societies, on case studies where resistance to industrialization has been found, and on extrapolations of the sequence of industrial development observed in England, the United States, and the other industrially advanced countries of the West. The anthropologists' "culture pattern" theory has also begun to appear in these analyses.

THE CLASH OF "INDUSTRIALISM" AND "TRADITIONALISM"

Theory of Uniform Sequence

The general line of argument in these analyses of economic development may be schematized by the following propositions:

1. There is a linear sequence of industrial development that is essentially the same wherever it occurs. The complete version of this sequence is provided by the history of industrialization in England.

2. This sequence is started, maintained, and accelerated by a specific complex of values and motives necessary for a functionally integrated industrial society and its associated "culture pattern."

3. Most of the newly developing countries are deficient in the required values and motives in this complex and are characterized by preindustrial and nonindustrial value patterns, which are inconsistent with it.

* I am indebted to Isabel Caro for research assistance in the preparation of this paper, which was written during my tenure of a Fellowship at the Center for Advanced Study in the Behavioral Sciences, 1957–58.

4. If the newly developing countries are to follow the sequence of industrial development, they will need to adopt the industrial value complex and get rid of their traditional value patterns.

This last proposition has direct implications for decisions on policy concerning economic development, and if valid, confronts the policy makers of these countries with a difficult choice between two courses. These implications have been drawn explicitly by McClelland:

. . . Western and Eastern intellectuals both frequently observe that they sincerely hope the East can develop economically without losing the many valuable features of its existing way of life and institutions, without becoming "materialistic" like the West. To a certain extent such sentiments, while admirable in many ways, are simply incompatible with the psychological requirements for a modern society. For instance, peacefulness and calm acceptance of life as it occurs are virtues the East might well wish to maintain and the West to acquire, but it is surely nonsense to think one can maintain those values and at the same time develop a nation of hustling entrepreneurs whose vigorous efforts are absolutely essential to economic advance. Underdeveloped countries must develop a strenuous, more achievement-oriented attitude toward life whether they like it or not, if they want economic development.[1]

If the theory summarized in these propositions is true, the development policies of some countries, such as India, seem self-defeating. The aim of these policies—to adapt industrial growth to preindustrial traditions—is in this view misguided, since it tries to mix the unmixable and puts off the basic decision to industrialize or not to industrialize. If the theory is not true, circumspect policies of compromise may be more effective than all-or-none programs of industrialization, and the all-or-none attitude may itself create unnecessary ideological barriers to industrialization programs by making them appear more of a threat to basic values than they in fact are.

Some Difficulties with the Theory

Present knowledge of comparative economic development is not sufficient to permit a definitive refutation or confirmation of this theory. The literature on the subject is meager and scattered and needs systematization and appraisal. The conference for which this paper was

[1] David C. McClelland, "Community Development and the Nature of Human Motivation: Some Implications of Recent Research," unpublished paper, Massachusetts Institute of Technology, Center for International Studies, 1957. By permission.

prepared was a timely step in this direction, and Feldman and Moore's analysis (Chapters 1–4 supra) offers a useful preliminary taxonomy. In this paper the applicability of their analysis to India is considered, but first a few comments are in order.

In several important respects their analysis departs from the paradigm stated in our four propositions. The conception of industrial societies used by Feldman and Moore does not point either theoretically or empirically to a single path for industrial development; they present a set of norms and actions required for an industrial society that is highly differentiated with respect to loci and the sequence of development; they recognize that some traditional values in preindustrial and nonindustrial societies may predispose their members to industrialization. Yet their desire to avoid a purely relativistic position leads them in the end to accept the essentials of the paradigm. Even if there is not a single path of development which should be repeated by latecomers, they say "recapitulation of the sequence is required in order to break apart the traditional network of relationships, since the gradual 'humanization' of the industrial structure is by no means a return to the status quo ante but rather rests upon the productive efficiencies made possible by a radical technical and organizational transformation" (page 365 infra). Whereas in Feldman and Moore's analysis the initial stages of industrialization do not require any over-all commitment to any particular value system, at the end of the transitional phase "commitment requires rejection of the most basic values, and a greater extent of substitution of new integrating principles than at any previous point" (pages 65–66 supra). The choice between two complexes of values must be made when individuals are already deeply involved in industrialization, not at the beginning of the process. This conclusion follows from several assumptions made by Feldman and Moore—that there is a progressive individual involvement in all the loci of the industrial system, that the loci constitute a mutually interdependent organic system, and that this system requires "system acts and norms" to integrate it.

The implications of their analysis for policy are not surprising; they engender a skepticism about efforts to mitigate the evils of industrialism and about a transitional strategy that seeks to adapt the structural features of industrial society to pre-existing social standards: "some forms of adaptation may result in 'traditional stereotyping' and therefore in decreased capacity for continuous adaptation and growth" (page 364). In the newly developing countries, the sequence that the older industrial societies underwent, including large-scale organization and impersonalization of work, is probably essential.

Feldman and Moore offer this analysis not as a dogmatic assertion of known truths, but as a set of hypotheses and as a conceptual framework to guide discussion and further research. They invite further study and analysis of the variety of industrial orders and the alternative paths to them.

It seems worth while here to develop the intimation of a variety of industrial orders. In doing so, there is no wish to minimize the value of the detailed analysis made by Feldman and Moore. However, the general assumptions underlying their analysis, particularly with reference to the value inconsistencies of industrial and preindustrial societies, are open to challenge on the basis of recent studies of industrialization in a variety of social and cultural conditions.[2] These studies emphasize a fact not considered by Feldman and Moore to be decisive: that the late arrivals at industrialization are confronted by a situation different in some essentials from that confronted by the early arrivals. The late arrivals, for one thing, do not have to start from scratch; they can take advantage of a highly developed industrial technology, as well as of

[2] Some of these studies are: Cyril S. Belshaw, *In Search of Wealth*, American Anthropological Association Memoir No. 80 (February 1955); Norman S. Buchanan and Howard S. Ellis, *Approaches to Economic Development* (New York: Twentieth Century Fund, 1955); Bert Hoselitz, ed., *The Progress of Underdeveloped Countries* (Chicago: University of Chicago Press, 1952); Marion J. Levy, Jr., "Contrasting Factors in the Modernization of China and Japan," in Simon Kuznets, Wilbert E. Moore, and Joseph J. Spengler, eds., *Economic Growth: Brazil, India, Japan* (Durham: Duke University Press, 1955), pp. 496–536; Margaret Mead, ed., *Cultural Patterns and Technical Change* (Paris: UNESCO, 1953); Manning Nash, "The Multiple Society in Economic Development: Mexico and Guatemala," *American Anthropologist,* 59:825–833 (October 1957), and *Machine Age Maya,* American Anthropological Association Memoir No. 87 (April 1958); Kunio Odaka, "An Iron Workers' Community in Japan," *American Sociological Review,* 15:186–195 (April 1950); Beate R. Saltz, *The Human Element in Industrialization,* American Anthropological Association Memoir No. 85 (December 1955); Kuo-Heng Shih, *China Enters the Machine Age* (Cambridge: Harvard University Press, 1944); Thomas C. Smith, *Political Change and Industrial Development in Japan: Government Enterprise, 1868–1890* (Stanford: Stanford University Press, 1955), and "Old Values and New Techniques in the Modernization of Japan," *Far Eastern Quarterly,* 14:358–363 (May 1955); Sol Tax, *Penny Capitalism: A Guatemalan Indian Economy,* Smithsonian Institution, Institute of Social Anthropology, Publ. No. 16 (Washington, D. C., 1953); John Useem and Ruth H. Useem, *The Western-Educated Man in India* (New York: Dryden Press, 1955); William F. Whyte and Allan Holmberg, "Human Problems of U. S. Enterprise in Latin America," *Human Organization,* 15:1–40 (Fall 1956).

the experience and mistakes of the past. This industrial technology and its institutional organization, moreover, have been changing in the older industrialized societies, so that a wider range of technical and institutional possibilities is available than was available 150 years ago. Nuclear and solar energy, hydroelectric dams, and automation were not alternatives then, as they are for newly developing countries today. The role of state intervention is far greater today than in the early days of industrialization. Considerations of this kind suggest that the late arrivals cannot repeat the earlier sequences of industrial development.

Feldman and Moore, nevertheless, choose to set aside these considerations on the grounds that a recapitulation of sequence is necessary "to break apart the traditional network of relationships" and so to make way for the segmental and total commitments required by an industrial society. This conclusion, they say, is based on a theoretical construct rather than on empirically observed phenomena.

Theoretical constructs are useful and necessary tools of scientific analysis and must be judged primarily for their relevance and fruitfulness rather than for their degree of realism. The construct of a functionally integrated industrial system unified by systemic norms that require total acceptance and internalization by individual participants should be so judged on the basis of studies of particular industrial societies. But the use of such a construct to appraise and guide policies for economic development invites scrutiny of its initial plausibility and general bias. It is in this context that the paradigmatic analysis of industrialization and the Feldman-Moore version of it are most vulnerable to criticism.

To set up requirements for industrialization that are highly idealized extrapolations from the most advanced industrial societies as measures for industrialization in newly developing countries is surely to put the process on too remote a pedestal. Where in the older industrialized societies are the integration and total commitment that this construct projects? Many peoples have learned to live with machinery of different kinds, but only in the theoretical analyses of professional ideologues has this many-sided fact been generalized into an "industrial system."

The incompatibility of such a "system" with preindustrial societies is further exaggerated when it is compared not with existing situations in these societies but with a hypothetical and idealized construct of "traditional society" and "traditional values," which are never supposed to change. Specific failures of industrialization in these societies are immediately referred to some feature of this hypothetical traditional system; and the diverse, concrete resistances are generalized into a monolithic conservative force of "traditionalism." The battle between this force and "industrialism" is a clash of hypothetical constructs, which does not realistically reflect obstacles to economic development.

PREINDUSTRIAL TRADITIONS OF THE INDIAN CRAFTSMAN

In the paper cited, McClelland uses an unsuccessful effort to organize hand-loom weavers in Orissa, India, as an example of the wrong approach to economic development. The entrepreneurial "values and motives" were missing, he believes, and this absence prevented the scheme from working. Some of these missing values are the importance of maintaining quality of workmanship, concern for a long-run relationship to consumers, and the assumption of personal responsibility for the product of one's labor. The Orissa weavers do not have an underlying drive for achievement, McClelland infers, because some weaver middlemen tried to sell inferior materials instead of assuming financial responsibility for them. These missing values are just the ones he finds in European entrepreneurial behavior and even among Western social and technical assistance workers. Unless some way is found to substitute these values for the traditional values, institutional rearrangements will not be effective. McClelland believes that these changes in values can be brought about by education and persuasion, by introducing changes in the social system, and by early character training. Of these methods, he favors early training in self-reliance, in high standards of performance, in cooperation, and in work with the hands, as the method most likely to succeed. If an entrepreneur brings the Orissa weavers out of their homes to work in one place, he can teach them these new values and others, such as limited contracts, achieved status, and "universalism," which are "required" for industrial development.

This diagnosis, in spite of the language and techniques of contemporary research on motivations, is curiously reminiscent of Samuel Smiles and the homiletics of eighteenth and nineteenth century England. As is now known, these did not succeed in bringing the English hand weavers out of their homes into the factories. The early factory population was recruited from the marginal population of women and children. Among the reasons the hand weavers resisted factory employment was their fear that it would deprive them of their personal relations to their work, their sense of achievement in identifiable products, their self-reliance and independence, their settled relation to customers, their habits of work, and their status as skilled craftsmen (since the workshop and factory disciplines were associated with poorhouses and orphanages).[3] These values are also important for the Indian hand weavers and craftsmen generally but are expressed within a different cultural tradition and scheme of social organization.[4]

Relation to Kinship and Caste

Handicrafts in India have been cultivated within particular families, usually belonging to similar castes, from generation to generation. The accumulated practical and technical knowledge is transmitted through an apprentice system in which the son or apprentice grows up with the craft in the house of the craftsman. Within the villages these artisans make up the regular complement of village craftsmen; particular families of artisans have served particular families of villagers for many generations. In the towns the artisans were organized into guildlike groups, consisting usually of all persons of a particular caste who practiced a particular craft, but including as well persons of a different caste who pursued the same occupation. These guilds (sreni) could act as law courts, had written rules, exercised some control over prices and quality, and established special market towns. They negotiated and supervised contracts, obtained special privileges for their members to march in processions with emblems, and acted as mutual aid societies.[5] Groups of artisans were also attached to temples and royal courts, the two most important markets for handicrafts.

The status of craftsman is usually associated with the sudras, the lowest of the four orders of Indian society. This, however, is a theoretical specification. In practice, the craftsman's status is generally low, but it varies with type of craft, locality, and position of the individual

[3] I am indebted to David Landes for information about the English hand weavers. See also M. D. Morris, "The Recruitment of an Industrial Labor Force in India, with British and American Comparisons," *Comparative Studies in Society and History*, 2:305–328 (April 1960).

[4] My chief sources of information on the traditions of the Indian craftsman are the writings of A. K. Coomaraswamy, Stella Kramrisch, and E. B. Havell, as indicated in subsequent footnotes. Coomaraswamy's *The Indian Craftsman* (London: Probsthain & Co., 1909) is a good brief introduction. During the autumn and winter of 1954–55 I observed surviving traditions. See also Nirmal Kumar Bose, *The Canons of Orissan Architecture* (Calcutta: R. Chatterjee, 1932).

[5] The organization and functions of the guilds in Southern India are described in A. Appadorai, *Economic Conditions in Southern India (1000–1500 A.D.)*, 2 vols. (Madras: University of Madras, 1936).

worker in a functional hierarchy.[6] The goldsmith, for example, generally has a higher status than other craftsmen. The ancient law books permitted all orders to practice crafts, and there are historical references to Brahman and royal craftsmen. Even the lowly *sudra* artisans aspire to raise their social status and sometimes succeed. In South India the ironsmiths, workers in wood, brass, and stone, and the goldsmiths have a legend of descent from Vishvakarma, the divine architect of the universe, and claim to be Brahmans, a claim not generally recognized by their neighbors. Even if artisans are otherwise considered "unclean," their association with ceremonial objects gives artisans a special prestige and status in ritual contexts. The consecration of temple images, for instance, calls for a special ceremony in which the image maker brings his tools to the temple to "open the eyes" of the image. One of Manu's rules is that the hands of the craftsman at work are always pure. Asoka decreed capital punishment for anyone who caused a craftsman to lose an eye or a hand.

The values of the Indian craftsman are expressed within this tradition and social organization. Since his craft is not only his occupation but his *dharma* and *karma,* the artisan regards his skill as a revealed mystery which he must guard, preserve, and transmit, just as the Brahmans have preserved and transmitted the Vedas. His workmanship must be as good as he possibly can make it if he is to live up to his *dharma*. The craftsman who produces inferior workmanship violates his *karma* and commits a kind of sin. The application of the doctrine of *karma* to the crafts is illustrated in the following list of punishments for misconduct:

[6] Surviving records give the scale of remuneration paid the designers and various architects and builders who worked on the Taj Mahal. Three principal designers each received 1,000 rupees per month, one architect received 800 rupees per month, six received 400 each, and nine received between 200 and 400 each, according to E. B. Havell, *Indian Sculpture and Painting* (London: John Murray, 1908), pp. 243–244. For some of the variations in status and economic conditions of the artisan crafts in villages and towns, see the following: F. G. Bailey, *Caste and the Economic Order* (Manchester: University of Manchester Press, 1957), pp. 109–117; S. C. Dube, *Indian Village* (London: Routledge & Kegan Paul, 1956); Stephen Fuchs, *The Children of Hari: A Study of the Nimar Balahis in the Central Provinces* (Vienna: Herold, 1950), Chapter 32; D. R. Gadgil, "Indian Economic Organization," in Kuznets, Moore, and Spengler, eds., *op. cit.,* pp. 448–463; R. G. Kakade, *A Socio-Economic Survey of Weaving Communities in Sholapur,* Gokhale Institute of Politics and Economics, Publ. No. 14 (Poona, 1947); McKim Marriott, ed., *Village India: Studies in the Little Community* (Chicago: University of Chicago Press, 1955), especially Chapters 1–3; M. N. Srinivas, ed., *India's Villages* (Calcutta: West Bengal Government Press, 1955).

A man's deeds follow him in his next birth. Thus one who knows amiss his craft will fall into hell and suffer after his death. Builders and painters taking money falsely from other men thereby grow poor. Builders and painters who know their business well will become rajas, lacking naught; so also cunning painters are meet to become nobles. Builders and painters both, who know naught of their craft, when here are given according to the work accomplished, take that money and (leaving their work) rush home therewith, though they get thousands, there is nothing even for a meal; they have not so much as a piece of cloth to wear, that is the reward of past births, as you know; dying, they fall into hell and suffer pain a hundred lacs of years; if they escape, they will possess a deformed body and live in great distress; when born as a man it will be as a needy builder; the painter's eyes will squint—look ye, what livelihood can there be for him? [7]

To assure the cooperation of his tools and his materials, the craftsman performs a religious ceremony, a *puja*, to them when he starts a new piece of work. Once a year during the Dashahra festival all artisans worship their tools. This practice has been extended to include such modern tools as surgical instruments, laboratory equipment, automobiles, and typewriters.

Innovation and Individuality

While originality is not a major value for its own sake in this tradition, innovations are known, and the distinctive styles of individual workmen are recognized and appreciated. J. L. Kipling describes the following practice as of 1881–82:

In building a house, for example, the work people are all paid wages more or less regularly, but for any extra spurt or during the execution of delicate or difficult details they are often liberally treated with sweetmeats, tobacco, sherbet, etc. In some districts when a carpenter has made a carven *chaukut* for door or window he takes a holiday to exhibit it, and spreading a sheet on the ground lays it down in front of the house it is to adorn, and sits there to receive the congratulations and gifts of his admiring townsmen. As much as Rs 100 have in one day been thrown to the carver of a particularly good piece of work.[8]

The individuality of the traditional craftsman's work is often overlooked because it is usually anonymous and because it follows fixed

[7] The Maya matya, quoted by Radhakamal Mukerjee in *The Foundations of Indian Economics* (London: Longmans, Green & Co., 1916), pp. 49–50, and in a slightly different version in Coomaraswamy, *The Indian Craftsman*, pp. 69–70. Quoted by permission of Longmans, Green & Co., Inc.

[8] E. B. Havell, *Essays on Indian Art, Industry, and Education* (Madras: G. A. Natesan & Co., 1907), pp. 129–130.

rules and processes. Coomaraswamy's description of the image maker's tradition undoubtedly characterizes the external transmission of all the crafts:

Images such as the dancing Shiva or the seated Buddha are the work of a school, not of any one artist. All essential details are passed on from father to son in pupillary succession through successive generations, the medium of transmission consisting of example, exact formulas in Sanskrit verse, and diagrammatic sketches. Thus during many centuries the artists of one district apply themselves to the interpretation of the same ideas; the origin of those ideas is more remote than any particular example . . .

We scarcely know the name of a single painter or sculptor of the great periods.[9]

An ancient manual quoted by Coomaraswamy links the esthetic qualities of a work with conformity to the craftsman's rules: "(An image made) according to rule (*shāstra*) is beautiful, no other forsooth is beautiful: some (deem) that beautiful which follows after (their own) fancy, but that not according to the rule (appears) unlovely to the discerning." [10] This passage at least suggests that there were craftsmen who preferred to follow their own fancy!

Disregarding these heretics—and heretics they were, for violation of the shastraic rules was also a violation of religion—a close examination of the products of the ancient craftsmen or observation of the surviving practices reveals a good deal of individuality within the tradition. General rules and recipes are transmitted, but for the individual craftsman these are bare outlines which, like the *Ragas* of Indian music, guide his improvisation. He could not reproduce exactly the same work twice simply by following the rules, even if he wished to, and the products of different craftsmen are distinctly recognizable even when unsigned. Moreover, in the tradition there is a sanctioned procedure for seeking inspiration from an individualized and concrete "fancy." This is the Yoga-like preparation of the imagination which the craftsman cultivated before starting a new work: "The Indian imager approached his work with great solemnity, invoking the god whom he would represent. In the Agni Purana, he is told, the night before undertaking a great work to pray: 'O thou Lord of all gods, teach me in dreams how to carry out all the work I have in my mind.' " [11]

[9] A. K. Coomaraswamy, *The Arts and Crafts of India and Ceylon* (London: T. N. Foulis, 1913), pp. 21–22. Quoted by permis ion of Peter Davis, Ltd., London.
[10] *Ibid.*, p. 16.
[11] *Ibid.*, p. 25.

As with modern artists, the finished product sometimes astonished its maker. On the Kailasanatha temple at Ellora, Kramrisch observed an inscription that records the reaction of the master to his own work: "Oh how did I make it?" Kramrisch, who has carefully examined sculptures and monuments all over India, has found names of individual artists and families of craftsmen on their work. One inscription reads: "There has not been and there shall not be in Jambudvipa any expert in the art of building temples equal to Narasobha." Her conclusions from these observations on the anonymity of the Indian artist-craftsman is not that he did not want to be known, but "on the contrary he wanted to be known as conveying surpassingly well what other artists then and in the future would endeavor to convey." [12]

This individuality of the craftsman may still be observed today, deeply embedded in the traditional routines. A worker of bronze images whom the writer met in Madras City knows brief Sanskrit verses describing how the image of each deity should be drawn. He does not understand as much Sanskrit as his father, from whom he learned the verses, but has memorized a great number of them, as well as verbatim translations of each into Tamil. When he receives an order for a temple or household image, only the name of the deity is usually specified; the form is specified by the Sanskrit verse, which is considered as important a part of the image maker's professional knowledge as skill in drawing, modeling, and metal casting. Ability to recite these verses is a major requirement for passing an image maker's examination. The verse for an image of Rama, e.g., prescribes: "the chest should be like the face of a young cow, the thighs like the plantain, nose like the sesamum flower, feet like the tortoise; this is the form of Rama." As he recited this verse, the image maker quickly sketched a figure of Rama and alongside it the items enumerated in the verse, to show its mnemonic value. The verse obviously does not describe every aspect of the figure, nor does it assure that the drawings of any two image makers would be exactly alike. For despite rules memorized by rote about the shape of images and their proportions, and despite highly standardized processes and materials, the work of different individuals is distinctive. This point was emphatically made by the image maker. He was also quite proud of having introduced some improvements

[12] Stella Kramrisch, "Artist, Patron and Public in India," *Far Eastern Quarterly*, 15:335–342 (May 1956). Additional evidence of a similar kind appears in her "Traditions of the Indian Craftsman," in Milton Singer, ed., *Traditional India: Structure and Change* (Bloomington, Indiana: *Journal of American Folklore*, 1958), pp. 18–24.

over his father's work. One of these was the discovery that a fine grade of sand from a particular river bed, when mixed with the traditional ingredients, would make a firmer and smoother cast.

DECLINE OF HANDICRAFTS AND THE PROBLEMS OF TRANSITION

For the traditional Indian craftsman his trade is a way of life supported by religious sanctions and expressed in religious themes and objects. His knowledge and skill are a divine revelation which he must carefully guard and transmit to his disciples; and his tools are inspired instruments which will do his bidding if he shows them the appropriate reverence. His occupation is his birthright, but this does not release him from the moral obligation to do his best and to strive for excellence. When he does so, he not only earns religious merit and avoids the fate of sinners, but he will also confer merit on his clients through the sale or gift of his products. His hands and eyes will be respected and the market for his products assured. Although his status is sometimes lowly, it may be raised by means of righteous conduct.

Adverse Effects of British Policy

The values expressed in this tradition are just some of those that McClelland found missing among the Orissa weavers and necessary for their economic advancement. For several reasons these values do not appear prominently in the life of this particular group of weavers: the study reported had a practical orientation and was not particularly concerned with the traditions of the hand weaver; social ideals are somewhat removed from everyday behavior; and, most important, the traditions we have been describing are no longer what they once were. When Gandhi started the Khadi campaign in his Satyagraha Ashram in Ahmadabad in 1915, he used factory-spun yarn. When he later decided to use homespun, he had great difficulty finding a few spinning wheels, and women to teach the art.[13] Even during this period there already was public discussion of the plight of the hand weavers and of the handicrafts in general.[14]

[13] Mohandas K. Gandhi, *An Autobiography: The Story of My Experiments with Truth,* trans. by Mahadev Desai (Boston: Beacon Press, 1957), Chapters 39–41.

[14] Alfred Chatterton, *Industrial Evolution in India* (Madras: The "Hindu" Office, 1912), Chapter 8; Sir Theodore Morison, *The Economic Transition in India* (London: John Murray, 1911), Chapter 6; Radhakamal Mukerjee, *The Foundations of Indian Economics,* Chapter 11 and passim. Records of earlier discussions of the problem at the administrative level are analyzed in R. D. Choksey, *Economic History of the Bombay Deccan and Karnatak (1818–1868)* (Poona: R. D. Choksey, 1945).

The conditions of the artisans recall those of their English counterparts at the beginning of the nineteenth century. In one respect these conditions were brought on by a similar force—the competition of cheaper manufactured goods. The Indian case differed from the English, however, in several important respects: most of the manufactured goods were produced not in India but in England, and these were given special protection by a foreign power that was not particularly sympathetic to Indian manufactures or to handicraft industries. In England (and in Europe, too) the example of superior Indian craftsmanship and materials, combined with restrictive legislation against Indian imports, stimulated English craftsmen to imitate them and then to develop new processes and materials in textile manufacture. Economic historians now see this as an important impetus toward development of the factory system in England.[15] This process deprived the Indian craftsman simultaneously of the European market and his home market. And the government of India not only pushed the products of Lancashire, but in many ways discouraged a transitional development in the direction of industrialization in India. For incipient Indian industrialists, capital, equipment, technical education, railroad rates, and government orders were difficult to obtain except on terms that favored their English and European competitors. Experiments in improving hand weavers' looms and skills were officially discouraged.

The result of this situation was that while the Indian craftsman was losing his market to manufactured products, very little in the way of alternative industrial employment was being developed. Both the urban and the village artisans were thrown back on the land; the proportion of the population dependent on agriculture actually increased from 61 percent in 1891 to 73 percent in 1921. After World War I the government's policy toward indigenous manufacturing changed, but too late to remove the economic dislocations produced by the decline of the handicrafts.[16] There were, of course, other causes for this decline: the decline of courts and temples as special markets and patrons, the passing of the guilds and indigenous merchants' organizations, and the coming of cheap transportation which brought European goods inland. These factors, however, had a negative effect on Indian economic development, chiefly in conjunction with foreign rule.

[15] A. P. Wadsworth and Julia de L. Mann, *The Cotton Trade and Industrial Lancashire, 1600–1780* (Manchester: Manchester University Press, 1931).

[16] Freda Utley, *Lancashire and the Far East* (London: Allen & Unwin, 1931).

Attempts to Revive Handicrafts

Now that India has her own government, there is a far more sympathetic attitude towards both handicrafts and indigenous manufactures. The policy of the government, as expressed in the first and second five-year plans, is to develop modern large-scale industry as well as cottage and small industry. This policy is based on the desire to build an "industrial tradition" continuous with the older preindustrial tradition. This means avoiding the evils of large-scale industrialism and urban concentration, but it also means the improvement of productivity and the conditions of life for all, through a decentralized economy with widely dispersed units. Under this general policy a serious effort is being made to rehabilitate the handicrafts and cottage industries by providing cooperative organizations for credit, purchasing, and marketing, and special facilities for technical training and research in design and market trends.[17]

It is too early to say whether these efforts will succeed in resuscitating the weakened traditions of the craftsman. Culturally there is a great deal to be said for such efforts to salvage a heritage of skill and art. Economically, too, a strong case can be made for using existing resources of capital and labor to provide employment and consumers' goods in the difficult period of transition to larger-scale industrial organization.[18] It will not be surprising if some groups of artisans resist the governmental efforts to improve their lot during this period. Historically they have good reason to distrust government policy, and there has hardly been time for them to discover that the present government is different and genuinely interested in their welfare. Perhaps, too, like the English artisans of the nineteenth century, the Indian artisans fear

[17] Ford Foundation, International Planning Team, *Report on Small Industries in India* (New Delhi: Government of India, Ministry of Commerce and Industry, 1955); Government of India Planning Commission, Second Five-Year Plan Committee, *Village and Small-Scale Industries* (New Delhi, 1955); Institute of Traditional Cultures, Madras, "Report on the Madras Seminar on the Role of Arts and Crafts," *University of Madras Bulletin*, 1957, especially pp. 211–216; *Traditional Cultures*, Proceedings of the Seminar Organized by the University of Madras under the Auspices of UNESCO, University of Madras, 1956, especially pp. 80–90.

[18] An economic as well as sentimental case for small-scale industry is now recognized by economists. See Peter T. Bauer and Basil S. Yamey, *The Economics of Underdeveloped Countries* (Cambridge Economic Handbooks; Cambridge, England: Cambridge University Press, 1957), pp. 252–254; H. G. Aubrey, "Small Industry in Economic Development," *Social Research*, 18:269–312 (September 1951).

that proposed changes will destroy the values of their surviving handicraft traditions. The fear of being displaced by technical improvements is widespread among these groups, and also has a sound historical basis. The artisans no doubt have other "rational" reasons for resistance.[19]

Factors Favoring Modern Industrial Development

Such cases of resistance should be analyzed in terms of the historical, "rational," and specific traditional factors that are involved. We have tried to sketch the outlines of an analysis that may be applicable to the weavers of Orissa, although we are not so much interested in explaining that particular case as in a method of approaching the problem. This method begins with analysis of the factors that can be shown to be operating in a specific situation, rather than of factors alleged to be absent in the given situation but required to be present if a hypothetical situation of a different kind is to be attained. An empirical examination of the situation actually reveals that many of the values alleged to be absent are in fact there, and that the problem of gaining acceptance for technical improvements is not one of changing the craftsman's character and values, but of assuring him continued opportunities for the expression of that character and those values during changes in the social and economic organization of the nation.

In the present situation one major value that is changing in India is the attitude toward manual labor. Among the upper castes and the educated there has been a tendency to despise such labor even if highly skilled. This attitude has two sources: the general association of the handicraft occupations with low castes, and the policy under British rule of encouraging literary and legal education for administrative careers and of discouraging industrial and scientific education. Even where engineering training was provided, its chief purpose was to produce civil engineers for the Public Works Department, rather than mechanical engineers. The present Indian government is keenly aware of this problem and is supporting special institutes for scientific and technical training. Children in elementary school are being taught

[19] This fear is reported by the Ford Foundation International Planning Team. Anthropological observers also have found many "rational" reasons for the Indian villagers' reactions to technical improvements. See, for example, S. C. Dube, "Cultural Factors in Rural Community Development," *Journal of Asian Studies*, 16:19–30 (November 1956); David G. Mandelbaum, "Planning and Social Change in India," *Human Organization*, 12(3):4–12 (Fall 1953); and McKim Marriott, "Technological Change in Overdeveloped Rural Areas," *Economic Development and Cultural Change*, 1:261–272 (December 1952).

about the dignity of labor. Patriotic movements, such as Swadeshi, Khadi, the revival of national arts and crafts, and community development and extension, have increased the upper castes' and the educated classes' respect for "body work" and have brought some of them directly into it.

The economic significance of the negative attitude toward manual labor is easily exaggerated. The attitude has never extended to the products of such labor and therefore has not affected commerce in handicrafts. Moreover, the people who actually perform this labor, the artisans, do not share this attitude, although it naturally influences their status aspirations. They are proud of their craft tradition and the manual skills of weaving, casting, modeling, drawing, carving and the like, which their families have cultivated for generations. The ancient craft manuals (*silpa sastras*) are still lovingly preserved on palm leaf manuscripts in these families. If craftsmen do not encourage their children to continue the traditional trades, it is not because they despise manual labor, but because they do not see very good prospects for making a living in them. If they leave their traditional occupations, it is because they are destitute and want to get into occupations that will give them better incomes, higher status, and work consonant with their skills. In one family of bronze-image makers in Madras, only one son, aged 34, is practicing the father's occupation in the family workshop. Another, aged 22, is assisting him but will not continue if something better turns up. A third, aged 28, has moved to North India, where he has found work at a temple. The oldest, aged 36, is a metal caster in the Madras School of Arts and is assisted by the youngest, aged 18. A sixth, aged 25, works as an illustrator for a local magazine.

Given public recognition, higher status, and opportunities for modern education, India's craftsmen are willing and able to furnish the technical skills needed in an emerging industrial economy. McCrory's observations on hereditary ironworkers, blacksmiths, and carpenters, who have set up their own small industries, give additional support for an optimistic conclusion:

The small craftsman-entrepreneur is not illiterate, backward, or downtrodden. He does not need to be awakened. He has the enterprise, the energy, the industrial outlook, and the skill *now* to make things efficiently and well. He would like more education, more technical know-how, and a better acquaintance with business and marketing practices, of course. But right now, he cannot even use what he has. For the present, he wants not to be fostered but to be listened to. And what he says is that in the beginning it would require nothing more—or less—than a judicious application of capital to enable him to start using the assets he already has effectively. At the very least, he deserves to be listened to.[20]

This entrepreneurial ambition of traditional craftsmen is particularly significant in view of the fact that, except for the Parsis, industrial entrepreneurs in India have come mainly from the traditional trading and money-lending castes—Gujaratis, Marwaris, Chettiars, etc.[21]

There are those who believe that the major barrier to India's economic growth is not the resistance of this or that group of craftsmen but the entire institutional framework. This argument is a familiar one. We have all heard about the sick sacred cows, the holy beggars, the irresponsible and lazy members of a joint family, the lack of mobility in the caste system, and the otherworldliness of Hinduism. The cogency of this argument rests, it seems, on a systematic selection of those features of India's institutional framework that appear to be in conflict with the conditions of an idealized free enterprise system, and on systematic neglect of those features of the same institutions that have played a positive economic role in the past and can support economic development today. Since this paper is concerned with the crafts, we cannot deal here with all sides of the institutional framework. Elsewhere the writer has suggested how India's "spirituality" and asceticism have inspired modern social and economic reform in the movements of Gandhi, Vinobha Bhave, and others.[22]

Religion and economics have always been mutually supportive in India and the partnership is not likely to be dissolved in the near future. The belief that modern technology is incompatible with traditional religious institutions and practices and will be resisted by such institutions cannot find much support in India. On the contrary, in this religious sphere the acceptance of technical improvements seems

20 James T. McCrory, *Small Industry in a North Indian Town* (New Delhi: Government of India Press, 1956), pp. 41–42. See also James J. Berna, "Patterns of Entrepreneurship in South India," *Economic Development and Cultural Change*, 7:343–362 (April 1959).

21 D. R. Gadgil, *Origins of the Modern Indian Business Class: An Interim Report* (New York: Institute of Pacific Relations, 1959).

22 Milton Singer, "Cultural Values in India's Economic Development," *The Annals*, 305:81–91 (May 1956); John Goheen, M. N. Srinivas, D. G. Karve, and Milton Singer, "India's Cultural Values and Economic Development," *Economic Development and Cultural Change*, 7:1–12 (October 1958). See also Hajime Nakamura, *The Vitality of Religion in Asia* (Rutland: Charles E. Tuttle Company, for the Congress for Cultural Freedom, 1956).

smoothest and least disturbing to traditional values and practices. No five-year plan was required for the installation of public address systems and neon lights in temples, for the use of airplanes, railroads, and automobiles for religious pilgrimages, or for cooking the pilgrims' food in pressure cookers. If the incompatibility does not exist in the sacred core of the culture, it is not likely to be of great significance in other spheres.

CONCLUSION

The gist of the preceding argument can be put in more general form by emphasizing the goal of the transition rather than its points of departure. What is an "industrial tradition"? Some of the things it is not are fairly obvious by now; an industrial tradition is not the factory system as it developed in England in the eighteenth and nineteenth centuries. Some elements of this form of economic organization will be found in newly developing countries, but there is no inherent necessity for the English experience to be recapitulated, nor is there any inherent reason why a factory system cannot coexist with cottage and small-scale industries in dispersed units. An industrial tradition is not a specific complex of values providing the motive force for industrialization. Even preindustrial and nonindustrial societies that have some values that differ from those of industrialized societies may be able to industrialize without destroying their basic values. The values usually adduced as necessary conditions for industrialization have their counterparts in many nonindustrial and preindustrial societies.[23] What differs is not the abstract values and motives, but the social and cultural contexts from which they have been abstracted. If these values have not propelled the newly developing countries into an advanced stage of industrialization, perhaps this only shows the limitations of values as motive forces in the absence of capital, skill, favorable government policy, and other concrete requirements of industrialization, rather than that the people of these countries need a different value system and "character."

The massive, personified force of "industrialism" doing battle with

[23] E. K. Francis, *In Search of Utopia: The Mennonites in Manitoba* (Glencoe: Free Press, 1955); Margaret Mead, ed., *Cooperation and Competition among Primitive Peoples* (New York: McGraw-Hill Book Company, 1947); see also Milton B. Singer, "Shame Cultures and Guilt Cultures," in Gerhart Piers and Milton Singer, *Shame and Guilt: A Psychoanalytical and Cultural Study* (Springfield, Ill.: Charles C. Thomas, 1953).

the equally massive, personified force of "traditionalism" is not an industrial tradition, nor is it equivalent to the more precise construct of "a functionally integrated industrial society," for that is a purely intellectual abstraction. Industrial traditions are "concrete" historical growths. While these growths in different parts of the world may have some elements in common, because of diffusion and mutual interaction, it is highly doubtful that this denominator will ever approximate an integrated, functioning society and culture.

Industrial traditions are plural and distinctive because they are aspects of societies and civilizations which are plural and distinctive. French industrial traditions differ from the English, and both of these differ from the Japanese and the Russian. It may be possible to specify a particular industrial process or product in abstraction from national and regional cultures, but if a particular society adopts such a product or process, its function and significance inevitably will be shaped by the receiving culture and social organization. These in turn may be changed by the new element. The resultant will be new and distinctive, but it need not be sharply discontinuous with what existed before the change. New words will appear in the language; new techniques of communication will change the culture media into mass media; and new habits of work and leisure will be formed. Not all such changes will be harmonious with older social and cultural patterns. But to the extent that such changes result in the formation of industrial traditions, these will be as grafts on preindustrial and nonindustrial traditions rather than as completely new species of plants. The problems of economic development confronting the newly developing countries might be fruitfully considered problems in the formation of industrial traditions in different types of societies and cultures, tribal and peasant, as well as industrial.

15 COMPETING STATUS SYSTEMS

Melvin M. Tumin

Two major themes are found in several of the papers presented in this symposium. The first theme forcefully asserts that the processes by which modernization takes place are numerous and diverse and that our knowledge of these is still so limited that the time is not yet ripe to attempt any all-embracing generalizations. The second theme acknowledges the diversity of the experiences of various societies, but strains toward provisional generalizations about the evolutionary processes of change and about the proper model of a modernized society.

The tension between these themes reminds us that we must view with suspicion any attempts to seal off questions by laying down propositions on what *must* take place in history, or what is sociologically unavoidable in the efficient arrangement of institutions. At the same time, the prolixity and incomparability of the data in the several papers remind us just as strongly that some genuine effort must be made to develop a more adequate comparative framework of concepts, and to attempt at least some provisional models of the relations among relevant variables.

A second noteworthy feature of these papers is the apparent ease and responsibility with which persons trained in one social science have managed meaningfully to utilize and incorporate data gathered by students trained in other disciplines. It is, for instance, impressive to discover how effectively a cultural anthropologist can take account of numerous political and economic factors while keeping kinship a central variable in his model of transformation. Political scientists similarly manage to keep various aspects of the political system in focus while considering the bearing of economic and cultural factors on political organization and process. And economists have not been insensitive to the numerous cultural and political factors that affect economic organization and reorganization. That these different scholars have taken the data and concepts of other disciplines out of the matrix of their original formulation does not mean they have done injustice to or distorted the facts.

RELEVANCE OF STRATIFICATION THEORY

Considerations such as those sketched above make it easier to deal with a rather large body of political, economic, cultural, and social psychological data within a framework of theory about social stratification and to try to apply these to the process of modernization. Two things must be said of any such theory: (1) Stratification is only one feature of any social system, and no approach through stratification theory can include or exhaust the phenomena relevant to the full analysis of a social system. (2) The study of stratification is primarily concerned with inequalities in the distribution and utilization of the good things in life. These are ordinarily subsumed under the rubrics of power, property, and prestige.[1] Study of such inequalities is therefore concerned with political structure and process, economic forms and functions, the cultural arrangements by which persons are differently evaluated in regard to their worth and desirability, and the social psychological dynamics underlying these arrangements.

The successful use of such diverse bodies of data requires the construction of some analytic apparatus that, while unavoidably compressing much detail, makes it easier to discern the interrelations of these materials. At this point in the development of our theory, no complicated or complex model of stratification that is relevant to modernization can be formulated. However, it is possible to list the aspects of social structure and action that are most pertinently involved in the recruitment of talent in any social system. With a schematic presentation of these aspects, it is possible to indicate the places at which political, economic, cultural, and sociological data may best be included, so that their more general relations can be analyzed.[2]

[1] Certain problems are created by the use of only these three categories. For instance, only by stretching the common connotations of the term "property" can we include such a valued item as "job satisfaction." Yet, in at least one theoretically possible major variant of stratification systems, job satisfaction must be considered a major "reward" in the system, and hence has to be allocated to one category of rewards. Other more complex matters, such as "style of life," similarly resist being subsumed by these rubrics. But for present purposes we assume that anything that does not refer primarily to the ability to get others to adopt one's own means and ends (power), or to a favorable position in some rank order of evaluation (prestige), is to be included under property. Thus property is used to mean "rights over goods and services, both tangible and intangible," and the term "goods" obviously refers to much more than is ordinarily connoted by it.

[2] The traditional view of the function of stratification in the efficient recruitment of talent is best stated in Kingsley Davis and Wilbert E. Moore, "Some Principles of Stratification," *American Sociological Review*, 10:242–249 (April 1945). The sharpest difference of opinion is expressed in Melvin Tumin, "Some Principles of Stratification: A Critical Analysis," *American Sociological Review*, 18:387–394 (August 1953). Bernard Barber's version of Parsons' theory of stratification, as found in *Social*

Although stratification is concerned with inequalities in power, property, and prestige, the focus of interest here is on the recruitment of labor and the development of its commitment to a new form of work and a new set of social relations. Our special interest, then, is with the recruitment of talent for the occupational sector of the society and the hierarchical distributions of occupations and incomes. We are concerned with the general questions that must be asked about any such system of recruitment and any such hierarchy of positions and rewards. These questions and the distinctions involved do not exhaust the relevant materials but are central to any case study and to any theory of stratification.

In the following outline of variables relevant to the location of individuals on occupational and income ladders, nine features of stratification systems are listed. The major possible variations appear under each of these: [3]

    I. Degree of proliferation and specialization of statuses
        1. Much specialization among many statuses
        2. Division into only two or three major statuses
    II. Manner of entrance into statuses
        1. Through competition (equal or unequal)
        2. Through maturation or assumption
        3. Through inheritance
    III. Fineness of measurement of role performance
        1. Finely calibrated measures
        2. Gross distinctions between the acceptable and unacceptable

---

Stratification (New York: Harcourt, Brace and Company, 1957), adds nothing to previous theoretical statements. Indeed, as Barber presents the case for the "inevitability" of stratification, it becomes clearer than in either Parsons' formulation or that of Davis and Moore that there is nothing inevitable at all about the need for unequal rewards for unequal work. Between the universal facts of differentiation of function and differential evaluation for moral conformity, on the one hand, and the "unavoidability" of unequal rewards for and invidious distinctions among such functions, on the other, there are no necessary and sufficient connections that have been described in any theoretical work.

[3] Surely this list by no means exhausts the relevant variables. The limits of the paper do not permit me to give a variety of illustrations, even hypothetical ones, which would clarify the ways in which these variables are strategically relevant to analysis of the process of recruitment of labor. Numerous other questions that are ordinarily asked about any stratification system, viz., concerning the degree and types of mobility and the barriers to mobility, do not appear in this list. But most, if not all, of these are here considered as derivative consequences of the combined effects of the variables that are listed. Finally, the changes in the stratification systems that are described in the following pages are meant only to be illustrative.

IV. Type of rewards emphasized
　1. External or extrinsic
　2. Intrinsic
　3. Social relational
V. Availability of rewards
　1. Scarce
　2. Abundant
VI. Mode of distribution of rewards
　1. Unequal (stratified)
　2. Equal, as much as desired, or both
VII. Consequences for other opportunities in life
　1. Greatly ramified and seriously consequential
　2. Restricted to particular area
VIII. Consequences for social rating
　1. Used as basis for differentiated prestige
　2. Used as basis for acceptance as equal
IX. Consequences for power
　1. Perfect correlation between property and power
　2. Completely random associations

INDUSTRIALIZATION AND STRATIFICATION

With this outline as our guide, we can specify some of the more general changes in stratification systems that occur *during the movement of a society toward industrialization.*

I. The division of labor grows increasingly complex and, as a corollary, the system of differentiated statuses, i.e., socially recognized and differentially evaluated positions and functions, also grows more complex.

II. Status tends to be allocated on the basis of achievement rather than ascription, or at least the ideal tends to shift from a socially approved award of status on the basis of membership in groups such as kin, to that of achievement such as is implied by the term "skilled worker."

III. Since the occupational structure and the attendant structure of rewards become specialized and elaborated, accurate and satisfactory measurement of performance becomes central to both the labor and the managerial sectors of the productive system.

IV. The traditional rewards for work that flow from the character of the social relations enjoyed at work give way to rewards that may be considered extrinsic to the work itself, in that they are rewards *for* the performance, rather than rewards *in* performance. The same change is noticeable in the attrition suffered by the "meaning" of work, in that gratifications formerly derived from the craftsman's relation to his work, or from the fact that one's work certified one as an acceptable human being, also tend to vanish. In short, work tends to become dominantly instrumental rather than consummatory in its gratifications. Orientation toward and motivation in work thus come to depend much more on marginal differentiations in extrinsic rewards, e.g. wages, than was traditionally true.

V. Ordinarily we associate the process of industrialization with the economic development of a society, marked by an increase in its gross national product and, in general, by greater production of desired goods and services. From the point of view of stratification theory, this change is seen as increasing the rewards to be distributed.

VI. We also tend to associate the process of industrialization with some general movement toward greater *equality* of rewards among the various sectors of the society. At the least, our visual image of the structure of rewards shifts from one with a large base rising to a very narrow apex to one with both a narrow base and a narrow apex, and a middle bulge indicating the greater homogenization of rewards.

VII. One important aspect of stratification has to do with the extent to which an individual's position on any of the hierarchies of rewards is determined by or determines the range of life chances to which he is exposed. Thus, we ask, in what social circumstances do the poor die at younger ages than the rich, and under what social arrangements do death rates among various income groups tend to approach equality? The evidence on this issue, as between agricultural and industrial societies, is mixed. On the one hand, we have reports on the ever-normal granaries which are maintained in various forms in numerous primitive and peasant societies, so that no one ever goes hungry as long as food is available. On the other hand, we know that in well-developed industrial societies a number of auxiliary agencies of social welfare are specifically charged with using public funds to reduce the unequal life chances flowing from differences in income. These are crude and gross contrasts, but they illustrate the variability of the conditions that determine whether, and to what extent, differences in position on the occupational and income hierarchies may be consequential for the whole range of other chances and expectations.

VIII. Among the most important and most desired opportunities in life in any society are those concerned with receiving a favorable evaluation of one's self from one's associates and of having this evaluation symbolized publicly by whatever criteria are currently recognized by the society. Again the evidence as to what transformations occur in stratification systems under the impact of industrialization is mixed. There are societies in which the relations between income and prestige strain toward a minimum of connection and interdetermination. There are also societies in which income virtually equals prestige. Both these types are found in nonindustrial as well as in industrial societies. There are sharp intersocietal differences in this variable in each major form of productive organization; and it is not easy to say which is empirically more dominant.

IX. The same sorts of observation must be made about the power correlates of a stratified position on the occupational and income hierarchies. The search for power may not be as ubiquitous as the search for prestige. Yet the connections of power with occupation and income are or can be as close as those between occupation and prestige. Moreover, the form of productive organization—whether agricultural or industrial—does not seem surely to determine the extent of the connections between the power, occupations, and income.[4]

In regard to the interconnections of property, power, and prestige, Inkeles has noted that two processes seem to occur most frequently in the transition from agriculture to industry or, better, in the transition from a traditional society to a modern one. He speaks of the three hierarchies as social "orders":

. . . the modernization of a traditional social system leads to a decrease in the degree of differentiation in each of the . . . subsystems or orders. That is, a process of relative homogenization takes place, reducing the gap or range separating the top and the bottom of the scale in income, status, power, experience (self-expression), and knowledge (skill). More important, in each hierarchy modernization brings about a marked increase in the proportion of the total population that falls in the same or adjacent strata near the middle of the distribution. . . .

. . . under conditions of modernization there is a tendency to equilibration within the stratification system as a whole, . . . that is, for standing on any

___

[4] Stratification theory, like any sociological theory, has two equally important purposes: (1) to describe in formal structural terms the possible variant forms; and (2) to account for the major gross empirical regularities of association and compendency among variables that have been found. The evidence suggests that power, property, and prestige are, at least theoretically, independently variable; and that when correlations do exist, they range from strong positive to strong negative relations. In certain circumstances the wealthy man is degraded by the fact of his wealth, and the powerful man suffers loss of prestige precisely because of his great power, etc.

one of the stratification scales to be the same or similar to the individual's or group's relative standing on the other scales.[5]

In brief, Inkeles is here asserting that the evidence is actually much clearer than we have been able to find it.

In applying these propositions to the case of the modernization of the Soviet Union, Inkeles is constrained to recognize that the case, at least for the second proposition, tends to break down when one considers the relative monopolization of power in that country. He contends, however, that the present great centralization there may be simply a "short-term reversal" of a different over-all trend—that the sharing of power has been increasing but has not yet reached its full extent. Even if the power system of the Soviet is exceptional, he thinks this need not impugn the value of the general model of transition, of which the Soviet case may be one distinctive variant.

However mixed the evidence may be, for our purposes it is most important to recognize that these central aspects of stratification theory are also central features of that social change called industrialization or modernization. We are dealing with fundamental aspects of social change when we focus on changes in the various hierarchies of power, property, and prestige. The ways in which the wide assortment of political, economic, and cultural facts can be classified to show their relevance to stratification theory should now be clear.

When we speak of the division of labor and its increasing complexity, we are obviously concerned with those changes usually focused on by economists. By considering these changes as the basis for new status arrangements, we translate the changes into terms relevant to the analysis of stratification. Similarly, when we speak of the systems of reward for work, we are concerned with the data derived from studies, for example, of the change from exchange by barter to wage labor. But we show the relevance of these data for stratification analysis by considering rewards for work in terms of their scarcity, their symbolic status significance, and their capacity to motivate men to conscientious performance, with or without considerable differentiation.

In considering such economic facts as the development of a system of wage labor, we are calling attention to the narrowing bases on which claims to social distinction may come to rest, as against the more dif-

[5] Alex Inkeles, "Summary and Review: Social Stratification in the Modernization of Russia," in Cyril E. Black, ed., *The Transformation of Russian Society* (Cambridge: Harvard University Press, 1960), pp. 341–342.

fuse claims to fame made by men in societies where status is primarily ascriptive and depends on membership by birth or lines of kinship. Each shift in the form of reward for work is intimately influenced by and strongly influences the modes and proprieties of inequality as these have been manifested in the society.

The elements of stratification theory that are most significant for the study of industrialization may serve as convenient categories within which to compare various systems in order to discover major lines of consonance and strain in social forms, and also may be used to ascertain whether certain general evolutionary developments tend to dominate the transformation from a traditional to a modern society. The interconnections of these categories may be studied directly, and any or several of them may be used in analyses of their relations with specifically economic factors, as by Udy and Gregory (Chapters 5, 9 supra). Or an examination of politics and social organization may be attempted by relating certain stratification variables to political organization, as Apter has done (Chapter 18). Similarly, the cultural anthropologist or historian concerned with integrating disparate facts from various disciplines into more inclusive gestalts may make selections from these facts in ways exemplified by Singer and Nash (Chapters 14, 17).

STRATIFICATION AND COMMITMENT: OBJECTIVE AND SUBJECTIVE ASPECTS

A more difficult problem now confronts us: What can be said about the bearing of these aspects of stratification on the commitment of labor to an industrial way of work and life? To answer this question we must first distinguish between two kinds of statements about commitment; one refers to objective conditions, while the other refers to attitudes and definitions of the situation.

The first type of statement would describe the degree to which the society contains the formal arrangements or structures that are thought to be required for efficient manning of an industrial system—including, for example, the various technologies and the charted numbers of organizational relations which efficient industrial organization is said to demand. Here, too, reference would be made to the quality and quantity of markets, including those for goods, labor, and money. Such descriptions indicate whether, or how well, a society is equipped for the industrial tasks which it assumes, or may wish to assume, but do not necessarily tell anything about the processes by which societies emerge from traditional, agricultural conditions, nor indicate the extent to which the population is subjectively committed to any way of life. Any statement concerning the latter must deal with habits and ways of thinking, feelings of satisfaction and dissatisfaction, reluctances and readinesses, and accepted and unchallenged patterns of social relations.

From at least one point of view, one may say that many persons in the most developed industrial societies do not accept, i.e., are not fully committed to, the industrial way of life. They find themselves seriously at variance with many of the pressures of life in such a society. They feel alien to the major impulses and kinds of behavior that seem to be required for success in the market place. They dislike the criteria of evaluation of the social worth of individuals. They deplore the inter-personal relations that develop when men view each other imper-sonally and instrumentally.

These objections to and alienations from the industrial way of life on the part of persons already involved in it may be indicative of the principal sources of resistance to moving into such a way of life. We can classify major resistances to industrialization expressed by people in preindustrial or quasi-industrial societies in terms of unwillingness to be subjected to the pressures implicit in industrialization; reluctance to break with forms of social relations that give assurance of security in the traditional societies; hesitancy to yield the comforting ratings and ranks they enjoy as members of their families and communities.

There is evident in these resistances the universal effort of normal individuals to maximize the favorableness of their self-images. This effort is of course always relative to perceived resources and perceived limits. Prospective self-images which are theoretically possible and which might, all other things changing appropriately, prove even more psychologically desirable to the individual may be rejected because they are not perceived as such, or because the attendant prospective risks and gains cannot intellectually and emotionally be brought into a satisfying balance.

Role Image and Commitment

There is also a universal strain to maintain the most favorable image of one's roles. The major guides to behavior acquired by any individual in the process of being socialized, whether as a child or an adult, in-volve certain images of roles that are related to the major statuses that one expects, and is expected, to occupy at various times in one's life. The normal adult statuses of breadwinner, husband, father, and citizen are examples. We all tend to make our behavior conform to those models of decorum and conduct that were sketched on our social memories, early in life. This is true even though the finer details are acquired only with the actual status, and even though the final manner of comporting ourselves in these roles depends largely on interaction with other persons.

In these images of major roles lie the dynamics of commitment, for the change to any system of behavior from any previous system depends on the ability of the particular individual to see himself as a player of the roles involved in that system. And this in prior turn depends on his ability to see himself as no longer playing the roles attached to the traditional statuses.[6] There are, then, at least two stages in the development of commitment. It is possible for a group of persons to be ready to change *from* certain status and role arrangements, without being ready to adopt and commit themselves to any other particular set of arrangements.

The restraining power of the traditional statuses lies not only in the habitual and customary nature of their requirements, which makes them easier to fulfill, but also in moral certifications implicit in the role images. Role prescriptions, in short, are not only descriptive; they are evaluative and normative. A father habitually or traditionally does this or that, but there are specific things a *good* father *should do*. And we all know what a *good* citizen *should* be like. Moreover, these general normative role prescriptions are frequently concretized, and their moral aspects introjected. The general statement is translated into a set of personal commandments in the form, "I am the kind of father who . . ."; the very *identity* of the person is thus defined by the personalization of the general role prescriptions. The importance of this identification of self with role lies in the fact that this is the self with which the individual actor confronts the world and, in that confrontation, measures out his own personal esteem for himself. He is encouraged to do so by the reactions to his role image on the part of those with whom he interacts.

The crucial resistance to industrialization found in peasant and primitive societies may come from the tendency of various major role images to be reasonably well-integrated with each other, although no one formula or pattern alone suffices as a model of such integration.

[6] For some of the dynamics of this process of change in one particular case, see Melvin M. Tumin and Arnold S. Feldman, "Status, Perspective and Achievement: A Study of Education and the Class Structure in Puerto Rico," *American Sociological Review*, 21:464–472 (August 1956).

There is integration in the sense that individuals in such societies generally have formulated a stable composite role image that includes the chief aspects of each of the component roles, even though their interconnections may involve the stressing of one as *compensation* for another. Thus, the utterly devalued untouchable in a caste system may be resistant to change of any considerable kind, even though one of his major roles may be a source of pain and deprivation.

The breaking of any aspect of a traditional society, then, immediately tends to involve much more change than that in the aspect where the impetus to change first appeared. This is why a peasant society frequently seems to recoil from the beckonings and bemusements with which it is confronted when it comes into contact with a culture of another world of understandings. It is not metaphorical to say that the total society is threatened by a change in any one of its major aspects, for such a statement tends to be true in a literal sense. Morals, habits, forms of community interaction, patterns of power and prestige, bases of self-esteem, as well as the general and impersonal arrangement of the society's institutions come into question when any *one* of these aspects is questioned.

The essence of the foregoing observations is that the way of work and the rewards for work in traditional societies are most frequently central to their way of life. To attempt to change the way of work is therefore to attempt to change the way of life. Naturally the resistance is much stronger than it is when a change in occupation implies little more than a change in the bus that one has to take every morning, or even such relatively large changes as moving from one city to another, changing one's community of peers, or acquiring new skills and attitudes essential for efficient performance.

The interaction of work with the total way of life in traditional societies has been discussed in several preceding papers. Thus, Elkan and Fallers have noted that wage work in town tends to be a phase rather than a way of life for the Baganda, many of whom commute daily from rural holdings where their wives cultivate food and cash crops, while others return to rural homes every weekend (cf. page 249 supra). Attention is focused throughout their paper on the tension between the attractions of town work and its level of pay, and the retentive forces of the traditional social system. We are led to understand why the Baganda maintain a strong affiliation with the traditional social structure, at the same time that they make some considerable ventures into the new labor market.

We also note that there is considerable difference between age groups in the frequency and depth of involvement in town life, as we should expect. One would assume that younger men, not yet integrated in their adult roles, and not yet privileged to receive the full rewards of participation in the traditional society, typically would be much more footloose and susceptible to the marginal attractions of the town. This is especially likely to be true when the prevailing definition of the worth of town work, provided by the words and actions of older men, tells the younger men to view such work as a temporary arrangement.

In the same vein, Singer points out that the problem of gaining the craftsman's acceptance for technical improvements is not one of changing his character and values, but of assuring him of continued opportunities for their expression under changing forms of social and economic organizations (page 272 supra). This formulation underestimates some of the difficulties that rise because at least some aspects of character and some values have to be changed if individuals are to adjust to the new system. But the more important truth is that, except where sharp breaks with former traditions are *forcefully* required, any population will tend to move into new work ambiences and to commit itself to the new ways only as it sees itself able to fulfill its traditional image of itself within the new. And this image is a configuration of a variety of separate but connected role images, which include prescriptions about how to think and feel, how to react to others, what to want from life, what is good and bad, and the proper course of life.

DEMOCRATIC FACILITATION OF SOCIAL CHANGE: THE PUERTO RICAN CASE

In stressing the probable resistances to change that must be expected in the process of modernization, one unavoidably gives the impression that all nonmodern peoples are yielding only with great reluctance to the inducements of the modern type of social order. That impression of what is happening is quite correct if it is recognized at the same time that, in spite of this considerable reluctance, rapid social change in the direction of modernization is occurring all over the world. We should hardly expect such rapidity of change if all the resistances worked to their fullest degree to retard the process.

What, then, can account for the current fact of rapid social change, in spite of the numerous and diverse resistances which have been noted? Many slogans attempt to account for this change but they are hardly satisfactory, for we learn nothing by talking about the inherent desire of people for a better way of life. We know that an "inherent" desire to continue the same way of life is an equally strong motive.

Must one not face the fact that the rapidity of social change from traditional to modern societies is often a function of the forceful impact of the developed on the undeveloped societies? Are not these changes sometimes made with little concern for native traditions, sometimes with only passing and token acknowledgments of these traditions, and a nominal interest in taking them into account and respecting them? But is it not also true that our judgment as to whether the change is rapid or slow depends largely on our individual and personal notions as to how fast change *should* occur? And do not these judgments in turn depend on the degree of our personal interest in reaching the outcome called "modernization," balanced against our inclination to make such a goal secondary to maintaining the "integrity" of the way of life of the peoples in question? The latter considerations obviously have nothing to do with the scientific issues at stake. At least, by common resolution concerning scientific method, they *should* have nothing to do with our estimates of the actual case and of possible future situations.

A case such as that of the modernization of Puerto Rico calls attention to the way in which our value questions and our scientific interests often become intertwined. This case of modernization, which is probably as rapid and as far-reaching as any the world is experiencing, exemplifies very rapid growth in the commitment of members of all levels of the labor force to the demands of the emerging modern society.

Most social scientists from the United States who have observed the processes of change in Puerto Rico tend to applaud what has happened, with few reservations. But some thoughtful scholars in Puerto Rico and others deeply concerned with the totality of Puerto Rican life find themselves highly ambivalent about the changes which have occurred, primarily because they see certain fundamental values in traditional Puerto Rican life being destroyed by the new market impulses and orientations that are coming to dominate the attention of virtually every segment of Puerto Rican society. The outside observers acknowledge these impacts on the traditional values but tend to be reassured, in their over-all evaluation of the process, by the fact that a democratic government is insisting that all segments of the society shall share in its new wealth and strength. It is precisely the Puerto Rican workers' perception and acceptance of this assurance by their government that enables them to experiment tentatively with new ways of work and of life. Puerto Rican workers approach the changes much more willingly and optimistically, and with a much smaller sense of danger to their way of life, than would be true under less democratic leadership and social organization.

It is quite possible for the majority of Puerto Ricans to develop new commitments gradually and apparently of their own will, and thus to shift their sensibilities and their orientations only *by barely perceptible degrees at any point in the process.* Most of the striving that one observes there is directed at improvement within the social system, rather than by change of the system. And this internal type of change is possible primarily because the majority of the workers, both urban and rural, continue to feel assured that they can express their character and realize their traditional values even if in slightly new ways. Of course, it is only the immediate, small, and hence relatively less consequential changes with which the individual workers must deal and to which they must adjust.

Typically we find that among Puerto Rican peasants who have entered upon the new ways of life there is virtually no sense of any danger to their conceptions of themselves as worthy individuals. This confidence is based in part on the shared concept of *dignidad,* and in part on the fact that the division of labor is not yet sufficiently differentiated to permit the development of multifarious invidious distinctions. These people are responsive and assured when officials tell them that they are the backbone of the nation. And there is sufficiently frequent confirmation, of a more than token nature, of this official estimate that the workers are not required to put their faith only in slogans.

These occurrences in Puerto Rico suggest that rapid change is possible, and that rapid modernization of a traditional society may give rise to little sense of threat to a way of life. For this, however, there must be mechanisms by which the members of the society can, in its estimation, continue to fulfill the major requirements of existing role images, at the same time that they are being revised by barely perceptible degrees to meet the demands of the emergent modern society. However successful other techniques of modernization may prove to be, there is a high probability of success for programs of modernization that contain the central feature that all portions of the population involved shall be helped to perceive the desired changes as rewarding in the ways in which they desire to be rewarded and are accustomed to being rewarded.

16 INDUSTRIAL CONFLICT AND UNIONS

*William H. Knowles**

LABOR UNREST

The labor unrest that followed World War II in the developing areas of the world cannot be described as industrial conflict because there is little industry in these areas; preindustrial unrest is a more appropriate term. Although the dislocations caused by even small amounts of industrialization can be great, particularly in cultures not receptive to it, the revolutionary foment in Southeast Asia, the Middle East, and Africa cannot be attributed to industrialization per se. The two central facts of the underdeveloped areas are grinding poverty, even by non-Western standards, and the predominance of agriculture. The bulk of the work force in these areas is made up of tenant farmers; few wage earners work in industry. The picture, provided by some social anthropologists, of primitive or peasant societies as integrated and unchanging with a perfect balance of social and natural forces is overdrawn.[1]

Labor Unrest in Preindustrial Societies

There is labor unrest in preindustrial societies because they are in a state of disintegration or transition. The decline and transition of indigenous cultures began with the arrival of the first explorer, missionary, or trader, and has been going on for some 300 years with increasing exposure to Western culture. The climax of this process was reached after World War II. Whether the labor force of a preindustrial society is made up of hunting or pastoral tribesmen, serfs or peons, landowning peasants or wage earners on large plantations, labor unrest has arisen because of some combination of the following factors or groups of factors:

* I am indebted to Van Dusen Kennedy and Anthony Koo for their careful reading and helpful criticisms of this paper.
1 E. Daya, "Freedom of Association and Industrial Relations in Asian Countries, Part I," *International Labour Review,* 71:365 (April 1955); Wilbert E. Moore, *Industrialization and Labor* (Ithaca: Cornell University Press, 1951), p. 70.

1. *Overpopulation, low productivity in agriculture, underemployment, and unemployment.* Characteristic of almost all developing areas is a "population explosion," which has been in the making for several generations.[2] Overpopulation is not yet a problem in Latin America and some areas of the Middle East and Africa, but will cause difficulties there, too, if present rates of population increase continue. Public health measures, including malaria control in recent years, are low-cost investments which have been readily accepted by primitive societies and which have phenomenally reduced death rates. Population pressure sets off a chain of events which eventually undermine the way of life of the indigenous society. Present methods of agriculture are sometimes the result of over a century of adaptation of a fixed amount of land to the needs of a growing population, with diminishing returns.[3] In some areas production per acre is actually falling. Attempts to support a growing population by traditional agricultural methods have led to soil depletion, erosion, overgrazing, and water scarcity. In peasant societies overpopulation has led to division of the land into uneconomic units. Abuse of the land leads to underemployment, poverty, debt, insecure land tenure, absentee control, and a body of landless agricultural laborers. Hunger for land gives rise to unjustified economic grievances against large commercial estates, which are generally units of optimum size for efficient production.

In most developing areas population pressure is excessive only in relation to traditional economic organization; the areas would not be overpopulated if the labor surplus could be shifted from agriculture to

[2] International Bank for Reconstruction and Development, *The Economic Development of Nigeria* (Baltimore: Johns Hopkins Press, 1955), pp. 3–5 [all the reports in this series were published by the Press; in subsequent citations, only the date of publication is given], *The Economic Development of Syria* (1955), p. 3, and *The Economic Development of Turkey* (1951), p. 16; National Planning Association, Special Policy Committee on Technical Cooperation, *Technical Cooperation in Latin America* (Washington, D. C., June 1956), p. 4.

[3] Ernest L. Fogg, "Labor Organization in Thailand," *Industrial and Labor Relations Review*, 6:243 (April 1953); Walter R. Goldschmidt, "The Interrelations Between Cultural Factors and the Acquisition of New Technical Skills," in Bert F. Hoselitz, ed., *The Progress of Underdeveloped Areas* (Chicago: University of Chicago Press, 1952), pp. 153; International Bank for Reconstruction and Development, *The Economic Development of Ceylon* (1953), pp. 13, 56, and *The Economic Development of Nigeria*, pp. 82–89; W. S. Mare, *African Trade Unions* (London: Longmans Green and Co., 1949), p. 111; Moore, *op. cit.*, p. 51; Oscar A. Ornati, *Jobs and Workers in India* (Ithaca: Cornell University, Institute of International Industrial and Labor Relations, 1955), pp. 19, 24, 52.

industry with more efficient use of known mineral resources.[4] Productivity of agriculture would rise in some areas, even with present primitive methods, if more people moved from the land. In other areas the food supply would be adequate if modern agricultural techniques were used, but then even more people would have to leave the land.

Endemic unemployment and underemployment are also characteristic of the developing areas. The resulting chaotic labor markets are not due to the refusal of workers to leave the land, for people are being driven from it, but to an unsettled rural proletariat that has no place to go. It would be a mistake, however, to conclude that industrial development can take place without being accompanied by an agricultural revolution. Balanced economic development rather than agricultural versus industrial development is the issue.

2. *Malnutrition and disease.* While public health measures can reduce infant mortality, population growth without an increase in food supply leads to malnutrition, which in turn increases susceptibility to disease. Treatment of some diseases is expensive, and a luxury that a poor economy cannot afford. In underdeveloped areas many people suffer from parasitic worms of the intestines and blood, malaria, incipient yaws, gonorrhea, syphilis, and vitamin deficiencies. Much of the indolence, apathy, inefficiency, and high rates of absenteeism and turnover, which are sometimes attributed to the culture patterns of developing areas, are in fact the consequence of malnutrition and disease. Lack of full industrial commitment is traceable, in part, to physical incapacity rather than cultural barriers.

3. *Urban slums.* Population pressure drives people from the land, the tribe, the peasant village, and the plantation. The developing areas of the world are characterized by the rapid growth of cities—a growth entirely disproportionate to their economic growth and opportunities for wage employment. Although urban growth may be attributed in part to expansion of commerce, communications, and government services, cities in the underdeveloped areas tend to be gigantic slums of underemployed and unemployed. Poverty, delinquency, labor exploitation, lack of sanitation, ill health, family disorganization, and a high ratio of males to females are all characteristics of rapid urbanization

[4] Conrad Bekker, "The Point Four Program of the United States" in Hoselitz, *op. cit.,* p. 237; Norman S. Buchanan and Howard S. Ellis, *Approaches to Economic Development* (New York: Twentieth Century Fund, 1955), p. 44; International Bank, *The Economic Development of Iraq* (1952), p. 1; Ornati, *loc. cit.;* U. S. Department of Labor, *Summary of the Labor Situation in Taiwan* (November 1956), pp. 1, 4.

without proper social planning and are not inherent in the industrialization process.

The displaced agricultural workers are "in the city but not of the city." Urban growth has undermined traditional religions, kinship patterns, symbols of authority, and value systems. Labor unrest is not the result of protest against industrialization, but rather of the absence of something to replace the traditional way of life.

4. *Social, recreational, educational, and other deficiencies in communities.* Underdeveloped areas are characterized by appalling deficiencies in educational, medical, recreational, transport, water supply, and refuse disposal facilities. Growing populations tax the limited existing facilities, and the economic structure cannot finance necessary expansion. In spite of the overcrowded city slums, the flight from rural villages continues. Although the casual visitor is shocked by the packing-crate and tin-can housing in the towns, building construction there is superior to that in rural areas. While the people may be committed to their traditional way of life in most respects, they have been exposed to nontraditional ideas long enough to expect and demand community amenities that are not forthcoming. Thus the governments of the developing areas are confronted with a newly awakened, widespread, and insistent demand for education, medical care, clean drinking water, and roads. In addition, a growing cause of labor unrest and high labor turnover is the lack of consumers' goods due to the backwardness of merchandizing methods.[5]

5. *Inadequate credit systems, usury, and growing debt.* Preindustrial societies are generally noted for primitive credit systems and usurious interest rates, which impede economic expansion and give a large portion of the return on agriculture to the moneylender. Population pressure and fixed quantities of land make nearly everyone a marginal producer. One crop failure places a family at the mercy of the moneylender. The crude system of credit which may have been adequate in the past is not satisfactory for people with rising aspirations who are frustrated by declining agricultural productivity. Labor unrest in developing areas is often the result of a growing burden of personal debt from which there is no escape.

[5] G. Balandier, "The Problems of the African Worker in the Gaboon and the Congo," *International Social Science Bulletin,* 6:456 (1954); International Bank, *The Economic Development of Jamaica* (1952), p. 189; Mare, *op. cit.,* p. 111; United Nations, Department of Economic and Social Affairs, *Processes and Problems of Industrialization in Underdeveloped Countries* (New York, 1955), p. 40.

6. *Feudalism*. In underdeveloped areas that are dominated by large landed estates, labor unrest results from tenancy laws that leave the tenant farmer insecure and give large shares of the crops to the landlord. Population pressure puts the sharecropper in a poor bargaining position and results in debt peonage. The landlordism of underdeveloped areas is usually associated with paternalism, arbitrary attitudes, and lack of managerial skill. The tenancy laws or customs, like usury, have been in force for centuries, and protests against them cannot be attributed to the impact of industrialization. Labor unrest under feudalistic forms of agricultural organization is probably the result of exposure to Western ideas and is part of the general upheaval taking place in the preindustrial societies of the world.

7. *Corrupt, autocratic, and apathetic government*. In many developing areas there are protests by labor against corrupt and autocratic governments which heavily tax the working and peasant classes while the hereditary ruling elite are virtually tax free. These governments have neglected to invest social capital in education and public utilities, which would help to create an environment favorable to economic development. The argument, sometimes heard, that agriculturalists in primitive societies are unwilling to change their techniques because of cultural barriers is not entirely true. They have learned that higher productivity leads to higher taxes, higher rents, and expropriation of land. Colonialism has also been associated with apathy because maintaining the public peace and balancing the budget are not adequate in the face of growing social and economic problems. These practices have been accepted in underdeveloped areas for centuries; protest against them is relatively recent. Labor protest against corruption, autocracy, and apathy should not be taken to mean that workers understand and are demanding democratic political institutions. The protest is more against present abuses than in favor of some specific ideology.

8. *Race and caste distinctions*. Barriers to economic advancement based on race and caste have been characteristic of indigenous populations and also have been imposed by colonial administrators and foreign directors of commercial enterprises. In either case discrimination is a practice of long-standing and for the most part has been accepted as normal. Racial discrimination is not inherent in industrialization. Demands for equality regardless of race, class, or nationality are part of the world-wide postwar labor protest. Growing nationalism in many developing areas, however, has created a new type of racial discrimination directed against white people, Chinese, and East Indians.

9. *Unstable world prices.* The underdeveloped areas of the world may be characterized as exporters of agricultural and mineral raw materials and importers of manufactured goods. These raw materials are sold in competitive world markets and therefore are subject to wide fluctuations in price and in demand, whereas the imported manufactured goods are noted for the relative stability of their prices. The fortunes of most underdeveloped areas are related to the export of plantation produce, timber, and minerals. Even some of the most primitive societies are tied to the world market by dependence on the cocoa or cotton market. Even without industrialization these societies have become part of the world economy and many of their members, like American farmers, do not approve of the way in which the market pricing system operates. Native growers believe they are at a competitive disadvantage with Western buyers and therefore feel exploited. Peasants and estate workers may not understand the economics of world commodity prices nor the pricing of manufactured goods, but they suspect that they are getting the worst of the bargain and call it imperialism. This type of labor protest eventually fosters nationalism and demands for industrialization in order to attain self-sufficiency.

10. *Poor personnel practices.* Wage-earning jobs in the underdeveloped areas are found principally in plantation agriculture and in small commercial and manufacturing establishments. Plantations, a form of capitalistic agriculture but not industrialized agriculture, have been important in the life of many underdeveloped areas for at least 200 years. Plantation practices affecting personnel may be summarized in general as involving poor housing, inadequate community facilities, low wages, seasonal unemployment, underemployment, insecurity of job and house tenure, lack of precision in the definition of terms of employment, and authoritarian management. Foreign ownership of many of the plantations adds to labor unrest through absentee control, the practice of racial discrimination, and importation of supervisors who are ignorant of local customs and values. Other causes of labor unrest on plantations and in mining operations are the use of long-term labor contracts and abuses in the labor recruiting and brokerage systems.

In spite of these aspects, however, working conditions on plantations are no worse than those generally prevailing in underdeveloped areas. Conditions in the small shops owned and operated by native capitalists are usually worse than on plantations, and a large part of consumers' goods are made in such shops. These shops can hardly be called industrial, for they are practically without capital equipment; they are sweat-shops in which conditions and wages are below the unenforceable standards established by law. The relations between employees and employer are complicated by feudalistic traditions and differences based on caste, tribe, kinship, and religion. Low wages and a surplus of labor make workers expendable. Labor protest in preindustrial societies is in part directed against the personnel practices prevailing on most plantations and in the native shops.

11. *Foreign competition.* Many consumers' goods used in underdeveloped areas are made by native artisans whose high-level craftsmanship has been in the family for generations. Although artisans suffer from poor credit as well as poor marketing and transportation facilities, their protests stem increasingly from the competition of lower-priced, machine-made goods that are imported. Again we note the effect of outside influences on the established way of life even before industrialization. In recent years native artisans have been protesting against the competition of goods that are locally mass-produced; for the initial result of small doses of industrialization is technological unemployment in societies already suffering from mass unemployment. Although the unskilled sweatshop worker loses relatively little, the artisan loses both his skill and his way of life. On the other hand, artisans in North Africa have enjoyed unprecedented prosperity as the result of increased purchasing power brought about by industrialization.[6] Artisans in North Africa, Syria, and Lebanon have found employment in skilled trades in industry.

Unrest of the Middle Class and Political Instability

Most underdeveloped areas are politically unstable, or potentially so, because they are throwing off the yoke of feudalism or of colonialism or are adjusting to newly won independence. The masses are dissatisfied but inarticulate; although their protest is often violent, it is without discretion.

Political instability in the developing areas is directly attributable to the problems of the unemployed middle-class intellectuals who provide the leadership for mass protest movements.[7] Expansion of educational

[6] Roger LeTourneau, "Social Change in Muslim Cities of North Africa," *American Journal of Sociology,* 60:533 (May 1955).

[7] Daya, *op. cit.,* p. 337; Goldschmidt, *op. cit.,* pp. 53–162; Bert F. Hoselitz, "Nationalism, Economic Development, and Democracy," *The Annals,* 305:2–10 (May 1956), and "The Recruitment of White-Collar Workers in Underdeveloped Coun-

facilities, inadequate as they are, in inefficient preindustrial economies creates a situation in which there are more people with high school and university degrees than there are job opportunities. Unemployment of middle-class persons is aggravated by local and colonial attitudes and customs that exalt the professional and civil service positions while disdaining the technical, engineering, and entrepreneurial occupations. Middle-class frustration is often complicated by racial discrimination and by the marginal position of individuals who reject their native culture and in turn are rejected by the white and native ruling upper-classes. As a consequence, middle-class intellectuals have become the leaders of nationalist, anticolonial movements, and are opponents of feudalism, corruption, autocracy, and racial discrimination. In analyzing their own personal problems and those of their countries, they are usually anticapitalistic—since capitalism is associated with colonialism —and ardent supporters of schemes for industrialization and economic development.[8] Ideologically, their protest usually takes some form of socialism or communism. Political instability is not only the consequence of middle-class criticism of the established order, but of ideological and personal rivalries between middle-class groups.

Although racial discrimination, nepotism, colonialism, and rigidity of class lines contribute to unrest of the middle class, it may be argued that this is due to the lack of industrialization. The frustration is based on the lack of jobs and of social status commensurate with education and ability. Although middle-class nationalists are committed to industrialization, they are not committed to technical and risk-taking occupations. In civil service tradition, they perceive themselves as the managers of industry. This lack of commitment on the part of educated middle-class persons to certain types of industrial employment is an obstacle to economic development. Nevertheless, middle-class nationalists make no protest against industrialization. Their enthusiastic embracing of industrialization only creates further unrest because of the imbalance

---

tries," *International Social Science Bulletin*, 6:436–444 (1954); William H. Knowles, "Social Consequences of Economic Change in Jamaica," *The Annals*, 305:136 (May 1956); Ornati, *Jobs and Workers in India*, pp. 108–110; David J. Saposs, "The Split Between Asian and Western Socialism," *Foreign Affairs*, 32:588–594 (July 1954); U. S. Department of Labor, *Labor in Chile* (July 1956), p. 2, *Labor in India* (July 1956), pp. 5–8, and *Labor in the Philippines* (December 1956), p. 17.

[8] E. Stewart Kirby, "Some Political Aspects of Far Eastern Economic Development," Institute of Pacific Relations, Secretariat Paper No. 4, Eleventh Conference (New York, 1950), p. 5; D. P. Mukerji, "Mahatma Gandhi's Views on Machines and Technology," *International Social Science Bulletin*, 6:423 (1954).

resulting from the neglect of agriculture, inflation, and unwarranted emphasis on heavy industry.

Impact of Industrialization

The developing areas of the world are now struggling toward industrialization, and their cultures are in varying degrees of decay or transition. Under the impact of industrialization the labor unrest attributable to this transitional state may become industrial conflict. A number of conditions are factors in or aspects of this conflict:

1. *Adjustment to industrial discipline.* That the discipline of industrial employment is different from that of agriculture and that adjustment to the new discipline is difficult for the recruit to industry have often been observed. The weight of evidence is that primitive peoples readily learn industrial skills; their real problem lies in adjusting to industrial discipline. The pace of agricultural employment depends on the season and weather conditions, and much of the planning of work procedures is left to the individual or to the work gang. Industrial employment is machine-paced, the method of work is prescribed by the industrial engineer, and the employee must put in a full workday and week. Tardiness, absenteeism, turnover, and unwillingness to accept initiative and responsibility become labor problems.

On the other hand, the effect on the worker of the difficulty of adjusting to the tempo of industry may be overstated. What is thought to be maladjustment may be passive insubordination in protest against low wages, poor working conditions, and poor supervision.[9] Primitive agriculture requires men to do backbreaking work that is neither dignified nor inspiring. Given good wages and fair treatment, the adjustment of workers to industrial discipline is not the traumatic experience that it is sometimes made out to be.

2. *Jobs with low pay and low status.* According to both native and European colonial traditions, manual labor is undesirable. Since labor is cheap and plentiful, traditional employment is of the beast-of-burden variety which carries no status. It is not surprising, therefore, that workers prefer industrial jobs to plantation work, although they are not enthusiastic about heavy work in industry at low wages which leave them no better off (and emotionally worse off) than they would have been had they remained in agriculture. With low wages and a shortage of skilled labor, however, it is logical that the industrialization process

[9] International Bank, *The Economic Development of Jamaica,* p. 208, and *The Economic Development of Nigeria,* p. 348; Knowles, *op. cit.,* pp. 138–139.

begins with the production of goods requiring quantities of cheap, unskilled labor. Workers do not give full commitment to this kind of industrial employment.

Another cause of industrial unrest, then, is a desire for industrial jobs that allow self-respect and respect from others. Jobs that give status need not be skilled craft nor white-collar jobs, but jobs that combine good wages and the supervision or care of power machinery. Status is lost when the machine controls the worker, but status equal to that of the lion hunter is gained when the worker has charge of powerful machinery. The criticism of workers in developing areas with regard to absenteeism, turnover, and inefficiency does not apply to those holding skilled jobs. We may expect labor unrest to continue until industrialization has advanced to a point at which jobs give workers more control and direction of the work process, and at which productivity is great enough to permit high wages. Workers may expect great satisfaction from industrial employment; their disappointment and shattered hopes may cause unrest in the initial stages of industrialization.

3. *Decline of traditional family and tribal organization.* Social anthropologists point out that industrial employment creates a new way of life at variance with the traditional and that this leads to both industrial conflict and unwillingness to be permanently committed to the industrial labor force. The worker who has a deep emotional attachment to the tribe, the village, the family, or the land is reluctant to give up the traditional way of life—with its values, economic and emotional security, and certain (although perhaps lowly) status—for the uncertain and the unknown. The approval of the primary social group whose values are preindustrial means more to the individual than the economic gain to be had by joining the industrial work force. Moreover, the tribal or kinship system may make demands on the worker's pay that destroy the incentive for regular industrial employment. In addition, the older generation, wives, relatives, and religious and village or tribal leaders see industrial employment undermining the traditional religion and systems of obligations and authority.

Nevertheless, anthropologists may overstate these problems. Many people in developing areas are refugees from disintegrating traditional religions, kinship obligations, low status, and oppressive authority. Even more are driven from the traditional way of life by hunger, poverty, and unemployment. In many cases the real problem, which has not been given adequate recognition, is that industrialization in developing areas has not given workers sufficient opportunity to make a clean break with the past. The industrial worker is unwilling to give up even the meager economic and emotional security offered by the family, tribe, or village for low wages, inadequate housing, insecure job tenure, separation from family, poor supervision, language difficulties, racial discrimination, and the lack of status and sense of belonging.

4. *Resistance to technological change*. Wages are low where labor is inefficient and there is a labor surplus. Many factories in developing areas employ more labor than necessary. The prices of locally produced goods are relatively high because of insufficient capital equipment, poorly organized manufacturing processes, and lack of a mass market. To create markets for export and to compete with imported goods, industrial processes must be made more efficient. Only in this way can there be more jobs at higher wages. But in the course of these adjustments technological unemployment occurs. Like the handicraftsmen and the sweatshop laborers, industrial workers protest against technological change, first, because they are already suffering from serious unemployment and, second, because increasing productivity is not reflected in higher wages. The reallocation of the labor force as a consequence of technological change is much more difficult and painful in a developing area than in one already industrially developed.

5. *Foreign control*. Industrial operations, like plantations, are frequently under foreign ownership and management, since most developing areas are short of capital and managerial skills. As noted above, foreign ownership is often associated with imperialistic exploitation in the view of middle-class intellectuals, who may fan the fires of nationalism and labor unrest. However, developing areas do need foreign capital for industrialization, and this antipathy often abates when nationalists win control of the government. More direct sources of industrial unrest are the racial discrimination that is sometimes a part of foreign supervision, and the honest misunderstandings that result from cultural differences and language barriers. The influence of these difficulties can be modified by training and promotion of qualified native workmen without regard to race; by the provision of equal pay and equal fringe benefits regardless of race, class, or nationality; and by instructing foreign supervisors in the customs of the host country. Nationalists have discovered that management skills as well as capital must be imported in order to start the industrialization process.

6. *Imbalance in economic growth*. Labor unrest may also grow out of imbalances in economic development. Expansion financed by inflation places a heavy tax burden on workers. Neglect of the agricul-

tural sector leaves the peasants and sharecroppers unproductive. Agricultural inefficiency results in food shortages when the industrial labor force is growing, and leads to a lack of purchasing power just when agricultural prosperity is needed to provide a growing market for new industry. Economic experts agree that agriculture should not be neglected in industrialization programs, but there is disagreement as to how much inflation is inevitable or even desirable.

It is sometimes alleged that industrial unrest will develop as a consequence of the growth of modern industry alongside primitive shops. Economic development is a long-term process that is likely to benefit certain sectors of the economy sooner than others. The industrial worker may enjoy job tenure, social security benefits, relatively high wages, and pleasant working conditions, while workers in the sweatshops will be no better off than before economic expansion began.

7. *Industrial grievances.* Industrial unrest in developing areas, as in industrialized nations, may result from disputes over the terms of employment. However, industrialization creates new forms of employment relations that disturb the values of the older culture. The traditional superior and subordinate positions usually found in underdeveloped areas are based on autocratic, benevolent paternalism which is not readily adapted to factory situations.[10] The function of management, the nature of relations between employer and employee, and the status of the employee must be re-examined in this context. These issues cannot always be disentangled from the general environment of limited commitments to the labor force, divided loyalties, urban slums, nationalism, and racial discrimination.

TRADE UNIONISM

Reasons for Rapid Union Growth

Union development, which has advanced rapidly since World War II in areas where it was formerly of little significance, has preceded industrialization and therefore cannot be regarded as the consequence of industrial unrest. Although unionism is relatively new to developing areas and the percentage of the labor force that is organized is small, the spread of unionism and the rapid increase in membership are among the most important social developments in those areas.[11] Rapid

10 Daya, *op. cit.*, p. 366; A. M. Malik, *Labor Problems and Policy in Pakistan* (Karachi: Pakistan Labor Publications, 1954), p. 14; United Nations, *op. cit.*, p. 19.

11 Robert J. Alexander, *World Labor Today* (New York: League For Industrial Democracy, 1952), p. 7; Malik, *op. cit.*, p. 16; International Labour Office, "Problems

union growth is the consequence of some combination of the following factors:

1. *Labor protest against conditions prevailing in most preindustrial societies.*

2. *Union leadership from middle-class intellectuals.* Since workers are inarticulate about their dissatisfactions, middle-class union leaders explain the problems of the workers from an intellectual viewpoint. The impetus to trade union development accordingly has had a middle-class ideology, emphasizing anticolonialism and self-government, against foreign influence, and favoring home-owned and operated industry. Unions under middle-class nationalist leadership are frequently no more than appendages of political parties. Nationalism under the same leadership, rather than the problems of the workers under rank-and-file leadership, has been the driving force for union organization. In the developing areas that have been granted independence, unions have experienced difficulty in reorienting their membership to new goals when anticolonialism is no longer their uppermost concern.[12]

3. *Positive government encouragement.* The colonial policy of Great Britain, in particular, has actively encouraged the development of unions in all its colonies. Recognizing the growing labor unrest, Great Britain "exported" its own type of trade unionism in an attempt to channel unrest into constructive action. The governments of the new nations that were formerly colonial territories have encouraged union development for the same reasons. Not all developing countries encourage trade unionism, however, and suppression of unions is itself a cause of labor unrest. The International Labor Office and the U. S. International Cooperation Administration, in response to requests from governments of developing areas, have given advice and organized training programs for the promotion of unionism.

4. *Competition of communist and anticommunist organizations.* Between the World Federation of Trade Unions, under communist con-

---

of Labor and Social Welfare in Southern and Eastern Asia: A Review of Major Postwar Developments," Institute of Pacific Relations, Eleventh Conference (New York, 1950), p. 8.

12 R. B. Davidson, "Labor Relations and Trade Unions in the Gold Coast," *Industrial and Labor Relations Review,* 7:593 (July 1954); E. Daya, "Freedom of Association and Industrial Relations in Asian Countries, Part II," *International Labour Review,* 71:492 (May 1955); Fogg, *op. cit.,* p. 4; Goldschmidt, *op. cit.,* pp. 154–157, 164; Malik, *op. cit.,* p. 26; Ornati, *Jobs and Workers in India,* pp. 38–40, 97–101; J. Norman Parmer, "Trade Unions in Malaya," *The Annals,* 310:143 (March 1957); U. S. Department of Labor, *Labor in the Philippines,* pp. 6–7.

trol, and the International Confederation of Free Trade Unions there has been strong and continuing rivalry.[13] The World Federation is an instrument of the Soviet government, which is interested in winning control of labor movements in the developing areas for the ultimate purpose of controlling governments. The International Confederation, on the other hand, is controlled by the free unions of the world, without government direction or subsidy, and is combating communist influence in the developing areas. The Confederation's objective is the development of unions along traditional job-oriented lines for the protection of the rights and dignity of the worker. By giving workers an organization that will handle day to day job problems, the Confederation removes some of the causes for communist infiltration. Aside from the conflicting objectives and ideologies, the competition between these two international bodies for the support of the workers of developing areas is a major cause of both rapid union growth and chaotic union rivalry.

Character of Unions

The character of the evolving labor movement in developing areas may be summarized briefly: [14]

[13] Alexander, *op. cit.*, pp. 3–6; Daya, "Freedom of Association and Industrial Relations in Asian Countries, Part I," p. 337; Fogg, *op. cit.*, p. 369; Goldschmidt, *op. cit.*, pp. 152–158; International Bank, *The Economic Development of Malaya* (1955), p. 159; Malik, *op. cit.*, pp. 17–21; Moore, *Industrialization and Labor*, p. 487; Ornati, *Jobs and Workers in India*, pp. 103, 157–174; Parmer, *op. cit.*, p. 143; Roberto Vernengo, "Freedom of Association and Industrial Relations in Latin America, Part I," *International Labour Review*, 73:455 (May 1956); U. S. Department of Labor, *Labor in Chile*, pp. 6–9, *Labor in India*, p. 9, *Labor in the Philippines*, pp. 5–7, 12, and *Summary of the Labor Situation in Taiwan*, p. 7.

[14] Davidson, "Labor Relations and Trade Unions in the Gold Coast," pp. 597–601; Daya, "Freedom of Association and Industrial Relations in Asian Countries, Part I," pp. 368–371; Fogg, *op. cit.*, p. 369; J. A. Hallsworth, "Freedom of Association and Industrial Relations in the Countries of the Near and Middle East," Parts I and II, *International Labour Review*, Vol. 70 (October, November 1954); International Bank, *The Economic Development of Malaya*, p. 159; International Labour Office, *Basic Problems of Plantation Labor* (Geneva, 1950), pp. 132–137, and "Problems of Labor and Social Welfare in Southern and Eastern Asia," pp. 8, 10, 20; Van Dusen Kennedy, "The Role of the Union in the Plant in India," in Industrial Relations Research Association, *Proceedings of the Eighth Annual Meeting*, Publ. No. 16 (1956), pp. 249–264; William H. Knowles, "Trade Unionism in the British West Indies," *Industrial and Labor Relations Review*, 8:1–7 (July 1955); Malik, *op. cit.*, p. 137; Mare, *op. cit.*, pp. 35–72; Moore, *Industrialization and Labor*, pp. 137–139; M. D.

Workers are dissatisfied but their protest lacks direction. With high rates of illiteracy and lack of experience in or understanding of unionism, their protest does not necessarily lead to effective unionism. In spite of rapid union growth the greatest obstacle to unionism is the apathy of workers.

Unemployment, underemployment, and the prevalence of casual labor make the payment of union dues almost impossible and weaken a union's bargaining power.

Since developing areas do not have much industry, most wage earners are in types of employment that present notorious difficulties for union organizers. The organizable workers, a small percentage of the total labor force, are in the strategic sectors of the economy: the railroads and other transportation, mines, utilities, public works, and the large factories in urban centers.

There are a multitude of small, independent unions that are "enterprise conscious" in a feudalistic identification with the employer. There are many rival federations of unions whose opposition is based on political affiliation, but few cohesive integrated labor movements.

Union leaders are usually outsiders—middle-class intellectuals who make nationalism a major union issue. These leaders are often ideologically committed to communism or some form of socialism, and their ideology is that of their unions. Most of these unions are tied to a political party and put its interest first. Ideological and political rivalries between middle-class groups have weakened union strength. Another type of outside leadership is that of the opportunist who capitalizes on workers' discontent by practicing extortion on employers and seeking political office for personal gain.

Collective bargaining is virtually nonexistent. Workers do not understand it, and the union leaders prefer politics. Although there are few legal barriers to union organization and most governments of developing areas encourage union growth, nearly all restrict collective bargaining by limiting the right to strike, enacting comprehensive labor codes, and providing for compulsory arbitration or labor courts.

In spite of these obstacles unions have made rapid progress. As workers become more experienced with unionism, their unions become

---

Morris, "Labor Discipline, Trade-Unions, and the State in India," *Journal of Political Economy,* 63:302–308 (August 1955); Ornati, *Jobs and Workers in India,* p. 176; Ornati, "Problems of Indian Trade Unionism," *The Annals,* 310:152–156 (March 1957); Vernengo, "Freedom of Association and Industrial Relations in Latin America, Part I," pp. 452–454.

better organized, better led, less entangled with politics and ideology, and begin to stress collective bargaining.

Unions, Labor Unrest, and Economic Development

Unions cannot by themselves remove all the causes of labor unrest in developing areas. They cannot bring about industrialization, agricultural reorganization, national self-determination, and land and tax reforms, nor eliminate city slums, nor improve communities. Since these issues cause labor unrest and are uppermost in the minds of union leaders, the emphasis placed on political action instead of on collective bargaining is understandable. Indeed, if these problems are not resolved it will be difficult for traditional unionism to function. On the other hand, traditional unionism, although foreign to the cultures of developing areas, can assist in the reduction of labor unrest and contribute to economic development.

1. *Poor personnel practices.* Through collective bargaining, unions can reduce labor unrest caused by the poor personnel practices generally found on plantations, in mines and logging camps, and in native shops. By defining workers' rights as a matter of contract and giving them the right of appeal, unions can improve the quality of supervision and contribute to workers' gains in human dignity.

2. *Higher wages.* The traditional union function of negotiating for higher wages can have several positive effects in developing areas. By campaigning for higher wages, unions can make labor more expensive. Workers then will have an incentive to become efficient, and management will be forced to become efficient. While workers accept low wages in traditional employment in the native village, a positive economic incentive is necessary to induce industrial commitment. Unions may establish a wage differential between industrial employment and nonindustrial employment sufficient to encourage full commitment to the industrial work force.

Although labor unrest arising from technological unemployment cannot be underestimated, resistance to technological change is intensified if labor does not share in the fruits of increased productivity. When labor surpluses exist there is no market force to include productivity increments in wage formulas, even though passive insubordination may be more costly than an organized strike.

The benefits of an aggressive wage policy will not be realized if unions are poorly organized, poorly led, and neglect job issues for political issues. Since few unions are job-oriented, and since security against technological change is of greater concern to workers than higher wages, unions of developing areas are not likely to be a force for a dynamic economy.

3. *Industrial citizenship.* Traditional job-oriented unions can also contribute to the alleviation of labor unrest that is caused by the frictions created in the transition from a preindustrial society to an industrial one. Labor unrest, the difficulty of securing industrial commitment, and obstacles to economic development are all related to the unintegrated amorphous masses of displaced agricultural laborers who must become members of organized urban communities in order to enjoy the benefits of industrial civilization. Unions through collective bargaining can help to bring about orderly processes of transition to industrial life.

Job-oriented unionism emphasizes the dignity, status, and prestige of particular lines of work. It brings workers together by craft and by industry to give them a sense of pride and identification with work. The informal social group in the workshop, which is the basis for unionism, gives the new recruit to industry an emotional sense of security and of belonging. Membership in an industrial primary group, which is in turn federated with other union groups, may serve as a substitute for membership in the extended family, tribe, or peasant village. Trade unionism, a form of modern tribalism, aids in securing commitment to the industrial work force. The certainty of job tenure through seniority, together with health and welfare plans, unemployment insurance, and old age pensions, replaces the security of the shared poverty of the tribe and extended family.

One of the problems of developing areas is that the culture of the preindustrial society is crumbling. It is with reluctance that the worker leaves the old society to become a victim of the impersonal forces of the market and of the arbitrary power of employers in developing industrial society. The worker in modern industrial society, however, is a partner in production rather than a factor of production. He is an industrial citizen with full rights in politics, in community affairs, and in social services. A function of the union is to give the worker status in a new environment as an industrial citizen.

It may be argued that job-oriented unionism is the product of a particular industrial environment rather than a force shaping the environment.[15] Job-oriented unions exist in developing areas in indus-

[15] Daya, "Freedom of Association and Industrial Relations in Asian Countries, Part II," p. 496.

tries employing literate and skilled workers, who enjoy higher than average wages and job tenure. They identify themselves with fellow workers and are fully committed to the industrial labor force. Unskilled, illiterate, casual laborers, who are agrarian refugees, it may be argued, can neither form job-oriented unions nor gain industrial citizenship. The truth probably lies between the extremes; unions both shape their environment and are shaped by it. The new recruit to industry makes poor union material, but a union can assist him to become a trade unionist and a member of the industrial community.

4. *Political stability.* In the absence of established trade unions and established political parties, labor unrest leads to both political and economic instability. The nature of the problems in underdeveloped areas together with the middle-class leadership of unions makes their deep involvement in politics inevitable, but when unions become merely a tool of rival political parties, serious problems follow. Unions that cannot effectively represent the interests of workers because this would be embarrassing to the political party in power are as irresponsible as those that use jurisdictional strikes and ill-timed demands to undermine rival political parties. Loosely knit mobs in the control of racketeering politicians can only be detrimental to the working class and to the political and economic well-being of developing areas. The unions that concentrate on collective bargaining, day to day grievances, organizing the unorganized, collecting dues, and building stable, democratic, and autonomous organizations, while maintaining alliance with a political party, contribute to the well-being of the country as a whole. By establishing stable unions they prevent opportunists from assuming leadership of labor to further their own goals.

Possible Adverse Effects of Unions

Autonomous unions enjoying free collective bargaining are not an unmixed blessing. Union objectives can conflict with the objective of rapid economic development in the following ways:

1. Union pressure for higher wages may promote managerial efficiency, but it may also help to discourage foreign investment and to increase inflationary tendencies.[16] The problem of maintaining a reasonable balance between rising wage rates and rising productivity is not automatically resolved by free collective bargaining. Programs for rapid economic development are of themselves inflationary, and free collective bargaining adds to the fires of inflation. Developing areas

[16] International Bank, *The Economic Development of Jamaica*, p. 71.

require foreign investment; one of the few attractions that they have to offer to foreign capital is low wages.

2. Genuine collective bargaining must be supported by the economic power of the threat of work stoppages, but developing areas cannot afford the luxury of strikes and lockouts. Mature collective bargaining may develop in the long run, but to the government financing a major program for rapid economic development, work stoppages appear to be irresponsible. As a consequence many governments, while encouraging unionism, do not permit strikes and in effect dictate the terms of employment.[17] Although such procedures are understandable under the circumstances, they undermine the basis of job-oriented unionism and invite political action or even strikes against the government. The tendency for unions to become primarily political bodies is thus encouraged.

3. Whereas it is understandable that unions in developing areas should be nationalistic and involved with ideological issues which may determine the form of national government, continued preoccupation with these issues to the neglect of the worker's welfare on the job can only contribute to economic and political instability.[18] The result is a political struggle for the control of unions, jurisdictional rivalries, and a close tie between collective bargaining and political issues.

4. Although unions sponsored by government and some socialist unions have favored technological change in the hope of benefiting the working class in the long run, no union in developing areas can command the loyalty of the workers without centering its attention on preservation of jobs at the expense of technological change. Unless industrial expansion can be maintained at a rate that will permit absorption of the technologically displaced, which is unlikely, resistance to technological change will continue to be a major obstacle to industrialization.

CONCLUSION

Labor unrest in developing areas is in large measure a protest against the existing way of life. Peasants and laborers have acquired new ideas

[17] Daya, "Freedom of Association and Industrial Relations in Asian Countries, Part I," p. 492; Malik, op. cit., p. 30; U. S. Department of Labor, Labor in India, pp. 15–16, and Summary of the Labor Situation in Taiwan, p. 10.

[18] International Bank, The Economic Development of Jamaica, pp. 222–225; Malik, op. cit., pp. 6, 30, 139; United Nations, op. cit., p. 385.

as to standards of living and human dignity. Even without industrialization, developing areas have long been part of the world market economy, confronted with the problems of selling raw materials and buying increasing amounts of manufactured goods. Population pressure has contributed to existing social and economic structures, making them unsatisfactory for meeting traditional needs. The conclusion is that those who continue to stress cultural resistance to change, the stability of preindustrial societies, and the futility of schemes for economic development have overlooked the revolution that has engulfed the developing areas. To a considerable degree, labor protest is against the failure to industrialize at a pace in keeping with population growth and rising aspirations, rather than a protest against the impact of industrialization on existing cultures.

Although reforms that do not involve industrialization are necessary to remove the causes of agrarian unrest, industrialization remains fundamental to the solution. Without industrialization there will be continued underemployment and unemployment; a farm labor surplus will cause further fragmentation of land holdings and soil erosion; without income from productive employment, there will be continued malnutrition accompanied by lowered resistance to disease; city slums will continue to grow. An unproductive economy cannot supply the amenities now demanded. A labor surplus encourages low wages and poor personnel practices, and impedes the breaking down of racial and caste distinctions. Continued population pressure on the land, due to failure to industrialize, puts the landlord and the moneylender in favorable bargaining positions; and continued dependence on raw material exports for money income renders the entire economy unstable.

The critical class in developing areas is made up of middle-class intellectuals, who are not only dissatisfied with their social and economic status, but provide the leadership of unions, political parties, and reform movements. Ideologically, they find themselves in the difficult position of (a) praising native culture as nationalists while condemning it as Western-educated reformers and planners, and (b) endorsing Western technology while condemning its association with colonialism and capitalism. The unrest of the middle class is a force for economic development, but the institutional framework within which it occurs depends on which ideology gains the ascendancy among the middle class.

Types of labor unrest that can be directly attributed to the industrialization process are those resulting from: (a) problems of adjustment to industrial discipline, (b) undermining of the traditional culture, (c) lack of a secure stake and status in industrial society on the part of the new recruit to industry, (d) technological unemployment, (e) imbalance in economic growth, and (f) industrial grievances that are complicated by a labor surplus and authoritarian management traditions. Three points should be emphasized regarding the impact of industrialization: (1) Much industrial unrest is not so much the consequence of industrialization itself as of the attempt to preserve a preindustrial way of life in an inappropriate environment. (2) Industrial unrest is not so much the result of workers' devotion to traditional values as of industrialization in an environment that does not permit the worker to become a full-fledged industrial citizen. (3) The problems created by industrialization are exceeded by those arising from the inability of countries to industrialize as rapidly as their people desire. Although industrial conflict will develop from efforts to adjust to changing values, there will be even more unrest unless industrialization is encouraged.

The rapid growth of trade unionism since World War II is not a product of industrial unrest, but rather of unrest stemming from nonindustrial causes. The type of unionism that developed in response to the problems of industrialization in the West is ill-suited to the problems of the developing areas, which encourage a pattern of unionism under middle-class leadership. The unions are loosely organized, with few paying members; tied to political parties and concerned with political issues to the neglect of the workers' problems on the job; fragmented and subject to extreme jurisdictional rivalry; and subject to government regulation of the bargaining process. Nevertheless, these unions are capable of exerting influence on employers and governments through strikes, rioting, and demonstrations. If trade unionism may be defined as an organized movement of wage earners with the objective of furthering workers' interests, the term does not describe most "unions" in developing areas. They may be described more aptly as heterogeneous masses of peasants, wage earners, sharecroppers, and unemployed who are momentarily loyal to a particular middle-class leader or group of leaders.

In spite of the difficulties confronting unions in developing areas, job-oriented unions have much to contribute to the welfare of workers and to economic development. Unions cannot solve the problems of the peasant, the tenant farmer, and the unemployed, but can modify the effects of general unemployment and of feudalism on the terms of employment in industrial and nonindustrial jobs. Such unions can promote economic development by correcting abuses in personnel policies, by forcing management to become efficient, by giving status and a sense of belonging to the recruit to industry, and by avoiding politically motivated labor disputes. Unionism that is job conscious, however, requires free collective bargaining, which may lead to serious strikes and inflationary wage-price spirals—a luxury that developing areas may not afford. The job-oriented pattern of unionism, under the influence of governments or of the International Confederation of Free Trade Unions has operated successfully in both the industrial and nonindustrial sectors of developing areas; but, because of workers' inexperience with unionism and politically oriented middle-class leadership, it is not now the dominant pattern.

Unionism is a foreign institution imported to control, channel, or take advantage of labor unrest. In the contest to shape the destinies of the developing areas many groups, other than the workers themselves, have sought to influence or control the nature of union development. There are, however, no laws for predicting the pattern that unions in developing areas may eventually follow. If the older forms of government and social structure are replaced by chaos in which rival middle-class groups struggle for power, unions may become increasingly fragmented and politically oriented. With political stability and economic progress, unions may become adjuncts of political parties, agencies of the state, or welfare divisions of corporate personnel departments.

The situation in many developing areas indicates that industrialization will be governmentally sponsored under middle-class nationalist management. Accordingly, there is a possibility that dependent unionism may become the dominant pattern. Although dependent unionism may solve many personnel problems in an honest and paternalistic autocracy, the working class is left without full industrial citizenship and without protection against the abuse of power. Although the environment of developing areas is not the best for the cultivation of job-conscious unionism, its cultivation by the governments of developing areas may help shape the environment.

17 KINSHIP AND VOLUNTARY ASSOCIATION

Manning Nash

This paper has a twofold objective: to explain the role of familial and kinship organization in the emergence and commitment of an industrial labor force in peasant and primitive societies, and to stipulate the grounds of development of those voluntary associations capable of playing a positive part in the structuring of a labor force suitable for sustained economic development. The procedure is to expound as much of a general conceptual scheme as is relevant for this objective and from that perspective to examine closely two rather well documented cases. One case is a Guatemalan Indian community which has relatively easily adopted a factory. The other is the difficult experience with industrial transformation in British East Africa, especially around Jinja. Empirical material is selected from studies of these widely divergent cultures, with the expectation that a set of extremes can be approximated as alternative paths to industrial commitment. The concluding statements attempt to provide the basis of a general understanding of the role of kinship and voluntary organizations in the process of labor force commitment in preindustrial, non-Western societies.

KINSHIP AND INDUSTRIALIZATION

General Kinship Characteristics

Kinship systems are a means of ordering and specifying social relations. A kinship system is a set of rules establishing behaviors, rights and duties, attitudes and sentiments between persons who are designated by special terms or by symbols which indicate the legitimacy of the reciprocal activities and sentiments involved. Kinship systems differ from one another in their range, i.e., whether the number of persons tied together by kin bonds is wide or narrow, and in the method by which they extend kin links—bilateral, unilineal, or double descent system.[1] It is agreed that kinship systems are determined by

[1] A. R. Radcliffe-Brown, "The Study of Kinship Systems," in his *Structure and Function in Primitive Society* (Glencoe: Free Press, 1952), pp. 49–89; Radcliffe-Brown

the general features of the social organization,[2] and that the latter is in part a response to other aspects of social life, particularly technology, pattern of residence, economic system, and the distribution of wealth and power.[3]

The social units, or groupings, based on kinship vary in size, structure, and function from society to society and over time. The family is a kinship group which combines socialization of the young, economic reciprocity without regard to price or other advantage, co-residence of sexually associating adults, and reproduction.[4] Other social entities may carry on similar functions, but the family is the social unit that combines these four. The form and function of the family and of the kinship system may be referred to as the domestic aspect of social organization. Analysis of this aspect is made from the perspective of the individual, and shows the kinship system's range, its method of ordering relations, its repertory of behaviors and sentiments, its rules of family duty, and its domestic and household features. Such an analysis enables the investigator to say what the web of kinship is for a given society at a given time and to specify the relative equilibrium of its tissue of kin connections.

Some societies utilize kinship for the structuring of social units whose tasks are political, economic, ceremonial, ritual, or military in the strict sense. These kinship groupings are lineages, clans, and dual organizations. Analysis of these social entities is made from the point of view of the total social system. This is a different level of analysis and shows what may be called the "web of clanship," to distinguish the tasks of kinship groupings in a total social system from those of kinship groupings at the domestic and familial level.[5]

Corporate Kinship and Industrial Labor

The emergence of a labor force means a change in the tasks that a social system is carrying on and therefore a change in the basis of

and C. Daryll Forde, eds., *African Systems of Kinship and Marriage* (New York: Oxford University Press, 1950).

2 Meyer Fortes, "The Structure of Unilineal Descent-Groups," *American Anthropologist*, 55:17–41 (January–March 1953); G. P. Murdock, *Social Structure* (New York: Macmillan Company, 1949).

3 Fred Eggan, *Social Organization of the Western Pueblos* (Chicago: University of Chicago Press, 1950); Fortes, *op. cit.;* Murdock, *op. cit.;* Radcliffe-Brown and Forde, *op. cit.*

4 Murdock, *op. cit.,* p. 3.

5 Fortes, *op. cit.*

social affiliations and the nature and distribution of social groupings in the society. Aspects of kinship and clanship are the predominant means whereby peasant and primitive societies organize their life and induct new generations into the social system. Hence, the successful emergence of an industrial labor force depends in part on the utilization or transformation of kinship and clanship so that individuals may be motivated in those primary social settings to enter and remain at wage work. On the other hand, the place occupied by kin groupings in performance of the legitimate tasks of the society is bound to be radically different if the operation of industrial organizations becomes one of its important activities.

It is clear that only certain aspects of kinship and clanship are strategic in promoting or hindering the development of an industrial labor force. A widely accepted proposition in social anthropology is that corporate kinship groupings (the clans, the lineages, and the phratries) are incompatible with industrial production. Despite Comhaire's contention that at least in Africa we cannot disregard corporate kin groups in the near future,[6] all theoretical expectations and empirical findings lead to the conclusion that corporate kin groupings are undermined and finally swept away by industrialization, whatever their fate may be in other encounters with monetary economies. Corporate groups arise in the middle range of social and cultural complexity, in what Fortes calls "relatively homogeneous, pre-capitalistic economies in which there is some degree of technological sophistication and value to rights in durable property."[7] These descent groups are the social units that regulate the political, economic, and religious life of this kind of society. Through the opposition of different corporate groups a balance of power and political control is maintained. Through their cooperation, the economic activities are carried out (chiefly but not exclusively in settled, farming societies), and the moral sanctions are maintained. When an economic situation necessitates the use of individuals as units of work and remuneration, the corporate nature of the clan is severely violated. Where the productive tasks are carried out on the basis of specialized skills and knowledges, the clan is too clumsy a mechanism to allocate tasks, rewards, and costs. In short, occupational differentiation, specialized skills, rapid and calculated response to economic situation, and individual units

[6] Jean L. Comhaire, "Economic Change and the Extended Family," *The Annals*, 305:45–52 (May 1956).

[7] Fortes, *op. cit.*, p. 24.

of manpower combine to make the clan incompatible with industrial work. The process of clan disintegration has been well described by Eggan, Spoehr, and Worsley.[8]

Variable relevance of noncorporate kinship. A large segment of the nonindustrial world has systems of kinship in which clans are not the prominent social features they are among, say, the Tallensi or the Hopi. In much of the underdeveloped world one finds a variety of extended kindreds, joint families, and loosely structured kin group- ings, which because of special circumstances have not crystallized into corporate and jural social segments. In these societies the role of kin- ship in industrialization is more problematic and must be sought in the interplay of finer features of social circumstance than the gross contradictions between clan-structured societies and wage labor forces. As may be shown in the following analysis of the Guatemalan Indian example, the role of these kinship systems in industrialization turns primarily on the differential productivity of generations, the control of income, the simultaneous emergence of other bases of social affilia- tion, and the reorganizations of paths of mobility and of obligations and positions that confer status.

KINSHIP AND VOLUNTARY ORGANIZATIONS IN GUATEMALA

The community of Cantel, in the Western Highlands of Guatemala, is made up almost entirely of Quiché-speaking Indians. Their social structure and cultural pattern are derived in part from their Maya ancestors, in part from their Spanish conquerors, and in part from the interaction of these two traditions over more than four centuries in changing social and political circumstances. The chief features of Indian communities like Cantel are a local social organization of civil and religious offices in a single hierarchy; a primitive farming tech- nology; a pecuniary, rotating marketing system; wealth distinctions, but no class lines; a kinship system based on nuclear families, which are the units of prestige and office holding; a feeling of community solidarity based on common culture, endogamy, adherence to a patron saint and local pantheon, and a body of belief and custom; and a num- ber of minor cultural differences in language, costume, surnames, eat-

---

8 Eggan, *op. cit.;* Alexander Spoehr, *Kinship Systems* (Chicago: Field Museum of Natural History, 1947); P. M. Worsley, "The Kinship System of the Tallensi: A Revaluation," *Journal of the Royal Anthropological Institute,* 86:37–75 (January- June 1956).

ing habits, etc.[9] Into Cantel, some 70 years ago, a textile factory was introduced. This factory, which is probably Central America's largest textile mill, continues to operate, using almost exclusively Indian labor. About a fourth of the working population of the community is employed in the factory.[10] In comparison with the penetration of industrial production in other parts of the world, the community has made a remarkable adjustment to this new mode of production.[11] It is still an identifiably Indian community, with its culture intact and its social institutions functioning.

Role of the Family

The role of the family system in neutralizing the tensions in the adaptation to wage work in Cantel has been large, while the family itself has remained relatively unchanged. It cannot be said that the family activity promoted, or even now promotes, entrance of workers into the labor force, or the commitment of those in it. Rather, the family and kinship system act as a kind of buttress that has made the role of factory wage worker tenable and legitimate, if not desirable. The voluntary organizations that have grown up around and because of the factory have played the positive role of inducing and tying wage workers to their jobs. Although the family and the voluntary organizations are not the primary influence toward factory work they play decisive parts in the making of a labor force.[12]

Structural features. The family in Cantel is a nuclear one according to cultural ideal: a man, woman, and their unmarried offspring should have a separate domestic household on a site of their own. Of course, not all Cantel families are of this type. Variety is in fact encountered —married sons live with their fathers, married daughters live with their mothers, and other combinations also exist. But the nuclear, independent family is the only form that does not raise some tension in the personality and that does not evoke efforts to change other forms into the cultural standard and the statistically dominant type.

Within such a nuclear family the male is clearly dominant and

[9] Robert Redfield and Sol Tax, "General Characteristics of Present-Day Mesoamerican Indian Society," in Sol Tax, ed., *Heritage of Conquest* (Glencoe: Free Press, 1952), pp. 31–39; Eric R. Wolf, "Types of Latin American Peasantry," *American Anthropologist,* 57:452–471 (June 1955).

[10] Manning Nash, "The Recruitment of Wage Labor and Development of New Skills," *The Annals,* 305:23–31 (May 1956).

[11] Manning Nash, *Machine-Age Maya* (Glencoe: Free Press, 1958).

[12] Nash, "The Recruitment of Wage Labor and Development of New Skills."

head. His wife is superordinate to the children but subordinate to him. It is he who, in the farming family, produces the income, determines the expenditures, gives the domestic orders, and decides the family's fate. However, the wife is consulted in all important decisions, plays a large part in determining spending patterns, and even keeps aside some of the household revenue for personal spending. This nuclear family is loosely tied to the husband's or the wife's relatives. Relations between brothers and sisters in separate households are not based on economic reciprocity, but squarely and unashamedly on the cash nexus. Fathers continue to be respected by their married daughters, but the cultivation of ties beyond the nuclear family is not automatically insured or demanded by kinship rights and obligations. Extension of kin bonds beyond the nuclear family to the kindred is not socially important, for there are only a few minor ritual gatherings at which nearly the entire kindred is assembled. Likewise, godparental relations (*compadrazgo*) are a weakly developed social institution and do not enjoin more than moral advice and some tokens at the appropriate times.

Functions of the family. In Cantel's social system, prior to the coming of the factory and most of the years since, the family has served as the unit of social structure. The civil-religious hierarchy was based on the conception that families, not individuals, take their turn in community service.[13] From this service families gained increasing social prestige and community-wide recognition. So the articulation of the separate nuclear families into a single social system was built on the mechanism of discharge of community obligation, rather than on superfamilial kinship structures.

The values of the community were inculcated within the nuclear family. A stress on hard work was manifested in the early age at which both boys and girls began making substantial contributions to the domestic economy, and in the scaling down of adult tasks and tools to the child's measure. For example, boys had small hoes, which they used when they worked in the fields beside their fathers. Girls were trained on miniature grinding stones and carried toy-sized water pots on their heads almost from the time they could walk. Discipline, respect for elders, and *costumbre* were also instilled in the home, chiefly through example rather than precept. The continual talk of the prices of things and the knowledge that money was necessary to

[13] Nash, "The Reaction of a Civil-Religious Hierarchy to a Factory in Guatemala," *Human Organization*, 13:26–28 (Winter 1955).

achieve social status (the communal offices are still an expense) helped to produce industrious individuals with a concern for money. The conviction that hard work is necessary to maintain life and that the good life itself consists in part of hard work has persisted from pre-factory times.

The Family and Commitment

The kind of family that exists in Cantel, promoting the cluster of sentiments just described, is especially propitious for the emergence of a labor force. No clan or lineage exists to be subverted; no traditions of leisured wealth stand in the dreams of the young. Continual physical labor is considered good and necessary. The factory originally was able to get recruits chiefly because of the poverty of most Cantelenses; many traditional needs and desires were not being effectively met by the traditional technology and economy. The family stayed together and continued to instill the virtues of work, discipline, and money (along with many other values and beliefs not germane to the labor force, but certainly important in giving meaning to effort and aspiration). The essential form of the family units continued through the operation of several simple mechanisms of social control. If a wage earner lived in the house of his father, he or she turned over his income to the father; this continued the pattern of parental dominance and control. The worker turned over his salary on the principle that if he lived under his father's roof, it was his father's right to control the income. The principle could be enforced in Cantel. A man did not earn enough, except through careful saving for many years, to buy or build his own house, and there are few vacant houses for rent in the *municipio*. One put up with paternal domination until the means to move were accumulated, for there was no recourse. It was the writer's observation that a greater than ordinary share of expenditure was lavished on the factory worker, and this of course lessened the sting of turning over an entire salary.

A further buttress to paternal domination of the young wage earner was the fact that as an unmarried individual he could not begin to move up the communal ladder of prestige. When he married, the wage worker tended to move into a separate household sooner than did his agricultural counterpart. The canon of paternal dominance was breached only in the cases where the older parent became dependent on the young wage earner for support. In this kind of family, which usually did not develop among farm families because of the pattern of inheritance, the greater earning power of the factory worker made him head of a household which contained his parents.

The role of women. For women factory workers the problems posed were slightly different, and on the surface more threatening to the family system. The role of "career girl" failed to develop, however, because single women have no place in Cantel, and there was no material or organizational basis for a revolt against their position (even if there had been a desire to revolt). Part of a woman's income, if she had young children, often went to hire a servant to take over some of her household duties. Women factory workers who were single were uniformly better dressed than farmers' wives. These uses of extra income helped keep women at what was always considered a not quite fitting job. Women did not develop into proletarians. They always regarded factory work as a kind of competition with their real life's work—the family. But their income and the help they could afford kept their families intact until they relinquished their factory jobs.

The foregoing discussion indicates, in brief, that familial controls of the kind found in Cantel continued to operate in the factory worker's family as they did in the farmer's. A detailed comparison of a factory worker's family and a farmer's family revealed their great similarity, at points verging on identity. The family in Cantel, then, continued to be the entity that socialized persons for work, but not specifically factory work. It prepared them for the larger economic and social world, but not particularly for wage work.

A survey of the school children in Cantel did not show an important preference for factory work as a future occupation, even among the sons and daughters of factory workers.

Role of Voluntary Organizations

Although the family was the social background for any kind of work—without which factory work could not successfully have been made a part of Cantel's roster of occupations—the voluntary organizations played an important part in providing the organizational framework and ideology that make factory work desirable and meaningful. The union is probably the organization most influential in tying workers to their jobs. The Cantel union was founded in 1945, the year workers' organizations became legal in Guatemala. Among the direct economic advantages the union achieved (and by 1948 nearly every employee was a member of the union) was the minimum daily wage. Despite the legal enactment of a minimum wage, only the organized industries of Guatemala, and not all of them, were able to compel employers to abide by the law. Furthermore, the union secured the abolition of corporal punishment on the job, initiated means for dealing with grievances, and provided a channel for communicating complaints to management. However, these economic gains were only some of the ways in which the union made factory work attractive. The union was a democratic *sindicato,* run by the workers themselves. Meetings were held weekly or more frequently. In these meetings workers first became familiar with, and learned to participate in the procedures of open debate and reaching a consensus on the basis of the desires of the majority rather than on that of age, wealth, and prestige. The issues on which workers voted ranged from small local affairs through questions of national federation, up to questions of international scope. The local union even sent an Indian delegate to the Vienna conference of the World Federation of Trade Unions.

Through these meetings and the issues they dealt with, factory workers came to consider themselves a pressure group, although not one completely distinct from the community. They used their organization for a number of community services: they helped build a bridge across the river that separated the factory from the town; they participated in the laying of the new floor in the local church; and they were instrumental in getting a new school built in Cantel. Workers believed they were better Cantelenses because of these services and realized that only through the union were such deeds made possible.

It was through politics and political contest that the union forged a partially separate identity for workers and an ideology suited to workers, rather than farmers. In local politics the factory worker and the union became the basis for one of the national parties; and through the power of the union this party won the top posts in the civil hierarchy. The union's participation in national politics made the factory worker feel capable of manipulating some parts of his work situation (for this was the decade of social reform and revolution which ended with Arbenz' movement toward communism). Politics gave the worker enhanced local power and greater possibilities of prestige. When the union was temporarily dissolved during the week of the late Castillo-Armas' entry into Guatemala, the factory had its largest single week of turnover in more than a decade.

Other voluntary organizations grew up around the factory nucleus—a bicycle club, a soccer team, and a basketball team. All these served to indicate the beginnings of leisure patterns appropriate to factory work. Some informal, personal association came to be based on the fact of factory employment. Moneylending groups, offering interest rates far below the usual usurious ones, came into being; and a kind of "pool" in which a half dollar or a dollar was contributed weekly gave a "payoff" to the worker whose number was drawn. Another important informal kind of association followed the opening of the factory—the emergence of bonds of friendship. Prior to that time the community of Cantel was marked by the absence of a notion or tradition of friendship, and this is still true among its farmers. Personal contacts were among kinsmen; visiting after dark was rare, and people saw each other in functional or formal fiesta contexts, rather than in informal social and personal ones. Some factory workers through their continued association on the job and in the union developed personal friendships. They and their immediate families began seeing each other in a "social" sense and joined in common recreational activities at other times than ritual days. These friendships made factory work more palatable and gave daily life a quality not enjoyed by those not in factory employ.

KINSHIP AND VOLUNTARY ORGANIZATIONS IN EAST AFRICA

Jinja, in Uganda, is now undergoing rather spectacular growth as an industrial center. A town of nearly 21,000 persons—14,900 Africans, 5,100 Asians, and 800 Europeans—Jinja presents the features typical of the emerging African industrial town. It is a center for migrants (more than 80 tribes are represented), both black and white; its population is predominantly male and young; it is stratified ethnically with the Europeans at the top, Asians in the trades and special services, and the Africans at the bottom.

Fractured Kinship and Ineffective Associations

Africans come to town to get cash, not to enter a labor force or take up an urban way of life, and consequently they develop a split orientation. The African in Jinja is torn between town and countryside, and this is reflected in the kinship system. Of the 945 households (a household is defined as a common domestic consumption unit), more than half had no female adults, 75 percent did not contain children, while only 62 percent were composed of relatives. These Africans came from lineage and clan societies, where the web of clanship is the regulatory machinery of social life. That kinship plays so small a role in Jinja clearly shows the operation of those forces that favor individualization and the destruction of lineage ties.

If kin life is so nearly destroyed, what gives Jinja's labor force its coherence? The labor force as such is not very stable. A constant coming and going of workers impedes the learning of new skills and the formation of social structures aimed at ameliorating the conditions of town life. Voluntary associations are not numerous nor important in Jinja; there are no unions, only works committees which present grievances. Recreational associations have not been formed, despite the popularity of games like soccer. Small wage pools of two to four members have been reported. Religious associations, especially the Balokoli (saved ones) have prospered through European backing. But as the Sofers summarize associational life in Jinja, "the outstanding features . . . have been the poverty of African associational life . . . lack of African participation in interracial association and the absence of voluntary interracial associations." [14] Kin groupings have failed conspicuously to function effectively, and voluntary groups have failed to fill the gaps left in the wake of the sinking lineage.

Jinja thus suffers from labor turnover, migrant labor problems, and the continual orientation of the transient worker to a life back in the countryside where kin and clan provide the framework of a meaningful life. Wherever European industry uses African labor, the results have been broadly similar. McCulloch says of kinship, "comparatively large well-integrated and interdependent units based on kinship are breaking down into comparatively small and independent units." [15] Associations tend to flourish in most African towns, but it is difficult to assess the extent to which African associations play any role in giving industrial wage work or urban life loyalties and social bonds appropriate to or functional in that milieu.

African associations tend to be of two chief sorts—the tribal association and the mutual aid association. The aim of the former is to unite members of one tribe who are resident in one town. These associations apparently promote law and order and at the same time encourage tribal loyalties and a rural orientation. This kind of voluntary association is a product of the assembling of a labor force but tends to retard the commitment of such a labor force and to inhibit the emergence of

[14] Cyril and Rhona Sofer, *Jinja Transformed,* East African Studies, No. 4 (Kampala: East African Institute of Social Research, 1955), pp. 111–112.

[15] Merran McCulloch, "Industrialization in Africa," mimeographed report of the International African Institute prepared for UNESCO (Abidjan, 1954).

sentiments and ideologies more compatible with the new productive life. Coleman has stressed the mutual aid functions of African voluntary associations—funeral benefits, repatriation, and illness payments. He sees these associations as a means of speeding acculturation in the countryside, and of providing a medium for the perpetuation of customary morality and discipline in the city or town.[16]

The overwhelming impression gained from the material on East Africa is that industrialization is creating something of a vacuum in social life by destroying kinship groups. Tribal associations and mutual aid societies take over some of the security and defense attributes of the descent group. But there are no family forms, or special action structures, or voluntary associations (except those which take on partial kin jobs) that tend to bridge the gap between traditional society and town life and wage work. Perhaps the virtual absence of unions and the interracial caste systems present nearly insurmountable barriers at this point to the commitment of many Africans to a labor force capable of bringing about sustained raises in levels of skill and productivity.

SUMMARY

Some rather general propositions about kinship, voluntary organizations, and wage labor may be offered by way of summary. These propositions appear to be consonant with the reported fact, and they may be fruitful for further elaboration and investigation:

1. Industrial wage work is subversive of the clanship aspect of social organization.

2. Family units can continue to function as they did preindustrially if the mechanisms of control of income are kept intact and if the differential productivity of generations is not great or is not given symbolic or social recognition.

3. The family structure is a passive agent in commitment to wage work. The role of the family is to instill generalized norms of work and discipline, rather than specific orientations to wage work as such.

4. Strong familial ties may be helpful in the transition from traditional work to industrial work, in giving incentive and personal coherence to new wage workers.

5. When the family acts to increase career opportunities for its

---

[16] James S. Coleman, "The Role of Tribal Associations in Nigeria," mimeographed paper, West African Institute of Social and Economic Research (Ibadan, n.d.).

members, rather than to preserve its social solidarity, the transition to wage work or industrial careers is substantially complete.

6. Voluntary organizations increase in the wake of industrialization, but not all such organizations are conducive to the recruitment or stabilization of a labor force.

7. Voluntary organizations directly connected with wage work, chiefly labor unions and recreational clubs and sometimes political parties, are important agents in promoting ideologies and sentiments that tie workers to their jobs and make the new occupational niche socially meaningful.

8. A developed labor force depends on the proliferation of ties and social relations connected with industrial work. Such ties are fostered by voluntary associations, but are not self-sustaining until new channels of social mobility and prestige are created.

9. In the transition period, associational life tends to be of a segmented character, focused on special purposes. When the labor force is stabilized, more personal and smaller groupings tend to emerge.

10. The family structure provides the basis for making any occupational role tenable, but the free choice of associates provides, at least in part, the attitudinal basis for personal commitment to wage work.

18 POLITICAL ORGANIZATION AND IDEOLOGY

David E. Apter *

This paper considers economic development from the point of view of political science. Our intent here is to indicate that the Western pattern of private entrepreneurship is a necessary but not a sufficient condition for economic development in underdeveloped areas; that in those areas political entrepreneurs are concerned with the development of multipurpose, omnicompetent organizations, which seek to use government enterprise as the main form of economic entrepreneurship, while retaining for political entrepreneurs a high degree of autonomous power. We assume that in an earlier day Weber was correct in his assumption that "Protestantism" was significant in the development of capitalism, and indicate that "socialism" in a loose sense has become the functional equivalent for political entrepreneurs in the contemporary underdeveloped world. In the case of Africa, at least, socialism has come to mean many things, including progress and development and anti-imperialism.

NATIONALISM AND THE DECLINE OF COLONIALISM

The first task of nationalism is to produce independence by the use of effective organizational power. The second task, once the first goal is achieved, is to provide greater economic satisfactions than were provided under the colonial regime. Therefore, unlike the original pattern of growth in the West, there is great urgency about economic development in the new nations. In spite of this urgency, few of them, without using very stringent measures, can show a greater proportionate growth in the same time period than can the developed nations. In all underdeveloped areas, then, the long-term goal of nationalists is self-sustained economic growth on a high level. Success is not easily achieved.

* The comparative scheme that underlies this paper was developed in an original draft which included a more elaborate conceptual framework. This was too cumbersome for treatment in a single article. The comparative scheme accordingly was omitted in revision of the present paper, and has appeared in a separate article, "A Comparative Method for the Study of Politics," *American Journal of Sociology*, 64:221–237 (November 1958).

Some nationalists come to feel that the products of their labors are not always fruitful. They fear relying on outside capital and technicians because of certain traditions that have grown up around nationalists in their fight against colonial domination. There are prejudices against foreign firms. Yet there is a signal need for development if nationalists are to retain support.

Nationalists argue that colonialism and imperialism have held back industrial development. Colonial rulers are alleged to have restricted education and barred local people from full participation in economic and social life. When colonial officials begin to depart, however, nationalists themselves inherit the difficulties of government, many of which they had been blissfully unaware of. Industrialization becomes for them an all-purpose goal through which many secondary goals can be satisfied. It restores national integrity since industrial states are powerful and independent. Wealth flows, and prosperity can come upon the land. The worth of the citizenry is enhanced. Hence national efforts must serve industrial ends.

Nationalists who do not show a strong desire for economic development are rare. Having come into prominence in environments of racial and cultural inequality, poverty and alien rule, nationalists capitalize on a prevalence of defiant shame, desire for social improvement, and the need to prove ability. Development thus assumes an importance that is not only economic but social and psychological as well.

However, economic development is easier to talk about than to accomplish. In rapid economic development political leaders face all the complexity of situations of radical change. The cultural traditions and structural features of rural, pastoral, and agricultural tribal societies, each with its own dynamic properties, are simultaneously present. The cultures of underdeveloped areas are not internally "simple," any more than was England in the nineteenth century when enclosure, famine, enforced mobility, poverty, and an extreme work discipline not only helped to produce an enormous industrial machinery, but also radically altered and reduced the range of difference in the array of social systems. Indeed, if the term industrial revolution has any meaning at all, it refers to the degree to which all social institutions are altered in meeting the requirements of technology.

The Soviet Union and China serve as contemporary models of rapid industrialization today. The industrialization process in the West has produced a superior standard of living, but has also produced a cultural superiority which has expressed itself in the ideologies of colonial powers. (The Soviet Union is not yet generally regarded as a colonial power.) Such ideologies include Christian "civilizing" missions, for example, and more recently a teaching role for colonial leaders by which the less "culturally advanced" peoples are to be more effectively "introduced to the modern world." The difficulty is that in both colonial and excolonial territories even a small degree of social and political development makes these colonial roles intolerable. The West is regarded as too rich, too swollen with success, and until recently too invulnerable. Here lies the common chord that nationalists can strike with the Soviet Union. The Soviet system has challenged that invulnerability and, using the language of nationalism, has given a great deal of vicarious satisfaction to political leaders who have fought against colonialism and for political and economic independence. The Soviet Union therefore has become a model for a type of economic growth. It represents a selfless bootstrap economic operation. Its emphasis is on sacrifice and hard work. If the question of freedom is raised, it is not answered in personal terms. He who is free to produce for his own society, and free of foreign domination, is a free man. The question of liberty is less relevant.

Development then has many compelling political aspects, and to some degree the Soviet Union serves as its contemporary symbol, not in terms of communist ideology but as a new approach to development. It is an intense organizational process in which the task is a restructuring of society to reduce social and cultural discontinuities and to effect orderly recruitment of skills and talents and mobilization of effort to achieve specific goals. In that sense the role of politics in underdevelopment is organizational rather than representational. Whatever the specific objectives may be, and these vary widely, politicians are concerned with changing things and creating militant multifunctional organizations than can efficiently provide both social and economic satisfactions.

Our discussion of organizational and industrial potentialities and their significance is based mainly on African territories. Most of Africa was under colonial rule until very recently, although the practice of colonialism varied greatly. Indeed, postwar colonialism is social welfare colonialism, and the interest in industrialization is by no means limited to nationalists. In former British and French territories most of the development that occurred had been under expatriate auspices with capital brought in from the outside. The same was true to an even greater extent in the former Belgian Congo. Nationalists are rarely disposed to cut off such a flow of investment funds, anxious as they are to control the political situation. Where no resident expatriate population controls both the political and economic life of a country, it has been possible for nationalist leaders to assume greater degrees of political responsibility until, as in the case of Ghana, they gain full political autonomy.

GOALS OF NATIONALISM

The Decalogue of Nationalism

It is important to distinguish the several goals of nationalism. Nationalism feeds off grievance, the elimination of which becomes the object of nationalism itself. Many of the issues that are profoundly important to people in underdeveloped territories can be expressed as demands for the following:

Political equality. Cultural or expatriate domination is becoming impossible. Whether in plural societies in East and Central Africa, for example, or elsewhere, political equality is manifested in "one man, one vote" concepts on the individual level, and in national autonomy on the territorial level.

Democratic structure of government. Arguments of nationalists against colonialists have been phrased partly in terms of the undemocratic nature of an expatriate oligarchy, ruling without the benefit of representative institutions. Indeed, if the Western influence is regarded as significant, it is not in the economic realm as much as in the development of parliamentary governments as a proper medium for self-government.

Rapid social mobility. As social welfare colonialism has produced trained and educated elites, there has been a demand on their part for greater eligibility for the higher power and prestige ranks of the system. Some colonial territories have attempted to create a class of *évolué's* or *asimilados* enjoying full citizenship rights with Europeans as well as equal access to jobs and facilities. In other territories such a pattern has served to intensify strivings for social mobility on the part of those not recruited into the upper ranks. The result was the application of equal citizenship and other rights to Africans, for example, in former French Africa. Still other territories adopt "separate but equal" doctrines, which attempt to set up multiple social hierarchies for Africans, Asians, and Europeans. These efforts are fraught with violence and scarcely accepted. The nationalists have identified social grievance in large part with denied opportunity for social mobility. When nationalists come to power, they are faced with a situation that they have helped to create. They must bend every effort to produce opportunities for mobility. These are satisfied only in part by ridding the country of expatriate officials and providing patronage jobs. More basically social mobility strivings put a heavy burden of economic development on nationalist leaders.

Equal opportunity. In most areas traditional eligibility for recruitment to important positions was on relatively ascriptive bases. Both social welfare colonialists and nationalists have had to provide alternatives in the form of expanded educational opportunities, and recruitment on the basis of talent and skill. The idea of equal opportunity has been one of the most compelling bases for nationalism. Social inequity has been a deep-rooted source of antagonism between emerging African classes as well as between expatriates and Africans. Although a sense of deprivation and lost opportunity has been expressed in demands for equal opportunity for all, the content of equal opportunity has been expressed primarily in political terms and only secondly in educational terms. It is being expressed increasingly in economic terms. Indeed, colonial and nationalist governments are engaging more and more in the business of providing loans for African enterprises and expanding African trade.

Racial tolerance. In relations with missionaries, traders, and administrators, Africans have suffered from presumed inferiority. The missionaries stressed moral weakness and inadequacy; the traders stressed the low level of crafts and civilization; and the administrators, governing large populations and territories with limited personnel, created something of a mystique about white and Western leadership. Sometimes expressed in separatist church movements, sometimes in revivalist traditional organizations, sometimes in art and drama, and in current nationalism, the consequences of racial intolerance have been profound. Indeed, the fact that Christianity is essentially a white European affair has greatly aided the growth of Islam.

Responsibility of the individual to the group. National leaders have placed great emphasis on group solidarity, which is often difficult to maintain, in the hope that prevailing and new social groupings can serve as mediators of cultural and social conflict. Through the reorganization of traditional groupings and the development of new ones, the corporate strength of national societies has begun to emerge.

Technological development. Material standards of life, especially those of the West, have increasingly served as guideposts for contemporary populations in Africa, by whom economic development is most desperately sought.

Government enterprise. In order to make assaults on economic backwardness, colonial and nationalist governments have sought first to initiate and improve health, education, and other welfare operations and, second, to undertake primary economic development, such as building of roads, port facilities, and the like. Because of obstacles to private economic entrepreneurship and particularly because of difficulties in the creation of large-scale industry, government has also served as a financial and planning base for economic growth. Nationalists increasingly look to government enterprise as the form in which economic growth most probably can be stimulated, with private enterprise as either an expatriate or relatively small-scale complementary effort.

A satisfactory explanation of imperialism. There is an effort to explain how Africans came to be dominated by the West and also to demonstrate the immorality of colonialism. Exploitation and plunder are the explanations most used.

Political puritanism. There is a search for beliefs that transform individual opportunism into socially necessary and valuable forms of activity and that favor the emergence of new forms of social discipline as older, and particularly tribal, forms alter.

These ten goals are among the most important on the African scene, where they are influential on many levels. To achieve these goals political leaders have been determined to create all-embracing organizations with great power. They seek to concentrate control over the several aspects of social change. Expression of the goals varies a great deal, but they are pervasive objects of considerable passion.[1]

Nationalism and the Economy

If we classify predominant forms of economic activity in Africa in three major types, subsistence, commercial, and industrial, of which the last may be considered the desired end, we find that nationalist goals are most widespread in the commercial societies. It is there that social dissatisfaction and grievance are most intense. The particular "solution" of the attendant problems, which is seized upon with increas-

[1] The organizational consequences of these goals are those of mobilization leading to industrialization. For a discussion of mobilization systems see David E. Apter, *The Political Kingdom: An Inquiry into the Political Sociology of Uganda* (Princeton: Princeton University Press, in press), Chapter 1.

ing frequency, is the "industrial" solution. In other words, industrialization has become the most generalized end because political leaders see it as capable of achieving the goals enumerated above.

The ultimate goal that seems to allow the solution of all intermediate but significant goals is industrialization. This particular form of economic growth is increasingly a measure of progress. It also is the symbol of success in modern life. The ideology of contemporary politics in underdeveloped areas, then, is an ideology of development. Scarcely a country in Africa does not have its five- or ten-year development scheme. Hardly a political leader does not envisage his role as creating opportunities that only industrial wealth can make possible. And barriers to industrial progress are identified with the slow and apparently halting measures of colonial governments. Political leaders are not necessarily concerned about the profitability of a particular enterprise; they may actually prefer to use protective tariffs in order to stimulate basic industries, even when their comparative advantage lies in continuing to import. Often, too, there is a belief that an industry not now profitable will become so later, as effective demand increases, and that further growth can be stimulated and enterprise made more profitable by a combination of inhibiting imports and raising income levels through domestic development. The question is: by what means can this be achieved?

POLITICAL ENTREPRENEURSHIP

Implicit in this discussion so far has been the idea that economic development depends in large measure on government enterprise. Political leaders want to control as much of the process of change as they can and to make it as efficient as they can. Once organized, an effective nationalist body overshadows all other organizations. It allows political leaders to form a self-perpetuating oligarchy, even when the form of government is representative, and gives them means of affecting more people in the population than any other organization can. The pattern of successful political opposition, for example, is relatively rare. The political party with an effective leadership is for a time relatively impregnable, particularly in formerly colonial states where nationalism takes over an established machinery of government. There is a natural propensity for nationalism—the logical outcome of which is antonomous power—to use government as its main mechanism for the achievement of goals. Indeed, a governmental framework that inhibits this achievement is likely to be replaced by another that is more congenial to nationalist purposes.

Most of the goals of nationalism are wrapped up in a wide range of social strivings, which are made more acute because the standards set by those who represented Western culture—missionaries, traders, administrators, and more recently settlers—are not normally attainable by the means originally available in the West, at least not attainable in the same degree. Even if such means were available, the urgency of change makes economic development through the Western pattern of private entrepreneurship seem gradual and slow. If it was the bureaucratic and stifling control over enterprise, characteristic of mercantilism, that was vulnerable in early Western experience, it is development through private means that is similarly vulnerable in new nations.

The difficulty is not that Africans are not enterprising or entrepreneurs.[2] Few of them are in a position to assemble capital, talent, and technological components on a large enough scale to begin an appreciable industrial process, by contemporary standards. The competitive position in any colonial country is bad from the point of view of economic entrepreneurs seeking industrial opportunities. With few exceptions, what can be produced by large-scale industry is more cheaply imported.

Since this is the case, the alternative approach to development is through political entrepreneurship. Here the emphasis is on establishing multifunctional organizations which can be directed at a number of targets. One target may be independence; another may be economic growth. The same organization attempts to achieve both by creating a following that gives it power. Thus political entrepreneurship uses public resources in order to achieve economic growth; economic entrepreneurship uses private resources.

Types of Economic System and Political Entrepreneurship

Our concern is with the political entrepreneurship of Africans. We shall make only passing comments about political entrepreneurship in multiracial systems as a special case of *compartmentalized commercial* system. We are interested mainly in two other types of commercial economy: a *bazaar* economy and a *participant commercial* economy. Africans participate in both, but in the first there is "horizontal"

[2] See, for example, Peter Bauer, *West African Trade* (Cambridge, England: Cambridge University Press, 1954), *passim*.

participation, i.e., in this single form of trading relationship there is wide participation; in other forms—large-scale commercial enterprise, for example—there is not. In the second type of commercial enterprise Africans participate on all levels. Differences between the participants in the bazaar and in the compartmentalized economies are determined by the basis of entry. If it is necessary to belong to a certain race, e.g., to be a European, although all other qualifications such as necessary capital and skill are available to a potential entrant, then the system is compartmentalized. A practical monopoly of certain forms of trade is normally supported by a host of discriminatory factors and is usually found where there are multiracial or "plural" societies—as in parts of East, Central, and South Africa.

Subsistence economies. There is an inherent difficulty in discussing pure subsistence economies because they are rare. Even in Karamoja in Uganda, where tribal warfare sporadically erupts and people are not overburdened with clothes, people sell their cattle in a market and have a well-defined sense of the things that money can buy.[3] Subsistence economies have meaning in one sense. Barring unexpected intervention, they provide for most of the basic wants of their members and are distinguished by a very limited division of labor. Subsistence economies do not produce political entrepreneurs, but do constitute a problem for them. Subsistence economies are poverty economies in the sense that poverty is a function of wealth, and wealth is normally reckoned in terms of real income, or readily transferable title to real income. However, subsistence economies are neither poor nor wealthy; their income simply is not usually reckoned in monetary terms.[4]

It is the culture of such economies that makes them important; traditional elements of their social life are strongly maintained. Neither exchange nor social relations have been altered drastically. Such systems show considerable resistance to both Islam and Christianity. Political entrepreneurs tend to ignore subsistence systems, since their participation in political and economic life is minimal. Where people living in a subsistence economy are able to vote, however, they rarely

[3] See Alan Moorehead, "A Reporter at Large: A Drop into the Stone Age," *The New Yorker,* September 6, 1958, pp. 39–87.

[4] However, in some areas the overwhelming preponderance of the population can remain primarily in the subsistence sector. Until World War II 90 percent of French West Africa's population was within that sector, and it is still estimated at 80 percent in spite of the rapid economic development taking place there. See Elliot J. Berg, "The Economic Basis of Political Choice in French West Africa," *American Political Science Review,* 54:392 (June 1960).

support political entrepreneurs unless the latter promote the goals held by leaders of the community. Such goals are rarely in accord with those of the economic system. Political entrepreneurs often view such peoples as "primitives" or as representing pockets of "nonrational behavior," defining nonrationality as unwillingness to recognize that change in behavior is required to produce both industrialization and political freedom. This attitude probably can be reduced to impatience with "bush" peoples who are not aggressive supporters of political entrepreneurs. More often than not, such peoples have had recent and friendly relations with expatriate administrators who "protected" them from the inroads of nationalism.

Political entrepreneurs need to draw peoples in subsistence systems into alliance with themselves and avert possible alliances with their opponents. One main way to gain the support of such peoples is to promote projects desirable to them. In subsistence systems a little usually goes a long way, inasmuch as very little has been undertaken in education, health, or welfare programs.

Commercial economies. Economic entrepreneurship is most developed, and economic "rationality" has penetrated farthest, even to the political sphere, in the commercial economies, of which three types may be considered separately.

Participant Commercial Systems

Although few African economies are subsistence economies, many are commercial economies with large subsistence sectors. Commercial economies originated in traffic with outside cultures. Commerce and exchange for money have always been widespread in Africa. Exchange was in cowrie shells, gold dust, and such other media as iron bars. Commercial systems became more developed after the intervention of Arab and European trading—first in salt, gold, slaves, and foodstuffs, and later in raw materials and such export crops as coffee, cocoa, cotton, and spices.

Even when commerce originates on a tribal basis, it tends to crode tribal exclusiveness by stepping up social interaction between increasingly dependent tribal groups through an increase in the number and nature of commercial transactions. The new social clusters do not respect the tribe as the most significant unit. Distinctions between town and rural areas become important, and social differentiation on the basis of wealth and occupation becomes established.

The phenomenon of "old families" began in mercantile houses and is still common in some areas. Many old families in Accra or Lagos, for example, were established when the English, Dutch, German, and Danish traders married local women. A larger proportion of the children in these families went into civil service, trade, and other prestigeful occupations than did those in other urban groups. Members of such families continue to intermarry and constitute a social elite. Nationalism often began when these old families had social advantages but were racially barred from political responsibility. Certainly much of the nationalism of West Africa was of this variety; the names of the early nationalists are the names of successful families in Sierra Leone, Ghana, and Nigeria.

Middle-class nationalism of this kind had a strong flavor of the church. This nationalism was commercial in its roots, clerical in its expression, and relatively exclusive in its organization. To behave as Christian gentlemen was an ideal, and to be treated as such was the objective. This type of nationalism served to enhance economic rather than political entrepreneurship. Few middle-class nationalists were career politicians, for example, and fewer of them engaged in the full-time organization of mass parties. They sought, instead, to put pressure on expatriate authorities, and did so with varying success. Their main contribution was to enable Africans to enter all levels of the commercial hierarchy. They succeeded in getting competence rather than color accepted as the major qualification for entry. The result was an increase in mobility, urbanization, commercial wealth, and education in the areas where middle-class nationalists were successful.

Expectations in the commercial sector were geared to economic entrepreneurship until crisis occurred. During the depression, however, it became apparent that independence of the subsistence sector brought dependence on the commercial sector of the economy, and this in turn was dependent on world markets. A second level of clerks, artisans, lorry drivers, etc. was made aware of this dependence through unemployment. Clerks, for example, found themselves possessing low status and no jobs. They joined both unions and political organizations. These used familial and kinship patterns of social organization and communication, and adapted them to all-purpose organizations, which went on to serve economic, political, educational, and other functions.

What we have described is the characteristic pattern in West Africa. Today the multifunctional nationalist organization has taken over government in many instances. No opposition organization is effective except possibly that of those trained in civil service under an expatriate staff and necessary to carry out administrative tasks. Indeed, the civil service is in some cases the only source of nonparty political pluralism in a system having relatively independent power.[5]

Bazaar Systems

A bazaar economy can be defined as the institutionalization of exchange without the institutionalization of savings and investment. Expansion of commercial enterprise takes place in a bazaar economy, but optimum expansion seems to be limited less by economic factors than by an interest in personal control over business. Indeed, the social bases of exchange relations become more important than financial consequences. The exchange relation is the satisfying feature of commercial life. A bazaar economy is also partly a stage between subsistence and participant commercial systems which can perpetuate itself for a considerable time.

Commerce, as the exchange of goods rather than the production of goods, develops a network of distributive social structures, which are distinct from the productive. A bazaar economy is a special case of a commercial system characterized by a lack of reliance on contracts and legal trust, and rather great reliance on family ties. In societies where families are major solidarity units, limitations to expansion by entrepreneurs are imposed by the needs of families and their capital resources. Risk taking in the economic sense is kept to a minimum. Indeed familial organization permits risk to be shared. A bazaar economy allows individual failure without personal responsibility. Many bazaar entrepreneurs have failed in business many times and have easily gone back into trade. When they fail, they borrow from their families or go to work for them. Such a system has considerable resiliency and, for a money economy, considerable security. Savings are often hoarded or turned over to family maintenance, or to old-age and burial societies. Taxes are assiduously evaded. Most of all, bazaar economies are characterized by a high degree of economic conservatism, particularly centering around the family.

Bazaar economies help to hasten political entrepreneurship. Indeed, they exhibit somewhat similar characteristics. Both place heavy reliance on kinship ties at the beginning of organization and in both there is a lack of individual onus for failure. Both have easy access and exit.

---

[5] See David Apter and Robert Lystad, "Bureaucracy, Party and Constitutional Democracy," in Gwendolen Carter and William O. Brown, eds., *Africa in Transition* (Boston: Boston University Press, 1958).

Both are essentially distributive, the one of goods and services, the other of positions of authority. And both provide profound social satisfactions —the one in exchange relations, the other with political power.

Given a bazaar economy, entrepreneurship is collaborative in the political rather than the economic sphere. Family support allows a measure of basic security in venturing into the political sphere, where success brings economic advantages to the family. While many of the practices institutionalized in a bazaar economy are self-perpetuating and make development difficult, the economy is further sustained because of difficulties in getting loans from banks to buy wholesale, for example, and because the costs of business expansion may be too large to be borne by a family-type system. The bazaar economy often feeds off the leavings of larger-scale commercial firms with foreign capital and control, receiving goods from them (often at retail prices) and selling them at a petty marketing level. Grievances against large expatriate firms are characteristic of individuals within a bazaar economy.

Political entrepreneurs, particularly as they seek to enter the arena of political authority, have much the same sense of grievance. In colonial territories in particular, their attack is on expatriates who hold positions of political responsibility and can dictate, or so it appears, the terms of political life in the particular territory. Political entrepreneurs seek to widen the scope of their activities and at the same time to achieve status, prestige, and personal dignity. Underdeveloped areas live in the shadow of presumed inferiority. Few inner resources of respect and pride can withstand the pummeling of cultural superiority by a colonial, industrial, or commercial expatriate oligarchy.

Obstacles to achievement are viewed as the agency of an outside force, rather than handicaps internal to the system. Exhorting people to invest or to cultivate accounting methods, etc. is rarely successful. Training people to become clerks, artisans, and school teachers seems unrelated to the sense of personal grievance so characteristic of the population of such territories. Political entrepreneurship in association with a bazaar economy is noticeably proficient in identifying its enemies, without identifying its handicaps. In practice it is not concerned with planning and productive enterprise. At least in certain stages, it does not encourage individual responsibility and often denigrates the values associated with skill, planning, and hard work.

Once the idea of economic growth and large-scale enterprise becomes accepted as the basis of modern society, however, bazaar economies are a fertile breeding ground for change. They provide an informational network that is highly developed for primary group contacts, and a durable kinship and financial basis for maintaining small-scale organizational nuclei out of which it is possible to build larger political entities.

Still, a bazaar economy poses difficult problems for political leaders who are development-minded. The economy lends itself to manipulation by petty politicians. Often these are "fixers," who hope to gain support by "deals" with the authorities and to curry favors from the wealthier members of the bazaar. In general they turn sharp commercial practice into political practice. Although expansion of commercial enterprise often takes place in a bazaar economy, optimum expansion is limited less by economic factors than by an interest in personal control over business. Within such systems politics retains local characteristics.

What the bazaar economy is able to do exceedingly well is to translate grievance into recognizable categories. It is precisely because of the pervasiveness of the ten nationalist goals in the system that educated political entrepreneurs can join with local "fixers" and, given the right circumstances, produce a common language and a common program.

Compartmentalized Commercial Systems; Combinations of Systems

In a compartmental type of commercial system, political entrepreneurs are often in a position of considerable danger, for they are engaged in breaking down compartments which are composites of racial discrimination, cultural exclusiveness and, most of all, political power. In fact, political entrepreneurship here runs maximum risks, but if it can put effective pressure on existing oligarchies, particularly of a different race, expanded opportunities for African economic entrepreneurship may result. To compensate for restrictive practices on the part of African political entrepreneurs, it is common for colonial governments in particular to expand economic opportunity. This has been the case in Kenya since the end of the Mau Mau.

Through the fostering of African economic entrepreneurship, some of the compartmentalization between races begins to break down. Opportunities for Africans follow quickly. This must lead eventually to the elimination of strict compartmentalization, as the economic and social activities of increasing numbers of Africans produce new social clusters around factors other than race. Indeed, in some compartmentalized systems this is a planned objective.

An interesting consequence of this compartmentalized situation occurs when political entrepreneurs are successful in providing opportunities for economic entrepreneurs but are less successful in providing opportunities for themselves. In such instances estrangement in the African community is common, at least for a time. During their estrangement, political entrepreneurs attempt to organize less fortunate members of the population, channeling grievances against African economic entrepreneurism as well as expatriate.

The most complex situation exists when a single political entity contains subsistence, compartmental, and bazaar types of commercial systems. This becomes critical if the bazaar and the subsistence sectors are open to local inhabitants, but the large-scale commercial enterprises are in the hands of expatriates. Typically, severe discontinuities in social structure allow effective organizations on the part of political entrepreneurs but do not allow effective outlets for their activities. The "solutions" are extreme, involving increasingly high degrees of coercion, partly because so many combinations of events and forces are possible. Because there is almost no way to provide durable satisfactions to the different membership groups in such societies, extremely effective organization is needed by political entrepreneurs for purposes of control. However, the loose structuring of the system makes it difficult to maintain stable organization membership.[6]

Characteristically, aspects of all three commercial systems are to be found in varying proportions in all African territories. Where the system is predominantly compartmentalized, the nationalist effort focuses on goals of political equality, democracy, and racial tolerance. Independence is the supreme goal, with industrialization as a more remote concern. In a bazaar system, political equality and rapid social mobility are the main targets of nationalist political entrepreneurs. Where a participant commercial system predominates, all ten goals receive attention. Political entrepreneurs try to instill political puritanism as the basis for internal abstinence from current consumption, and stress loyalty to the group as a means of devoting social institutions to the simultaneous struggle for economic growth and political independence.

[6] In such systems industrialization is the only possible "solution." Except when there are outbreaks of various sorts, the main mediator against coercion is corruption. In this respect it serves a useful purpose. Political entrepreneurs attempt to control corruption as a form of patronage and use it as a means of maintaining support. A modest degree of corruption can soften the processes of cultural integration until some order and discipline are imposed and until new organizations devoted to welfare and productive activities can be established.

The strategy of leadership and the degree of coercion required to create change will vary, depending on the components of compartmentalization and the significance of bazaar and commercial participation. Where all the components are present in appreciable degrees, especially if there is a mass political party and individuals can participate in politics on a universal franchise system, political entrepreneurs walk a tightrope between coercion and patronage. They use corruption and inveigh against it; attack tribalism and offer alternatives to those in the subsistence sector, hoping to gain support; use old families in the civil service; attempt to modify the bazaar by rationalizing productive and exchange relations; and expand opportunity by facilitating the growth of credit and providing jobs in government corporations and joint governmental and private enterprises. The more complex the mixture of systems, the more likely industrialization is to be viewed as the urgent task. Grievance must be directed against stereotypical enemies so the people will unite around both organizational and ideological goals.

Political Significance

Coming from backgrounds of oligarchical control via political or administrative service, political entrepreneurs demand a widening of the franchise and political equality. They argue for the use of democratic structures of government. Western colonial powers are most vulnerable in these terms. How can they deny to others the highest expression of their own cultures? Local leaders demand rapid social mobility. In compartmental societies they attempt to break down barriers on the basis of race; in subsistence systems they attempt to break down kinship, familial, or other obstacles to mobility. In the bazaar system they strive for greater opportunities for credit and for expanded opportunity for economic entrepreneurs. They demand equal opportunity in education and jobs and plead for racial tolerance. They remind expatriates in compartmental systems that their tenure is based on force and thus is vulnerable.

In their organizations political entrepreneurs demand loyalty to the organization. Such loyalty in compartmental systems is based on the unity of shared danger and mutual complicity. In bazaar systems loyalty is inculcated more through symbolic leadership, patronage, and corruption. In highly participant systems loyalty is normally produced by a combination of both forces with the added characteristic that the party becomes the self-constituted society to which anyone who expects rewards must give service and devotion. The party leader becomes the symbol of nationality and society. The means open to political entrepreneurs are increasing through the operations of government, with its financial majesty. Obstacles to economic development via government and obstacles to successful organization are said to result from imperialism. Finally, political entrepreneurs implore their followers to a higher morality, that of selflessness and sacrifice.

We must now specify the relationship between the various forms of economic system, the recruitment of political entrepreneurs, and the propensities of the latter toward socialism. Subsistence economies do not as a rule provide a country with political entrepreneurs, as we have pointed out. Bazaar economies, on the other hand, have been the breeding grounds for small-scale political entrepreneurs who fill the middle leadership ranks of mass political parties. These are the "brokers" and "fixers" of nationalist parties, on whom senior and more highly educated nationalists are dependent for information, organization, and support, particularly as the small-scale entrepreneurs are in daily touch with the public and with semitraditional organizations—benevolent societies, sports groups, trade unions, cultural unions, guild associations, and the like. The tendency toward socialism among political entrepreneurs of the bazaar is based on their developing sense of status deprivation, which is only partially appeased by positions of political authority. Socialism and its emphasis on equalitarianism provide an ideology of power for benevolent purposes, while permitting the political entrepreneur to retain his pride in affiliation with the public. His generalized antagonism is against expatriate firms (in the market) and senior nationalist elites (in the party).

In participant commercial systems which produce a fairly large elite, conflict between different sections of that elite soon appears. Older educated nationalists tended to enter the professions and, having been part-time politicians, were easily displaced by younger educated groups. This process is only beginning in some new countries of Africa, but this sort of conflict contributed to the breakup of former French West Africa. It occurred in Ghana with the ousting of the United Gold Coast Convention, and is to some extent present in the party conflict between the Action Group and the National Council of Nigeria and the Cameroons in Nigeria. Political action becomes the alternative road to power and prestige while, by governmental means, access to professional and other roles is increased. Commerce itself is regarded with contempt not because it is plebian, which would derive from an aristocratic point of view, but because it is antisocial, that is, irrational in the economic sense and socially seductive in the political sense. Once again the result is an emphasis on government activity, although few new nations are willing to deny themselves the advantages of outside investment on the largest scale on which they can obtain it.

In compartmentalized economies, mutual ethnic exclusiveness serves to deter all but the most restricted social and economic relations between major groups. Indeed, relations between ethnic groups are characterized by highly ritualized patterns, such as those of master and servant, merchant and consumer, professional and client. Violations of ritually correct relations, through which the different races can meet only tangentially, bring ostracism and other penalties. For political entrepreneurs in such situations the combination of status, racial, and economic differentials which tend to cluster around ethnic compartmentalization are the most difficult to accept and the most dangerous to challenge. The tendency for extremism is thus very great. Socialism provides a liberal ethic for extremist positions.

Thus we see that in each case political entrepreneurs are drawn toward socialism as an ideology. Nor is it without significance that socialism is the ideology of the pan-Africanist movement. What are some of the consequences of this tendency?

SOCIALISM AND THE CRISIS STATE

To summarize briefly, nationalist organizations are designed to take over the state and produce changes in society. Economic entrepreneurship is less able to accomplish rapid change under present circumstances than is political entrepreneurship. The political entrepreneur's first devotion is to his organization. The bazaar system allows nationalists some freedom to organize, but it is where there already is a relatively high degree of economic entrepreneurship, i.e., in the participant commercial systems, that political organization and nationalism have genuine possibilities for furthering industrial development.

In the organizational stage, which is not entirely dissimilar to the initial campaigns of trade unionists in the West, all efforts are made to build an organization of an inviolate character. An opposition under such circumstances is simply a form of treason if it divides the movement. Such an organization of course requires money. The commercial systems in which there is high participation provide sources of income for nationalist purposes. Expatriate firms are anxious to provide for their own security by providing money to political leaders. Political entrepreneurs who have been successful in building organizations seek to make them the primary means of mobility, i.e., to create a system of stratification alternative to those prevailing in the society. They begin to bureaucratize their party government.

Such organizations are possible in any meaningful sense only in a participant commercial system or a compartmental commercial system. It is no accident that mass political parties have emerged only in West Africa or in Kenya; in the latter, once the party was organized, it had no outlet other than violence. Political organizations face their first difficulties in their initial efforts; once the crisis of organization is over, other crises take their place. The bureaucratization necessary for efficient party work begins to produce internal difficulties. Hence nationalist organizations are fragile in the midst of their strength. Ceaseless vigilance must be maintained to keep them in trim. In the process tremendous demands are put on political entrepreneurs; they need a selflessness and spiritual quality that can sustain enthusiasm even in the midst of success. We can now show how such circumstances propel nationalists toward a socialist ideology.

Successful nationalism is directed by political entrepreneurs in such a way that social welfare colonialism is transformed into socialism. The widely pervasive nationalist goals need to be supported by an ideology, and organizations become increasingly ideological as time goes on, since the possibilities for splitting the party increase as its tasks become more concrete. These become more concrete as the party achieves more power and responsibility, depending on the extent to which appeals have been made on a symbolic level rather than a programmatic one. Each of the goals is less than programmatic.

Success in organization tends to be undermining unless political entrepreneurs are able to control and discipline the organizations themselves and the societies over which they may come to rule. Oligarchy becomes the alternative to chaos or subordination. This leads us to a theory about political entrepreneurship. Briefly stated, the theory is that socialism is to political entrepreneurship what Protestantism was to economic entrepreneurship. The goals of nationalism have increasingly become identified as socialist goals; socialism has become a useful ethic for political entrepreneurs. It justifies the use of government for economic development and it stresses economic development. It has the associations of Western humanism without identification with the church. Indeed the party becomes the "church." By being the credo of the disadvantaged in some sense, it feeds on a common identification with "exploited" people both in the West and elsewhere. Socialism insofar as it is accepted as a higher stage of evolution than capitalism is a symbol of modernity. Capitalism is identified with foreigners and exploitation.

That socialism, industrialization, and organization have mutually reinforcing qualities is most important for political entrepreneurs. In order to maintain their support, they must begin to achieve some of the goals of nationalism. Most of these goals require organizing society for far more stringent efforts than colonial officials would ever have considered possible. In addition, social welfare costs rise as attacks on immobilities in the system are made. The political entrepreneur must provide a useful all-purpose goal in order to permit subordinate goals to be attained, but he cannot allow his support to diminish as he takes concrete action. Industrialization becomes the all-purpose goal. Through organization, and thereby industrialization, all subordinate goals become attainable.

However, nationalists soon recognize that industrialization does not come about at once. Organization is used to direct state enterprise simultaneously toward both developmental and welfare objectives. Forced savings become necessary—a costly means for political entrepreneurs because their followers may become disaffected. Discipline then must be tightened further. The political entrepreneur must cajole and coerce to keep his organization intact until he can begin to send out a stream of benefits. He transforms his political entrepreneurship into economic entrepreneurship via government enterprise and directs his energies to success at that level.

State enterprise serves a number of purposes. At the very least it provides rewards for loyal party followers. At the most it attacks prevailing social organization. With industrialization as the all-purpose goal, party and government actions have their own justification, because industrialization itself sets impossible social tasks. Crisis is produced by the objectives and process of industrialization because of the very difficulties that it imposes. Yet once a large-scale attempt to industrialize is made, at least up to the point at which enterprise is so established that net economic growth is registered, all social groups in the system are largely dependent on government and its economic activities. Sources of pluralism in the system are weakened, and all voluntary associations except trade unions become functionally more precise. Everyone becomes dependent in large measure on the government, and political entrepreneurs become the organizational leaders of a changing society. Industrialization then serves to preserve organization, and it seeks industrialization as a way to gain subordinate goals.[7]

At this point socialism as an ethic becomes significant. Organization, which is the object of political entrepreneurship, tends to be regarded with hostility by colonial officials. In compartmentalized systems it is regarded as dangerous. In participant commercial systems organization takes on invidious characteristics by recruiting into mass movements people who have not been socially, economically, or politically successful. In bazaar economies organization fastens on grievance and is, by its very nature, irresponsible. Organization consequently has a history of presumed "irresponsibility," which has been a source of "risk" for political entrepreneurs. On coming to power, they speak for society and with the voice of responsibility. In other words, they need an ethical code that will be widely accepted.

Christianity is identified with imperialism in underdeveloped areas and is not conducive to meeting their organizational and industrial needs. By contrast, socialism is an expression of the welfare state. Built into it is modesty about the personal use of power, but a justification for unabashed use of power for industrial and welfare purposes. Further, contemporary socialism in non-Western areas expresses firm beliefs in individual dignity. Some of the values embodied in Christianity are now embodied also in socialism.

Socialism is used, first, to justify accumulation of capital for government enterprise; hence taxes, forced savings, and even conscription become morally and organizationally desirable objectives. Both capital and labor are regarded as sources of wealth. Socialism emphasizes disciplined labor and abstinence from current consumption via governmental control. Second, socialism provides for heavy reinvestment in industry as the means of inducing progress, and is heavily weighted with a technological notion of progress. Third, socialism provides the ethics of individual abstinence by emphasizing responsibility to corporate groups—society, party, and work group—while individualism is regarded as potentially antisocial. Thus devotion to party leader,

---

[7] See David E. Apter, "Nationalism, Government and Economic Growth," *Economic Development and Cultural Change*, 7:117–136 (January 1959) for an analysis of optimal conditions for economic growth and mobilization. See also Rupert Emerson, "The Erosion of Democracy in the New States," in his *From Empire to Nation* (Cambridge: Harvard University Press, 1960), Chapter 15.

organization, and state are justified as socially necessary and part of the selflessness required to bring about dramatic social development.

Socialism in both its ideology and its practice has a high regard for rationality. The rationality of capitalism is measured in the market place; that of socialism is measured in planning. Its guide to success is the number of followers and supporters retained by the political entrepreneur, for these determine the effectiveness with which changes that facilitate the industrial process are brought about in the system.

Finally, socialism is a form of contemporary puritanism. It emphasizes social thrift, hard work, the dignity of labor, and selflessness. All these are necessary to political entrepreneurs if they are to use government as a major source of industrialization, and the political party as the means. Socialism makes political entrepreneurs respectable leaders of society and makes colonial and business oligarchs disreputable.

19 CHANGING SOCIAL STRUCTURES

Clark Kerr

The world is currently undergoing a great economic and social transformation. In essence, this transformation is in the commitment of man to a new way of life. Throughout history most of mankind has been committed to a constant way of life, even though particular ways have varied from one place to another and, to a much lesser extent, from one time to another. Commitment to a constant way of life seems to be the natural state of man.

The current period of history is distinguished from all others, however, by the immensity of the process of destroying old commitments, no matter how constant they may have been, and by the world-wide uniformity of the new commitment. Men everywhere are transferring themselves fully and finally into the industrial way of life. Great uniformity is developing out of great diversity. *Industrialism, itself, is the significant new form of social affiliation.*

This transformation may be viewed from its end result, the way points between, and its points of origin. The end result is marked by great similarity; the way points, by both great similarity and great dissimilarities; and the points of origin, by great dissimilarities. Viewed from the end result, the transformation is one great process of such overwhelming impact that the current and local variations are almost unimportant. Viewed from points in between, there are roads and alleys and even dead ends; some societies choose one of these and some choose another. The great questions are: why was one choice made rather than another, which choice is best, and how may the choice be influenced? Viewed from the points of origin, the transformation is a complex, confusing process, yielding to few generalizations, and the final outcomes are somewhat uncertain. Each situation is unique and deserves unique consideration. Each view has its merits and each is necessary to a full understanding of this "greatest transformation."

INEVITABILITY OF COMMITMENT

The best place to start is with a view of the end result; for industrialism is a great magnet which is drawing all human life to it and ordering the orientation of this life. Whether a society has been matrilineal or patrilineal, whether based on family or tribal ownership of land, whether responding to the Protestant ethic or the Bantu ethic, or whether it goes through a prior commercial revolution or not, it ends up following the logic of industrialism.

The logic of industrialism requires that many things be done. The new society must be on a reasonably large scale, at least as compared with many pre-existing societies; the logic of industrialism may even insist eventually on a single world-wide economy. There must be urban centers of some size. An increasingly diverse occupational structure must reflect an increasingly advanced technology. An educational system must be created to feed this occupational structure and advance the technology that lies behind it. A wage structure reflecting the supply of and demand for the various occupational skills must be developed, although it may reflect, of course, more than these forces alone. A labor market mechanism must be established to sort out and distribute and redistribute workers into a myriad of jobs. There must be managers and there must be the managed—those who give the orders and those who obey them; and these two groups must be related by a whole web of rules governing their relations. There must be industrial discipline at the level of the individual worker and of the group; and the imposition of this discipline requires means for handling the inevitable protests which arise in the industrial order. The state must be reasonably strong to govern the industrial order, and may perhaps become excessively so. Finally, the men who live within the industrial order must accept its imperatives. There is no place for anarchy in the logic of industrialism.

This is not to suggest that industrial societies may not be diverse among themselves, at least for a time, but only that their similarities are very great, that they will be much more nearly alike than pre-industrial societies, and that these similarities are important for labor commitment, however significant the variations may be in terms of human welfare or in other respects. The variations are found mainly in the emphasis on state as against private initiative, in the character and the role of the elite classes, and in the rate of economic progress which in turn relates to both of the other major variations.

To fulfill its logic, industrialism will sweep before it many of the behavioral patterns of prior times, as it has certainly done with almost astonishing success. There are few things so changeable as "customs." In terms of the daily lives of men, however diverse they may be in parts of the world today, one can foresee with great clarity what they must become. The present can be penetrated best from the vantage point of this future because the motto of the future is *e pluribus unum* and *unum* (the new industrial society) is fairly well known. Labor forces have been, are being, and will be created and committed by one process or another.

The more interesting, but also the more passing, question is how commitment will take place; for there is no one way. However, commitment is not really very hard, impossible as the transition in some cases might seem at first glance. The Bantu of Central, Eastern, and Southern Africa, to give one illustration, are currently being taken straight from the "bush" and being turned into mine and factory workers and "townsmen" almost overnight. New industries and new towns often rise where even maize had never grown before; and these "work" albeit not altogether smoothly. They "work" because the Bantu work.

The Bantu work, although they move between highly contrasting ways of life. As subsistence agriculturalists, they enter a society that emphasizes specialized skill. As members of small tribal units, they submit to the rules and the discipline that take the place of custom and personal decisions. Raised in a traditional system with a high degree of security and equality, they enter a life noted for its insecurity, inequality, and constant change. Responsibility comes to be toward the job and themselves instead of the tribal or family community, which loses its significance. The new government is remote and impersonal and belongs to somebody else; and group action, instead of being the normal response to problems, is always suspect and often prohibited. Even the ethics governing personal conduct are quite different. Despite all this, production goes on.

The secret of the Bantu and other rapid and largely successful transitions to industrialism is the great adaptability of man. It is not the resistance to change but the acceptance of change that is the more remarkable. The real problem is not in the adjustments to be made by men, but in the effectiveness of social processes and the suitability of institutions. Individual man is generally better at making his adaptations than society is in adapting processes and institutions to the new requirements of the emerging industrial order.

COMPLEXITY OF THE PROCESS OF COMMITMENT

Commitment may be looked at as a current process, as well as an assured fact of the future. As a current process, the comparative uniformity of the future dissolves into the complexity of the present. Yet there is a certain "normal" pattern in the process of commitment of workers to industrial life. Four stages may be distinguished, or perhaps it would be more accurate to say that four points may be identified in the continuum of behavioral change which marks the transition of the worker from traditional society to full adherence to the industrial way of life. These four stages may be designated as follows: (1) the uncommitted worker, (2) the semicommitted worker, (3) the committed worker, and (4) the overcommitted worker.

Stages of Commitment

The uncommitted worker is well represented by the "target worker" of the South African gold mines. He has no intention of entering industrial life on any continuing basis. He goes to the gold mines for a specified period of time, usually a year, and may set as his goal the saving of a certain sum of money, often the price of a bride. At the end of his sojourn he returns to his native area where his family has remained. The South African gold miner maintains his tribal contacts while on the job through the influence of the *induna*. He is a tribal member temporarily away from his tribe. But the sojourn marks a break from the tribal background and is frequently the first step into industrial life. He is in industry but not yet of it.

The semicommitted worker is a man on the margin of two civilizations. He works more or less regularly in industry but maintains his connection with the land. He has a foot in both camps. The "bachelor" worker in Nairobi is an illustration. His wife and family remain on the tribal land whcre she largely supports herself and her children. The "bachelor" will send her small amounts of money and return home periodically to help plant or harvest a crop or build or repair the family hut. He gets cash and a more interesting life from his industrial employment; he gets security and a larger total family income from his connection with the land. In South Africa the semicommitted worker may have his family with him in the city, but the children are often sent back to the tribal area to be raised. The whole family returns there periodically, sometimes for extended stays, and retirement normally takes place in the tribal area.

The committed worker has severed his connection with the land and with his tribal background. He is fully urbanized and never expects to leave industrial life. His family is permanently resident in an urban area, and it is not unusual for the wife also to enter the labor market. In fact, one good test of the degree of commitment of a labor force is the percentage of it comprised by women. An uncommitted or semicommitted labor force is predominantly male. The committed worker depends for his security on his employer and on the state, not his tribe. His way of life is industrial.

The overcommitted worker is committed not only to industrial life but also to his particular occupation or his particular employer by training, by seniority rules, and by pension and welfare programs. He is not just a member of a permanent labor force, but of a small and closely prescribed segment of it. He is back in the closed circle of the "tribe," subject again to custom and to duty to the group.

The first two of these stages are clearly transitional ones and the workers involved in them are subject to considerable adjustments in their patterns of life, to divided loyalties, and to sharp jolts from their environments. They bear the personal costs of the transition.

Commitment, the Labor Market, Protest, and the Wage Structure

Workers in the four respective stages of commitment behave quite differently in the labor market. The first type is on a work schedule of planned and frequent turnover. The second type usually experiences either a heavy turnover or heavy absenteeism, or both. As a consequence, these two types of workers accumulate little skill or seniority to protect them in industrial life, and their low productivity is rewarded by low wages. Between the second and third types, a great drop normally takes place in both turnover and absenteeism, and the opportunity to acquire skill is vastly improved. The overcommitted worker has largely lost his mobility; turnover is low and security is high as industrial life becomes bureaucratized and feudalized.

The nature of the labor market changes as commitment increases, but so does the pattern of expression of protest. Protest is inevitable in industrial life, perhaps in any form of group life, but varies both in its level of intensity and in its means of outlet. The level of protest rises and then falls again as the process of commitment advances. At first, the worker is so little connected with industrial life and so bereft of power and the basis for organizing power that he has neither a great desire nor sufficient means to protest. As his involvement in and experience with industrial life increases, his power to influence the industrial environment also increases, and his tendency to protest rises. Industrial life is now his life, and he wishes to mold it closer to his heart's desire. Later on, as machinery is established to meet his grievances and as the cost of conflict begins to bulk larger, industrial protest may tend to fade away. The surrounding industrial environment comes either to be accepted or, at least, to be acknowledged as inevitable. What protest remains tends to be highly structural and formally expressed. Finally, in the overcommitted worker, organized protest tends to disappear.

The form of protest also shifts from the individual's protest expressed through turnover and absenteeism, to the guerrilla warfare of the quickie strike or boycott over immediate dissatisfactions, to permanently organized economic or political action or both, and finally to the petty and covert sabotage of the trained bureaucrat whose chains can be rattled a bit but never lost. This is the normal life cycle of protest and it is closely related to the normal life cycle of the process of commitment.

A word may be added on the behavior of the wage structure in the course of commitment and partly as a result of the process of commitment. In the first stage, that of the uncommitted worker, wage differentials will be very wide. The uncommitted worker will receive just enough to draw him from the rural pool, and this wage usually will be at about the subsistence level for a single man. At the other end of the scale a small number of skilled workers and supervisors will receive particularly high wages if they are paid at an expatriate level. In the South African gold mines the European workers average ten times as much as the Africans. Differentials will begin to narrow for the semicommitted worker, but particularly for the committed worker. The committed worker can more readily attain skill so that the premium paid for skill goes down and at the same time the pool of rural workers often starts to dry up. Differentials, when allowed to operate without restraints such as a "color bar," close very fast, and in industrialized economies the premium for skill will range from 10 to 50 percent instead of 1,000 percent. At the overcommitted stage many and perhaps most wage rates are not subject to the direct influence of the market forces of supply and demand but go their own ways, largely directed by custom.

Thus labor force commitment affects the operation of the labor market, the nature of labor protest, and the character of the wage structure. The committed labor force means a labor market active principally at the relatively few ports of entry where new workers are hired, a low or moderate level of organized protest which is expressed through formalized procedures, and a narrow wage structure which is responsive to the maintenance of customary relationships.

Although it has been suggested that the process of commitment normally progresses through four stages, it need not follow this path. It is

highly unlikely that what has been suggested as a later stage has preceded, or will ever precede, one of the suggested earlier stages; but
stages have been and can be either entirely omitted or at least so greatly
shortened in their life span as to make them of little importance. For
example, it is possible to enter stage two, semicommitment, without ever
going through the stage of the uncommitted worker and to shorten
greatly the duration of this second stage.

Factors in the Commitment Process

The process of commitment can be aided or impeded, accelerated or
delayed by developments in several important areas, five of which may
be noted here:

Agricultural policy and practice. Developments affecting life in rural
areas can have a major impact. The enclosure system in England, the
collective farm system in Russia, and erosion in the Ciskei of South
Africa all drove people from rural areas into the cities and helped
break the connections with traditional life. The successful perpetuation
of the family homestead, as in Uganda (cf. Chapter 13 supra), serves to
maintain contact with the old society.

The role of the family. The wider the family and the longer it is
preserved unchanged, the less rapid will be the transition to a committed labor force. The extended family removes much of the incentive
for individual initiative and much of the basis for savings and investment, as in Ghana. If the family is held in the tribal reserves, as in the
case of the native gold miners in South Africa, the adherence to industrial life will be made more difficult. The family, however, can also be
used to commit an industrial labor force. In the Belgian Congo, generally, and the Copper Belt of Northern Rhodesia, specifically, workers
are encouraged to settle down with their families from the very beginning of industrial employment. In Russia and China women are put to
work early as part of the process of committing the labor force.[1] In
Japan primogeniture pushes the younger sons out into industrial life.[2]

Labor market policy. The policy of the employers or of the state, or
both, in organizing and operating the labor market can have a major
impact on the process of commitment. In the Belgian Congo the policy
is to commit the worker as fast as possible. He is encouraged to bring

[1] H. F. Schurmann, "Organization of Response in Communist China," unpublished
manuscript.

[2] James C. Abegglen, "Subordination and Autonomy Attitudes of Japanese Workers," *American Journal of Sociology,* 63:181–189 (September 1957).

his family along, to buy a house, to acquire skill, and to rise in the occupational hierarchy. Excellent medical services are provided. A benevolent paternalism is directed toward quick commitment. In Kenya, under the "bachelor" system, the worker keeps his family in the tribal area, has no chance to buy a house, and receives little encouragement either to acquire skill or to attempt to move upward occupationally or socially. In South Africa every effort is made to force the African to maintain his tribal contact—this is the essence of "apartheid."

These policies have quite different results. For workers with the same general background in Sub-Saharan Africa, depending on the policy, absenteeism may be 2 percent or 40 percent, and turnover 10 percent or 300 percent per year. Absenteeism and turnover rates relate more to labor market policy than to the chronological age of the process of industrialization. Heavy absenteeism and turnover are not an inevitable aspect of early industrialization (see Chapters 9 and 10 supra). In the United States, in early times, slavery and the indenture system were developed in part to offset tendencies toward heavy turnover.

Race and class structure. When there are barriers to upward social mobility, the incentive to identify oneself with industrial life can be much reduced. The "job reservation" program in South Africa and the "color bar" in the Copper Belt of Northern Rhodesia set limits to the occupational advancement of the Africans which can only serve to discourage their permanent attachment to industrial life. In Kenya and Natal the Indians form a layer of craftsmen and merchants into which the Africans find it difficult to penetrate. They bump their heads on this low ceiling. In the Congo, on the contrary, there is no formal "color bar" and the immigration of Indians is actively discouraged. On the positive side, efforts are made to elevate Africans into skilled work and middle-class pursuits. They are pulled up into some of the choicer spots in industrial society.

The management of protest. The basis for protest exists in any industrializing society (see Chapter 16). This protest can be incited or channeled or submerged. How it is managed depends largely on who is managing it. Protest can be used by "political entrepreneurs" (to use Apter's phrase) to excite the workers, or it can be controlled by "economic entrepreneurs" to permit greater productive effort. How protest is managed depends on whether it is managed by opponents of the society or by its supporters. A revolutionary union can heighten protest measurably; a "job conscious" union can channel it into specific gains instead of the attempted destruction of the system; a "partner in progress" union, like Histradut or the *sindicato* of Mexico,[3] can turn the energy of protest into constructive effort; an "agent of the state" union can help suppress protest in its organized forms.

Political parties with a mass base can also affect the ebb and flow of protest and the operating effectiveness of the system. While unions and political parties of workers generally serve to commit workers to the industrial way of life and subject them to disciplined action, it makes a great difference whether these organizations are oriented toward protest or toward production. Generally a "protest approach" impedes full commitment to and acceptance of industrial life, whereas a "production approach" can aid commitment and acceptance.

Through control of agricultural policy, the family system, labor market operations, the class and racial social structure, and the management of protest, the process of commitment can either be accelerated or substantially prolonged. In particular, stage one (the uncommitted worker) can be largely or even entirely eliminated, or continued, if not forever, at least for a very long time. In South Africa this stage has already lasted more than 70 years. If pressure is to be applied to the commitment process, the attempt can be made in five strategic areas.

Some Additional Conditions

The process of commitment involves more than the four stages and five critical pressures noted above. Three additional considerations are especially important. First, commitment is much more difficult when industrialization is being fought by the workers, as in England at the time of the Luddites, than when it is avidly desired, as in most of the world today. England is not the standard case, but the exception. Workers no longer revolt against industrialization; in general, they favor it. Second, a nationalist interlude in the economic development of a nation is almost bound to hold up the commitment process in the days before independence, and may well accelerate the process in the early days after independence. Such an interlude will almost certainly affect the rate of flow of commitment of the labor force. Third, wherever the state controls the economic and political systems or largely influences them, the conscious guidance of the commitment process is both more possible and more probable. This guidance may be directed toward a negation of the normal tendency toward commitment, as in South Africa, or toward a rapid acceleration of it, as in Russia.

[3] Wilbert E. Moore, *Industrialization and Labor* (Ithaca: Cornell University Press, 1951), pp. 283–284.

THE DIVERSITY OF THE PAST

The shadow of the past lies over the commitment process but is usually a surprisingly soft shadow. The commitment process, as we call it from the vantage point of industrial society, is an uncommitment process when viewed by the traditional society. People not only arrive in the new world; they also leave the old. The new world is in a roughly fixed position, and the old worlds may be located fairly close to it or quite far away. Also, their holding power may be strong or weak. The nature of the old world affects both the social distance to be traveled and the likelihood that the trip will be undertaken at all. The Yoruba of Nigeria with their established town life are much closer to the new world than are the cattle herding Masai of East Africa. The Indians, with their long-established traditions of craftsmanship and commercial pursuits, are much closer than the Zulu subsistence farmers. The social distance to be covered varies enormously.

But does it make much difference how great the social distance is? The Zulus adjust to town life in Durban or Johannesburg with such alacrity that the social distance they travel has only a temporary effect. It may be argued that the greater the distance traveled, the faster will complete commitment to the new way of life be achieved.[4] The old has so little to offer, once the journey has been made, that it can less readily pull the traveler back and hold on to him. Even geographical distance may have this effect. The Uganda African, whose industrial place of work is close to his ancestral home, maintains more connections between his two worlds than does the Congo native who undertakes a long journey to Elisabethville. Social and geographical distance may hasten full commitment more than social and geographical proximity.

The holding power of the traditional society has an impact of quite a different order. Aristocratic tribes, such as the Masai and the Watusi, seem to be able to hold their members better than the less aristocratic, such as the Kikuyu; the aristocratic tribes may thus condemn their members to lesser progress. The greater the holding power of a traditional society, the fewer of its members will slip away from it and the greater will be the group and personal disruption caused. The holding power is probably related more to the strength of the social web of the old society, which is based in part on its successful operation in its environment, than to the distance it lies from the industrial world.

On the basis of the most casual observations, it seems that the im-

4 *Ibid.,* Chapter 10.

portant influence of a traditional society on the commitment of a labor force to industrial life is not how far that society is situated from industrial life, for the journey can be made so quickly over social space, but rather the holding power of that society. This would suggest that the components of holding power are the items crucial for further study. Some societies have substantial rejecting power—as in the case of the younger son in Japan or the young hunter or warrior in some Bantu tribes.

The disruption caused by the transition is a somewhat different phenomenon than the process of commitment of the labor force. A textile factory fitting into a receptive community in Guatemala (see Chapter 17) or miscellaneous plants in Puerto Rico entering into village life conditioned by plantation agriculture (see Chapter 9) will cause less social disruption than the creation of a new commercial and manufacturing center drawing in people from many tribal backgrounds, as in the case of Jinja in eastern Uganda (see Chapter 13). Adapting old forms to the new social situation, as in the substitution of the *induna* or the shop steward for the tribal chief (see Chapter 8), may ease disruption. Commitment of an industrial labor force, however, can go along more or less independently of the amount of disruption in traditional patterns of behavior, important as such disruption may be to individuals and to groups.

How nearly alike the old and the new societies may be generally does not seem to be a crucial factor. Rather, regardless of how far apart they may be, it is a question of the magnetic power of each. In the tug of war over individuals, which has the greater strength? Holding power can slow the development of an industrial labor force quite substantially; social distance cannot. The similarity of the two worlds is much less important than the comparative strength of the old world and the new.

Conclusion

In conclusion, two generalizations about the commitment of an industrial labor force may be emphasized. They apply to the employee labor force and not to the development of a managerial elite, which is quite a different and in some ways almost an opposite kind of problem. First, the future into which workers are going is much more determinative of what happens to them than the past from which they are drawn. This particular history gets written mainly from the future into the present—what is currently happening comes from what is to be. The future is the cause and the present is the effect.

Second, the real problem is not the adaptability of man, which is almost infinitely greater than we once supposed, but the suitability of institutions and their policies. The contact of civilizations, the traditional and the industrial, can be managed well or managed badly. The social management of this contact, not the adjustability of individual men, is the heart of the matter. This management can greatly ease or greatly hinder the commitment of an industrial labor force. Beyond commitment, it can vastly affect both the liberty and the welfare of the new industrial man.

20 MOOT POINTS IN THE THEORY

Arnold S. Feldman *
Wilbert E. Moore *

It would be patently false to pretend that the expert opinion represented in the preceding chapters yields a unanimous view of what are the important questions or what are the reliable answers. There remain a number of issues, some of which have been sharply joined by the authors of several papers and can be recapitulated here in a somewhat different context.

The focus of these studies has been the involvement of persons in novel patterns of social activity. The acceptance of and adherence to these patterns has been called commitment. The relevant patterns are those hypothetically associated with the process of economic development or, more narrowly, industrialization. This equation of development with industrialization is, however, one of the moot issues, as are the exact requirements of social change and the importance of commitment itself.

INDUSTRIALIZATION, ITS COMPETITORS, AND COSTS

It would seem that, of all the proposed patterns of economic development, industrialization requires the most radical transformation of existing ways of working and living. There seems to be widespread agreement that the forms of activity introduced by virtue of industrialization are extremely novel. The one exception to this is reported by Udy in Chapter 5. His analysis indicates that many tribal societies, in their work organizations, have institutionalized norms that are quite similar to those of "rational legal" bureaucracies. Thus it would appear that the equation of industrialization and radical change is somewhat more tentative than is commonly assumed.

Actually, each of the two equations regarding industrialization—economic development equals industrialization, which in turn equals the most radical process of socioeconomic change—has a problematical

---

* As editors the authors have had the opportunity to have the last word and to base that word on revised papers by other participants and their own reflections on the debates at the time of the original conference. This puts opponents at a disadvantage, but one that we have attempted to minimize by a "fair" representation of conflicting views.

character. Both sets of "problems" are the consequence of a third relationship: the more radical the character of the process of change, the higher the social costs, part of which is the increased difficulty of gaining commitment. For if industrialization is associated with extremely high costs and extremely severe commitment problems, the assumption of its inevitability should be carefully scrutinized. Three moot questions are: (1) Is industrialization necessary? (2) If necessary, does it involve the most radical program of change? (3) If it does involve the most radical program of change, does that involve the highest social and personal costs?

Industrialization and Alternatives

Naive socialists to the contrary, the economic problems of newly developing areas are not amenable to solution solely through altering the distribution system. If an economy is to grow, it must produce significantly greater amounts of something of value, whether raw materials or manufactured goods or services. Altering the distribution system may encourage the accumulation and use of risk capital, but there is considerable doubt that simple alteration of the distribution system can supply the levels of investment required for sustained economic growth, no matter how efficiently it is "liberated." [1]

The bulk of the available evidence indicates that significant increases in extractive, manufacturing, and service industries are all interdependent. Thus continuing growth in either agriculture or services will depend on and cause growth in the manufacturing sector of the economy. It would appear that economic growth inevitably requires development of the manufacturing sector of an economy, even though the relationship is not exclusive. Knowles presents this position persuasively in the particular context of agricultural underemployment and labor "unrest" (Chapter 16).

It is frequently argued that increased production in the manufacturing sector of an economy does not require large-scale industrialization. The claim is that development programs that stress cottage or small rural manufactories offer the most efficient means for increasing output

[1] See John A. Buttrick, "The Formation of Capital," in Harold F. Williamson and John A. Buttrick, eds., *Economic Development: Principles and Patterns* (New York: Prentice-Hall, 1954), Chapter 5; Henry G. Aubrey, "Investment Decisions in Underdeveloped Countries," in National Bureau of Economic Research, Universities — National Bureau Committee for Economic Research, *Capital Formation and Economic Growth* (Princeton: Princeton University Press, 1955), pp. 426–431.

in this sector of the economy. By avoiding the establishment of large factories, radical transformations in workers' life styles are avoided. Accordingly, commitment difficulties might be significantly altered.

A cottage or widely dispersed rural factory program is severely limited in regard to kinds of products. Although it might save the labor force the costs of geographic mobility, it transfers these costs to the sources of development capital, public and private. Some objections to mass industry stem from the brutal conditions of urban life for the migrant. However, working conditions in small rural factories may not be much better. What some scholars portray as craft centers that do not disrupt the even tenor of traditional culture frequently turn out to be rural sweatshops. To paraphrase Morris (Chapter 10), this position might be called "The Myth of Paradise Slightly Altered." It could be argued that although cottage industries are exploitative, workers are not likely to perceive them as such and therefore are more likely to accept this form of development. The obvious answer is that the exploitative nature of a relationship is not reduced by lack of awareness by one of the parties, and such lack of awareness cannot be expected to endure.

In sum, it would appear that sustained growth in the developing areas of the world requires industrialization.

Variability of Industrialism

Given agreement that the goal of economic development must include industrialization, there remains the question of its specific character. This argument is precisely over the kinds and amounts of social change required for successful industrialization—whether industrialization must involve radical processes of social and economic change. The argument is carried on at two levels. In its theoretical form, it is another case of the traditional battle between the adherents of structural uniformity and those of cultural variability. Practically, the argument turns on the question whether development plans should be designed to maximize or to minimize the changes in a population's style of life.

Arrayed on one side are those who hold that although the structure of an industrial society may not be randomly variable, a significant amount of variation is possible and quite efficient. This position is extended to encompass sequences and rates of change as well as patterns of social organization. Singer makes an excellent case for this position (Chapter 14). Belshaw, Hammond, and Herskovits (Chapters 6, 7, 8) all adopt the same general position, with Belshaw giving special attention to possible variation in the sequence and rate of change.

Those who favor adaptability and gradualness in industrial development believe that significant changes in productive processes can be introduced into a newly developing area without radically altering the traditional fabric of life. Hoselitz and Nash (Chapters 12, 17), for example, maintain that the subversion of the extended kinship system by industrialism has not been demonstrated, although they agree that as household or corporate political entities the extended groups lose significance.

Some analysts think that insistence on a set sequence and structure involves costs that will be extremely heavy and possibly destructive of development. Among the costs cited is the considerable misuse of preindustrial skills and talents with the consequent high levels of economic waste. As Singer argues, in a society where productive skills are at a premium, it is a particular sin to waste those that are readily available. Another cost cited results from the failure to employ interaction patterns traditional in the preindustrial society. Thus, Belshaw points out that there is considerable scope for entrepreneurship in preindustrial Melanesia. Further, such native entrepreneurs as exist might be destroyed if support were limited to enterprises that adopted "Western" management practices. Hammond stresses the commitment difficulties that resulted from a failure to employ, or a misinterpretation of, tribal patterns of social organization. In this instance the consequence was wide rejection of a modernization program by the labor force.

Thus the failure to accommodate any modernization program to traditional practices possibly involves waste of existing manpower resources, destruction of nascent entrepreneurs, and rejection of the program by those most concerned.

Arrayed on the opposing side are those who question the possibility of significant variations in the sequence and structure of industrialization. They argue, among other things, that the costs of variation are likely to exceed the costs of radical alterations in life styles. The attempt to minimize the costs attendant on industrialization is thought to place the entire development program in jeopardy. Thus, industrialization historically and contemporarily has involved sizable costs, including commitment difficulties. Although it is certainly desirable to keep such costs at a minimum, ameliorative efforts are necessarily limited by the requirements of industrial production.

Both types of costs are real and both positions involve comparable dangers. It was argued that gradualness could lead to apologies for carrying preindustrial patterns of exploitation into the factory. Correlatively, insistence on a revolutionary change may lead and indeed has led to apologies for some of the brutal and coercive recruitment tactics commonly associated with initial periods of industrial development—forced labor camps come particularly to mind. Alongside the myths of "Paradise Lost" and "Paradise Slightly Altered" should go the myth of "Paradise About To Be Gained."

The emphasis on limited structure and sequence does not exclude the possibility of cultural alternatives. Nevertheless, although the specifications vary, violations of appropriate patterns can be theoretically specified and have been empirically observed. Thus industrialization is viewed as a process that creates cultural homogeneity, in that certain patterns of belief and behavior are necessarily common to all industrial societies. Moreover, commonality is not limited to the single act or norm but applies as well to the configurations into which they are formed, for example, the interrelations among machine technology, division of labor, and authoritative coordination. The violations of the boundaries of these configurations are as capable of being identified as the violations of any single element.

The specification of some of the social and economic requisites of industrial societies greatly facilitates the analysis of possible alternative paths toward development. If the boundaries of the interrelated acts and norms are capable of identification, then limits of the process are at least located. If it can be demonstrated that a particular path would inevitably lead to violations of prerequisites for structure or sequence, this path must be rejected. Such rejection can be based on theoretical grounds and not primarily on criteria of efficiency, since the theoretically possible paths can vary and be equally "efficient." In sum, lacking a determinate dynamic principle, the method of comparative analysis can satisfy some of the analytic needs and aid search for the dynamic.

A closely related question is the extent to which industrial organization or any other structural feature of industrial societies is adaptable to pre-existing social standards as a transitional strategy. The empirical or the theoretical range of feasible structural forms is not actually known. It does appear, however, that some forms of adaptation may result in "traditional stereotyping" and therefore in decreased capacity for continuous adaptation and growth.[2] Thus Hammond, although generally favorable to organizational adaptation, noted the negative consequences of attempting to utilize the traditional figures of authority

[2] See Talcott Parsons, "Introduction," in Max Weber, *The Theory of Social and Economic Organization* (New York: Oxford University Press, 1947), pp. 47–49.

and thus frustrating the changing standards of youthful recruits (Chapter 7).

Questions regarding the required degree and sequence of social change involve the moot issue of historical repetition. The precise form of the query is the possible advantage of late starters. It is commonly noted that growing countries do not have to recapitulate either the rate or the sequence of technological developments in the older industrial countries. (It is of course also noted that advanced productive technologies do not necessarily fit the functional context of newly developing areas—labor abundance and capital shortage, lack of skilled operators and maintenance men, readily available replacement parts, etc.) It may also be unnecessary to repeat the gradual evolution of large-scale administrative organizations in finance, manufacturing, and distribution, and especially unnecessary to segregate and depersonalize work roles to the extent indicated by the formal model of a rational bureaucracy, only to reinstitute more functionally diffuse relations.

The alternative line of argument maintains that recapitulation of the sequence is required in order to break the traditional network of relationships, since the gradual "humanization" of the industrial structure is by no means a return to the *status quo ante,* but rather rests on the productive efficiencies made possible by a radical technical and organizational transformation. Apter notes that native political leaders themselves often accept a doctrine of recapitulation, but perhaps with the Soviet Union rather than capitalistic countries as historical models (Chapter 18).

Although nobody maintains that an exact recapitulation of the European experience is necessary, some argue that viable variations are likely to be peripheral to the central core of industrial institutions. Variations that are central to the developing economy are perceived as aberrations that are likely to be destructive of industrial development in the long run. Holton argues this position with regard to deviations from the sequence of industrial development (Chapter 11). Kerr stresses the homogenizing properties of industrialization, which is a view insistently presented in Part 1.

The interdependence within industrial systems, whether viewed in terms of structure or in terms of commitment, thus has temporal dimensions also. One principal manifestation of this is a dynamic pattern of evolution that is simultaneously cumulative and retroactive. Change is cumulative in that multiple involvements reinforce one another and yield an increased general level of commitment. It is retroactive in that a high level of commitment may be dependent on previous commitments in other contexts, but further involvement in these contexts may depend in turn on the intermediate step.

An example of this evolutionary pattern may be found in the sequence of development between the commodity market and factory employment. Because of the culture of the hypothetical society in the preindustrial phase, commitment starts in the market. Once a market has at least started and developed to some extent, commitment can start in factory employment, in that the nature of commitment in the market was such as to remove the previous cultural blocks to commitment to wage labor. However, full commitment in the market in turn may depend on the development of a high level of commitment to factory work. Thus the sequence between these two loci reverses itself and is "retroactive." The theory is not a determinism of "prime movers" and rectilinear sequences, nor simply a functional correlation, but a sequence with alternating directions. Now, interestingly enough, this hypothetical illustration has a precise confirmation in Gregory's data on Puerto Rico (Chapter 9). An analogous pattern of change operates in economic systems, as where an initial agricultural revolution makes possible a diversion of productive factors to manufacturing, which in turn makes possible agricultural mechanization, chemical fertilizers, and rapid delivery of agricultural products.

Thus we conclude that the initial feasible variations in paths and sequences of industrialization are fairly restricted and tend to converge substantially short of infinity.

The Problematics of Commitment

We come now to the final moot issue: given the radical processes of change that accompany industrialization of newly developing areas, how problematical will labor force commitment be? The various chapters contain a number of different answers to this question. Starting from one extreme, there seems to be some support for the position that commitment, as defined, will rarely be problematical. Some subscribe at least partially to the view that as soon as the opportunity for industrial labor presents itself, people will take advantage of it with reasonable promptness. The initial sections of Morris' chapter can be interpreted as providing supportive evidence for this position (Chapter 10).

Morris persuasively argues that various Indian factories were able to recruit a labor force with considerable ease and that once recruited this labor force displayed high levels of stability. He then, quite reasonably, suggests the broader relevance of his analysis for comparable societies, i.e., China and Japan. At least in regard to these societies, Morris re-emphasizes the predictive value of labor surpluses, the lack of alternative opportunities, levels of poverty, etc. As such, his analysis represents a healthy corrective to those that employ such concepts as "the inscrutable Oriental mind," or the mystical irrationalities of ancient beliefs. He also reminds his colleagues that the conditions that obtain in the nonindustrial sectors of many newly developing areas may provide great impetus for change. Knowles, in his general survey of "labor unrest," indicates that displays of dissatisfaction may represent the industrial workers' distress at the slow pace of industrialization, or at his lowly position in the new order (Chapter 16).

Nevertheless, this evidence must be interpreted with great caution. Morris limits the interpretation primarily to India, China, and Japan. The evidence from tribally organized societies (Chapters 7 and 13, by Hammond, and Elkan and Fallers) indicates that a number of factors intervene between the creation of opportunity, its recognition, and labor force commitment. Even for India, a number of crucial questions remain unanswered. How selective is migration? Are new factory workers recruited at random from the total population, or do they represent a selective minority? Is the supply of "easily" committed workers inexhaustible, or are there imminent limits? Given a full-scale industrialization program, how rapidly would such limits be reached? Hoselitz suggests that these questions are not picayune in view of his diagnosis of the Indian labor force.

A second position on the ease or difficulty of gaining commitment is related to the previous argument over structural variability. The students who favor variation hold that since ease of gaining commitment varies inversely with departures from traditional life styles, it is desirable and possible to keep such departures at a minimum. This course of action would presumably minimize commitment problems. The opposite view holds, with Kerr, that industrialization is truly revolutionary and that radical transformation may be easier, as well as more rapid and viable, than patchwork compromises between inconsistent systems.

Commitment, it has been noted, involves at least for the transitional actor a process of adult socialization. Consistent with the notion that radical change is necessary, it has also been argued that commitment is best maintained when it exists for the total matrix of social involvements. These positions, in turn, are linked to the hypothesis (stated in

Chapter 4) that generalization of a common level of affect is a more tenable position than the competing principle of frustration and diverted activity. That hypothesis provides the possibility of linking theories of social change with theories of individual change. Put in extreme terms, social change is potentially an agency for releasing but also for *creating* participatory energy. The circle may be enlarged but it remains a circle if we note that deliberate change is itself an important component of industrial systems. When change takes on a moral character, innovation and rapid adaptation are requisite orientations for the committed participant.

THE "PERMANENT REVOLUTION" [3]

One reason that problems of economic transition can be identified with some confidence is that they are never solved. The tensions and conflicts of industrialization are also persistent features of industrial societies. A stage of "complete industrialization" or "full commitment" is a theoretical construct rather than an empirical type. For some purposes the construct must be abandoned in favor of dynamic models, lest the continuous tensions and transformations of industrial systems be quietly neglected or discreetly hidden from the scholar's view.

Tensions persist and are "normal." Tumin has highlighted the discontent involved in systems of social inequality, however closely they may approximate the ideal of rewards for differential merit (Chapter 15). Wherever one turns in the observation of industrial societies, the dynamic potential is evident—in the polity and the economy, the family and the work place, and in the inconsistent role demands on fully committed participants.

The present volume has been concerned with developing areas in transition. The conclusions, as well as the unsolved problems, can surely be transported in part to "developed" areas, and thus redress the historic error of supposing that history ends when the industrial revolution occurs.

[3] The phrase "permanent revolution" was apparently first used by Marx in 1844. See E. H. Carr, *A History of Soviet Russia*, Vol. I, *The Bolshevik Revolution 1917–1923* (New York: Macmillan Company, 1959). More immediately it is, of course, borrowed from Leon Trotsky; see *Permanent Revolution*, 1st Indian ed. (Calcutta: Gupta Rahman and Gupta, 1947). The phrase is applied to German National Socialism by Sigmund Neumann in his *Permanent Revolution* (New York: Harper & Brothers, 1942). It is perhaps needless to add that both Trotsky and Neumann use the term "revolution" primarily in the traditional narrowly political sense, and only indirectly in the sense of transformation of social institutions generally.

INDEX OF NAMES

Abegglen, J. C., 37n, 38, 354n
Abercrombie, K. C., 207n
Abramovitz, M., 38n
Aitken, H. G. J., 72n, 73n
Alexander, R. J., 302n, 304n
Allen, G. C., 37n
Anstey, V., 174n, 188n
Appadorai, A., 264n
Apter, D. E., 72, 73n, 75n, 284, 326n,
   331n, 337n, 346n, 355, 365
Arbenz, J., 321
Arensberg, C. M., 14n, 15n, 34n, 42n, 217
Aubrey, H. G., 208n, 271n, 361n

Babchuk, N., 27n
Bailey, F. G., 265n
Bakke, E. W., 23n
Balandier, G., 30n, 68n, 294n
Baldamus, W., 19n
Bales, R. F., 11n
Banerjea, P., 182
Barber, B., 278n–279n
Barkin, S., 34n
Bauer, P. T., 126, 233, 271n, 333n
Beal, E. G., 13n
Bekker, C., 293n
Bell, D., 18n, 29n
Belshaw, C. S., 70, 92n, 95n, 98n, 99n,
   102n, 106n, 124–127, 261n, 362, 363
Belshaw, H., 37n
Bendix, R., 34n, 56n, 257n
Benjamin, H. C., 6n
Bennett, H. S., 230n
Benoit-Smullyan, E., 46n, 58n
Benson, W., 244
Berg, E. J., 334n
Beri, S. G., 174n
Berna, J. J., 274n
Beveridge, W. H., 244n
Bhave, V., 274
Black, C. E., 283n
Blau, P. M., 11n, 47n
Blum, F. H., 27n
Bogue, D. J., 23n
Bose, N. K., 264n

Brown, W. O., 337n
Brozen, Y., 45n, 59n, 210n
Bruner, E. M., 204n
Buchanan, D. H., 174n, 183n
Buchanan, N. S., 6n, 203n, 261n, 293n
Buttrick, J. A., 45n, 210n, 361n

Caro, I., 258n
Carr, E. H., 368n
Carter, G., 337n
Casis, A., 12n
Castillo-Armas, C., 321
Chang, P. K., 206n
Charlemagne, 229
Chatterton, A., 269n
Chinoy, E., 46n
Choksey, R. D., 269n
Clark, J. M., 8n
Coleman, J. S., 324
Comhaire, J. L., 315
Coomaraswamy, A. K., 264n, 266n, 267

Dalton, M., 16n
Davidson, R. B., 303n, 304n
Davie, M. R., 89n
Davis, A., 52n
Davis, K., 12n, 13n, 22n, 68n, 74n, 80n,
   177, 179, 278n, 279n
Daya, E., 291n, 297n, 302n, 303n, 304n,
   307n, 309n
Desai, M., 269n
De Schlippe, P., 135
Deutsch, K. W., 6n
Deyrup, F. V., 73n
Dickson, W. J., 14n, 16n
Dobb, M., 25n
Dube, S. C., 265n, 272n
Dubin, R., 24n, 27n, 33n
Durkheim, É., 28n

Eggan, F., 314n, 316
Elkan, W., 287, 367
Elkin, H., 37n
Ellis, H. S., 6n, 203n, 261n, 293n
Emerson, R., 346n
Evans-Pritchard, E. E., 252n

INDEX OF SUBJECTS